D0192891

ABOUT THE AUTHOR

TREVANIAN was an elusive figure, writing under at least five different pseudonyms in at least five different genres. He is probably best known for the spy thrillers *The Eiger Sanction*, *The Loo Sanction* and *Shibumi*. His obituary in the *New York Times* described him as "the only writer of airport paperbacks to be compared to Zola, Ian Fleming, Poe and Chaucer."

OTHER TREVANIAN BOOKS
PUBLISHED BY
OLD STREET

The Summer of Katya

THE CRAZYLADIES OF PEARL STREET

THE

CRAZYLADIES

OF

PEARL STREET

A Memoir

TREVANIAN

OLD STREET PUBLISHING

Copyright © Trevanian 2005

All rights reserved.
First published in Great Britain 2007 by Old Street Publishing Ltd,
14 Bowling Green Lane, London EC1R 0BD
www.oldstreetpublishing.co.uk

First published in the United States by Crown Publishers, an imprint of the Crown Publishing Group, a division of Random House, Inc., New York

A CIP catalogue record for this book is available from the British Library.

ISBN13: 978-1-905847-16-7

10 9 8 7 6 5 4 3 2 1

Printed by Creative Print and Design, Wales

For Diane

Author's note to the US edition, published as fiction

Although the characters and incidents of this novel are set in a closely observed and carefully described block of Albany, New York, during the Great Depression and the Second World War, a lively desire to thwart the litigious impulses for which Americans have become renowned obliges me to declare that all the characters and names are products of my imagination and exist in no other reality than my own.

Trevanian Website

The Trevanian Buff is a strange and wonderful creature: an outsider, a natural elitist, not so much a cynic as an idealist mugged by reality, not just one of those who march to a different drummer, but the solo drummer in a parade of one. It is for the Trevanian Buff that I prepared cybernotes to broaden or deepen this last book. A friend has put these cybernotes on a dedicated website along with other bits and oddments collected from my desk. Feel free to download them, should you wish. Please accept these tokens of gratitude for having followed me through so many genre and eras. The website is www.trevanian.com.

THE GREEN CAKE

MY SISTER, my mother and I sat in a row on the front stoop of 238 North Pearl Street, feeling overwhelmed and diminished by the unfamiliar bustle of the big city. Beside the stoop was a stack of twine-bound cardboard boxes bulging with bedding, clothing and kitchen things. Around them were clustered our few scraps of furniture looking scuffed and shabby in the unforgiving glare of daylight. It was Saint Patrick's Day, and the mid-March sun felt good, but chill winter air still lurked in the shadows. The year was 1936; I was six years old, my sister was three, my mother was twenty-seven, and we were beginning a new life.

We had been sitting on that stoop long enough for the gritty brownstone to mottle the backs of my legs between my short pants and my knee-high stockings. My sister wore a starched, frilly dress that Mother had bought out of money meant to tide us over until we got on our feet because she wanted Anne-Marie to look pretty the first time her father saw her, but the dress had got crushed during the long drive with the three of us crammed into half of the front seat of my uncle's rattletrap of a truck. And now we sat hip to hip on that step, Mother in the middle, my sister and I drawing comfort from contact with her, while she drew maternal strength and determination from contact with us. Anne-Marie was hungry and sleepy and close to tears. Taking her onto her lap, Mother looked anxiously up and down the street for my father whom she hadn't seen for four years, not since the morning he went out to look for work and didn't come back, leaving her with a toddler, a baby, and two dollars and some change in her purse.

She didn't hear from him again until a letter arrived just three days earlier saying how sorry he was for running away from the family he loved, the family he had worried about every single minute since he left. There was no excuse for behaving like that, he admitted, but he just couldn't stand being made to feel he wasn't man enough to support his own wife and children. He had been sure that her family would give us a hand once he was out of the picture. He knew that Mother's father considered him to be little better than a flashy hustler and a con man—exactly what he was, in fact. The letter said that he had found a job and an apartment in Albany. Not much of a job and not much of an apartment, but it would be a start, and he had something big in the works. That letter had come in the nick of time, because the owner of Lake George Village's only all-year restaurant had just told my mother that he wouldn't be needing her as a waitress when the tourist season began. Her frequent absences during that winter when she was sick with lung trouble had shown him that she was unreliable, and he had decided to replace her.

During the whole trip down to Albany, my uncle had grumbled about the time and money this was costing him, and when we didn't find my father waiting at the address he had given us, my uncle just unloaded our stuff in grumpy haste and left us there, saying that he had to make it back before nightfall because he didn't trust the headlights of his old truck. He was in such a hurry to get away that he drove off without shutting the passenger-side door, which flopped open. As he reached over to shut it he stepped on his brakes, causing the door to pinch his hand. He roared a curse as he furiously stomped on the gas to get the hell away from that goddamn hole of a goddamn slum, but the truck stalled and a car behind him sounded its irritated horn, so he shouted at the driver to go to hell and started up again, and he drove off pounding his good fist on the steering wheel, glad to see the end of his wife's goddamned freeloading cousin and her goddamned brats!

Mother and I exchanged glances and couldn't help smiling.

My father's letter had said that we should wait for him on the steps of the building because he was planning a big surprise for us, but now Mother was tired of sitting there with people peering at us from windows and stoops all around. She rose to go inside and look for him, but I grabbed her wrist. Like most kids, I loved surprises, and I didn't want her to ruin this one. Let's wait just a little while longer.

A couple of boys detached themselves from a knot of kids and sauntered past our stoop, disdainfully eyeing our cardboard boxes and our shoddy furniture, then letting their sassy eyes slide over me. I knew that my short pants and knee socks made me an object of scorn to these two boys dressed in knickers. From school I was familiar with those universal rituals among boys when they puppy-sniff one another for the first time, measuring and hefting for rank and dominance. I could tell that the smaller of the two boys, a big-eared kid about a year older than I, was wondering if this skinny new kid would turn out to be a regular guy or a sissy, if I would fight my way out of school-yard challenges or run to the teachers. I kept my eyes on him as he strolled by, but I held him in a soft, tired look. To look hard-eyed would be to send a challenge; to avoid his eyes would be to submit. Boys are born with this canine pack-hunter's instinct for caste and nipping order. After the kids had passed, one of them crossed the street and spoke to a flat-faced, boneless woman sitting on her stoop, obviously his mother, and I could see she was asking him about us, especially about my mother, who wasn't anything like the faded, marshmallow mothers of other kids. My mother was young and slim and had short bobbed hair; she could dance and run and play games, and she wore slacks in an era when few women did. I don't know what the kid said, but his mother sniffed in a way that was both competitive and dismissive. I was used to that sort of reaction to my mother, but still sensitive about it. It wasn't that I wanted her to be the same as other mothers. I was proud of her youthful good looks and her feisty independence, but I sometimes wished she could be different in a less obvious way because it's hard having a mother who's different.

Some bigger boys, fourteen or fifteen years old, loitered in front of a cornerstore diagonally across the street from our stoop. Fully aware of the gaggle of girls who admired them from two stoops away and whom they ostentatiously ignored, the boys talked loudly, pushed one another in gruff play, snorted out forced laughs and repeatedly glanced at their reflections in the cornerstore window with satisfaction, although now and then one of them felt obliged to hook a comb out from his back pocket and drag it through his Brylcreem'd hair, then press the sides into place with a caressing palm. They played an endless round-robin of that finger game in which paper covers rock, rock smashes scissors and scissors cut paper, known by different names in various parts of the country, but called 'Rochambeau' in the urban Northeast by genera-tions of kids who had no idea that a French general who had helped our infant republic defeat the British at Yorktown had been immortal-ized in a child's game, much less how to spell the chanted sound as they threw their fingers out on the '-bow!' of the third syllable. The loser of Rochambeau had to let the winner 'knuckle' him, hit him on the top of the head as hard as he wanted to with the knuckle of his middle finger. The one who got knuckled would snort disdainfully although the pain sometimes dampened his eyes with fugitive tears, which he quickly blinked away as he rearranged his hair in the store window. Two of the boys were smoking, the biggest one, who was the leader, and a small ugly one who played the role of flunky and clown. They smoked like kids new to smoking do, trying to appear supremely casual, but fussily examining the burning ends of their cigarettes with grave frowns and tapping off the ash more frequently than it could gather. These older boys wore long trousers and were bare-headed, while the younger boys of the block were in knickerbockers and caps. Only very young boys wore short pants. Except for me, of course! The principal bane of my life was my mother's need to dress my sister and me better than other kids, in compensation, I suppose, for our lack of a father and a secure breadwinner. Because she couldn't afford new clothes, the hand-me-downs my sister and I wore were always cleaner and more freshly ironed than those of our playmates, yet another of those differences that kids will not endure.

The strange new sounds and gestures of life and play that I ob-served with a mixture of fascination and malaise from our stoop that first afternoon would, in the course of the eight and a half years I was to live on North Pearl Street, become the unremarkable and unremarked ambience of 'my block' with its noise, its squalor, its childhood rites and ordeals, the awkward rutting rituals of its adolescents, and its shoals of dirty brats with runny noses, nits and impetigo playing their screaming games of kick-the-can or stick ball, sassing icemen and pushcart vendors, blocking traffic and exchanging insults with truck drivers who wanted to get through.

On that first day, the game of stick ball in the middle of the street broke up when second base drove off. The preening boys in front of the cornerstore drifted away down Livingston Avenue toward the deserted warehouses between the freight yards and the river where, as I would learn by being one of them, they would snoop around the dripping, echoey, broken-glass-crunchy-under-foot, piss-smelling vastnesses of abandoned buildings, and they would chuck stones at the few window panes that remained tauntingly intact. North Pearl Street was a typical slum of the first half of what would be called the American Century. These slum blocks were identical in their essence and social effects, varying only in the cultural decoration of their ethnic concentrations. Pearl Street was Irish. More precisely, it was bog Irish.[1]

Pearl Street was the sort of place that appeared, laundered and tempered with humor and hokey sentimentality, in films starring the Dead End Kids: sassy-mouthed but essentially good boys who only needed one of Hollywood's grittier stars to sort them out and make honest, hard-working citizens of them. But the violent, reality-calloused kids of North Pearl would have scoffed at the efforts of a tough (but warm-hearted) Father Pat O'Brien or a wryly knowing Father Spencer Tracy to 'save' them by opening a boys' club and showing them that priests could be reg'lar fellas.

While we were sitting on the stoop anticipating the surprise my father had prepared for us, a thin layer of milky cloud began to spread over the sky, and the chill of a March afternoon settled on us. I was ready to give in and suggest that we go inside to look for my father, when the front door of a building across the street flew open, banging

---

[1]This tale is complete without footnotes, but there are also social, historical, political and personal observations available to you. You can download these cybernotes from www.trevanian.com, or have a friend download them for you. Cybernote 1 will deal with 'bog Irish'.

against the brick wall, and out poured a yelping, shrieking pack of children belonging to what we would come to know as the Meehans: a wild, drunken, dim-witted tribe that inhabited three contiguous houses on the east side of the street. All the Meehans were related in complex and unnatural ways. The four old Meehans, two brothers and two sisters, had produced half a dozen loud, dirty, boozy Meehan adults; and random, transient matings between and among this second generation of brothers/sisters/cousins and their parents had spawned some twenty offspring, who combined among themselves and with the earlier generations to produce a scattering of son/nephew/uncle/cousin/grandsons and daughter/niece/aunt/cousin/granddaughters. While all the Meehans had earned their family name at least twice over, only one of them was called 'Mrs Meehan'. The rest were known by their full names: Old Joe Meehan, the tribal chief, Young Joe Meehan, the heir apparent, Patrick Meehan, the dangerous one, Maeve Meehan, the nasty one, or Brigid Meehan, the willing one.

Ironically, the one called 'Mrs Meehan' on the block was the only woman of that tribe who was not related to the rest of the adults by blood. One of the Meehan men had been put into an institution for the dim-witted for a while, and he returned with a woman he had found there. It was she who did most of the tribe's cooking, cared for the younger children, and did such cleaning as took place in their warren...mostly scattering the litter around by batting at it with a ratty broom.

This 'Mrs Meehan' was the epicenter of the consternation and wailing that erupted through their front door and poured down the stoop. She was clutching a smoking iron skillet, and the kids surrounding her were sobbing and screaming, 'Drop it, Ma! Drop it!' Her face was twisted in agony because the skillet handle was burning her hand, but still she clung to it, whimpering. A Meehan male appeared at the top of the stoop wearing a sweat-stained undershirt, beer bottle in fist. He shouted at 'Mrs Meehan' to put the goddamned skillet down, for the love of Jesus! What did she think she was playing at, there?

"Help me!" she beseeched, the pain causing her to bare her teeth.

But he only sniffed and shook his head. "Crazy bitch."

A tousled female opened the front window of the next Meehan

house and thrust out her inflamed face, a cigarette glued to her lower lip. "What the hell?"

"It's only herself," the man informed his sister/cousin/mate in a tone of weary exasperation. "Up to her old tricks, she is."

The woman shrugged and closed the window.

One of the children tried to wrench the skillet out of his mother's hand, but he yelped and sucked at his burnt fingers. Just as my mother took Anne-Marie off her lap and was rising to dash across the street to help the poor woman, Old Joe Meehan, the doyen of the clan, appeared at the doorway. His sunken cheeks were white-stubbled and he had obviously just pulled on his tatty low-crotched trousers because the flies were agape and he was still thumbing his suspenders up over his bare chest and tufted shoulders. "Jesus, Mary and Joseph!" he complained as he swatted his way through the swarm of kids. With one skillful gesture born of practice, he kicked the skillet out of Mrs Meehan's hand, and she screamed as some of her skin went with it. Clutching her wrist as though to pinch off the pain and keep it from rising up her arm, Mrs Meehan docilely followed him up the stoop. Two of the kids kept watch over the still-hot skillet so that no one would steal it before another kid had returned from inside with a wad of rags to wrap around the handle so they could bring it back in, followed by the rest of the runny-nosed Meehan flock, all chattering and laughing now that the crisis was past. And suddenly the street returned to normal, and the rumble and clatter of the city around us re-emerged.

My sister and I exchanged big-eyed looks. What kind of place *was* this? What kind of people?

This was my first encounter with one of the crazyladies of Pearl Street, some of whom were not really crazy at all, just eccentric or 'different', although a couple were crazy by anyone's criteria. Over the ensuing years, my dealings with these crazyladies would punctuate the lurching, uneven stages of my growth and self-awareness.

We had been sitting on the stoop for over an hour, expecting my father to come walking around the corner at any minute. When a man did approach, Anne-Marie and I looked up at our mother to read her reaction, because neither of us would have recognized him. But none of them was our father. The March air was cooling rapidly, and Anne-Marie in her thin party dress was rubbing her upper arms to warm them, so my mother rose and looked up and down the street one final time before saying, "Well, we can't sit here until the cows freeze over! I'm going to take a gander inside. Maybe Ray told someone where he was going and how long he'd be. You kids keep an eye on our stuff." And she went up the stairs and into the red brick tenement.

She came back with an envelope she had found stuck into the crack of the door of apartment 2 on the first floor. Number 238 had no apartment 1, a designation the mail carriers reserved for basement apartments that looked through the iron bars of their low windows into wells sunken below the level of the sidewalk. But the brick row of seven identical five-story buildings that included 238 had only half-basements across the front, and that space was occupied by coal bunkers, huge old iron furnaces and boilers in varying states of dilapidation. Mother sat down between us and opened the envelope to find a note and a big old-fashioned key with a bow of green crepe paper tied around it. The note was from my father; it said that he had gone out to find a bakery that had a green cake for the party and he'd be back in a jiffy. A party? Green cake? Anne-Marie and I exchanged eager glances.

"Well, we might as well get ourselves moved in," Mother said.

Leaving Anne-Marie to watch over our things, Mother and I struggled up the stairs carrying her old Saratoga trunk with its scuffed leather bindings. Out of the corner of my eye, I saw the kids across the street watching me stagger under the weight of the trunk. I'd have given anything to be able to hook one finger in the leather handle and lift it...just like that!...whistling to myself, maybe. Yes, and carrying something huge in my other hand! That would have been great!

I have always been particularly sensitive to smells, even squeamish, and when I stepped into that hall I drew my first breath of that medley of mildew, Lysol, ancient grease, rotting woodwork, sweat, rat droppings, coal dust, baby urine and boiled cabbage...the residue of a hundred and fifty years of poverty and hopelessness, damp and eternal in the nostrils.

My mother and I staggered across the threshold of apartment 2, my arms feeling drawn out of their sockets by the weight of the

Saratoga trunk we had dragged and scooted down the hallway's scuffed and scruffy linoleum. We went into the kitchen to get a drink of water and were greeted by a vision. Obviously, the celebration my father planned was to be a Saint Patrick's Day party, and he had pasted strips of green crepe paper ribbon into chain links that he had looped back and forth between overhead water pipes. He must have spent hours doing it. On the narrow kitchen table there were four green paper plates with shamrocks, and standing in the middle of the table was a big bottle of green soda, presumably lime.

After drinking water directly from the faucet and getting our fronts wet in the process, Mother and I returned for more boxes and pieces of furniture. When we stepped back out onto our stoop Anne-Marie was standing in front of our boxes and furniture, her eyes shining with unwept tears of fear as she bravely interposed her little body between our possessions and the kids who had gathered to watch us move in. People had come out onto the stoops on both sides of our building and across the street, where they sat, the men sucking at quart bottles of ale, the women observing and frankly evaluating our efforts and our possessions. I would learn that watching people move in and out was a traditional community entertainment on North Pearl Street, not only because it offered an opportunity to see things that were usually hidden away in apartments, but also for the tantalizing narrative conjectures the event spawned. For those moving in, there were questions of where they had come from. What misfortune—or, better yet, disgrace—had brought them to North Pearl? What sort of people would they turn out to be? (The gossips of Pearl Street deplored two kinds of women, those who were 'loose' and those who were 'snooty', the one being every bit as objectionable as the other.) For those moving out, the suppositions were more dire and the gossip more juicy. Oh, a move away from Pearl Street *might* result from a bit of remarkable luck, like getting a job in some other town, or marrying a man with a job, but more commonly it was a final family dispersal caused by someone dying, or being sent to prison, or by losing their child-support benefits, and the family, no longer able to sustain itself as a whole even in such a last-ditch place as Pearl Street, had been evicted by the slum landlord. Where could they go? How could they live? Would they ever be seen again? And what if they had borrowed something from you? You'd better watch that they didn't take it with them.

Mortified to be the focus of this attention and conjecture, I worked hard to get us moved in quickly and away from their eyes and comments. To show the circle of kids that I was strong enough to take care of myself, I picked up things that were too heavy or too bulky for me to handle. To their sniggering amusement, I invariably had either an awkward struggle or a mortifying mishap in my effort to get whatever it was into the apartment, like when I finally managed to get a big box of mixed cleaning products to the top of the stoop, only to have the bottom fall out, leaving me holding the empty box while all kinds of stuff clattered back down the steps followed by a roll of toilet paper that unwound as it went, leaving a paper trail across the sidewalk and into the gutter. After chasing it down I had to re-roll it carefully, sure that all eyes were on me and that everybody was chuckling and snorting, but we couldn't afford just to waste it. In my rush to get this humiliating task over with quickly I got the paper on crooked several times and had to unroll it and start again.

While I fumbled in angry, unproductive haste I could see out of the corners of my eyes that the women were watching my mother lift big boxes and carry them with ease. She wasn't all that strong, but she was adroit. She was only a little over five feet tall, but she was wiry and she moved with the grace that had won her trophy cups for dancing the Charleston and the Varsity Drag when she was a seventeen-year-old flapper, only ten years before. I could tell that the women, mostly flaccid and dumpy with eating bad food, felt an immediate dislike for my mother's short page-boy hair, her bell-bottomed slacks, and her pert, even saucy, movement and gestures. "Probably both snooty *and* loose," their sniffs said.

Eventually we got all our boxes and bits into the apartment, which was rented 'semi-furnished', meaning there were four straight-backed wooden chairs each of a different design, color and epoch, two chiffoniers, one with drawers that stuck open, the other with drawers that stuck shut, a sagging double bed and a hand-made child's cot in the back bedroom, a narrow table in the kitchen, and in the front room an iron daybed and, incongruous in the limited space, two wicker chairs with broken spines that caused them to twist and squeak when you sat in them and whose split canes scratched your legs and clutched at your clothes. But we were off the street and our possessions were no longer under the gaze of scoffers. Worn out with having done most of the work, Mother lay down on the daybed in the front room while Anne-Marie and I wandered through the apartment, looking into nooks and dark corners, imagining what our lives would be like in this strange new place. We flushed the toilet to see if it worked, and opened the tap in the old iron bathtub until the rust-brown water thinned to tan, then ran clear. (Apparently, the prior renters weren't great bath-takers.) We peeked into cupboards and the apartment's only closet. We opened the door of the lead-lined icebox and quickly closed it, gagging at the knee-buckling smell of a stale icebox. Being a big brother, I threatened to push her head in and make her breathe the stink; being a little sister, she threatened to tell our mother if I did, then I'd get it. She claimed the little child's cot in the corner of the bedroom; just right for her, be-cause she too was little, and she would be close to Mother in the big bed, just in case someone had bad dreams and wanted to crawl in next to someone else.

As Anne-Marie looked on, her head through the railings in the back hall, I crept down the dark stairs to the basement from which a clammy, ominous chill rose to meet me. Being watched by my kid sis-ter, I was obliged to go all the way down and even open the basement door a crack and peek in, but then I heard something—or thought I did—and I came dashing back up, shouting as I ran so it would seem as though I were trying to scare Anne-Marie, not that I was scared my-self. But time and again, we found ourselves back in the kitchen, at-tracted to the looping festoons of green crepe paper and the Saint Patrick's Day paper plates and napkins and green soda for our party. We kept an ear cocked for our father's return with that green cake. A green cake!

Number 238 was at the center of seven identical brick row houses that had been built as private homes in the 1830s, when Pearl Street was a middle-class residential street that had the advantage of being close to the teeming commercial wharves where merchants did their business. To reflect the social aspirations of its original owners, the en-trance halls of all seven houses were wide, so there was room for only three interconnecting rooms on the first floor, rooms that were used for entertaining and impressing guests, so they were high ceiling'd, had ogee moldings and chandelier rosettes (but no longer any chandeliers), and the room giving onto the street had two tall windows. In most of the houses in our rows, these spacious first-floor rooms had been converted into three one-room studio flats with little kitchen nooks in the corner, a sofa that opened into a bed, and a shared bathroom at the end of the hall, just right for single old people who couldn't manage the stairs; but ours had been left as one apartment with a formal receiving room in front, giving on the street, a windowless middle room that had formerly been the dining room but now was more like a big hall and all-purpose storage space that you had to pass through to get to the other rooms, and a smaller back withdrawing room that had been partitioned into a bedroom and a small kitchen, with a door that gave onto a bathroom so narrow that the toilet, the tub and the washbasin were all in a row. The original kitchens had been in the basement, and all meals had been carried up to be served. The second floors of the seven identical houses had contained a withdrawing room ('drawing room), a study or office, the master bedroom, and a generous dressing room cum lady's retiring room at the back of the building. These had been converted into two three-room apartments, each with a minute bathroom. Second-floor apartments were considered the best in any tenement and always cost more than others because they had biggish rooms and you only had to walk one flight up to get away from the noise, grime and threat of the street. Few on welfare ever lived on the second floor, which was reserved for 'a better class of people'. The third and fourth floors had originally been the family bedrooms, which had been converted into flats sharing an end-of-the-hall bathroom. Typical of Georgian fenestration, the windows were smaller the higher you went, so the fifth floor had the very small windows and the low ceilings of what had been servants' quarters. The cramped rooms on the fifth were the cheapest, not only because of the long climb up, but also because they were beneath the uninsulated flat roof and therefore were hot in summer and cold in winter. A bitter street joke said that people living on fifth floors had no right to complain about simmering all summer and freezing all winter because, in fact, the average yearly temperature up there was just about perfect.

The overall effect of our building, with its traces of erstwhile re-

finement in the intricate plasterwork now muffled beneath coats of ancient paint, was one of fallen gentility, of tawdry elegance. An old gen-
tlewoman with her front teeth knocked out in a bar brawl.[2]

We thought ourselves lucky to have three big rooms, but we soon
learned that first-floor flats were cheap because they were not considered desirable, in part because their windows were within reach of
drunks and vandals leaning out from the stoop, so people could never
sleep with them open, no matter how hot the weather got. Also, the
rooms were awkwardly shaped because of the space lost to the big entrance hall and two flights of stairs, a broad one ascending to the second floor 'drawing room, and a dark narrow one down to the coal
bunker and furnace in the basement. The front receiving room, however, with its high ceilings and ornate if paint-clogged plaster cornices
had retained a certain forlorn grandeur, and here I was to sleep on the
iron daybed for the next eight years, and here I listened to adventure
programs on our Emerson radio, and here, late into the night, I knelt
on a pillow at the big front window in the dark, and I daydreamed as I
watched the street, when winter snow sifted down diagonally across
the pane, or when plump drops of spring rain burst upon and wriggled
down the glass, and sometimes in summer I would open the window (it
was safe to open because it only came up about three inches before its
warped frame jammed) and let the cool late-night air flow over my face
as I listened to the melancholy sound of trains down in the freight
yards that separated Pearl Street from the wharves and warehouses of
the Hudson. In all seasons I was intrigued by late-night life on Pearl
Street: sleepy lovers walking because they had no place to go, her head
on his shoulder; befuddled drunks stepping off the curb with neck-
snapping jolts, then looking back and swearing at the pavement for
its duplicity; the rotating light of prowl cars grazing smears of red over
the brick walls when the cops came to investigate a complaint or arrest
someone...and sometimes the obscure wanderings of Pearl Street's
crazyladies.

Having investigated our new home, Anne-Marie and I were in the
kitchen, looking at the bottle of green soda and thinking about that
green cake. She sighed and said she was really, really, really hungry.
Poor Anne-Marie. We hadn't eaten since breakfast, and food was more
crucial to her sense of well-being than it was to mine or Mother's.

When she drank hot chocolate, she would look into the bottom of her cup and hum with pure pleasure, and she got light-headed and frightened when she was hungry; but she hadn't said a word because she didn't want to spoil the Saint Patrick's Day party by eating just before it started. I went into the front room and woke Mother to tell her we were hungry. She dug into her change purse in that tight-fingered way that meant she was almost out of money and clawed out a quarter, and she sent me across to the cornerstore to get a loaf of bread and a small jar of peanut butter. Mother believed that peanut butter offered the best food value per unit of money you could buy. Meanwhile, she would locate the box containing our kitchen things and unpack it.

"But don't mess up the kitchen," I reminded her. "We've got to keep everything ready for the party."

I crossed the street and passed, head down, through the knot of older kids that had returned to loiter in front of Mr Kane's cornerstore.

"Hey, kid! Where you from?"

I didn't answer. I had developed the tactic of pretending to be lost in my own thoughts to avoid having to deal with people.

"What's the matter, kid? Your ears broke? I asked where you was from."

He said 'axed' for 'asked'. I shrugged and reached out for the door to the shop, but a kid grabbed my collar and pulled me back, so I muttered, "Lake George Village."

"What's that? George what? Talk up, why don't you?" He said 'tack' for 'talk' and 'ya' for 'you', and that troubled me. These local tribes didn't even speak our language. It wouldn't be long, however, before I learned to slip into the metallic, dentalized, slack-mouthed idiom of Northeastern street talk when I wanted to sound tough, and save my own accent for when I wanted to seem intelligent or polite.

"We're from Lake George Village," I said more firmly than I felt.

"Where's that?"

"Up-state."

"Hey, kid, got any money?" another asked.

"No."

"Why you going to the Jew's then? He don't give kids no credit."

I tried to open the shop door, but someone grabbed my arm. "Come on, kid. Give us a nickel!"

"No!"

"You looking for a fist sandwich, kid?"

The door of the cornerstore opened. "Well, well, what have we here? A gathering of the neighborhood's best and brightest, is it? Our nation's hope for the future?" It was the shopkeeper wearing thick glasses and a green cloth apron. "And who are you, young man? Well, come in if you're coming in. I can't stand around here all day. Time is money, as the watchmaker said."

I followed him into the store, hoping the kids would disperse before I had to go back home.

In response to my request for a small jar of peanut butter, Mr Kane took up a long wooden pole with metal fingers that were manipulated from a grip in the handle. He grasped the jar of peanut butter on a high shelf of his narrow shop, plucked it away, then opened the metal fingers and let it drop. As I gasped, he snatched up the hem of his apron to make a nest for receiving the jar with a plop, the deft performance of a man who had show business in his blood. I would learn before long that only bad breaks and the Depression had brought Mr Kane to North Pearl Street as a shopkeeper. And it wasn't show business he had in his blood, it was socialism.

"And what else, young man?"

"A loaf of bread," I said. "...wait a minute. How much is the peanut butter?"

"For you? Fifteen cents. For others? A nickel and a dime."

"Okay, and how much is a loaf of bread?"

"Eleven cents. One thin dime and a somewhat thicker penny... which isn't logical, but who said life has to be logical?"

"Do you have small loaves?"

"Eleven cents *is* the small loaf."

"...Oh. I don't think I can..."

"Of course, day-old bread is only a nickel."

"Do you have any day-old bread?"

He looked down on me, his eyes huge through thick lenses. "Well, I close up shop pretty soon. Tell you what; I'll sell you a loaf of tomorrow's day-old bread. How's that?"

I hated people giving us stuff or doing us favors, as though we couldn't make our own way. I hated it because my mother resented it so much. But...

"Okay."

There was a shout outside as one boy 'sizzled' another by snapping his fingernails down across the kid's butt in a way that stings like hell. The sizzled kid took a swing at the other, who ran down the street, and a couple of kids ran after him, laughing and shouting. If I could only give them a little more time, maybe the rest of them would go away somewhere.

"We just moved in," I told Mr Kane brightly.

"Yes, I saw you sitting over on the stoop of 238, surrounded by your possessions, like a band of Arabs in the desert. When business is slow, so it shouldn't be a total loss, I use my time to keep an eye on the street. After all, if I don't keep an eye on it, who will? I heard you tell one of your tormentors that you're from Lake George Village."

"Oh, do you know Lake George Village?"

"Never heard of it. But if I concentrate I can almost..." He closed his huge eyes. "An image is coming to me through the mist. I see a small town. No, no, it's more like a village. And I see...I see water! Is it a river? The ocean? No, it's...a *lake!* And it's named after a person...wait a minute, wait a minute, it's coming to me. Is it Lake Nathan? No, not Nathan. Lake Samuel? No, not Sam—Ah! I've got it! George! It's Lake George, by George!"

I didn't mind his teasing. I could tell he loved to perform, and there were still a couple of kids outside the cornerstore, so I said, "We came to Albany to be with my father. He made a party for us."

"A party?"

"A Saint Patrick's Day party. He's out getting us a green cake."

"A green cake? H'm, I *did* see a man come out of 238 this morning. Dapper-looking gentleman, he was. And, you know, I remarked at the time that there was something in the way he walked that suggested a man on the trail of a cake. But I've got to be honest with you. From across the street I couldn't tell it was a green cake he was after. It could have been any color for all I knew."

"Yes, we're waiting for him to come back for the party."

A woman's voice from the back room called out in an exasperated

whine, wanting to know if Mr Kane was going to close up or did he intend to stay open all night! His soup was getting cold!

"Ah. My life-burden calls." He chanted back, "Coming, dear."

"Well, I better be getting home." I put my quarter up on the top of
the glass candy case that served as a counter.

"Why don't I just put it on the slate until your welfare check
comes in?"

"We don't have any—"

But he was already opening the scuffed and thumbed notebook
that was his 'slate'. "Now, what name shall I put down? Mr and Mrs
George, from the lake of the same name?"

My mother had punitively reverted to her maiden name after my
father abandoned her with me still in her arms and Anne-Marie 'under
her heart'. To avoid confusion and comment she had entered me in
school as Jean-Luc LaPointe, not using my father's name. "LaPointe,"
I said.

"...Mr and Mrs LaPointe," he droned as he carefully printed the
name at the top of a page. "The LaPointes from France, I assume?"

"My grandfather came from Canada. We're part Indian."

"Oh-oh. Not one of those tribes notorious for scalping shopkeepers and making off with his penny candies!"

"No, not that kind."

"Whew! Talk about your close calls! So that's fifteen cents for one
jar of butter of the peanut variety..." he wrote, "...and five cents for a
loaf of bread; size: small; age: one day old. Neonate bread, the bakers
call it." He closed the slate with a snap and waggled his thick eyebrows
up and down above his huge eyes.

When I returned to our apartment with the bread, the peanut butter, and the quarter still intact, I had to explain to my mother that we
were down on Mr Kane's slate and didn't have to pay until our check
came in.

"What check?"

"I don't know."

"And he gave you credit, just like that?"

"I guess he gives everybody credit. The boys said he's a Jew and he
doesn't give credit, but he does. He has a book that he calls his slate."

"H'm!" She didn't like the sound of that. She hated feeling be-holden. Especially to strangers. "It'll be a hot day in hell before I go begging from strangers! What were you thinking of, Jean-Luc?"

"I don't know, I just—"

But she said never mind, she'd straighten things out in the morning.

We ate our peanut butter sandwiches at the kitchen table from which I had carefully cleared the paper plates and napkins so they could be replaced exactly where they had been for our Saint Patrick's Day party. I could tell that Mother didn't like my fussing that way. She was seething inside over something, so I kept my head down and didn't say anything. But Anne-Marie kept eyeing the bottle of lime soda. I told her we had to save it for the party, so everything would be green.

Mother sniffed. "Party! If I could find our bottle opener among all this crap, I'd open that soda quick enough. And I'd pour it down the sink!"

"But you can't. That'd spoil everything!"

"A big goddamn Saint Patrick's party! That's just like your father. You don't know his ways. I do. Always the big noise. The big show! He leaves us in the lurch for four years without so much as a word, and we don't know if he's alive or dead or what the hell, and now he's going to throw a big party, and that's supposed to make everything just fine and dandy! And the worst of it is that he's probably going to get away with it. Sure! When you kids are grown up, it won't be the years I've shrimped and saved and worked my fingers to the knuckle that you'll remember. It won't be how I've had to worry and fret, scared that I'd get real sick, and then what'd happen to you, I'd like to know. No, what you'll remember will be Ray's goddamn green Saint Patrick's Day cake! He runs away leaving me with all the work and worry, then he comes back with a big splash and we're all supposed to forgive him! Goddamn him to hell! And we're not even Irish!" But she shook her head and I knew that she was perversely proud of his cheek and élan. Who else would have had the brass to throw a party instead of saying he was sorry? Throughout the years we had been alone, whenever Mother got fed up with struggling to keep us in food and clothing, and especially when she was afraid she might be hospitalized with one of her lung attacks and social workers might come and take us kids away from her, she would give vent to her disappointment and fury. But after accusing him of being weak and irresponsible and selfish, she always ended up mentioning, in a give-the-goddamned-devil-his-due way, that he was a smooth dancer and a nifty dresser and that he had buckets of charm and what she called 'real class'. Ruby Lucile LaPointe wasn't the sort to fall for just any pair of trousers. No, sir.

My sister and I knew our father only from a photograph taken during their two-day honeymoon in New York City in 1929: a slim, handsome man in a white linen summer suit, the jacket held open by a fist on one hip to reveal a silk waistcoat, a straw boater tipped rakishly over one eye, his smile at once knowing and boyishly mischievous. After their honeymoon, he sent Mother back to the village of Granville to stay with her cousin Lorna and her husband while he went down to Florida to join up with friends who had let him in on a foolproof enterprise that would make him lots of money fast. Something to do with land speculation. He would return at the end of the summer and they could begin their life together. On Easy Street, Toots! Over the next two weeks, my mother received a letter from him every day, then one a week for the next month, then silence, and her letters to him were returned 'Address Unknown'. I was born nine months and six days after their marriage, and as soon as she was strong enough after a difficult birth (I heard the clinical particulars of this exceptionally long and arduous birth many times) we moved away from Lorna and her husband, who always grumbled about having to share his house and food with a cousin-in-law and her squalling brat. Mother got a job as a waitress in the summer resort where she had met my father, and we lived there until a letter from my father was forwarded to her by her cousin. He had run into some 'trouble' that led to his becoming an honored guest of the state of Florida for a year and a day. He hadn't written because there was nothing she could do to help him, so what was the point of distressing her? But he was a free man again, and a wiser one, and he was coming back north to meet some friends in Montreal who were letting him in on a sure thing. He stopped off on his way and spent one night with us at Lake George. I think I remember a man who came bearing a very big teddy bear, but I might only be remembering my mother's description of his arrival on our doorstep, tipsy, singing, and bearing an oversized teddy bear with which he staged a comic wrestling match to my giggling delight, ending up on the floor with the teddy bear triumphantly astride his chest as he begged for mercy. I wonder what happened to that teddy bear? Mother never said so, but I suspect she threw it out in a rage when he disappointed her again. The only time she ever spoke of this one-night visit she shook her head fatalistically and said, "All that man had to do was unbutton his suspenders and I got pregnant." The deal in Montreal fell through and my father disappeared from sight for a month or two. Then another letter came asking us to meet him in Schenectady, where he had reason to believe he could pick up a little action. His letter went on to say, "I know what anxiety and worry you've been through, Toots. All I ask is a chance to make it up to you. And remember...'You Were Meant for Me'." This song title had little notes written around it. The citing of 'their song' and the coyness of '...as an honored guest of the State of Florida...' are typical of the letters from him I found among my mother's things after her death. She had saved every one of them, a total of nineteen, all written in a blend of jocular Runyonesque style, sudden sincerity, unabashed sentimentalism, and kittenish duplicity. In short, a con man's letters.

I should mention that my mother never told us that our father spent time in prison, presumably to protect us from the shame. I learned about this later, when reading over the letters she left behind.

We joined my father in Schenectady in the winter of 1932–33, the nadir of the Depression, when dazed men stood on street corners, the collars of their suit jackets turned up, and begged passers-by for jobs or handouts, hopelessness muting their voices to mantra drones. We survived on a series of short-lived scams he ran, penny-ante hustles that didn't require much setup money. One of these was the Sure-Fire Employment Agency that disappeared from its storefront office within a month. (Mother had one of the business cards for this fraudulent enterprise in her photograph album, its corners held by stick-on tabs.) Another hustle was selling exclusive franchises to market Jiffy Fifteen-Way Mirakle Kleener (Fels Naphtha bar soap cooked down in water, bottled, and labeled in the kitchen of our basement apartment to flash as samples of the product). I remember standing in the front room looking up at the window to see the legs of people passing by, sometimes followed by little doggies that sniffed the window and sometimes cocked a leg at it, their leashes leading up from their collars to... nowhere. The room was full of the nose-stinging steam of yellow bar soap being cooked down to make Mirakle Kleener.

The Sure-Fire Employment Agency scam provides an insight into the con-man mentality that reasons: If you can't find a job, then it must be possible to make money off other people trying to find jobs. And the jobs my father offered were opportunities to become franchised door-to-door salesmen of Jiffy Fifteen-Way Mirakle Kleener. This double-barreled scam shows how hustlers automatically think on the diagonal. Lots of men with no work and a family to support might have bottled and peddled Mirakle Kleener from door to door; but only cons like my father would have sold other out-of-work men *franchises* to sell it: offering them not only a chance to survive but an opportunity to 'Make a Killing in the Cleaning Industry!' because, let's face it, no matter how good or how bad things are, there'll always be dirt! My father had the con man's instinct for the jugular of human greed.

These low-grade scams ultimately built up a body of victims eager for an opportunity to inflict retributive damage (if I may imitate my father's hokum/comic style, à la W. C. Fields), so it is not surprising that after seven months in Schenectady he accepted an offer from 'some friends' to go to South Dayton, New York, and supervise the transport of what his first letter back to Mother called 'prohibited merchandise' from Canada to 'deprived communities'. National prohibition had just ended, but the old supply systems remained functional because there were still dry states and counties. A second letter told her that he missed her more than he could say because 'You Were Meant for Me', Toots. Following this letter, there was a three-year silence, during the first month of which my sister was born.

It was while we were in Schenectady that I ran away from home for the first time. For some reason, perhaps because the return of my father suddenly deprived me of my mother's undivided attention, I began to wet my bed at night, although I had been toilet-trained for a year. The first couple of times this happened, my mother dismissed it as a 'phase', but she was ultimately obliged to accept that it was full-blown regression. She decided to correct my urinary insouciance using a method

she had read about in a book on 'modern' child-raising, a book that was
against corporal punishment, preferring bloodless tactics that caused
only emotional and developmental damage. One evening she came
back from shopping with a package for me. I eagerly tore off the wrapping and discovered to my surprise, but not to my horror, a dress that
she had picked up in a second-hand clothing shop. Following the advice in her book, she told me that if I was going to act like a little wet-
the-bed girlie, then I would have to dress like a little wet-the-bed
girlie, and she made me take off my clothes and put on the dress. At
first I didn't realize this game was meant to be a punishment. Dressing
up like a girl seemed strange, but not shameful; and I was far from dis-
pleased by the attention I got as I pranced around the room in my
dress. It was only when my father grasped my arm angrily and said
that I would have to wear the dress like a little girlie until I decided
to stop wetting my bed that I realized the costume was meant to be
humiliating. I was first confused then hurt by the realization that my
mother...my *mother* was trying to shame me. And this big man was
angry because I had found the punishment amusing. I threw myself to
the floor and kicked and screamed and tried to tear the damning dress
off me. But I was put into my crib wearing the dress, and long after my
incensed screams had collapsed into sobs and gasps, I lay in the dark,
my teeth clenched.

I had overheard my mother talking about a naughty boy in the
apartment above ours who ran away from home, not caring how much
his parents suffered and worried until he was found and returned to
them. This equipped me with the means to avenge my humiliation. I
would run away to my grandfather LaPointe, who had been the only
man in my life before the return of this *father* who had changed my
loving mother into a woman who liked to shame me. They would suf-
fer and worry about where I was, but I would never return to them; instead I would go live with my grandfather who had choo-choo trains
and would give me rides all the time.

The next evening, when this...father...was safely out of the house
and my mother was upstairs having coffee with the neighbor lady, I
collected my knitted winter hat with a green tassel, a folded-over piece
of bread for sustenance, and my red Christmas tricycle for transporta-

tion, and I left home forever. I can recall only blurred snapshots of the great escape: pushing my tricycle along the edge of a sidewalk crowded with impatient workers swarming out of some big factory; then night fell, and I was cold and scared. I remember waiting forever for the courage to cross a wide street with floods of noisy, speeding traffic, then being helped across by an old lady; and I asked a gasoline-smelling man in a service station with green-and-orange pumps which way it was to the choo-choo trains; and later I got tired of pushing the red tricycle, so I left it in a dark narrow space between two buildings where I could find it when I needed it. But I never found it again, and it started to rain, and I needed to poo very badly, but didn't know where to go, so I poo'd in my pants. A car pulled over to the curb and a police-man got out and asked me my name and where I was going, then he told the policeman in the car that I was the one the lady had called about, and that I smelled pretty 'high'. I remember being obliged to sit on newspapers in the back seat with the windows open as they drove me back home.

My mother cried and yelled and kissed me and smacked my legs and hugged me and cleaned me up and got me warm by bathing me in the kitchen sink, then she fed me and told my father that he'd better get rid of that damned dress or he'd have to deal with *her*, believe me you! I slept in my cozy crib that night, and never wet the bed again. I don't know what happened to the book on modern child-raising. I never saw it again.

My father went out the next morning to look for work. After a few days our money ran out, and my mother was obliged to accept that he wasn't coming back. She had been abandoned...again. She sent a letter to my grandfather and he took a day off from his job as station master of the whistle-stop railroad depot in Fort Anne to help us move back to Lake George Village. We were tided over by small amounts of money from my grandfather, who depleted his savings by helping to support his children and his nieces through the Depression. My first sure, un-fragmented memories come from the time Mother and I and my new baby sister lived in Lake George Village with only a tin kerosene heater to combat the cold that seeped through the uninsulated walls of a two-room summer cottage. As a special treat after she got back from work late at night, my mother used to make us toast on the top of that kerosene heater: toast that browned in the intricate hole patterns of the heater's lid. I loved the char taste of that toast, and the crunch of it between my teeth, and the late-night celebration of all being together. And I remember my grandfather's weekly visits. He used to smell of talcum powder and leather and he always took me on his lap and asked me how the world was getting on, then he gave me a lollipop. After supper, he would play two-handed pinochle with my mother and make her laugh by pretending to be furious about the rotten cards he'd been dealt. His visits were not only to give us the little money he could spare, but also to sustain us morally. I was enormously proud of my grandfather, and not only because he was in charge of trains and could click messages down a wire all the way to New York City, if he wanted to, but also because he was a half-blood Onondagan whose parents had immigrated to the United States from their unproductive farm on a tributary of the St. Lawrence. This meant that I was an Indian[3] too, although my grandfather's marriage to a woman from a New England family and my mother's marriage to a man of English extraction combined to dilute my Indian blood terribly. Nevertheless, I used to feel a secret and thrilling kinship with a bronze statue of an Indian drinking water from his palm in Lake George Village.

My grandfather's car skidded off the road in a blinding snowstorm when he was driving from Granville, where he had given money and encouragement to his niece and her husband, to Lake George, where he was going to do the same for us. When the news of his death came, my mother was sick in bed. She had caught a bad chest cold walking to work through the snow, and for days she had been lying in the back room, a wracking cough denying her sleep and bursts of high fever causing her to drift along the edges of reality—a recurring pattern of illness that was to become familiar over the years. The neighbor lady who was looking in on my sister and me assured us that Mother would make it through, "...so don't you worry your little heads." It hadn't even occurred to me that my mother might not make it through until the neighbor's assurances suggested that terrible possibility. And it was this same neighbor who got the telephone call about my grandfather and decided that the news of his death would be easier for my mother to bear if it came from me. This neighbor lady whispered into my ear that my grandfather had been killed in a car crash, then she pushed me into the dark bedroom, and when I paused, unwilling, she urged me forward with impatient flicks of her fingers.

I sat on the side of my mother's bed—she smelled of sleep and the mustard tang of Balm Bengué—and I stroked her damp forehead as I told her that her father had gone to heaven. I was four and a half and she was twenty-five, and on that snowy evening I became my mother's confidant and 'good right hand', roles that were to continue throughout my childhood. I was proud of my newfound importance; but my retreat into long and complex story games began at this time.

Two years passed, and my mother had just been told that she wouldn't have a job come the summer because her bad health made her unreliable, when she received a letter from my father, a letter I have before me on my desk. He had made an 'error in judgment' for which he had been given five-to-seven in 'an institution dedicated to the moral reconstruction of those who take shortcuts to success and comfort'. But he had proved 'a contrite and willing pilgrim on the road to redemption' and had received early release after working as assistant to the prison librarian. He was now in Albany, the state capital, and he had rented us temporary lodgings until he was able to find a decent job...maybe in a library somewhere. He was all through with chasing rainbows. He was ready to settle down and make a life for his family. He knew he didn't deserve a second chance (or was it a third chance?), but...'You Were Meant for Me', Toots. Remember?

Although Mother had vowed never to accept another thing from her cousin's husband after the way he had complained about being burdened with us, she swallowed her pride and wrote, asking if he could bring us and our stuff down to Albany in his old truck. During the trip, I looked out the side window at passing farmland, at the blur of bushes beside the road, and up at the telephone wires that seemed to part and re-weave, part and re-weave above us. And now we were eating peanut butter sandwiches in the kitchen of 238, and Anne-Marie and I were anticipating the Saint Patrick's Day party to celebrate our family's finally getting together to start a new life.

It was growing dark, so Mother turned the old-fashioned porcelain switch for the kitchen's naked overhead lightbulb. Nothing.

"Just like him! Didn't even think to get the electric turned on!"

I had an idea. I went into the bathroom and turned its switch, and the light came on. The kitchen bulb was only burned out. So we finished our sandwiches by the light from the open bathroom door. For some time Anne-Marie had been dipping and dozing on the rim of sleepiness, then her head would snap up as she fought to stay awake until her father came home with the green cake, which she was determined not to miss.

But Mother stood up with a sigh and said he'd come when he came, and there was no point in our sitting up all night. She unpacked the box containing our sheets and our most treasured possession, three Hudson Bay blankets given to her as a wedding present by my grandfather, and we made the beds together. The blankets were thick, top-quality, 'five-tail' Hudson Bays with those bands of bright color that fur traders thought would appeal to primitive Indian taste sufficiently to make them part with five beaver hides to get one. I had seen pictures of Indian chiefs wearing 'five-tail' blankets, and I wished the neighbors who had scoffed at our battered possessions out on the sidewalk knew that we also owned three of the best woolen blankets in the world. Mother put her reluctant but comatose daughter into the little bed in their bedroom, where, after making Mother promise to wake her up for the party, Anne-Marie instantly fell into a deep sleep, sucking her fingers. Mother and I sat at the kitchen table for a while, silent and with that metallic emptiness in the stomach that follows long periods of excitement. Then she said we might as well go to bed too. I could help her unpack in the morning. I kissed her good-night and told her I'd just set the table first, and I began putting the green paper plates and napkins back into place around the bottle of lime soda, while Mother watched me, shaking her head.

"You're my good right hand, Jean-Luc. I don't know what I'd do without you."

She kissed me good-night and turned out the bathroom light, and the crepe paper chains disappeared into the dark of the high ceiling.

I lay on my daybed in the front room, which never got totally dark because a streetlamp cast a diagonal slab of light from one corner to the other. I was looking up at the ceiling, intrigued by how, each time a car passed out on the street, the edge-ghost of its headlights slid through and around the chandelier rosette in the middle of which a single light-bulb dangled from a paint-stiffened wire. I lay there for what was, for a kid, a long time, maybe ten minutes, until I thought Mother was asleep, then I eased out of bed stealthily and went to the window to watch for my father's arrival. He'd be the one coming down the street carrying the string-tied baker's box with a green cake that he'd finally found after going from one end of Albany to the other, and I would sneak out onto the stoop and beckon him in, putting my finger across my lips to signal him to walk on tiptoes, and we'd put the cake in the middle of the kitchen table and open the green soda carefully, so the *pfffft* sound wasn't too loud, and we'd get everything ready, then we'd go into the bedroom and wake Mother and Anne-Marie, and they'd be surprised and all smiles and...

I heard a faint sound from the back bedroom. I knew that sound, and hated it. My mother was crying softly to herself, as she did only when the bad breaks and the loneliness and ill health built up until they overwhelmed her. She cried when she was afraid, and the thought of my mother being afraid frightened me in turn, because if that buoyant, energetic woman couldn't handle whatever the problem was, what chance did I have? Sometimes, I would go to her and pat her shoulder and kiss her wet, salty cheek, but I always felt so helpless that the pit of my stomach would burn. Precocious at games and arithmetic, I had learned a couple of months earlier how to play two-handed 'honeymoon' pinochle, her favorite game and one that reminded her of her father. Sometimes playing pinochle took her mind off our problems. But the cards were deep in one of our boxes somewhere, and anyway, I didn't feel like sitting with her, helpless and hopeless. Everything would be fine when my father got back. Even if he hadn't managed to find a green cake...but I was sure he would...he'd care for Mother when she was sick and kiss her tears away when she was blue and play pinochle with her and take responsibility for keeping the family well and happy, and I'd just play my story games, and everything would be fine. I put my cheek against the cool window pane so I could look as far up the empty street as possible. People passed by occasionally: lone men walking slowly, their fists deep in their pockets, wishing this night were over; women hastening to get somewhere on time; young couples

with their arms around each other's waist, keeping hip contact by stepping out with their inside legs at the same time, wishing this night
would go on forever. When a car passed, the edge of its headlights rippled over the brick facades on both sides of the street and lit up my
ceiling briefly. I considered slipping into my shoes and going out onto
the stoop to await my father's arrival, but the night was cold, so I sat on
the edge of my bed with my Hudson Bay blanket around me Indian-
style and watched the street, as I would do night after night.

My father never came. But, of course, you have anticipated that for
some time.

Settling In

B ACK IN Lake George Village, I had been used to waking up to the sounds of birds chirping and little creatures rustling in the woods behind the summer cottage we rented, but that first morning on North Pearl Street I was wrenched out of sleep by the sound of my mother thrashing around angrily back in the kitchen. I went in to find her wobbling precariously atop the narrow kitchen table as she snatched down the green crepe paper festoons. One loop was just out of reach and she almost fell stretching out for it. I suggested we move the table, and she told me the last thing she needed was a six-year-old telling her what to do, goddamnit! Then she came down and hugged my head to her stomach and said she didn't mean to snap at her first-born and good right hand, but she was determined to get rid of all this green party crap that reminded her of that no-good, lying, irresponsible bastard!

Always spiky and short-tempered the morning after a night of grief or regret, she would rage against 'the big-shots' and 'the rotten way things are'. Although she always assured my sister and me that it wasn't us she was mad at, just the goddamned world out there, we were the ones who winced as she unleashed the famous French-'n'-Indian temper that served as both a purgative for depression and a source of flash energy in her struggle to keep our family together against the odds. This explosive safety valve of hers frightened Anne-Marie and angered me. Sometimes her shouting, door-slamming, pan-throwing rages against life's injustices would make me yell at her in defensive counter-rage, and we'd have a brief, hot word-fight that would make my sister recoil into herself. Then suddenly the storm would pass and we'd both be sorry. Mother would hug me and suggest that the three of us go out and play tag or Simon Says or some other kids' game. She was wonderful about playing games with us. Even after we came to Pearl Street and were under the eyes of the block's gossips, she would sometimes come out and play with us, shrugging off the harsh glances and captious muttering of neighbor ladies who thought she was just showing off her youth and energy and suppleness. As, indeed, she was, to a degree.

Silent now, but simmering within, Mother gathered up the green paper plates and napkins and crammed them into a bucket that would serve as our garbage can until she could afford to buy one (we used that bucket for eight years), then she grasped the warm bottle of lime soda by its neck, stepped out into the sooty backyard and, throwing side-armed like a boy, hurled it over the weathered board fence into the back alley, where the bottle burst with an effervescent explosion that I'd have given anything to have seen.

But what a waste! I'd never tasted green soda because my mother was against our drinking 'fizzy crap', in part because it wasn't good for us, and in part because it was expensive.

Anne-Marie came padding sleepy-eyed into the kitchen and she knew immediately what had happened. She was painfully sensitive to Mother's rages and could always smell the sulfur in the air. She looked at the paper plates in the bucket, then at me. I shrugged. She smiled faintly and waited until Mother was not in the kitchen before she dared to retrieve a couple of the crumpled plates to play 'Saint Patrick's Day party' with.

After a breakfast of peanut butter sandwiches Mother held the first of many 'war councils' around that kitchen table. Here's how things were: We were marooned on this slum street in this strange city where we didn't know anybody and nobody gave a damn about us, and we had only a little more than five bucks to our name. But we weren't beaten. Not by a damnsight. Nobody beats Ruby Lucile LaPointe! No, sir! In all the years she'd taken care of us kids alone, her pride had never let her seek public assistance, and it burned her up to have to do so now, but she'd been thinking about things all night long, and she couldn't let pride stand in the way of us kids having food on the table. There must be agencies and people that she could turn to, just until we were on our feet again. First she'd contact them and ask them for help...*make* them help us, goddammit! Then she'd look for work as a waitress. A hard-working, experienced waitress can always find work, even if it's only split-shift, or standing in for girls who call in sick. She'd go around to every goddamned restaurant in the city putting her name in with the managers. But first, she had to find out the addresses of the welfare agencies. If only she knew someone she could ask about things like this.

"What about Mr Kane?" I suggested.

"The grocery man? Oh, I don't know. I don't think we want any more favors from his sort."

"...His sort?"

She shrugged.

"But he's nice," I said. "And smart, too."

She thought about that for a moment. She didn't like being be-holden to strangers, but...Oh, all right, she'd go over to thank him for giving us credit. That was just common courtesy. And maybe while she was there she'd..."You know, come to think of it, this Mr Kane of yours just *might* help us out because if he doesn't, we won't be able to pay what we owe him. You can only count on people if there's something in it for them."

"He'd help us anyway. He's nice."

She humph'd. She often said, and honestly believed, that she was not prejudiced—well, except in the case of Italian mobsters and drunken Irish loafers and stupid Poles and snooty Yankee Protestants, but then who wasn't? Among the cultural scars left by her early years in convent school was a stereotypical view of 'the people who slew Jesus'. "On the other hand," she said, always wanting to be fair, "I served some very nice Jewish people in Lake George Restaurant last season. They always chose my station. Real good tippers. But then they had to be, didn't they? To make up for things."

I accompanied her across the street, and Mr Kane spent half the morning looking up the appropriate welfare agencies and using the pay phone at the back of his shop to call people and make appointments for my mother, while I took occasional trips back to our apartment to make sure Anne-Marie was all right, but she could just look out the front window and see us in Kane's Cornerstore. Mr Kane gave Mother a dog-eared map of downtown Albany so she could find the addresses and he drew her up a list of things she should bring with her to the welfare offices: her marriage license, our birth certificates, her most recent address in Lake George, the telephone number of his store, where messages could be left for her...things like that. I looked up at my mother to give her an 'I *told* you he was nice' look, and I was surprised to see tears standing in her eyes. She said later that she didn't know what got into her. I think that Mr Kane's kindly manner sapped the constant background rage that gave her the grit to face difficult situations. Whatever the reason, the next thing I knew she was telling him about my father, and how he had run out on us twice before, and about our coming to Albany in the hope of starting life as a family, and about the Saint Patrick's Day party with the green cake...everything. Pushing the tears back into her eyes with the heel of her hand, she confessed that she didn't know what she would do if somebody didn't help her. One thing was sure: she wouldn't let her kids starve! No, sir! She'd steal—kill even!—before she'd let her kids starve. Distressed by her tears, Mr Kane rubbed his hands together, not daring to pat her shoulder compassionately lest she misunderstand the gesture (or, worse yet, lest his wife do so). He told her he didn't want to pry or anything, but maybe he should also contact the local ward heeler. See if the machinery could be oiled to make it turn a little faster. Otherwise, we might have to wait months for our case to make its way through the turgid system. She thanked him for his help, but now there was a chill in her tone. I could tell that she was ashamed of having broken down before this stranger. As we crossed the street back to 238 she told me that I must always be careful with these people.

"But Mr Kane was just trying to be..."

"They have a way of worming things out of you."

"He wasn't worming any—"

"You just be careful what you tell them, and that's final. Period!"

Later that month, when we were able to begin paying something against our slate, my mother felt vindicated in her mistrust of 'these people'. She discovered that Mr Kane had charged her a nickel for each call he made on her behalf. I explained that this was only fair because he had put a nickel into the slot for each call, but she waved this aside, saying she was sure he made a little something on each call. Why else would he have a phone taking up space in his shop? No, they work every angle, these people, believe me you.

With that 'believe me you' I think I'd better pause to explain that my mother's defiant independence extended to refusing to speak like everybody else. She had a tendency to get common idioms and clichés just that annoying little bit wrong. You may have noticed, and winced at, some of the askew figures of speech in the dialogue I've recorded for her, and perhaps you put them down to shoddy copy editing or to the writer's having momentarily nodded. In fact, I was trying to suggest my mother's slippery grasp of popular vernacular. She complained, for instance, of always having to 'shrimp and save', and she would declare that it would be 'a hot day in hell' before she'd do this or that, rather than a cold one which, presumably, is somewhat rarer. Uninteresting things were 'as dull as dish water' for her, and a pious, hypocritical woman 'looked as though her butter wouldn't melt'. I learned many of these twisted idioms from her only to experience the smarting humiliation of being corrected by people who were attuned to more conventional usage. The effect of this was to make me abjure hackneyed expressions from an early age, so I suppose I benefited from my mother's phrasal insouciance in the long run, although it's possible that my automatic eschewal of clichés occasionally drove me from the Scylla of ridicule into the turbid Charybdisian eddies of sesquipedalian obfuscation...though I trust not.

Mother's battles against the machinery of official compassion could not begin until the following morning, so we spent the rest of that day unpacking and putting things in order, making a home for ourselves, and Anne-Marie's spirits rose with the fun of playing house. Twice I was sent over to Mr Kane's, first to get a bar of Fels Naphtha soap and another of Bon Ami window cleanser (with the chick that 'hasn't scratched yet'), floor wax, cockroach powder, and...mortifying cargo for any little boy to have to carry past other children...a large package of toilet paper; and a second time to get groceries and milk for our lunch and supper. Both times Mr Kane did his vaudeville turn of getting things off the high shelves with his long, steel-fingered can-grabber and dropping them into his green apron, all the while joking and prattling so that I hadn't time to be embarrassed about asking him for more credit. While he was bagging up my purchases his wife, an unsmiling woman with features that seemed too big for her crowded face, came out from the back room and watched him to make sure he didn't drop a free piece of candy into my bag, as he had the first time. She made a tight-lipped comment about her husband having wasted enough time helping 'that new woman'.

The next morning my mother appeared at her bedroom door ready to take on the big-shots. She spread her arms in a 'Well, how do I look?' gesture. She was dressed in a slacks suit she had recently made by hand from a glossy royal blue material. It had a close-fitting jacket and wide belled trousers that flopped when she walked, and on the side of her head she wore a cocky little bellhop's hat that she'd made from the end of a cylindrical oatmeal box and covered with the same bright blue fabric and a bit of netting. It was her version of a costume Bette Davis had worn in a film. She saw strong parallels between herself and the characters Bette Davis played: women struggling in an unjust world ruled over by unreliable males. Bette Davis didn't have to rely on men for anything. No, sir! Not Bette Davis!

I told her she looked great, just great! But I secretly wished she had chosen something like other people's mothers wore, something dowdy and simple, the kind of unchallenging clothes that people who need help from officialdom should wear.

Leaving me to take care of Anne-Marie and buy something for our lunch over at Mr Kane's, Mother went down the street, her bell-bottoms flopping with each pert step. I had suggested that she wear a coat because the March weather was unreliable, but she said that her old wool coat would spoil the effect of her Bette Davis suit...which was pretty much what I'd had in mind. But I was also afraid she might catch a cold that would lay her up for days or weeks with one of her 'lung fevers'. Over the time we lived on North Pearl Street, she would end up in the hospital four times with pneumonia, which was often fatal in those pre-penicillin days, and each of these episodes gave the social services a chance to take Anne-Marie and me away from her on the grounds of her being, in the literal sense, an unfit mother.

It was dark out when Mother got back to our apartment after a day of those demeaning delays, opaque instructions, complicated forms and accusatory interrogations that welfare systems use to protect society from fraud or laziness on our part, or excessive compassion on theirs. Her face was drawn and her eyes sunken with fatigue and hunger. She hadn't brought any money for lunch because she didn't have a purse that matched her Bette Davis creation and there were no pockets in the close-fitting slacks, so she had passed the bureaucrats' long lunch break on a park bench, simmering with rage. I was afraid she might have caught a cold, but she was feeling triumphant. She described her day over the supper of tuna fish sandwiches and reheated Campbell's tomato soup that constituted the limit of my culinary capacities. All in all, she thought she had been victorious in her skirmishes with the Lords of Misery. I wasn't so sure, and I winced at every '...so I gave *her* a piece of my mind, don't think I didn't!...' and '...well, I didn't let him get away with *that* crap!...' and '...I told *them* a thing or two, believe me you...'. But at least she had come home in fairly good health and with her spirit unbroken, ready to continue the fight tomorrow.

As it turned out, she was not obliged to engage the Establishment in battle the next morning. She had dressed up in her glossy blue Bette Davis slacks suit and was checking through the list of names and addresses that Mr Kane had made out for her, when there came a knock at our door. Our visitor was a rotund, tightly packed man in a shiny black three-piece suit and a derby, the first derby I had ever seen outside of comic strips, where their primary function seemed to be to get blown off by a wind that then rolled them into the road where they

promptly got flattened by a steamroller that just happened to be passing by. The man wiped his hat band with a large handkerchief that he
then applied to his copiously sweating face, before asking in a broad
Irish accent, "Would you mind terribly, Missus?" Without waiting for
an invitation he came into our apartment, lowered himself with a grunt
into one of the creaking wicker armchairs, and began to fan himself
with his derby. Mother stood at the door, her arms crossed, ready to
throw this intruder out; and I stood beside her, ready to help, if that
was necessary. "So then, Missus," the ward heeler began. "We got a
telephone call from your Mr Kane, explaining your situation. Have I
the right of it when I say you're an abandoned woman?"

I could feel my mother tense up beside me. "What business is that
of yours?" she asked.

He explained that he represented the Third Ward, and that North
Pearl Street was part of his turf. "You've been around to see the welfare
people." He swabbed his glistening forehead with his handkerchief as
he consulted an official form that my mother had filled out the day before at the Aid to Dependent Children office. "You should have come
directly to us, Missus. That's what we're here for. But no harm done.
No harm done. Now I assume you're married to the man who abandoned you?"

"Now, just a goddamned min—"

"And I assume these fine children here are the legitimate product
of that marriage...darlings that they are, the poor abandoned things."
He smiled at Anne-Marie, who had slipped into the other wicker armchair and was looking at him with frank and frowning solemnity, wondering how anybody could sweat so much on a chilly day.

"What are you trying to say?" Mother wanted to know. "Are you
suggesting that my kids are—?"

"I'm not suggesting a thing, Missus. But if these are the children of
a legitimate and documented marriage, and if you have definitely been
abandoned—I don't mean just walked out on in a huff and maybe
his lordship will be coming back in a few days—then the Ward could
give you an emergency payment of ten dollars, five for each child, to
tide you over until welfare people process your paperwork. It's just one
of the little services the O'Conner brothers are happy to perform for

those in need of a helping hand. You couldn't possibly give me a drink of water, could you, young fellow? It's purely burning up that I am. You see, Missus..." His voice dropped to a confidential timbre. "...I have this thyroid. It makes me hot and thirsty all the time. It's the cross I bear. Oh, and sonny? You'll run the tap until it's cold, won't you, fine young man that you are?"

By the time I returned with the water, the confrontational atmosphere had cleared and Mother was sitting on the edge of my daybed with Anne-Marie on her lap. Whatever mistrust she had felt for the ward heeler had turned towards Mr Kane for telling strangers her personal business.

"Well, you know, Missus, they're all a little nosy and pushy," the ward heeler said. "It's in their born nature. But old Kane's heart is in the right place, and he's a Democrat to the bone. Which reminds me, Missus. You *are* a Democrat, aren't you?"

Like most of the poor of the Depression era, my mother idolized President Roosevelt, and would be a Democrat for the rest of her life, so the ward heeler didn't have to worry about that. In his smarmy, circumlocutory way, he made it clear without saying it in so many words that the help he was offering was from one good Democrat to another, and he shared with us the fact that 'the boys' always knew how everybody voted, though he was damned if he knew how they found out, crafty devils that they were. In the end, he wrote a little note on the back of a form my mother had filled out the day before (we later wondered how it had ended up in his hands) and he told us that our case would be processed by the end of the month, when we would receive our first welfare check. There would be no further appointments for my mother to keep, no papers to fill out, no queues to stand in, no documents to be shown. The power of the O'Conner political machine had swept all these inconveniences aside. But of course, we understood that that which had been so easily bestowed could be taken back without trace of its ever having existed. After asking for another glass of water to slake his thirsty thyroid, the ward heeler grunted up from the squeaking armchair which clutched at his trousers so that it took a moment to disengage himself without excessive damage. He peeled two five-dollar bills off a damp roll he had dragged out of his pocket and gave them to Anne-Marie, who had never held that much money in her life.

After he left, I made a point of saying that we were lucky Mr Kane had decided to contact the ward heeler. Mother shrugged as she threw away Mr Kane's carefully drawn up list of names and appointment times. "We're lucky that I'm a good Democrat, that's what we're lucky about," she said, and I realized that Mr Kane's efforts on our behalf had just lost their value.

"Well!" Mother said. "Now that I'm on a lucky streak, maybe I'd better go hit up some restaurants for work! You kids finish putting things away and cleaning up. And Jean-Luc, you go across to the cornerstore and get something for your dinner. When I get back, the three of us will take a long walk downtown. Do some window-shopping. Take a look-see at this Albany. How's that strike you?"

As offhandedly as I could, I suggested that if she was going to look for work, maybe she should change her clothes...I mean, you know, because her silky blue slacks suit was too good for everyday and...I mean, well, it was so dressy and pretty that people might not believe she really needed work...or...well...Who knows? Maybe it was just the right thing to wear. You look great in it, Mom! Just great!

It rained that afternoon, a cold diagonal rain driven on a March wind, and Mother came home with dark wet patches on her Bette Davis slacks suit and her bellhop hat a sodden mess. She was sniffling and feverish, and all through the night I could hear her hacking cough. The next morning she had a raging fever and was unable to lift her head from the pillow. "Don't call for a doctor unless I tell you," she said in a thin, raw voice. "We don't want welfare people poking their noses around here. You know what to do, Jean-Luc. You're my good right hand."

I did know what to do. We'd been through it three or four times every year since my grandfather skidded off the road in a snowstorm and crashed into a cement viaduct.

The front room with my iron daybed became our sick room because it was too gloomy in her bedroom with its small window giving onto the sunken back 'area'. For the next five days I nursed her. Sitting on the edge of the bed, I bathed her forehead and neck with a wrung-out washcloth when the fever was upon her, and hugged her within her Hudson Bay blanket when the bone-wracking chills came, and put my hand on her back and made comforting sounds when she was hanging off the bed, coughing and gagging and spitting phlegm into a basin that I would empty into the toilet, my face turned away from the greenish slime. I made up and applied mustard plasters to 'loosen her up'. Her bouts of lung fever were so frequent that we kept in a drawer ready for use a box of dried mustard and half a dozen squares of cotton cut from an old sheet. The thick mustard and flour paste had to be made with boiling water to be effective, but I was always afraid that I would burn her skin, and I was distressed by the bright red rectangles the mustard plasters left on her back, rectangles into which I could push a white spot with my finger.

Anne-Marie was so miserable and frightened that she retired into the back bedroom, where she walled off her fear by playing doctor and nurse with her paper dolls with desperate intensity: games in which the paper-doll doctor assured the paper-doll nurse that everything was going to be all right. The sick paper-doll mother would get well in no time, and then they'd all go out and have hot dogs and birch beer. She began to suck her fingers again, and when I tucked her into bed that night before going back to sleep in one of the creaking wicker chairs beside Mother, she clung to my hand until she slipped into a profound, frowning sleep, her eyes moving beneath her blue-veined lids in some desperate nightmare struggle. At times of emotional pressure, Anne-Marie would fall into so deep a sleep that I sometimes feared she would never awaken. She needed large draughts of calm and peace each day, like she needed food and drink, and she suffered if she couldn't have them.

I woke in the chair at dawn one morning, sweaty and with my clothes all twisted. The apartment smelled of mustard and eucalyptus, but Mother's breathing was better and her skin was cool, even a little clammy. But that evening the fever and coughing began again and she had a three-day relapse that left her wan and frail.

Finally the crisis broke and Mother lay back against the pillows and looked at me with vague, defocused eyes. She squeezed my hand to thank me. I squeezed back three squeezes, our secret family code for 'I love you', then I went in to her bed and slept the rest of that night and half of the next day.[4]

Another typical attack of her lung fever had passed. In a couple of days she would be full of pep and playfulness again, ripping through the housework with her mania for cleanliness, playing street games with us, singing songs from 'Your Lucky Strike Hit Parade' or showing us dances from her heyday back in the 'Twenties. Her bouts of lung fever frightened me, of course, but not so much as they frightened my sister, who could only look on and dread the outcome of something she could do nothing about, while I had lots to do, and I took pride in the important role of carer and healer that made me, for a few days, boss of the house. I relished being permitted to stay home from school to care for her. So I coped fairly well with the physical fragility that lay just beneath the surface of my mother's stubborn vivacity. Her emotional frailty, however, was a different matter.

Just as her health could be shattered by the slightest chill or fatigue, so her moods could plunge overnight from resilient self-confidence to the darkest acedia, where life seemed hopeless and pointless. And there was the omnipresent threat of that famous French-'n'-Indian temper of hers, but while her self-indulgent, short-fused temper could punch a raw red hole into the middle of an otherwise good day, it always passed off quickly, leaving her sorry for having shouted or smashed something and eager to play with us or make us a treat to compensate for having behaved badly. The condition she called 'the blues' or 'down in the dumps' was longer lasting. For a week or more the spark was out of her and she couldn't see how we could ever get free from the centripetal cycle of poverty, ill health and bad breaks. She continued to make meals, clean the house, wash and sew and mend, but there was no life in her voice, no lightness in her movement. She was a gray presence that dragged dully through the house exuding chill and despair.

In time, she would pull herself out of the slimy depths of depression, back into the light of hope, but not without considerable emotional cost. And not only to herself.

We children knew that Mother had had more than her share of bad luck and disappointments, and we knew that the struggle to keep us with her sometimes absorbed so much of her energy that she was

left unable to ward off bouts of depression or to control her occasional rages. Anne-Marie and I understood this in that intuitive, non-
verbal way that children perceive the emotions and attitudes of the
adults around them. But for all our understanding, we still resented her
bad moods, and felt guilty for resenting them. She was a wonderful
woman, but not an easy woman to live with; her health was always
close to collapse, her emotions always teetering on the threshold of
black depression.

It was during Mother's first bout of lung fever in Albany that I
learned her trick of using rage as a weapon. While she lay limp and
helpless in bed after a night of fever and coughing, I went across to the
cornerstore to buy food for breakfast. I offered to pay out of the ten
dollars the ward heeler had given us, but Mr Kane said I'd better keep
that for medications we might need from the drugstore. When I asked
how he knew that my mother was ill, he drew his shoulders up to his
neck in a thoroughly Levantine shrug.

"Logic. Observation. Deft reasoning. And a dash of raw guess-
work. A woman comes home in the rain without a coat. The next
morning, a boy comes in to buy groceries when he should be starting in
school. Deduction? There is sickness in the house. Alternative deduction? Or maybe not."

In fact, we had run out of Balm Bengué and were low on aspirin, so
after breakfast I told Anne-Marie to look after our fitfully dozing
mother while I ran down to the drugstore on Clinton Avenue. "But
I don't know what to do!" Anne-Marie said. "Just sit here and hold
her hand," I told her. "But what if she coughs and can't breathe?"
"That won't happen." "But if it *does?*" "Sh-h-h, you'll wake her up.
Just do what I say!" "You're not boss of me!" "I'll give you a slap!"
"I'll tell Mamma!" "Oh for Christ's sake!" "*And* I'll tell Mamma you
swore!" "Look, I've got to go. I'll be right back!" "No, don't leave me
alone." I left.

The woman behind the drugstore counter took my money and
gave me the Bengué and my change. When I reminded her that I also
needed aspirin, she asked how old I was. I told her, and she said she
wasn't allowed to sell aspirin to a six-year-old. I started to explain that
my mother was ill and—but the woman just pursed her lips and said

that rules were made to be obeyed, then she flashed a smile at the next customer and ignored me. I left and stood on the street corner looking up and down for another drugstore, but there wasn't one in sight. Suddenly I panicked. What was I going to do? Mother needed aspirin to keep the fever down. I couldn't leave Anne-Marie alone with her for long. What could I do? Then I got mad. *My* French-'n'-Indian temper flashed. I returned to the drugstore and told the woman I wanted the aspirin right now! She repeated that she was not allowed to sell—

At the top of my voice I screamed that my mother was dying! Customers gasped and gaped. A prissy man in a white jacket came around the end of the counter. "Now, little boy—" But I continued to scream that my mother was dying and she needed aspirin and she was dying and she needed aspirin and she was dying! People out on the street stopped and stared through the shop window. The man in the white jacket whispered harshly to the woman, who slipped me a bottle of aspirin and told me to get out. And stay out! She didn't even ask me to pay. I ran home with the aspirin and the Bengué. I had learned a lesson that would serve me well for several years. The use of only partially controlled rage would save me from being bullied when I enrolled in P.S. 5, just down the street from 238.

It was mid-April by the time Mother was well enough to sit up in bed and play honeymoon pinochle with me, her grip so weak that sometimes the cards would slip from her fingers and she'd laugh feebly at her feebleness, and I knew she was going to get well. Anne-Marie's paper-doll games no longer had to do with doctor and nurse, and she slept through the night without waking up in gasping panic. She stopped sucking her fingers. The most salient sign that Mother was herself again was a late-night gab session after pinochle in which she sketched out our future once 'her ship came in'. I would become a rich and famous doctor or lawyer, or a business tycoon making money hand over glove, and we'd all live in a grand house on a hill somewhere. Her eyes came alive as she described in detail the fine furniture we would have, and the delicious things we would eat: T-bone steaks and watermelon every day, just the sweet seedless heart of the watermelon, we'd throw the rest away, and we would never again have to shrimp and save, not after our ship came in!

As soon as she was strong enough, Mother enrolled me for what was left of the school year. She had wanted me to go to a Catholic school where I would get a better education, but in the end she sent me to P.S. 5 just down the street because if I was close by I could continue my schooling even when she was in bed with lung fever. I could make breakfast and care for her in the mornings and return during lunch period to see how she was doing and make her some soup, then I could get home immediately after school; but if I were at Our Lady of Angels school seventeen blocks away up the Lexington Avenue hill, I would have to take days, even weeks, off from school every time she got sick, and that would not only ruin my education, but it would alert the authorities to the fact that she was ill, and they might try to take us kids away from her. So I was to go to P.S. 5 for the time being...just until her lungs got stronger.

MISS COX

A s it turned out, I went to P.S. 5 for three years before transferring to Our Lady of Angels, while Anne-Marie was able to begin at the little convent school only two blocks from our apartment. The parish paid her fees, and the sisters made her uniforms, so it didn't cost us anything to send her, and she loved the convent school and the sisters, who were delighted by her shy grace and her refined features. When it came to looks, Anne-Marie had inherited all the beauty genes, both from my mother who, although a plain, petulantly frowning little girl in the one sepia photograph we had of her, had metamorphosed into a vivacious knockout of a flapper by the time she was sixteen years old, and from my father, whose mischievous good looks were a major asset to his life of conning and conniving. One of the younger nuns enjoyed plaiting Anne-Marie's long blonde hair, and they would ask her to sing and dance for them, then they would applaud while she blushed, very pleased.

I had gloried in school in Lake George Village, where I was treated as something special because I could read and write while other kids were still chanting their ABC's. I was allowed to sit at the back of the room reading at a little table of my own, and from time to time the teacher would come and ask me about what I was reading, or give me a little writing task to do. I can't remember a time when I couldn't read and write. Starting before I was a year old, my mother read me picture books from the library, and later she read the cereal boxes to me each morning before she went to work: ingredients and recipes from the sides of the boxes, stories from the back, and the practical 'cowboy life' tips that were printed on the cardboard spacers between layers of Shredded Wheat, like the trick of putting your lasso in a circle around you when you're sleeping on the ground during a cattle drive, because rattlesnakes hate to crawl over rope. I've never forgotten that bit of wilderness lore although I confess I've never had occasion to use it, but if I had, I'd have wanted assurance in advance that the rattlers knew the rules. Mother would read the cartoon or the card so I got the idea of it, then she'd go over it again slowly, pointing to each word as she said it until one day, according to her, my face lit up as I suddenly understood that the letter cluster and the word sound meant the same thing!

One morning, my mother was changing my newly arrived baby sister while I was eating breakfast, and she suddenly became aware that I was reading the cereal box aloud to get a little attention. At first, she thought I must be repeating what I had memorized from her earlier reading. But you could have knocked her down with a feather bed when she realized that this was a new kind of cereal and I was read-ing...really reading.

Typically, my mother immediately decided that I was a genius, and that I would bring success and riches to our little family by appearing on station WGY's weekly 'Child Wonder' slot, a tri-city precursor to the nationally popular program, *The Quiz Kids*. She used to brag to whoever would listen that "Not only can he read, my boy, but he's de-veloped a *vocabulary*," and it was true that I sought to elicit praise by trucking out my most exotic words. 'Riboflavin' was a favorite gleaned from my in-depth reading of cereal boxes, but a little difficult to work into a conversation. As you see, I was well on my way to becoming an insufferable little wiseass. But as it turned out, being a wiseass was the one thing about me that was universally applauded by the kids on North Pearl Street, even the dimmest. They admired cheekiness in all its forms, and particularly cheekiness in the face of authority.

I was anxious to get back into school after missing a whole month because I was afraid I would be behind and have to work hard to catch up. I needn't have worried. Expectations were low at P.S. 5 where most of the kids were unmotivated, few had models of excellence at home or praise for intellectual accomplishment and many were just stupid. Nor were the teachers much better. Some of them had long ago forsaken real teaching and had settled for policing, some were disenchanted after years of frustration, and some had been low-grade teaching material to begin with. Because I had been far ahead of my first-grade class at Lake George, my mother decided to put me into the second grade at P.S. 5, where I was astonished to discover that these bigger kids read haltingly and some still didn't even know the alphabet. I had been miles ahead at Lake George; here I was a visitor from a distant planet. I could see that I was in for long days of boredom.

But first there was the humiliating ordeal of being introduced to the class, which looked at me as a robin looks at a worm. The pretty young second-grade teacher was new enough to the profession to be still making an effort. I don't remember her name, but her bright little eyes above an up-turned smile made her look like an umlaut U. She twittered how *interesting* it must be to have a French name. Don't we think so, class? Then she wrote 'Jean-Luc LaPointe' on the blackboard and pronounced it in a French-ish sort of way. She said she was sure the class would be interested to know how my family pronounced it. Wouldn't we, class? I told them we pronounced it John Luke LaPointe (with no nasal in the last name). But for the next couple of weeks I had to deal with being called Jean, a girl's name. During recess out in the fenced-in playground of cracked and scabby macadam I was teased about my name, and this led to more bullying after school and to confrontations and fights, the usual ritual ordeal all new kids face. I was wiry and quick, but the opponents I tangled with were a year older and bigger than I, and they were tough street kids. Fortunately, I had an edge...well, two edges, really. My first edge was the tactic of focused rage I had learned in the drugstore that had refused to sell me aspirin.

While my tormentors were still in the chest-pushing, 'Wanna make something of it?' preliminaries to battle, I would be totally silent, afraid and nauseous as I hovered for a moment on the rim of battle, then I would unleash a flood of blind rage and get two or three shots in before my antagonist realized we had gone to Fistcity. I would strike out with a jugular fury that squirted adrenaline into my blood, making me stronger and oblivious to incoming damage and pain. I punched kicked bit elbowed and gouged anything I could reach, while my opponent clumsily tried to stifle my frenzied attack as one might try to smother a grass fire by flapping a damp handkerchief at it. My second edge was that I absolutely refused to give up. Bigger kids could throw me down or knock me down, but as soon as I managed to struggle out of their grasp, or they got tired of holding me down I plowed into them again. I almost always lost in the end, but although I would come home messed up, they never got away without a few bruises and some blood. After a while they gave up teasing and bullying because there wasn't much glory in beating up a smaller kid, and they were sure to reap a harvest of pain for their trouble. They saved face by just walking away from showdowns shaking their heads and muttering that this new kid was crazy. I mean *crazy!* In time, my existence in school and on the block came to be accepted, and I was left alone. In return, I often concealed my intelligence and bookish curiosity, sometimes by pretending not to know the answers to teachers' questions, and occasionally by making wisecracks in class, or funny faces behind some admiring teacher's back after she had complimented me. This involved treachery against my own intellectual caste, and I always felt a little ashamed afterwards.

I only had to put up with that saccharine, intensely *concerned* second-grade teacher for a couple of weeks before she brought me to the principal's office, complaining that I was too far ahead of her class and she just didn't know what to do with me. And there was another thing. I was always starting fights. It seemed I was a little bully. (Teachers never know what's really going on.) The principal, a sere woman with colorless hair twisted into a bun so tight that the corners of her eyes were drawn back, pointed out that there was only a month left before vacation, so I might as well be sent directly to the third grade, so Miss Cox could get to know me before I started regularly with her the following autumn.

Neither the second-grade teacher nor the principal worried about the fact that I would thenceforth be with kids two years older and bigger than I, and some of them even more, for this was before teachers dodged responsibility by falling back on the 'social pass' that would fill urban high schools with sullen sub-literates. In the 'Thirties, a student stayed in the third grade until he was able to do fourth-grade work, or until they gave up on him and sent him to a manual arts school, where he was taught how to bang out copper ashtrays or make a crystal radio by winding wire on a toilet roll. When he reached the school-leaving age of sixteen, he went out into the world to look for work on the basis of his copper bashing and toilet roll winding skills.

Miss Cox was P.S. 5's dominant figure. I suppose she was in her mid-fifties when I met her, but you would no more think of her in terms of age than you would ask how long gravity had been around. She was tall and broad-shouldered, although surprisingly thin when viewed from the side. Her face was wide, but even so her features seemed crowded together: a prominent hooked nose with a red birthmark on one side, large deep-set glittering eyes beneath thick eyebrows, full, rather pendulous lips accented by bright red lipstick and dyed orange hair, which was so thin that her white scalp showed through. Her taste in clothing was expressive to the verge of eccentricity. Her long skirts, a different one for each school day, were made from what looked like upholstery fabric, and she wore white satin blouses with stand-up collars, padded shoulders, and full sleeves that buttoned tight at the wrist and rippled with each gesture, like a swordsman's shirt in a cloak-and-dagger movie. She often tucked two or three patterned silk handkerchiefs into a broad leather belt, and these fluttered around her as she moved, as did the long-tasseled oriental scarf she draped over her shoulders, its ends flipped over her wrists. She wore copper bracelets and long loops of colored glass beads that swung and rattled and clinked with her quick, angular movements. The timbre of her voice ranged from rich chocolate-contralto speech through to cascading soprano laughter.

Miss Cox was determined to broaden the minds and lift the spirits of every slum child whom Fate had placed in her care, and the class-room over which she reigned for more than a quarter of a century reflected both her mission and her personality. In her exquisite Palmer hand she wrote aphorisms and maxims in various colors of chalk on the blackboard, reminding us that 'The lost minute can never be recovered', or enjoining us to 'Reach for the stars', or warning us that 'Senseless haste is the enemy of speed'. She added new admonitions and adages when she thought the old ones had had time to soak into our collective unconscious, but because she often had to erase to make space for classwork and illustrations, it was not uncommon for only fragments of the maxims to be left on the blackboard for a week or two: messages such as 'Reach...' which was what a cowboy said when he drew his gun on a bad guy, or 'Senseless haste is...', a baffling existentialist affirmation. There was a pin board covered with layers of constantly refreshed pictures from *National Geographic* and other magazines showing us what life and people were like in Africa, Asia and Europe, so we wouldn't get the idea that the universe ended at the corner of Pearl and State Streets. "There is a whole wide world out there, children, and it's yours for the taking." And there was a large modern globe next to a globe showing the world as it was conceived during the Age of Discovery. She often compared these two to demonstrate that the accepted truths of a given time can change, and that there are new truths all the time. Most interesting of all to me was what Miss Cox called an orrery, a complex model of the solar system with wires and strings and a crank that she would sometimes turn so we could see the relative motion of the Earth and its moon, and the other seven planets (no Pluto because the orrery was pre-1930). And there was a scuffed and battered upright piano on which she played every morning, lifting her wrists high from the keyboard and holding that graceful balletic gesture for a moment before slamming down on the emphatic chords of the morning sing-song, which she believed was good for both our lungs and our souls.

Covering every surface—tables, windowsills, bookcases, the piano top—was a gallimaufry of broken pottery, driftwood snarls, 'interesting' bits of rock, twisted metal...anything she thought might inform or inspire our aesthetic sensibilities and make us realize that beauty was all around us; and hanging from the nails she had pounded into the walls with the heel of her stout shoe, there were swatches of fabric and ribbons and feathers and colored paper, anything that caught her eye and seemed stimulating.

Alone of all the teachers at P.S. 5, Miss Cox never had trouble maintaining order, despite her willingness to let us move about the classroom with a freedom that other teachers didn't dare to permit, lest it lead to stampedes, even insurrections. She would suddenly order us out of our desks and onto our feet whenever she decided that it would be good for us to move our bodies in 'free dance' to the thumping rhythms of her piano. The sheer mass and intensity of her personality awed the class into good behavior. Even the sullen older boys who sat, root-bound, in small desks at the back of the room responded when she smiled dazzlingly at them and chanted in two bell-clear notes, "pos...ture, gentlemen! Pos...ture!" They would sit up straight, although they did so with the bored listlessness necessary to affirm their roles as tough kids. She used to bring in large prints of famous paintings to show to the class, and she would tell us why they were famous and what we should look for "...because art is for everybody." In addition to the usual third-grade subjects, she introduced us to the joys of elocution and clear diction. "...because ideas are expressed in words, and the clearly spoken word reflects a clearly understood idea." I leave to your imagination the sounds produced by the tough older boys in the back row when obliged to 'round their vowels' and 'be mindful of terminal consonants'. But they would do their best, then they'd glower around the class, daring anyone to laugh...or even smile. I loved the sound of her 'elocution' voice and I was a natural mimic, so it wasn't long before I was imitating the precise diction and rich pronunciation of radio actors as I talked animatedly to myself in the course of the intricate story games that occupied most of my free time; but I always fell back on the flat, dental sound of urban New York when dealing with people on North Pearl Street because that was the only sound they took seriously. When that aggressive street speech was bolstered by profanity, it was more likely to produce respect and compliance than the fruity sounds of Claude Rains or Orson Welles, which would probably have earned me a sneer and a fat lip.

Each afternoon as four o'clock grew near, the allure of freedom would become too great to ignore, and your soul would twist within your body with the need to be *elsewhere*. Over the teacher's head in every room of P.S. 5 there was a Regulator clock whose long hand did not crawl around the dial but remained frozen for an eternal fifty-nine seconds then suddenly clunked to the next minute, giving a jab of excitement to hundreds of young bodies, stiff with accumulated boredom and yearning to run screaming out across the macadam playground and down the street. But not in Miss Cox's third grade, where we enjoyed the inestimable privilege of ending our school work twenty minutes early, when she would say calmly and without breaking the flow of whatever she had been talking about, "...and now we have five minutes to tidy up the classroom...silently!...and then it will be storytime." With busy—but silent!—efficiency, we lifted our hinged desktops and put away books and pens then closed them...silently!...then the assigned chair-straighteners set about their task (always girls, as boys tended to scrape the chairs across the floor), and the book-putters-away and wastepaper-basket-emptiers discharged their responsibilities, and the window-closers (the big older boys at the back of the class) manipulated long wooden poles with blunt brass hooks at the end to close the windows which Miss Cox insisted be open at least a crack during class, even in winter, because "the brain requires oxygen", and the best student of the preceding week (me, usually) collected the blackboard erasers and took them out onto the iron fire escape, where he clapped them together vigorously until the chalk dust was dispersed into the air. When this privileged functionary was daydreaming, as often he was, he would forget to stand upwind of the erasers and would return to the classroom with white eyebrows and hair, to the scoffing amusement of the big boys. "Yeah, sure. The smart one!"

Then, for the last quarter of an hour, Miss Cox would read to us, not dull, stuffy 'good' fiction, but cracking stories with plenty of action and danger, and with kids as the heroes. She would act out all the roles, letting her voice become tense with danger or breathless with excitement or hysterical with fun. Sometimes these stories came from Miss Cox's collection of children's books with pictures of boys and girls in outdated clothes, other times she would read from handwritten notebooks, for Miss Cox was a writer of children's fiction, although, she admitted, "...as yet to be discovered." She somehow always managed to be at a moment of danger or discovery when the Regulator's minute hand lurched to straight up, and the school bell jangled. All the class would groan and beg her to read on, just to see *what happens next*, but she would shrug fatalistically and close the book until the next day, reminding us that "If you always leave the table a little bit hungry, you will never sit down without an appetite." With this, she would slowly turn over one hand so that the fingers pointed to the cloak room at the back, and that was the signal that we were free to leave. That gesture was the boundary between the world of school and the world of freedom, and as Miss Cox, Queen of Chaos, sat smiling, we would rush back and grab our jackets and hats off their hooks, pushing and shoving and babbling and playing tricks, and on snowy days, those of us who had rubbers or galoshes would hop around on one foot, slipping on the still-wet floor and pinching our fingers to pull them on. Then we would dash out of the cloakroom and immediately slow to a walk and stop babbling because each student said, 'Good-bye, Miss Cox' as he passed her on his way to the door, and she would hold each of us in turn in her affectionate gaze and say: Good-bye, Joseph or Mary-Elizabeth or Margaret, always using the full name rather than nicknames, to the slight discomfort of a Bart who was Bartholomew or an Al who was Aloysius, and we would go out into the hall more orderly and better behaved than any other class because we had had a moment to let off steam in the cloakroom.

Often Miss Cox would begin story time by reading a short poem, which nobody liked as much as the stories, although some girls pretended to, trying to convince somebody that they were more refined than boys. She tried to tempt the boys to taste the riches of verse by occasionally reading things like "The Shooting of Dan McGrew", which she described as a cowboy poem, but all that stuff about the lady known as Lou seemed awfully gushy to us, although the gunfight in the dark was pretty good. Shortly after I returned to Miss Cox's class the following September to begin the third grade in earnest, she read the class Kipling's "Gunga Din" and told us that she would give any boy who could recite it a 'special treat'. I checked it out from the library and memorized it, despite the funny spelling that was supposed to represent a cockney accent. After rehearsing before my admiring mother and long-suffering sister, I informed Miss Cox that I had "Gunga Din" down by heart, and she told me that the 'special treat' was not so much for me as for the entire class: I would be allowed to recite the poem to them! Both the class and I felt terribly let down, but I went to the front of the room and ground my way through the poem, lavishing generous measures of histrionic excess upon the last gasping words of the mortally wounded water-bearer. Later, I would learn to play to my audience under similar circumstances, sheltering myself from their mocking antipathy by making fun of the poem, or the assignment, or myself, or them; but this first time on stage I had no armor but melodramatic sincerity as I shifted roles and bitterly lamented my recent death, manfully fighting back the tears as I made what was, for a leather-hearted white soldier, a difficult confession: "You're a better man than I am, Gunga Din." Throughout my recitation, Miss Cox listened, her eyes closed in receptive ecstasy, while my classmates tried to distract me by rolling their eyes or pretending to strangle themselves with both hands.

Each grade of elementary school has its own ethos, its own shibboleths, its own taboos, even its own jokes that linger through the summer in the chalk-dusty air to be rediscovered, dusted off and found hilarious by each succeeding wave of children. Each generation of third-grade kids at P.S. 5 was intensely loyal to Miss Cox while under her thrall, but the moment they became sophisticated fourth-graders they felt obliged to ridicule her and to disdain the next batch of adoring third-graders. Boys would mock her by speaking in a snooty, fluting voice, and even the best-behaved girls sometimes put their heads together and giggled at her bizarre clothes. It was universally accepted that she was 'crazy'.

Miss Cox was a teacher for all students. Her inexhaustible flow of information, ideas, images and inspiration was sufficient to satisfy the curiosity of the brighter minds and send them into books to learn more, while average students learned enough to do well in the fourth grade, and the bumptious tendencies of the dimmer kids were allayed by the unaccustomed attention and individual recognition she gave them. She embraced all her students with her absorbed, responsive gaze as she reached out for them with her rich, many-layered voice; and she was in almost constant physical contact with us, placing her hand on the shoulder or head of one while she answered another and looked into the eyes of a third, somehow giving every one of us the feeling that she was aware of your particular needs and interests or, sometimes, of what mischief you'd been up to.

Miss Cox was a uniquely colorful example of those generations of splendid, often lonely, women who devoted their lives to teaching in urban slums, small towns, and one-room rural schoolhouses from the last third of the nineteenth century until the end of the Second World War, women whose personal sacrifice made American public education effective despite its innate weaknesses of structure, organization and resources. Most of these martyrs to learning never married; in many school districts they weren't allowed to. They lavished upon succeeding generations of children the energies and talents that other women put into marriage and motherhood, energies and talents that a modern woman might devote to a career in commerce, government or industry, the doors to which professions were either closed to women at that time, or just barely ajar. Grand and noble though the achievements of these lay saints were, no compassionate or just-minded person would want to see a return to such exploitation of talent as was necessary to make a jury-rigged and neglected educational system work.[5]

One afternoon in late fall Miss Cox said she wanted to speak to me after school. Apprehensive, I lingered as long as I could in the cloak-room. The only reprehensible things I'd done that day had been the vivid daydreams I slipped into while waiting for the rest of the class to finish a word problem. I let my fertile, furtive imagination settle on the girl who sat in front of me...what would the nape of her neck feel like if I stroked it?...and the golden hairs on her arms—I glanced up and saw Miss Cox looking down on me, smiling. Oh-oh! I had often had the uneasy suspicion that Miss Cox could read minds!

Perched on the edge of her desk, she whipped the corner of her shawl over her shoulder and looked down at me, hot and cramped in my jacket and feeling vulnerable without the insulation of my fellow students around me. "Have you ever been tested, Luke?" Right from the first day, she had had the sensitivity to use the American version of my name that I preferred. I was 'different' enough as it was without having a different kind of name.

"Ma'am?"

"Have you ever taken an IQ test?"[6]

I said no, I didn't think so.

"H'm. But surely you know that you're quicker than other children...and that you learn more easily, yes?"

I didn't answer. It sounded like one of those trick questions adults are always decoying their quarry with.

"I think you ought to be tested, Luke, and I intend to arrange for it. Unfortunately, our Board of Education is behind the times and still uses the adult tests for children, and that can produce wild measurements, especially at the higher ranges of ability. I'm sure you'll turn out to have a high IQ, perhaps very high. And that's a good thing. But it's not everything. Do you know what IQ means?"

I admitted that I didn't.

"A person's Intelligence Quotient is an expression of the difference between his mental age and his physical age. If a child of, say, ten years old, did as well on an IQ test as most other ten-year-olds, he'd have an IQ of 100, which is what they call average intelligence. If he did as well as a child of thirteen, he'd have a 133 IQ. Above average."

I nodded tentatively, still not sure where all this was leading.

She went on to tell me that no one had ever defined 'intelligence' in any useful way. Indeed, the man who invented intelligence testing, a Frenchman named Binet, ended up by admitting that: "The most accurate definition of 'intelligence' is: the quality my test measures." And what Binet measured was a cluster of aptitudes and skills that made certain kinds of learning relatively easy, particularly the kinds one needs in a technological culture. "It's what I call round-peg/round-hole intelligence," Miss Cox said dismissively, adding that she personally found such human qualities as kindness, fairness, gumption, honesty and compassion more valuable than the ability to figure out quickly which direction the sixth cogwheel of a system was turning.

"Do you understand what I'm saying to you, Luke?"

"That it's good to be intelligent, but it isn't the most important thing in the world and I mustn't get a big head."

"Exactly. I'll let you know when it's time to take the test." She turned her attention to some desk work she was doing.

I rose and began buttoning up my jacket. "Miss Cox?"

"H'm?" she hummed without looking up.

"I sometimes have the feeling that you can look right into my mind. I know you can't, of course, but..."

She continued scanning her page.

"I mean, you can't really see what I'm thinking, can you?"

She looked at me owlishly. "Can't I?"

I left.

When I got home that afternoon I was careful to mention the forthcoming IQ test in an offhand way, adding untruthfully that all new kids had to take them to keep my mother from making something big out of this. She was quick to build castles of expectation on the shifting sands of hope and longing.

Shortly thereafter, Miss Cox excused me from class to go to the principal's office, where I found a large woman with thick glasses, a red face, and a molten head cold that made her sniff constantly. She was a psychologist from the State Department of Education, and she gave me a long test to do against the wall clock that chopped off a minute with each click. It was a game, and I enjoyed it. I knew most of the answers even before looking at the multiple choices, and so I finished each section in less than half the time allotted, which the sniffing psychologist seemed to take as a professional affront...as though I were making light of her test and, by extension, of her expertise.

By the next morning it had got around the school that I had been sent down to the principal's office to meet a psychologist, and kids began to tease me about being a nutter. This gave birth to a new, happily transient, playground chant that followed me around during recess for a few days. Little girls would make the shame sign at me, scraping one forefinger on another as they chanted:

> *Mickey Rooney is a loony.*
> *Like his ma, he's really goony.*

I rankled at being called Mickey Rooney, a reference to my overacting the role of Gunga Din. This stung because Mickey Rooney was my least favorite actor after Rin-Tin-Tin (whom, come to think of it, Mickey Rooney resembled in his moist-eyed, canine need to be loved). I didn't even mind their calling me a loony, but I was sorry to have my suspicion confirmed that the block included my mother among its crazyladies. Fortunately, street gossip never grouped my mother with the block's full-blown nutters like Mrs Meehan across the street, or the old woman from around the corner who used to get away from her grandchildren a couple of times a year and run down the street screaming that she was the queen of heaven and the common-law wife of Jesus Christ. My mother's craziness was understood to be only a mild case that manifested itself in her 'funny' clothes, her 'tomboy' behavior and her repeated attempts to get part-time work, despite the danger that if she were caught working we would lose our welfare allowance.

Just before the Christmas vacation, I was given a note to carry home to my mother, asking her to come to school, where the principal and Miss Cox revealed my IQ score, which they told her in confidence because the then-prevalent theory was that a child shouldn't know his IQ because if it were low he would be discouraged and give up trying, and if it were high he might stop working and rest on his laurels. Naturally, my mother ignored this injunction and told me everything she had learned. On the adult test they had given me, I had scored a little better than the average fifteen-year-old, which, considering that I was only seven, gave me an IQ of something over 200, which Miss Cox had said was patently ridiculous and served only to point out the foolishness in using adult IQ tests for evaluating children as young as I. But my mother was delighted. More than 200! Well now!

I wasn't nearly as impressed. In fact, I was a little annoyed to learn that I was only as smart as an average fifteen-year-old. Vic Ravelli, a swaggering dolt from down the block, was fifteen years old, and to be told that I was only as smart as Vic Ravelli...Jeez! Hoping to deflate her optimistic dreams lest she get carried away, I said that I was probably already as smart as I was ever going to get, and that if I took the same test in, say, five years and did exactly as well, my score would fall from over 200 to 125. But that wouldn't mean I was getting any dumber. It was just a number thing. And if I went on in the same way, by the time I was fifteen I'd have an IQ of 100, and by the time I was thirty my IQ would be 50.[7]

But Mother dismissed my self-abnegating manipulation of the IQ scores. The principal had told her that my performance put me in the top fifth of the top one percent of the population. "The top fifth of the top one percent of the population," my mother repeated, as though to cement it in her memory. "...the *top fifth* of the *top one percent!*" She was in awe of this brainy phenomenon she had produced (after such a long and difficult labor) and not a little proud of the woman who had produced it.

I had been afraid from the first that my mother would convert any good IQ score into yet greater confidence in, and reliance on, my ability to cause her ship to come in and transport us from North Pearl Street to Easy Street, so I explained to her that being in the top fifth of the top one percent of the population meant that one kid in every five hundred was like me, and this meant that Albany, with its one hundred thirty thousand residents, had two hundred and sixty people every bit as smart as I was; and among New York City's seven million, there were fourteen thousand of us! But this failed to puncture my mother's balloon of hope; indeed, it reinforced her faith in my genius. "How many boys could have worked all that out so fast in their heads? You've got a gift for figuring out the percentages, Jean-Luc, and if there's one thing I know, it's that being a success in business is mostly a matter of figuring out the percentages."

So now I was going to be a businessman? Just when the example of Miss Cox had persuaded me to devote my life to teaching?

Even after the tests, I didn't think of myself as particularly gifted. I was smart, sure. Smarter than anyone I knew. But then, I lived on North Pearl Street and went to P.S. 5. What kind of standard was that to measure myself against? My idea of a gifted person was one who could think up new inventions, new methods, new systems, and that wasn't me. I wasn't so much intelligent as quick-minded. More than half the class would get the right answer to the mathematical word problems. My answers weren't any more correct than theirs, it was just that I got them while Miss Cox was still dictating the problems. If I had a gift I was proud of, it wasn't 'intelligence', it was my ability to create situations and characters for the story games I constructed from fragments of reading and, later, from adventure programs I heard on that most absorbing and evocative of all media, radio.

One morning during that winter vacation the mailman brought a letter addressed to me. The first letter I ever received. It was a Christmas card from Miss Cox, a snowy old-fashioned street scene with smiling people and kids skating on skates with blades that curled up in front, the kind of card that is appropriate for people of all religions, or none. Inside she wrote: 'To Jean-Luc. Your quick understanding and intelligent questions make teaching a pleasure. And a challenge, too!" My mother read the note and beamed. "I'll bet you're her pet. Why else would she send you a Christmas card?" I shrugged, embarrassed but pleased. I was later to learn that she sent cards to all of her students, each with an appropriate supportive message.

Mother had found split-shift work in two restaurants during that Christmas season, so she was able to afford special gifts for us: an expensive doll for Anne-Marie that could wet its diapers as it emptied its bottle (girls' toys are so dumb!), and for me a three-volume compendium called *High School Subjects Self-Taught* that offered condensed courses on everything from Astronomy and Biology to World History and Zoology. At first, I felt ambivalent about this present that was so obviously intended to move me along more quickly to the time when I could get out into the commercial world and drag that damned ship into port. But I became intrigued by the self-graded tests at the back of the book that you could rip out along dotted lines and mail to the publishers together with five dollars in cash or stamps, and they'd send you an embossed imitation parchment high school diploma issued by the fully accredited American National High School Association, which had the same address as the publisher. Any fear that dishonest people might cheapen the value of this diploma by looking up the test answers in the book was dispelled by a notice declaring that 'these tests must be taken in accordance with the strictest Honor System, which obliges all candidates for a diploma to act fairly and honorably.' Well, you can't ask for more protection than that. I worked it out that if I applied my newly discovered IQ to this book with diligence, I could get a high school diploma by the time I was ten, finish college at fourteen and, if I fulfilled my mother's wish that I become a doctor, I should be ready to perform my first brain surgery at the age of nineteen.

I could have used my potential medical skills a little earlier because the stress and fatigue of working late shifts in those restaurants night after night, then walking home through the snow and slush to save the trolley car money had the usual effect of giving my mother a terrible cold, and she passed Christmas Day in bed with chills and fever, and me doctoring her with aspirin and mustard plasters so hot that they burned my fingers, so I'd plop them quickly onto her bare back. She had a particularly hard night, hacking and coughing, gasping for breath as she hung over the edge of her bed to help the phlegm 'come up', a process that tested the limits of my squeamishness. I sat on the edge of her bed, trying to relieve her wracking cough by rubbing her back with Balm Bengué. (As a little kid I had marveled at how Dr. Bengué managed to sign each and every tube, and later I was embarrassed at having been so gullible.)

Late one night, after Anne-Marie had gone to bed with her incontinent doll and my mother had finally fallen into a shallow, rasping sleep, I opened *High School Subjects Self-Taught* and began to learn those random, unconnected facts that have clung to my memory ever since: the Great Wall of China was begun by Shih Huang-ti, Charlemagne was crowned Holy Roman Emperor in Rome on Christmas Day of 800 AD, sulfuric acid is H_2SO_4, the three kinds of solid-state carbon fuel are peat, lignite and anthracite. Although age and illness now cause me to forget things that happened yesterday, hundreds of facts gleaned from that book more than sixty years ago are still with me. I even remember where they were on the page.

I stayed home taking care of my mother for two weeks after Christmas vacation was over. When she was well enough for me to leave her bedside and go back to P.S. 5, I found Miss Cox's room stripped of its decorations, its blackboard aphorisms, the swatches of bright cloth and paper, the inspirational objets trouvés. Even the piano and the fascinatingly complex orrery were gone. Miss Cox was dead.

What?

She's dead.

...Dead?...

...and in her place was a dry-voiced man with pallid, rain-colored eyes and creases of bitterness at the corners of his mouth. He stood looking out over our heads as our slant-eyed principal explained to the class that Miss Cox had been in a glee club that dressed up in old-fashioned costumes every Christmas and sang carols on downtown street corners, urging passing shoppers to donate for Christmas baskets for the poor. Miss Cox had caught a cold which had developed into pneumonia and...

...Dead? Just like that? I could not believe it.

In the middle of that afternoon, I slammed my book shut, suddenly angry. Why did people have to die? Like my grandfather had died that Christmas two years earlier when his car skidded off the road in a blizzard! And like my mother might die with her next bout of lung fever, leaving Anne-Marie and me alone!

The new teacher asked me why I wasn't copying the arithmetic problems on the board. I didn't answer. He leaned over my desk and in a cigarette-smelling hiss said that the principal had told him I was Miss Cox's favorite—high IQ and all that—but to him, a pupil was just a pupil. He didn't have pets. Did I understand that?

I looked up at him. Then, without answering, I turned my eyes and looked out the window.

Aware that the class compared him unfavorably with Miss Cox, the new teacher—my memory does him the favor of not retaining his name—often sneered at the unorthodox methods of the eccentric woman he had replaced. Under his firm hand the big boys crammed into little desks at the back of the room soon reverted to their sullen, class-distracting ways, and he told me that he couldn't understand how I had been Miss Cox's pet, considering that I never raised my hand to answer questions, hardly ever did my homework, and wasted the class's time with my wisecracks and skylarking. One day he said something snide about his predecessor's peculiar belief that funny clothes made the creative teacher. I got up and walked out of class, while he called after me: Come back here! You just come right back, you hear me?

I spent a fair amount of that year sitting on a bench outside the principal's office, awaiting punishment, and I went into the fourth grade with lower than average grades. By the time I passed on to the fifth, my chronic daydreaming, my satiric sallies at the expense of teachers who got a fact wrong or mispronounced a word, and my new-found role as class clown made me even more dreaded than the often-flunked kids who threatened the peace of the class from their desks at the back of the room. So much for the 200 IQ.

I have often wondered what happened to Miss Cox's intricate orrery. Old pale-eyes probably threw it out, the turd.

$7.27 A WEEK

A ID TO Dependent Children paid a 'rent allowance' of twenty dollars a month directly to our faceless slum landlord instead of giving us the money and letting us negotiate for our own accommodation. This bound every family on welfare to one of the 'designated' landlords, which made bargaining impossible. But then as now the Lords of Poverty didn't trust the poor not to squander their money. I need hardly add that slum property owners were expected to respond to the fund-raising solicitations of the party machine in return for being 'designated'. In Albany at that time, these slum landlords were not, as they would be today, large development companies squeezing a few dollars out of the poor while they waited for the tides of fashion to bring the comfortable classes back in search of inner-city re-colonization. Our landlords were petty nickel-and-dime entrepreneurs who seldom owned more than four or five buildings broken up and cheaply remodeled into apartments.

Our three-room first-floor apartment rented for twenty-five dollars a month, which meant that we had to find five dollars each month to fill the gap between our rent allowance and our actual rent. Each week, a dollar and a quarter had to come out of our seven dollars and twenty-seven cents for this purpose. Actually, because our rent was monthly and our living allowance was weekly, there were four weeks in each year when we could put that dollar and a quarter to other purposes, and that's the kind of thing you look forward to when your budget is as tight as ours.

So after setting our rent supplement aside, our allowance of seven dollars and twenty-seven cents per week was really six dollars and two cents, which had to cover not only food and clothing, but also hundreds of necessities that go unnoticed by those who do not have to count every penny: soap, medications, ice for the icebox, towels, clothes pins, baking powder, tooth powder, roach powder, soap powder, matches, fly paper, toilet paper, waxed paper, writing paper, lightbulbs, fuses, envelopes, thread...all of which my mother managed on less than thirty-five cents per person per day. We inched along on the tightrope of our budget, teetering from week to week, but the end of every month brought us a blow that buckled our knees and made us wobble precariously: the gas and electric bills. (In my day northeasterners spoke of the 'electric', not the 'electricity'. Perhaps they still do.) Mother kept our heads above water, or at least our upturned mouths, but making it through the week required strict planning, stretching every nickel, a Spartan diet and, above all, no bad luck. 'Bad luck' meant anything getting lost or broken, for any unforeseen need could cause our fragile financial raft to founder, leaving us no option but to economize the only place we could...food. My mother never let us go hungry, but variety often had to be sacrificed. Every month there were at least five or six days when we had potato soup for dinner and supper. Our budget was so tight that it took her all that first summer and well into the fall before she could to pay off our slate at Mr Kane's cornerstore. In fact, I'm not sure that we ever paid him off totally. Like everyone else on the block, we were always a week or so behind, and every time we almost closed the gap, something would happen to set us back. Mr Kane was gracious about extending credit and never once pressed us for payment, and he was helpful in a hundred ways when my mother was learning the ropes of life on welfare, but inevitably she came to share the block's feeling that Mr Kane profited from our poverty and misfortune.

My mother's imagination was fertile when it came to making our money stretch. She had dozens of ways to make something 'do' for another week or month. Skillful with a needle, she could darn and re-darn our socks without making the heel or toe uncomfortably thick; and there were strict rules requiring us to think ahead when we used the icebox in summer, picturing where things were stored, then opening the door, grabbing what we wanted, and closing it quickly, so we didn't waste ice. We always saved the boxes our shoes came in because shoeboxes could be mined for two pieces of cardboard (top and bottom) that were just the right size for cutting out 'insoles' that would extend the life of worn-out shoes an extra couple of weeks, unless you were unlucky or careless enough to step into a rain puddle, which would turn the cardboard into a pulpy wad. Clothing and shoes were always bought a size or two too big because it would be a crying shame if we out-grew anything before we wore it out.

In working out our weekly menu my mother displayed a knowledge of good nutrition that was rare in that era, and she had a gift for creating variety, or at least a sense of variety, out of very little. Our big meal was in the evening, except for Sundays, when it was at midday. She carefully planned each week's meals around three basic 'baked dishes': tuna fish casserole, corned beef loaf, and vegetable 'surprise', each of which was made to last for two meals. She bought the canned meat for these dishes and the bones for soup stock as soon as the check came in, and only then did she feel safe about feeding us that week. This meant, of course, that we only rarely ate butchers' meat...two or three times a year, at most. To save on gas, she would prepare two dishes and put them into the oven together, and to avoid monotony she would serve half of each baked dish on alternate nights. For Saturdays she made Boston baked beans with a small piece of salt pork if we could afford it, without if not, and there was always enough left over for baked bean sandwiches to take to school on Monday and Wednesday, once again trying to avoid having the same thing twice in a row. Occasionally our budget let her replace one of the baked dishes with a special Sunday dinner of what she called chicken 'frigazee'. She would go down to the open-air market at Washington Street and buy a tough 'boiling chicken' (euphemism for a layer that had entered menopause) which she cut up and stewed with potatoes, onions and carrots until it was tender, then she thickened the broth with flour, topped the dish with baking powder biscuit dough, and put it into the oven. The biscuit crust soaked up enough chicken gravy to stretch the frigazee through to Monday's supper as well. But when things 'went wrong' (something had to be replaced or repaired, or clothing was needed, or medicine) then one or even both of the baked dishes had to be scrapped and potato soup was called on to fill the gap, usually for two days, occasionally for four. Fortunately, I particularly liked potato soup, and still do to this day. Mother varied our vegetables as much as she could, buying whatever was in season and cheap. We always arrived at the Washington Street Market half an hour before closing time so she could bargain with stall-owners who didn't want to have to take unsold vegetables back with them. The remaining produce had been picked over, of course, but Mother would cut out the bad bits and prepare the vegetables so you couldn't tell. She even varied the three casseroles, sometimes making them with rice and sometimes with macaroni, sometimes with cream of mushroom soup as 'binder', more often without.

Luckily, the ingredients for our safety-net potato soup were often to be had free at the Federal Surplus Commodities Corporation warehouse. The welfare people had issued us a green 'two children' card, and once every two weeks for eight years and in all weathers, I walked the twenty-two blocks north to the FSCC warehouse and twenty-two blocks back pulling my sister's rattling, loosely jointed wagon containing our ration of whatever was on offer from crops the New Deal government had bought from farmers. Thousands of tons of food were destroyed to keep it from flooding the market and undermining the farmers' already low prices, but a portion was given out to the poor on the assumption that this would not harm the farmers' markets because the poor couldn't have afforded to buy it anyway. We never saw people from Pearl Street at the FSCC warehouse, in part because they were too lazy to walk over forty blocks for handouts, and in part because the technology of dehydration was in its infancy and few people knew what to do with the dried potatoes, onions and milk, as they were all nearly inedible in the state in which we received them.

My mother's determination that her children should have wholesome food inspired her to invent ways to use the dried potato flakes which, when mixed with water, produced a glutinous, un-swallowable paste, and the dried onions that rattled into the dish like flakes of granite, and the dried milk powder that could be broken down only by the hours of simmering necessary to make her potato soup. Oh, and powdered eggs! I'd forgotten those powdered eggs that were even more stubbornly insoluble than the dried milk. Adding water to the dried eggs in the hope of getting something usable was hopeless. Regardless of how long or fast you stirred and whipped, the end product would be a bowl of dirty water upon which floated frothy globs of yellowish powder, and any effort to fry or boil the ugly mush produced a ghastly sulfuric smell that made most people give up experimenting. But Mother found a way to use both the dried eggs and the dried milk to give us additional nutrition. When both were in their relatively mixable and un-smelly dry states, she would blend them with flour to make healthful, if stodgy, pancakes for cold winter mornings. They didn't taste all that bad, but they took a bit of swallowing. My mother did everything she could to save us from the undernourishment that was so widespread in the Depression 'Thirties that our generation was shorter on average by an inch and a quarter than the generations that preceded and followed us, generations that had the same genes as we, but were raised in more affluent times.

In addition to dried foods whose insolubility would challenge the most resolute and resourceful alchemist, there were sometimes welcome surprises at the FSCC warehouse, such as split peas or dried beans when pulses were flooding the market, or two-pound bags of flour from which baking-powder biscuits could be made, and sometimes there were dried apples that Mother made into applesauce or, after soaking them overnight, apple pies. A man at the warehouse door would punch our green 'two children' card to make sure we didn't get more than our allotted share of free food.

. . . .

One afternoon, Mother, Anne-Marie and I were going downtown for something. Mother was humming to herself, brimming with energy and cheer. She had recently recovered from a bout of depression and was in the high spirits that always followed an extended session of the blues. We passed the three buildings that were the Meehan warren and Mrs Meehan was sitting on a stoop surrounded by a shoal of kids, the same kids we had seen the day we arrived on Pearl Street, swarming around her, begging her to let go of the skillet. When Mother smiled at her and said, "Good afternoon," Mrs Meehan glared at us and scowled. We had walked on a distance when I heard slapping footsteps behind us and turned to see the crazy Mrs Meehan bearing down on us in her crushed-down-heels slippers. My first impulse was to run, pulling Anne-Marie and Mother after me. But Mother turned and stood her ground, and Mrs Meehan caught up with us, panting and gasping. Anne-Marie slipped behind me. When Mrs Meehan caught her breath, she said, "Good afternoon, Missus!"

Mother threw an anxious glance at me then said tentatively to Mrs Meehan, "A-a-h...good afternoon."

Mrs Meehan grinned and nodded, then she turned and shuffled back to her stoop, where she was met by her flock of babbling children.

We walked on in silence; mine stunned, Mother's thoughtful, Anne-Marie's worried. After half a block, Mother said, "I'll bet I know what that was all about. I wished a good afternoon to her for no reason...just because I was feeling good. But no one ever talks to the Meehans, so she didn't expect it and didn't know what to make of it. That's why she stared at me like that. But after a while, it sank in that I was just being friendly, so she came running after us to say good afternoon back to me."

"Maybe so. But it could also have something to do with her being a nut."

"She's not a real Meehan, you know. She's the only one of them who isn't. One of the Meehan men found her in a loony bin where he was doing time, and he brought her home...or so Mrs Kane says. But that could be just a lot of hooey. You've got to take everything an old gossip like Mrs Kane says with a dose of salts.[8] You know what I bet? I bet Mrs Meehan was brought up around polite people, and she misses it."

"But she's the craziest of all the Meehans," I said. "You don't want to get mixed up with her."

"She's not dangerous, poor thing."

Anne-Marie and I exchanged glances. We weren't thinking about danger. We knew that if Mother started having anything to do with the Meehans, the block's gossips, who already thought she was far too 'different', would be confirmed in their belief that she was a borderline crazylady.

After that day, whenever my mother walked downtown, even if she was on our side of the street, the Meehan kids would rush indoors screaming, "The Missus! The Missus!" And Mrs Meehan would appear on her stoop, wiping her hands on a rag or pushing hair out of her eyes. She would grin and wave at Mother, who would call "Good morning!" or "Good afternoon!" and Mrs Meehan would return the greeting, beaming with pleasure as she watched Mother walk down the street for a while before returning to her warren, her day brightened.

· · · · · · · · · ·

Through determination and invention Mother managed to keep us healthy on $7.27 a week, but when it came to providing the little extras that make life worth living, she had to find occasional part-time work as a waitress, regardless of the risk to her health. The first, and by far the most important, of these life-embracing extras was an extravagance, a beloved extravagance: the Emerson radio that became our principal contact with the great external world of learning and life and love and laughter. One night when she was walking home from a late shift in a hash house where she'd been filling in, my mother spotted the Emerson in the darkened window of a pawn shop on the corner of South Street and Herkimer. The next day, a Sunday, the three of us were returning from Washington Park where there was a wooden four-person 'gondola' swing that we could queue up for, then ride it until our arms and legs were heavy with pumping and our heads were light with swooping through the air. Mother brought us home the long way around, down State Street to the closed A-One Pawn Shop, where we stood before the window looking at the radio and imagining all the drama, comedy, music and news that could come pouring out at the click of a switch. We knew about this because we'd had the use of a friend's radio for a month during our last summer at Lake George Village and we'd spent several hours each day listening to programs coming to us from as far away as Glens Falls and Schenectady. I wondered how much the shopkeeper would ask for this radio, considering that its walnut cabinet was cracked and some of the inlaid bits were missing. I liked its reliable, old-fashioned key-hole shape and its upside-down face with an arched dial of a mouth above two turn-knob eyes. If it had been newer it would probably have been Bakelite molded into that universal design idiom of the 'Thirties: Streamlining. This smooth, swept-back look was logical for automobiles and locomotive engines, but throughout the 'Thirties streamlining was applied to all kinds of products and articles, even the least appropriate: toasters, lamps and handbag clasps were streamlined, as well as bookends, exit signs, money clips, barrettes for girls' hair, ashtrays, facades of buildings...all sorts of things were designed to come flying at you through the air. No wonder it was a nervous decade.

Mother said we were lucky the radio's cabinet was old and cracked because that would be useful in bargaining with the pawnbroker, and she knew how to haggle with these people. You had to stand your ground and—

Just then a spring bell above the shop door *ping'd* as the door opened. "There's something?" asked the pawnbroker, an old man with a thousand years of craft and suffering in his face and twice that much complaint in his voice. In height, he was about halfway between me and my mother, and he wore a woman's apron and dust bonnet, presumably his wife's. I guessed he had been cleaning up his merchandise. My mother told him we were just looking.

"Looking's free. Enjoy." And he turned to go back into the shop. My mother tipped me a wink and asked the man how much a pair of binoculars in the window was. (Ah, she doesn't want him to know she's really interested in the radio. Crafty.)

The old man smiled at her. "I could have sworn you were looking at the radio. Quality merchandise. Absolutely guaranteed to carry the finest programs available on the airwaves. And all in English for ease of use."

"Radio?" my mother asked, puzzled. "I didn't notice any...oh, you mean that one down there? The old one with the broken cabinet?"

"The crack lets the sound out more freely."

"How much?"

"A bargain at nine dollars."

Mother sniffed a note of laughter and turned away.

"But for you, lady, seven dollars fifty cents."

Mother shook her head and made a puffing sound.

"Lookit, lady, I'll tell you what. Because it's Sunday and because I'm not officially open for business and because you're my only customer and because I like the look of your kids and because I'm too soft-hearted for my own good, I could make it six seventy-five. A penny less and I'm in the poorhouse."

"Six dollars even."

"Oy ayoy! Such a stubborn lady! All right, six dollars. But my wife's a proud woman. She's going to hate living in the poorhouse. By the way, we're talking cash here, aren't we?"

"I get paid at the end of the week."

"You're saying you don't have the cash. Why are you wasting my time like this, lady? What did I ever do to you?"

"I'll have the money at the end of the week."

"Lady, I just can't...! Oh, all right, all right! Come back with the cash at the end of the week. The radio will be waiting for you."

"Yes, but I need—"

"Don't even think it, lady."

"There's lots of good programs on Sundays, and I—"

"I asked you to don't even think it."

"My kids would love to listen to—"

"You're thinking it, even though I begged you not to!"

"I could give you a dollar right now, and the rest when I get paid at the end—"

"Lookit, lady, I don't know you from Adam. Or Eve either, for that matter."

"I've never cheated anybody in my life!"

"Who's talking cheating? A trolley car could hit! The world could come to an end! Things happen!"

"I could make it two dollars down. That's every last cent of my tip money."

"Help, somebody. A man's being robbed here!"

"What do you say?"

"What do I say? I say I'm being robbed. Tell those kids not to look at me like that. Why did I open the door? All right, two dollars down, four fifty at the end of the week."

"We agreed on six dollars even."

"That was the cash price. The robbery price is six fifty."

"All right, it's a deal."

"My wife's going to kill me. Then they'll send her to prison. First the poorhouse, then prison."

As we walked home, me carrying the Emerson proudly and Anne-Marie green-lipped from sucking a striped candy stick the shopkeeper had given her, my mother muttered, "You see how he jacked up the price on me at the last minute? They're all alike."

I couldn't believe it. After the way she had whittled him down like that, and the way he'd let us walk away with his radio for only two dollars down. But that's how she'd been brought up to see things.

We tried to work out a schedule for listening to the radio so we could hear all the best programs without wasting electricity. But in the end we listened greedily and without method because radio not only brought drama, comedy and world events into our lives, but we were also avid followers of the fortunes of the popular tunes that were featured on the weekly *Your Lucky Strike Hit Parade*. We would cheer the climb of our favorites up the hit-parade ladder, then lament their inevitable decline into the shadows of history.[9]

As it turned out, the pawnbroker was right when he said that things happen. For one thing, he didn't get his four fifty at the end of that week as we had promised. Mother fell ill from late hours and overwork, and the manager of the restaurant held back part of her wages because she hadn't worked the full week. At twenty-five cents a week, it took us more than four months to pay off the four fifty we owed for the radio, and that quarter was enough to strain our budget to the extent of at least one extra day on potato soup each week. But it was worth it. A radio! At the time we got ours, only a few people on our block had radios. When President Roosevelt made a Fireside Chat to the nation we radio owners would put our receivers on the sills of our front windows and turn the volume up, so the people who gathered on the pavement could hear. I used to look down benevolently on the sidewalk listeners we were informing with our Emerson, and I would keep my hand on the volume knob, so everybody knew who was in charge of things.

Each Saturday afternoon Mother would give me a quarter and I would walk all the way down to South Street and Herkimer. The spring bell above the door of the A-One Pawn Shop would *ping* as I entered, and the old man would always greet me with the same words: "Ah! So you and your mother haven't run off to Mexico with my radio yet, eh?"

And I would always respond, "No, still here, Mr A-One."

"Mr A-One! That's a hot one! Such wit! You should tell jokes on that radio you stole from me on false pretenses." He would take the quarter and write out my receipt on a scrap of paper which I would put into my shoe for safety because my mother carefully saved all the receipts. You can't tell with those people.

He would tell me how much we still owed; I'd say: See you next week, Mr A-One; he'd say: Such wit; and I'd open the *ping-ing* door and start the long walk back home, thinking about the special Saturday night comedy hour with *Amos 'n Andy* and *Fred Allen's Town Hall Tonight* both of which could make my mother laugh until tears stood in her eyes.

It is difficult for the modern reader to appreciate the effect of radio upon the pre-television audience, because the functions and the impact of radio differed from those of television in fundamental ways, not the least of which was the fact that the radio audience was innocent and receptive to a degree unimaginable today.

Introduced on the eve of the Age of the Consumer, television quickly became a throw-away narcotic for the reality-stunned. Its messages bypass the censorship of the brain and are injected directly into the viewer's central cortex. It is a babbling background irritant to modern life, always present, never significant, except to the lonely, the dim, and the damaged. Radio, on the more joyful hand, engaged us, busied our imaginations, and obliged us to paint its images on the walls of our minds. On radio, a handsome man was *your* personal image of a handsome man, and a brave woman was *your* idea of a brave woman, and a beautiful sunset was *your* sunset, *your* beauty. News broadcasts were gritty, immediate and potent, science was fascinating and significant, humor was side-splitting, drama touched our hearts, and the adventure programs, particularly those directed at children, were the very stuff of daydreams: absorbing, involving, challenging, frightening and totally satisfying. (If you were a boy, that is. It must be admitted that radio drama arrived in an era when the female character was still limited largely to romantic and domestic settings, which is too bad, because few women look back on radio with the affection men feel, and one cannot blame them.) I used to stand before our Emerson for hours, one foot hooked behind the other ankle, my eyes defocused, thoughtlessly tearing up little bits of paper as my imagination battened on the radio as on an unending flow of ambrosia, food for the mind and the soul that sustained you when you needed support, exercised you when your emotions or intellect were flabby and cosseted you when you needed rest and escape.[10] And radio was a liberator. For me, radio was the quickest way out of North Pearl Street. And that was important because I was chilled by a nagging fear that I might end up on public support the rest of my life until, like most of the people on my block, I became so spiritually enfeebled that I lost all dignity, grit and ambition and came to view the dole not only as a necessary condition of existence but as a basic civil right.

But Mother was determined to save my sister and me from accepting the values and limitations of North Pearl Street as our own, and radio wasn't her only means of accomplishing this. On Saturday afternoons when admission was free, she would pack a lunch (usually bean sandwiches) and take us for an enlightening visit to the Schuyler Mansion. Confident that her French ancestry, however distant, endowed her with innate good taste, she would openly criticize the decor of the rooms, describing what colors she would have used, or what fabrics, and I would cringe at the stares she collected from the tight-lipped volunteer guides. It never occurred to me to doubt my mother's aesthetic judgment, I only wished she expressed it less freely...and loudly. But she thought it was best to be frank with people who were in error. How else would they learn? On those weekdays when there was no school because of religious holidays, we would walk up State Street to the

Natural History Museum to broaden our understanding of the world and its wonders by standing in awe beneath the high-arching skeleton of a dinosaur held up by a metal armature; or, wandering alone through those vast halls, we would gaze at the realistic woodland dioramas of plaster Indians sitting around glowing lightbulb fires, or we would peer down into glass display cases, browsing on such scientific wonders as birds' eggs, ore samples and arrowheads, and Mother and I would take turns reading the inscriptions in half-whispers that hissed in the echoing marble corridors.

On Sundays, when the weather permitted, we would walk all the way up to Washington Park to eat our sandwiches beside the little lake before going over to the big four-man wooden 'gondola' swings. Anne-Marie and I would sit on one side facing Mother, who would push the bottom bar with her feet and pull the crossbar with her arms until we got the considerable bulk swinging, slowly at first because our legs were too short to help much, then faster and higher as Mother pumped harder and harder until we swung high enough to rock and shake the framework. At the apex of the swing, our stomachs went weightless and Anne-Marie and I giggled helplessly, then we swooped down through space and our stomachs rose within us as fright moistened our palms and weakened our grips on the crossbar. One of the old men who served as park wardens would shout up at us not to swing so high, and Mother would laugh and shout down to him: go to hell! and he would shake his head and go away muttering. Just as her encounters with the guides at the Schuyler Mansion left me proud of her refined taste but uncomfortable about her willingness to share it, so these confrontations with park authority made me proud of her feisty independence and yet embarrassed. You shouldn't swear at old men.

Washington Park's wide lanes were tended by WPA crews that wandered through, each man taking personal responsibility for picking up five leaves. The late-Victorian esplanade had been laid out as an ambulatory park for 'promenading', which Mother, who read historical novels and knew about such things, described as a social ritual in which pairs of snappy young men in boaters and candy-striped blazers strolled along in the hope of meeting two modern young women in wasp-waisted, pigeon-breasted Gibson-girl dresses walking in the opposite direction, arm in arm. Nods and half bows might be exchanged the second time around, and perhaps a smile or even a word the third. And if, by astonishing coincidence, they met again the following week, who knows? Names might be exchanged. Snappy sayings might be produced and laughed at. Dynasties have been founded on such oblique negotiations between urgent genes.

Washington Park was my favorite of Mother's no-cost cultural expeditions designed to remind us that there was a world beyond North Pearl Street, so it was natural that I usually ended up there the handful of times I played hooky from school, which I did for the thrill of wrong-doing, or out of boredom when I knew that a teacher would be grinding her way for the third, fourth, fifth time through some matter that was self-evident to anyone with an IQ larger than his shoe size. I also played hooky out of duty to my self-image as a real boy, in imitation of Mark Twain's Tom Sawyer and Thomas Bailey Aldrich's Bad Boy.[11] As with so many social trespasses, most of the fun of playing hooky was in the planning and anticipation...in fact, just about all of it, because there was almost nothing that a boy wandering alone on a school day through strange streets and back alleys could find to do, with no destination, no money, and not daring to come too near his own neighborhood for fear of being recognized and reported to his mother. The night before, I would make up story games about the adventures a lone boy prowling through the city might get involved in. Most of these came from books and radio and had to do with foiling crooks, spies, blackmailers or kid-nappers. Unfortunately, the heroes in the books were always big, brave, handsome crack shots, so I was obliged to work out story games in which my advantage as a crime fighter lay in my having the appearance of a skinny little kid, so no one suspected me of being, in fact, a heroic protector of the oppressed and the endangered. The basic lead-in to my adventures would be something like this: I'm wandering down some street, and a beautiful woman rushes out onto her stoop and looks desperately up and down the street for a kid; and I'm the only kid around because it's a school day. The reason she needs a kid is that she can't get into her apartment because (a) she has lost her keys, (b) some cruel guy has locked her out, (c) it isn't her apartment, but that of a fear-crazed friend who has telephoned, begging her to rush over and help her, but when she got to the friend's apartment, the door was locked and no one responded to her frantic knocking. There is a narrow transom above the door that a kid might be able to squeeze through, and that's why she so desperately needs a kid, particularly a skinny kid. Well, I would set my lunch bucket aside and roll up my sleeves, and the beautiful woman would interlace her fingers and I'd put my foot into the hand-stirrup and she'd boost me up and I'd wriggle through the transom, drop down on the inside and open the door. And from there the adventure took any of a hundred paths, all of which ultimately led to the bad guys being thwarted ('thwarted' and 'foiled' were verbs applied only to villains), and in the end the beautiful woman invited me to drop in any time I wanted to sit by the fire in their richly appointed salon and read any book in their huge library while I nibbled on the delicious things their servants left out for me. I don't remember any romantic enticements—I was, after all, only seven when these story games began—so I don't know why the heroines were always beautiful. Just narrative convention, I guess.

I usually ended up in Washington Park after wandering through the prosperous streets abutting it, tacitly offering my services to any beautiful heroine who might be in need of a kid to shinny through her transom. Finally giving up, I would drift into the park where I would stylishly out-fence then ruthlessly decapitate a few weeds with a stick-rapier, chuck pebbles into the man-made lake to see the ripples spread like Mrs Kane's rumors, then climb the flat-topped artificial hill that had been created out of the spoil from digging the lake it overlooked. Up there, I would be out of sight of the omnipresent truant officers with which my guilt populated the park: truant officers disguised as bums, as park wardens, as old men sunning themselves on benches, maybe even as women pushing baby carriages...the sly rats!

While the story-weaving and the anticipation of coming across some great adventure were rich and rewarding, the reality of playing hooky was not. It was usually a long, boring day of aimless wandering, and even worse when it rained and I was obliged to spend time in doorways or in dark, silent churches from which I returned home tired, cold and saddened to have been born too late for the great era of discovery and adventure. For lack of anything else to do, I almost always ate my lunch in mid-morning, so by the time I got home I was not only grumpy about being born too late, I was also very hungry.

After visiting the Schuyler Mansion for our refinement, the

Natural History Museum for our understanding, or Washington Park for our spirit of adventure, my sister, mother and I would walk home, playing 'Name That Tune' or 'I Spy', or trying to avoid stepping on cracks in the sidewalk while not appearing to do so to anyone who might be watching our progress down the street. It's hard not to break out laughing as you do this because you have to keep your head up and look down your nose to spot the cracks, which makes you cross-eyed, and you have to take shorter or longer steps while trying to appear perfectly natural. We would arrive at 238 after dark; Mother would make soup and sandwiches; then we would end our perfect day sitting in the dark, listening to the radio. Somehow, radio programs were always best listened to in the dark with only the amber glow of the dial.

PEARL STREET BLUES

M Y MEMORIES of Pearl Street are set against seasonal and me-
teorological backdrops that might be termed 'folkloristically
correct'. Most of the old fairy tales and story books that established the traditional settings for America's seasons were written
and illustrated in New England, where March is indeed windy and
April showery, where Halloween obligingly rustles with the ghostly
susurrus of crisp fallen leaves and there is a crust of early snow for
Thanksgiving. I used to feel sorry for children from the West and the
South who were obliged to accept these literary givens despite the evidence of their senses...sweating, sunburned kids in Hawaii or Galve-
ston who had to make do with cotton wool snow for their windows. I
felt lucky to have been brought up where the seasons were folkloristically correct.

Pearl Street, Fall. Illustrations in the dog-eared old primers we
used at school showed boys in knickers and girls in pinafores happily
jumping through piles of fallen leaves, but our block had no trees to

shed leaves, so fall is symbolized for me by the beginning of the school year. Book covers were made from brown paper bags and we bought new notebooks that I promised this year for sure—for *sure*—I would keep neat and un-scribbled-on, but sooner or later my bored hand would begin to doodle autonomically, and by the time I noticed what I was doing, it was too late, the purity of the notebook was compromised and, on the virgin-or-whore principle, I felt free to fill the notebook with doodles, multiplications of massive numbers, and lists of words from one of my boredom-slaying pastimes, seeing how many words of more than four syllables I could think of beginning with the letter...[12]

Pearl Street, Winter. I can envision those eternal narcotized afternoons during my last year at P.S. 5, before Mother transferred me to Our Lady of Angels school because I had been getting bad grades and warnings about my 'behavior and attitude' ever since Miss Cox died. Chalk dust hangs in the air, momentarily defining a pale winter sunbeam. Bored, I let my mind drift...drift...my dip pen stops and a furry blot blossoms where the nib touches the paper...my heavy-lidded eyes rest on the unfinished portrait of George Washington that makes him seem to be emerging from clouds...beside him, a limp flag to which we pledge our allegiance every morning, flinging our arms straight out, palms down, as we say '...*to* the flag of the United States of America'. With the coming of the Second World War, the teachers would discontinue this gesture that seemed too close to the Nazi salute, and tell us to keep our hands over our hearts.

Pearl Street, Spring. A fleeting few weeks between the searching cold of winter and the oppressive heat of summer, Spring was as perilous as it was ephemeral. Although your mother warned you not to, and although you knew from experience that you shouldn't, you always shed your winter jacket too soon and let your winter-stiff legs stretch as you ran, scudded along from behind by the March wind, and you inevitably ended up with a tenacious head cold. Because she always had a stuffed-up nose, the urban Goddess of Spring pronounced her name 'Sprig', and that, for the etymologically curious, is how new spring branches came to be called 'sprigs'.

Pearl Street, Summer day. Roller-skating up and down the street to the click-clack of the cracks beneath your wheels as your roller-skate key swings from a string around your neck. We had only one pair of roller skates bought from a woman whose child had died of polio, they were too wide for Anne-Marie and too short for me, but we managed, taking turns, she slipping around on the skates, me with pinched toes. My feet still remember how, when you've unclamped the skates from your shoes after hours of skating, the soles of your feet continue to tingle, remembering the pavement.

Pearl Street, Summer night. People sit on their stoops on hot nights, talking lazily. I walk down the street, looking up at the full moon, which seems to travel with me at the speed of my walk, weaving its way through the power lines, and I wonder if there is another boy in some other town, maybe some foreign country, looking up as he walks and assuming the moon is following him, too.

And through all seasons, our radio offered *Your Lucky Strike Hit Parade* and brought the Big Bands to us from dance halls and ballrooms across the nation, providing the songs that formed a musical background for the troubles and joys that textured our lives on North Pearl Street.

> Let's Face the Music and Dance...
> There's a Small Hotel...Easy to Love...
> I've Got You Under My Skin...
> I Can't Get Started (with you)...Little Old Lady

Most of the games kids played on our block were the same as those we had known in Lake George Village. Aside from those anonymous roughhouse games that give boys a chance to knock one another around and barge into clumps of girls, who protest and squeal, but continue to stand about, hoping to be barged into by a boy they think is 'cute'; boys had marbles and mumblety-peg, both played in the vacant lot beside Kane's cornerstore where there was some sooty dirt for drawing marble circles and for jack knives to stick into. Quick-handed little girls played jacks on the wide top step of the stoops, or skipped and dipped over chalked hopscotch patterns that blossomed on the sidewalks each morning only to become foot-smudged palimpsests by nightfall. Bigger girls jumped rope to the rhythm of those chants, some modern, topical and ephemeral, others ancient, metaphorical and eternal, that were, and I hope still are, the folk poetry of the slums. Most of these chants ended with counting the number of times 'Bonnie Johnny kissed ya sistah' or how often 'the ghost of Cindy Flinders came a-tappin' atcha winders', or the number of crullers the jumper could eat at a sitting, or the number of lovers she would have, or of children, or the number of miles she would run to avoid a certain boy (or to catch another one). The pace and volume of the enumeration rose until the ordeal ended with high-speed 'hot pepper' skips that separated the mediocre jumpers from the stars and made frustrated younger sisters yearn to beat triumphant older ones—just once! Soon, too soon, the arrival of 'the curse' would thrust each girl in turn into gawky, giggling puberty, which would oblige her to scorn both sidewalk games and the insufferable babies who still played them.

Boys were prohibited by tacit sex taboos from jumping rope, but they could turn the rope for their sisters and their sisters' friends, so long as they did so with bored, sardonic expressions on their faces and eventually whipped the rope up to trip the girls and spoil their fun. Failure to ruin the game, or turning the rope for anyone who wasn't your sister, got you teased for being 'sweet on' some girl, which obliged you to fight the accuser to prove he was a dirty liar whose pants were on fire.

As soon as the snow was gone and the sidewalks were dry, baseball cards were brought out onto the street to be swapped and gambled for, three or four boys standing back about five yards from a building and flipping the cards against it. You won the other kids' cards by getting closest to the wall, or by overlapping them. It was better to overlap, because flipping a card hard enough to get really close to the wall risked denting its corners, thus reducing its swap value. Baseball cards came wrapped up with thin, rectangular, one-for-a-penny slabs of pink gum that tasted like the inside of an old woman's purse smells, sweet and powdery. This gum didn't 'blow' as well as Fleers, which came as a chubby pink cube wrapped in paper with twisted bow-tie ends and had a waxed 'funny paper' with a couple of stale jokes, a riddle, and an 'amazing fact', but you didn't get baseball cards with Fleers, so the sales of this superior bubble gum fell off drastically during the spring card-flipping season.

You only flipped duplicate cards, never risking one of your collection and hoping through skill and luck to win cards that would fill gaps in your pictures of baseball players arranged by teams. It may seem odd today, but before the Second World War, all the major-league teams of America's 'national' sport were located in cities east of the Mississippi and north of the Mason-Dixon line, except for Washington, D.C.'s two teams. In addition to baseball cards there was a series of automobile cards depicting everything from the Model T and the Stutz Bearcat through to the newest 'airflow' models, and a series of æroplane cards (yes, with that 'æ' ligature) including fragile bi-planes, stumpy Schneider Trophy seaplanes that were little more than motors with cockpits, and modern all-metal planes, like the Ford tri-motor that flew over our street every morning just before school started, causing all the kids to arch their backs and squint up through 'binoculars' made of two hollow fists to watch it pass over carrying the airmail south to New York City. But most desirable of all during the spring of 1937 was a new line of 'War Cards', gaudy and ghastly images of Japanese atrocities against Chinese women and children that were printed in China and distributed as propaganda to solicit sympathy and assistance in their war against smaller but more modern Japan. When the attack on Pearl Harbor came almost five years later, a whole generation was preconditioned to hate the 'vile Nips' by these war cards depicting slaughtered children, their mouths agape in silent screams.

Every kid in Albany played these games, but a game unique to North Pearl Street was 'ledgey', in which a ball was aimed at an inch-wide, up-angled decorative ledge across the face of certain buildings on our block, about three feet up from the sidewalk. The bald, flabby tennis ball was thrown so hard that it hit the wall with a hollow *fwop!* that could be heard a block away. If the ball missed the narrow target of the ledge, as it usually did, it would simply bounce off the wall, and the opponent had to catch it before it bounced a second time. If he failed, the other player got a point and remained 'at bat'. But when a ball hit the ledge it would arc high, and if the opponent caught it in the air, the other fellow was 'out', but if the ball arc'd over the opponent's head, that counted as a four-point 'home run'. Because the game depended upon an architectural oddity that was particular to just three houses on our block, ledgey belonged to the kids of North Pearl Street and to no others, and we all became more or less skillful at playing it. One of my early humiliations was discovering that all the boys on the block and most of the girls could beat me at ledgey, which they won through their ability to throw the ball so hard that it was difficult to catch, even a flabby worn-out tennis ball with very little bounce left in it. But slowly over a couple of years I became the street's best ledgey player despite the fact that most of my adversaries were stronger than I. My advantage lay in wiry quickness and low cunning: I would run my opponents from side to side for a while, then I would place a soft little ball that made them rush forward, almost into the wall, and the best they could manage was a desperate, stabbing catch and a limp return, which gave me a relatively easy shot at the ledge, and if I hit it, the ball would arc out of reach. Home run! Gee, it's sorta hard to get those high ones, isn't it. Sorry, pal! Who's next?

In time I gained acceptance and even a certain amount of status among the kids of the block. Some of this status was earned by my skill at ledgey, but most of it came from the tough, sassy mouth I developed defensively. People who lived in the buildings with good ledgey facades were driven mad by the constant *fwop*. They didn't seem to appreciate the finer points of the game that caused kids to scream and shout outside their windows and occasionally to send a stray ball crashing through one of their panes, instantly dispersing the kids into side alleys and basement doorways as the street became absolutely silent for a few minutes, like a forest after a gunshot. At least once in the course of each animated game somebody would open a window and stick out his head. "Hey! I'm trying to sleep for the love of God! You kids get the hell away from here, you hear me?" I would pull my cap down tight by the brim and remind the complainer that he didn't own the world, and he'd tell me that I'd better get going if I didn't want my ass kicked, and I'd say: Oh yeah? You and who's uncle? Then I'd turn and walk away slowly with an I-don't-give-a-damn swagger, but quaking inside and ready to take to my heels if I heard the sound of a door being opened. The kids never recognized that my swagger was a cocky sham. "He don't take shit offa nobody, that kid! He's like his crazy mother." Not taking shit offa nobody was an admired quality on Pearl Street.

North Pearl might have been a sump for society's lost, damaged and incapable, but my sister and I never felt inferior, not even to those lucky kids in the movies who lived in small towns with big lawns and had wryly benevolent fathers who remembered what rascals they had been when they, too, were young. We didn't feel inferior because my mother wouldn't let us. She made it clear that, unlike most of our neighbors, we didn't belong on North Pearl. Bad luck and the Depression had dumped us there, but we weren't going to stay. No, sir! One of these days we'd be out of there in a flash. Boy-o-boy just you watch our smoke!

Society provided our basic shelter and food, but we were on our own when it came to those little extras that separate life from the daily grind of survival, such things as birthday or Christmas presents, or a nice dress for my sister who was very sensitive to clothes and fashion, or the coffee that was my mother's only hedonistic vice, or special holiday meals like our long-awaited Easter treat of 'Virginia Baked Spam' made from two cans of Spam, a small three-slice can of pineapple and a bottle of imitation maple syrup. Mother used to shape and score the Spam, arrange the rings of pineapple, then pour a little maple syrup over it and bake it so that it came out looking almost exactly like a miniature glazed ham, and we used to have it with yams on which we melted margarine. It was my job to color the margarine, putting the white, lard-like block into a bowl then sprinkling orange coloring powder over it and mixing with a fork until it was more brazenly yellow than any butter would dare to be. Not until the war came along to absorb all of dairyland's produce did the butter lobby allow pre-colored margarine onto the market in dairy states like Wisconsin and New York.

Christmas presents, coffee, Virginia Baked Spam, these little indulgences and pleasures required money beyond our 35¢ per person per day, and this had to be made either by Mother working as a waitress, or by me carrying my home-made shoeshine box on rounds of the bars on Friday nights (black and brown polish only, no two-toned shoes). But even when things seemed their grimmest, my mother would assure my sister and me that one of these days we'd wake up and find ourselves on Easy Street.

'Easy Street' was one of my mother's favorite songs. The surest indication that she had emerged from a spell of the blues was hearing her sing such up-beat songs as she cooked supper. The three of us sang together almost every night as she sat at the table darning and Anne-Marie and I did the supper dishes, me washing, she wiping, standing on a chair because she was so little. Among our favorites were those defiantly optimistic songs that appeared during the first years of the Depression. Not only did these songs urge you to live your life 'On the Sunny Side of the Street' but they insisted that it wasn't all that bad to be poor, because 'The Best Things in Life Are Free', and love was among those finer things in life that were to be had on the cheap, like the man who 'Found a Million-Dollar Baby (in a five-and-ten-cent store)'; so you should keep your chin up because 'Beyond the Blue Horizon (waits a beautiful day)', and all you had to do was to 'Wrap Your Troubles in Dreams (and dream your troubles away)'.

Occasionally, when she was down in the dumps, Mother would sing one of the embittered Depression songs, like 'Remember My Forgotten Man' or 'Buddy, Can You Spare a Dime?'

In her heyday, my mother had had one of those quintessential symbols of the flapper 'Twenties, a ukulele. When the magic of short-wave brought *Hawaii Calls!* to our radio all the way from those distant islands, Anne-Marie would put on a grass skirt she had made from newspapers cut into long strips and she would hula with graceful, expressive hand movements while Mother strummed and fingered an imaginary ukulele and I imitated the falling whine of a Hawaiian guitar by humming in falsetto while blocking one nostril and flicking the other. Show Business!

Pennies from Heaven...These Foolish Things...
The Way You Look Tonight...Goody-Goody...
It's De-Lovely...The Music Goes Round and Round...

My mother always attacked the housework chores with unbounded energy. Saturday was laundry day in our apartment, and I worked with her in the bathroom while clothes boiled on the gas stove and filled the kitchen with steam. Bending over our old-fashioned claw-footed bathtub I would rub the sheets up and down a corrugated washboard with such reckless vigor that I always skinned a couple of knuckles, which would stiffen and sting for half the forthcoming week. Doing the laundry in those days was not just a matter of washing, rinsing, wringing out, then hanging on the line; the job involved several operations that are either combined today or dismissed as unnecessary. There was also bluing, bleaching, boiling and starching. Not only my school shirts and Anne-Marie's white school blouses got starched, but also the sheets and pillow cases. So a single item might be boiled, then bleached, then washed, then rinsed, then blued, then starched, then hung out to dry, then taken in, then sprinkled, then ironed, then folded away. My first encounter with the marvels of domestic technology designed to end housework drudgery was a new washboard we bought when our old one got too rusty to use. The corrugated scrub board was made of glass (no rust!), and this Nu-Mode Self-Soaping Glass Washboard (patent pending) introduced an innovation into the shallow wooden rectangle that held the bar of soap: holes had been drilled in the bottom board, allowing the soapy water to drain from the bar of Fels Naphtha and run down over the clothes being scrubbed on the corrugated glass. Nothing wasted. O, brave new world.

The only thing Mother couldn't do by herself was wring out the sheets because the strain of leaning over the edge of the bathtub always started a bout of coughing. So I used to help her, me twisting in one direction, she twisting in the other. When I was little, she was too strong for me and she would twist the sheet out of my grasp, which used to make me roar with frustration. We would coil the wrung-out sheets in the bottom of our clothes basket, which we would carry between us to the backyard to hang them out. Because Pearl Street traversed a hill that ran down to the river, the front windows of our apartment over-looked the street from a height of about ten feet, but we stepped out the door of our kitchen into a cement area that was four feet lower than the impermeable hard-pack of our sunless backyard. A central drain re-ceived the rainwater that cascaded down from beneath a rickety plank fence of weathered, dangerously splintery boards that separated our barren backyard from the alley where I used to play. One reel of our clothesline was attached to this fence, and the other was screwed into the frame of our kitchen door. Only people with first-floor apartments could hang out their washing while standing on the ground. Everyone else had to hang theirs from back windows using one line from the complex web of lines that looped off this way and that from the back of every building on the block. To hang out your clothes you had to bring them to your bedroom window, if you had a back apartment, or to the hall window on your floor if yours was a front apartment. You opened the window and leaned out to attach your wet clothes with clothespins, then you reeled them out far enough to attach the next pin, a difficult task if you were dealing with big things like sheets, which were always heavy with water, because no one on Pearl Street had a washing machine with rollers that squeezed the water out of sheets. Nor did our women want washing machines because they had all heard chilling urban factoids describing careless women who caught their fingers between the rollers and were dragged through the wringers up to the shoulder before their screams alerted passers-by. (Such are the dangers of being rich and so la-de-da as to need a machine to do your washing.) The reason the newspapers never carried stories about these ghastly accidents was that the big washing machine companies paid them to hush things up...or so we were assured.

Threading wet clothes out through a window without letting them brush against the sill and pick up soot required skill, strength and, on windy days, a little luck, but there were times when reeling the clothes back in was even more difficult. In winter, the sheets froze stiff on the line, and the rigid rectangles would not fit back in through the window, so you had to cuff and punch them until they 'broke' and could be folded. All this work was done leaning halfway out an open window as high as four stories up, while your neighbors complained about the cold drafts you were letting in. And even when you managed to get your sheets in, they would become damp again as they thawed out, so you had to string them around your kitchen and bathroom, where they gave off waves of clammy moisture until finally they dried.

When your house was back-to-back with the one on the next block, the far reel of your clothesline would be screwed into the woodwork of your back neighbor's window, and hers into yours. These attachment points were always within reach of the windows so that repairs and replacements could be made and, in some particularly irritating cases, so that tangles could be unraveled after windy nights. Since people whose houses backed on one another's did not, by definition, live on the same block and were therefore alien, this occasional need for cooperation involved negotiations with people you didn't know. Sometimes friendships were established this way; but more often quite the opposite.

Ole Buttermilk Sky...That Old Feeling...Remember Me...
It Looks Like Rain in Cherry Blossom Lane...
Rosalie...Harbor Lights...September in the Rain...

I can see Mr Kane's eyes, huge behind thick glasses. We were sitting on his side steps in the evening after the cornerstore was closed, having one of our talks as we looked out across what he ironically called 'my garden', a narrow strip of vacant lot, bare sooty earth that glittered with shards of broken glass, a clump of sumac growing out of a crack in the wall of a building, its prehistoric leaves turning over to show their light side when it was going to rain, and here and there a clump of indestructible ironweed breaking through the hard-packed ground.

These talks were neither regular nor frequent, perhaps four or five a year, but they went on as long as I lived on North Pearl Street. Most of them, and especially at first when I was seven or eight years old, consisted of Mr Kane amplifying on things he had heard on the shortwave radio that kept him in contact with what was happening in Warsaw, London, Madrid and Berlin. I picture him in the small hours of the night hunched over his radio, a shock of white hair caught in the head strap of his earphones, while his wife snores upstairs. These were, I believe, among the happiest moments of his life...certainly the most peaceful. I realize now that he must have been very lonely, isolated on North Pearl by his race and by his role as the block's credit provider. Why else would he talk to a kid who could add nothing to the conversation but the occasional nod or hum to indicate attention?

Our first talk was occasioned by something I said one spring evening just before closing time while I was buying a penny's worth of Spanish Red Hots (three-a-penny cinnamon disks). It must have been a Saturday because that morning I had attended catechism class up at the priests' house across from Saint Joseph's Church. The class was taught by an intense young priest with pink-rimmed eyes, a scratchy voice and incandescent acne. After battering his way through the difference between complete contrition and incomplete contrition (which, as best I could make out, depended on whether you confessed your sins because you cherished Jesus Christ who was all good and deserving of all our love, or because, unspeakable coward that you were, you dreaded spending eternity in Hell), the priest asked if we had any questions, and seeing that I was about to pose one said, "Well then! Let's all kneel and offer up prayers for the poor priests and nuns who are being martyred by those Godless, blood-thirsty Spanish Republicans." So we said a few Hail, Marys and Our Fathers after which, ignoring my eagerly raised hand, he blessed us and we filed out into the street.

I had wanted to hear more about these blood-thirsty Republicans. My mother never had anything good to say about Republicans, whom she described as a bunch of fat cats who were against everything President Roosevelt was trying to do for the poor, and who had caused the Depression by an evil act called 'buying on margin'. I was willing to accept that any enemy of President Roosevelt was my enemy too, and that buying on margin was a base and unforgivable vice, but it seemed odd to me that when cataloguing the Republicans' iniquities and misdeeds my mother had failed to mention the juicy fact that they were in the habit of butchering priests and nuns.

I was in Mr Kane's cornerstore just before closing time, negotiating to exchange my penny for two Spanish Red Hots and two Jelly Babies, both of which were three-a-penny candies. In the course of the babble-blur I kept up to prevent Mr Kane from adding up and realizing that I was trying to get one and a third cents worth of candy for a penny, I said I sure hoped these Spanish Red Hots weren't made by Republicans.

Mr Kane gave me the candy and, as he dropped my penny into the cash drawer, said, "So what's all this about candy made by Republicans?"

"Well, I mean...the Spanish Republicans?"

He raised his eyebrows. "You've heard about the Spanish Republicans?"

"Sure. They kill priests and nuns."

"*This* is all you know about the Revolution?"

"The Revolution?" I couldn't understand what Spaniards had to do with the Revolution which, according to my mental swatchbook of historical images, had been fought out between brave Colonial Minutemen and Hessian mercenaries in red coats, while a bunch of frozen guys crossed the Delaware standing up in the boat, and Paul Revere rode through the night shouting, 'The British are coming! The British are coming!' so guys in Boston got dressed up as Indians and threw their tea into the ocean...oh, and there was something called the Stamp Act.

Mr Kane closed his eyes and shook his head sadly. "It's a crime against the future that the schools haven't taught you about the most important event in the world today. Even you, a smart little boy, don't have the slightest idea what's going on. There should be a law against such ignorance."

"The most important thing in the world? Tell me about it."

"What's the point?" He opened the door for me to leave, then followed me out, locking the door behind him.

"Tell me."

As he pulled down the metal shutter and locked it, he said, "It's too complicated."

"The Republicans are the bad guys, right?"

"Wrong."

"But they murder priests and nuns."

"Yes, that happens sometimes. Out of rage. Out of frustration. There are evil men on both sides. And madmen, too. That's the way it always is. If things were black and white, taking sides would be easy. But in life, good and evil are always in shades of gray, so it takes courage to pick a side. One must consider motives as well as deeds."

"But the Democrats wouldn't kill priests."

"In Spain, the republicans and the democrats are the same people."

"What?" I knew *that* couldn't be right.

"And the revolutionaries are the fascists."

"Fascists?" I had never heard the word before.

By this time, we had walked around the outside of the cornerstore. Mr Kane sat on the wooden steps that led to his side door and took a flat Bugler Cigarette Machine out of his shirt pocket. He limited himself to two cigarettes each day, one before work, one after, both of which he smoked sitting on his side steps because his wife wouldn't let him smoke in the house. Perhaps his admirable self-control was reinforced by the complexity of the cigarette-making operation. First he pinched some shag-cut Bugler tobacco out of its blue tin and carefully distributed it across a little slot at the top of the machine, then he lifted a lever, which action rolled the tobacco into cigarette shape on a rubberized belt within. He licked the adhesive on a cigarette paper and placed it carefully into the slot, then he slowly lowered the lever, which turned the internal mechanism again and voila! a cigarette popped out. He trimmed off the little tufts of tobacco that hung out the ends of the cigarette with a clipper designed for the purpose, carefully brushed the clippings back into the tobacco can, then fished a wooden match out of his pocket, scratched it on the side of the step, lit up, and took a long draw, which he released slowly, his eyes closed as the harsh tobacco made his senses swim for a second. The voluptuously complicated sacrament involved hedonistic teasing and anticipation before satisfaction.

After his second deep draw and slow exhale, he quietly sketched out the history of the Spanish Civil War up to that date. I learned that the bad guys, the Nationalists, were made up of businessmen, the army, land owners, and the Church, and they were trying to overthrow the elected government of good guys, the Republicans, who were workers, farmers, labor unionists, socialists, communists, anarchists, and a few middle-class liberals. He gave me thumbnail definitions of the various 'ists' and 'isms' in terms of what they thought the world ought to be like, and how they intended to bring that ideal state about.

Mr Kane had the gift of being able to weave history into a good story, an adventure with heroes, villains, quests, danger, and dramatic-sounding names: Asturias, Franco, Negrín, Córdoba, Guernica. Fighting on the side of the Republic were the Soviet Union, Mexico and the George Washington and Abraham Lincoln Battalions of young Americans;[13] helping the Fascists were Italian soldiers, *Croix de Fer* rightists from France, Ultra-Catholic Blue Shirts from Ireland, and the Condor Legion of German pilots who practiced tactics by bombing defenseless cities. All the people, places and events came in too thick a flow for me to remember in detail, but I got a feeling for the romance and tragedy of Spain.

It grew dark as I listened, entranced and muddled in equal parts, to Mr Kane's version of the causes and progress of the Civil War. From within his shop, his wife summoned him to supper in a sing-song, long-suffering voice, although it was the first time she had called. I rose, stiff-butted from sitting so long. I could tell he enjoyed having someone who was interested in what life had taught him. I was about to dash across the street to my apartment when he called after me: "By the way! Don't think you got away with anything. I know you cheated me out of a Jelly Baby. I've got my eye on you."

My Funny Valentine...Where or When...
In the Still of the Night...The Nearness of You...
You're a Sweetheart...Little White Lies...A Foggy Day

Albany must have been in a ten-year sartorial time warp, because I later discovered that few men of my age had worn knickerbockers as boys. But in my day, Albany boys wore knickers from the time they graduated from short pants until they entered the ninth grade. We never felt our knickerbockers were peculiar because all the boys in our old textbooks, most of which dated from the 'Twenties, wore them. For Catholic boys, the rites of passage from short pants to knickers and thence to long trousers were synchronized with religious events. First Holy Communion was celebrated in a short pants suit of white with a flowing white satin bow tie, and this was your last pair of short pants; from then on you wore knickers, until your first long-trouser'd suit for Confirmation. The following fall, having worn out your last knickers over the summer holidays, you emerged from the stylistic chrysalis in long trousers, a confirmed man capable of manly sins.

Standard school dress for boys was matching corduroy knickers, jackets and caps, but in the poorer districts this ideal of matching clothes that fit was achieved only seldom and briefly because caps tended to get lost and knickers wore out more quickly than jackets, which were worn until they were tight in the chest and at least two inches of bony wrist dangled from the cuffs, then they were passed down to younger brothers and from family to family on the block. The widespread use of hand-me-downs that fit 'well enough', the practice of buying all clothes, including shoes, at least one size too big so they wouldn't be too quickly outgrown, and the uncooperative tendency of kids to grow by spurts all combined to make our school clothes a medley of floppy and tight. One element of dress, the jacket for instance, might fit for a month or so as the boy grew through it, but the mathematical likelihood of shoes, jackets, knickers and caps all fitting at the same time was too slight to be a practicable ideal.

New (too large) knickers were bought, inherited, or bartered for each year just before school started. The cheapest place to buy school clothes was JC Penney, where Weaver Overhead Cash Carriers zinged along on wires attached to the ceiling, bringing little canisters containing money and sales slips to a central cashier's nest suspended overhead, and the change came zinging back down to clerks on the floor from the gods of commerce above. We had to save up for the school shopping trip for at least three months because in addition to clothes there were school supplies to buy: protractors, rulers, pencils, erasers that were soft and pink on one end for pencil and gritty and white on the other for ink (but they didn't really erase ink, only shredded the paper), a couple of dip pens with cork grips, a little blue box of Crown nibs which always got splayed because in my efforts to write quickly I pushed down too hard, a bottle of blue-black ink, as many free blotters with store advertising on them as you could get away with and a brand-new ring notebook that you promised yourself you would keep neat— and this time for crossyourheartandhopetodie sure! This year you would not doodle in it, or make up secret codes, or start writing stories that had nothing to do with school. But, of course...

By the end of the school year the knickers had become too short to be buckled below the knee, so they were worn through the summer vacation without socks, something like long, ungainly shorts. No matter how hot it got, no boy on our block went around without his cap. We were convinced that nothing looked so fine and sassy as a cap worn slued to the side of the head or with its brim low over the eyes. Nuns, mothers and teachers never tired of telling us to put our caps on straight, which we would do, until they were out of sight.

What a dapper lot we were in summer. Cap bills tugged down because you looked tougher with your narrowed eyes peering out, short knickers with buckles flapping if not missing, no socks to cover skinny shins embossed with bruises that were blue at first, then yellowish, and finally gray.

No one wore denims (which were not then called jeans) except cowboys in the movies whose denims had three-inch cuffs over their boots. The legs of jeans were all the same length, long enough for tall men, so the shorter you were, the thicker or wider your cuffs had to be. Comic hicks wore denim bib overalls, chewed on blades of straw and rocked up on their toes as they said things like 'yessiree bob'. No one on Pearl Street would have been seen dead in denims.

Nice Work If You Can Get It...
They Can't Take That Away from Me...
Love Walked In...Our Love Is Here to Stay...
Johnny One Note...The Lady Is a Tramp...

The ice man came down our street twice a week in summer, his horse-drawn wagon dripping melt water. People who wanted ice put cards in their windows, right side up for a 25-pound piece, upside down for a 50-pound piece. Nobody's icebox was big enough to hold a 50-pound piece, so if someone's ice card was upside down that meant they were having a party and wanted to put ice and bottles of beer into a wash basin. Mrs Kane's fertile imagination manufactured the rumor that an ice card put sideways into a window meant that the woman wanted service of another kind from the ice man. I don't think any woman on the block actually believed this, but they always let their eyes slide over the windows opposite, checking for sideways ice cards...just in case. Our ice man, an Italian with bulging, writhing muscles and a neck wider than his head, would grab a block of ice with his hinged tongs and with one smooth motion slide it off the back of the wagon and up onto his shoulder which was protected by a thick piece of leather. He'd carry it up to the apartment with an ice card in its window, leaving his old horse to wait in the breathless city heat, its head down, a shoulder muscle fluttering like a tic in the corner of a tired eye. As soon as the ice man was out of sight, kids would descend on the wagon, some to dabble their hands in the cold melt water and pat it onto their faces and arms, while older boys used their jackknives to chop off slivers of ice for sucking before the ice man returned and chased them off, bellowing hideous threats, all the more dreadful for being in Italian.

The boy whose responsibility it was to empty the water pan under the icebox in summer would get engrossed in some story game or radio program until a heel-skid in a trickle of water on the kitchen floor brought his attention to his duties, which he had to attend to quickly if his slackness were to pass unnoticed. He had two options, the one slow, the other dangerous. He could carefully dip water out of the pan with a cup, making many trips from beneath the icebox to the sink, until the level of the water pan was low enough that he could carry it over to the sink without making a mess, or he could gamble and try to slide the brim-full pan out slowly, slowly, without letting it slop over the edge (not easy because the pan always stuck to the linoleum), then pick the pan up and walk to the sink carefully, carefully, with short steps calculated to break up the slosh-rhythm of the water. The first was the prudent method, the second was what the boy always did; and the water, of course, always slopped over the boy's clothes and onto the floor, and he ended up having to put the pan back down and dip the water out cup by cup, slopping a good bit in the process, then wipe up the floor (including the long evil-smelling reach under the icebox) then rinsed out his mother's favorite coffee cup, the total cost in time and effort being roughly three times what the prudent way would have been. But you never know. Maybe the next time...

The ice man was also our coal man in September each year because that was when central heating began in the apartments, and it continued until Easter, regardless of the weather. Through fall and winter he delivered coal in the same wagon, pulled by the same horse, which stood with its head down as its master and fellow beast of burden carried hundred-pound sacks of coal on his back, wearing a kind of hood made from a burlap coal sack over his head. Nobody used ice in winter. Everyone nailed an orange crate to the side of a window and things like milk were kept there, although the milk often froze in the bottle, expanding and causing a little tower of frozen cream to lift the cap off. This free 'ice cream' was treasured by kids, who would try to wake up early to get it before other kids in the family did, but mothers complained that this left them with nothing but skimmed milk.

In each building one renter was responsible for taking care of the boiler, banking it with coal each night and stoking it up again in the morning. In the winter of our second year, Mother managed to get this job in our building, and during the subsequent winters the rent agent forgave us the five dollar surcharge we had to pay over our rent allowance in return for four trips down to the basement each day to shake down the ashes and shovel in coal, then to put the ashes into the battered ash cans we set out on the curb to be collected once a week. That worked out to something like four cents for each time we tended the fire, but we were glad to have the extra money through the heating season, which began about the time school started, just when we needed the money for school supplies and clothes. Attached to the job of tending the furnace was the chore of sweeping and mopping all the halls and stairways. From Easter to Labor Day there was no heat, so the five dollars a month was reduced to two to cover the hall cleaning. When Mother was sick, I took over tending the boiler, a wearisome chore in the early years when I was small and the coal shovel was so big and heavy that I couldn't lift it with more than a quarter load of coal, so stoking the furnace took me a long time, particularly when we were low on coal, and it was a long walk from the furnace to the little pile remaining at the back of the bunker.

The Merry-Go-Round Broke Down...
The Love Bug Will Bite You (if you don't watch out)...
Too Marvellous for Words...
I've Got My Love to Keep Me Warm...

Mr Kane and I were sitting on his side steps overlooking his urban garden of sooty dirt, broken glass and ironweed as he smoked his evening cigarette. He had been hearing disturbing things from daring amateur short-wave operators in Europe, and he described to me the indignities and injustices the Nazis were inflicting upon Jews. (Even Mr Kane didn't know about the nastier crimes at that time.) His voice was sad rather than angry, a tone of fatigue that was centuries deep. I asked why the Germans let their leaders do these things, and he told me that for more than two thousand years Jews had served their European hosts as scapegoats after natural disasters and as whipping boys for personal failure, and he gave me brief narrative glimpses of crusaders running wild through mediaeval ghettoes, the Inquisition in Spain and Portugal, pogroms in Russia. When I praised the way he described these things, as though he had been there himself, he said, "But, I was. I was there."

"You were there, Mr Kane?"

"If you're a Jew, you are wherever Jews are persecuted."

I sensed something profound in that...but I didn't quite get it and I was uneasy with the muted passion of it, so I changed the subject.

"Does 'nazi' mean something in German?"

"Yes. It's short for National Socialist." He sniffed an ironic chuckle. "They are, of course, the very opposite of socialists. Their natural spiritual allies are the captains of industry, the landed classes and the military establishment."

"What *is* a socialist, then?"

"Well...me. I'm a socialist." And he went on to describe his very personal and quixotic brand of socialism, which he called 'enterprise socialism'. According to him, the classic socialist's insistence on public ownership of the means of producing wealth was a serious error because it overlooked such basic qualities of human nature as the desire to accumulate good things and pass them on to one's children. He explained that the capitalist believes that, after defense of the nation, the primary concern of government is to facilitate 'the pursuit of happiness', meaning the acquisition of wealth, property, and comforts; while the socialist views government's principal task, after defense of the nation, to be the welfare of the people, which, by the Darwinian nature of things, means particularly the welfare of the poor, the old, the weak and the disadvantaged.

In Mr Kane's 'enterprise socialism' such basic human rights as medical care and the best education your mind is able to absorb would be paid for, but not *provided by*, the government. The government would give vouchers (Mr Kane called them 'health tickets' and 'school tickets') with which individual citizens would 'pay' whatever private doctor, medical service, or educational institution they thought was right for them and their children. Experience had taught Mr Kane that everything run by the state is run badly, because the overriding motivation of the politician is to remain in office at all costs, and the guiding imperatives of the bureaucrat are to escape responsibility, dodge problems, and gather power to himself.[14]

"And all of this...tickets for free doctors and hospitals and schools... this is what socialism is?" I asked.

"Well...it's *my* kind of socialism."

"And there are people out there trying to make all this happen?"

"Not many, alas. But who knows? You, maybe, one of these days. And when it's your time to try to set the world aright, remember this: when it comes to providing basic necessities like health care and education, you need both the efficiency of capitalist competition *and* the compassion and humanity of socialism. The money must be made by Capitalists and spent by Socialists."

"...Jeez."

Where Are You?...Let's Call the Whole Thing Off... Shall We Dance?...That Old Feeling...Caravan...

'The Block' is a geographic concept; but not solely or even primarily so. The Block is a cluster of cultural, ethnic, social, tribal and economic characteristics. People were identified in terms of what block they came from, and the block also served as a basic unit of social measurement; a really tough kid was 'the meanest guy on the block', or a girl might be described as 'the prettiest girl on the block'...or the plainest. If a girl from your block was unattractive but nice, she was called plain; if she came from another block, she was ugly. And if she was very unattractive but very nice, then everyone assumed she would become a nun and the whole block felt proud of her...but a little sorry for her, too.

Blocks had individual personalities. There were good blocks where people cared about and stood up for one another, and mean blocks where they didn't. There were 'ritzy' blocks where many of the men had jobs, and dangerous blocks where you could get beaten up for straying onto alien turf; there were old people's blocks where children got yelled at for just looking around too hard, and there were Black blocks, Jewish blocks, Polish blocks, Italian blocks, Irish blocks, each with its characteristic ambience, smell and rules of conduct. And then, there was your own block, where things smelled as things ought to smell, and where you didn't dare cut up too wild because everybody knew your name and where you lived.

You were used to the smells of your own block, which in time your nose identified as neutral. This made the richer neighborhoods, which were clean and odorless, smell flat and insipid by comparison; so no smell was a kind of smell too. All the poor blocks had the basic slum basso ostinado I had met when I first stepped inside 238: mildew, leaking gas, Lysol and rat feces, with grace notes of baby diaper, lye soap and sweat, and through these were threaded the cooking smells that had soaked into the plaster of the hallways: Polish sausage, Irish cabbage, the sharp tang of Black people's greens, the lonely metallic smell of Jewish cooking with its goose grease and fish, the splendid olfactory symphony of Italian food. When something brought you into the hallways of blocks other than your own, you found the cooking smells odd and alien. And rather ominous.

The most salient characteristic of any block was its ethnicity. South Street, for instance, was Black and Jewish, the former crowded into decrepit tenements, owned by the latter, who lived over their rather seedy pawnshops, liquor stores and corner groceries. The Black block I knew best was called Blacktown, and was not a block in the strictest geographic sense, but a tangle of short streets—De Witt, Rathbone, Lawrence—surrounded by warehouses and light industry. Some Sundays after mass, I would pass through Blacktown on my way to a deserted brickyard down by the river docks where there was a huge pile of sand that I used as the Sahara in the intense, day-long Foreign Legion games I used to play all alone...except for my comrades of the Legion and several thousand very angry Arabs eager to throw off the cultural benefits of French imperialism. With its scattering of run-down brick houses, a grocery store, a barbershop and three storefront churches, Blacktown was a transplanted southern hamlet in the heart of a northern city, and it felt different from those neighborhoods in which Albany's Negroes had lived for as long as anyone remembered. The soft-spoken residents of Blacktown were recent arrivals, having been attracted north during the First World War when Whites rushed into profitable war work, leaving many hard, dirty, undignified jobs unfilled. Although they suffered from mass unemployment when the Depression struck and their jobs were lost on the rule of 'last hired, first fired', Blacktown maintained its gentle, old-fashioned ambience. After its ministers, the leaders of Blacktown were its uniformed railroad sleeping car attendants who had traveled widely and knew something of the world, as their air of unspoken wisdom revealed. These 'Georges' (all sleeping car attendants were called George) had a union of their own, and in Blacktown they set a tone of dignity, reliability and responsibility. Their opinions mattered, and their approval was sought.[15]

I never felt threatened (as one might today) as I passed through Blacktown on Sunday mornings, on my way to the Sahara, but I did feel intrusive and glaringly white. People sitting out on their wooden stoops would interrupt their soft-voiced gossip and watch me walk by, then start talking again after I had passed; and little kids would stop skipping rope or playing finger games and look at me with big-eyed, disconcertingly frank curiosity until I was well down the street and they felt free to get on with their play.

I was intrigued by the storefront churches with hand-painted bible pictures and mysterious names including words like Nazarene, Glory, Eternal, Assembly, Salvation and Tabernacle, sometimes several of these in the same name. I used to slow down as I passed them so I could catch some of the singing, so much more spirited than ours. And sometimes, if no one was around, I would pause and listen for a moment to a fast-talking, gasping, repetitious preacher in the throes of being penetrated by the Holy Ghost (enthusiastic in its etymological sense) and the shouted responses of the congregation that asked the brother (rather than 'father') to lay the Word of God up*on* them! For a long time, the only Protestants I knew were Negroes, and it seemed that being a Protestant was a more lively and interesting affair than being a Catholic. That was before I met White Protestants and learned that this is not the case. But at least most Protestants eventually get over their relatively rigid and sanitized childhoods, while Jews and Catholics struggle with their uncertainties and guilt for the rest of their lives and, what is worse, feel obliged to tell everybody about it.

The blocks east of us, down the hill between North Pearl Street and the Hudson River, were entirely Negro. Most people called them niggers or spades or blacks or coons or smokes or jigs, not in anger or contempt, but simply because that was their street appellation, just as we were polacks or wops or micks or canuks. When people did say 'Negro', you could often hear ironic quotation marks in the long *e* in the North. In the South the *e* was a short *i*, and the *o* reduced to a schwa, so that it came out 'niggre', only a breath away from nigger. My mother never let my sister or me use any other word than Negro, perhaps because she was sensitive to the racial slurs she had faced as a quarter-breed child in a very Yankee village.[16]

This Can't Be Love...My Heart Belongs to Daddy... Louise...You Go to My Head... I Get Along Without You Very Well...

Sometimes I was able to get Mother to retell the stories of how her father had begun life as a half-breed laborer, but had worked and studied to improve himself and eventually surmounted barriers of culture, race and religion to win the hand of my grandmother. I knew these stories by heart, but I loved hearing about my grandfather whom I hero-worshipped and tried to emulate—indeed, still do. The images I retain of Edmond LaPointe come mostly from my mother's stories, because he died when I was five, so I have only fragmentary sensory memories of his visits to us at Lake George Village every Sunday: the smell of leather polish and of the Johnson's baby powder he used to cover his raspy cheeks. Half-blood though he was, he had not inherited the Indian male's advantage of having little beard. His cheeks were usually blue with stubble because it was his habit to shave just before going to bed. Mother explained to me that businessmen shave in the morning, because they love their jobs, but men like Edmond LaPointe shave at night, because they love their wives. It would be some years before I understood this.

My grandfather used to arrive at our cottage in Lake George Village bearing 'safety lollipops', which had flexible loop-sticks designed to protect the child who ran with a lollipop in his mouth from falling flat on his face and driving the stick through the back of his neck...an ever-present danger, according to the prevailing folk wisdom of the era. A packet of the loop-stick safety lollipops contained five different flavors (five colors, really, as the flavors were only slight variants of 'sweet'), and we had to choose one, first Anne-Marie, then I. The moment of choice was difficult. It wasn't so much deciding which one I wanted, but which three I was willing to leave behind.

The LaPointes came from a small mixed-blood farming community in Quebec, where their ancestors had lived since they had been driven out of their homeland in the Finger Lakes near the end of the eighteenth century. Their tribe, the Onondaga, had fought on the side of the French and against the English in the French-and-Indian Wars because the French fur traders had no intention of settling in Onondagan territory, while the land hunger of the English colonists was insatiable. But the English colonists won, and several decimated Onondaga clans made their way up into Canada and settled on thin, rocky farmland near the juncture of the Ste. Anne and St. Lawrence rivers, where they found themselves surrounded by Algonquin-speaking tribes, their traditional enemies. (Well, not so much their enemies as their livestock, as the Iroquois economy included a regular harvest of the possessions, furs, and women of the Algonquin tribes within their catchment.) So it is understandable that this band of displaced Onondagas was unloved by their new Algonquin-speaking neighbors.

Because the stranded Iroquois remnant consisted almost entirely of women, children and old men, their warriors having fallen in battle, the community quickly became mixed with local French blood. Thus, the part-breed character of later generations did not result from intermarriage between a lovely Indian princess and a brave White woodsman, as the romantic traditions of so many métis families assert, because Victorian sensibilities could not abide the thought of an Indian male astride a White woman; the people of my grandfather's generation were breeds descended from breed parents, who had descended from breed great-grandparents, and so on. They had little contact with either the Whites or the Algonquins of the Three Rivers country, and after the last of the Onondaga returned at the end of the nineteenth century to that part of their homeland that had become the United States, the Algonquins remaining behind got a belated revenge by writing these Iroquois interlopers out of the folk history that they packaged for White tourists.

Over-farmed and badly farmed,[17] the LaPointe land was too fatigued to support the clan through the agricultural depressions of the 1860s and '70s, so, together with most of the displaced Onondaga mixed-bloods, they gave up and drifted south, settling in French-speaking communities that provided unskilled labor for mills and factories throughout northern New York and New England. My grandfather, Edmond LaPointe, began working for the New York Central

Railroad at the age of fifteen, gandy-dancing with a line crew in the draining heat of summer and the drifting snows of winter. But he was bright enough to see that life was better for those who toiled indoors and wore ties, so he worked on his English and taught himself Morse code and ultimately became a railroad telegrapher. Step by step, he worked his way up until, at the age of twenty-five, he was appointed station master in the town of Fort Anne, New York. If you picture the all-powerful station master of a major railroad terminal presiding over a staff of several hundred clerks, ticket agents, baggage men, book-keepers, yard bosses, freight handlers, cleaners, maintenance crew and signal men, you will not have a very accurate image of Ed LaPointe's work and life, for in little whistle-stops like Fort Anne at the turn of the century, the station master *was* the clerk, telegrapher, baggage man, freight handler, cleaner, yard boss, signal man and maintenance crew. These versatile one-man-bands were so valuable to the New York Central Line that they were seldom considered for advancement into mainstream administration; instead, they were moved from one tank-town to another, lucky if they ended up having one trainee-assistant by the time they reached retirement age, after which they usually spent three or four years as a semi-retired 'floater': an experienced man who could replace any station master in the system in case of illness, death or, very rarely, a vacation. But it was indoor work, and the station master was an important man in his village, not only at the center of its transportation but of its communications too, as he was also the Western Union telegrapher. A station master got news from the outer world first, so his views were listened to around the pot-bellied stove of the general store. He wore a suit and tie and was called Mister—a big step from being an anonymous French-speaking, half-breed gandy-dancer.

Although the station master was at the center of his community (in addition to being the entire staff of the station, Edmond LaPointe used his access to transportation to establish an independent enterprise in coal and ice), he was viewed as an oddity and an outsider by the stiff Yankee village of Fort Anne, not far from the Vermont border. Not only was he French, but he was half Indian—a savage, not to put too fine a point on it. Worse yet, he was a Catholic. And if all that wasn't enough, he was also a Democrat, which in those ultra-conservative rural up-state villages was akin to being a bomb-throwing anarchist.

But any harassment or overt hostility he might have met because of his race, religion or political orientation was mitigated by the general knowledge that Ed LaPointe was an avid amateur boxer who was not only quick with his fists, but who took a delight in fighting. (A *savage* delight, some added archly.) He had a powerful grip and bony fists he could throw at your face like rocks, and it was his practice to go to Fistcity while the other fellow was still strutting and blustering, a tactic I imitated.

The village of Fort Anne was dismayed to learn that this Catholic, Democrat, half-breed scrapper had successfully wooed Maud Prescott, the daughter of a Puritan family that lived on the Vermont farm their ancestors had worked since before the Revolution (indeed, before there had been a Vermont). The Prescotts had come to the New World in the 1640s and they could (and often did) boast that the four men of their name who died fighting in the Revolution were fifth-generation Americans. Maud was the eleventh generation of Prescotts in America, which makes me the thirteenth and my grandchildren the fifteenth; this in a country where few people can claim more than four or five generations of American-born ancestors, and most of those who can are Black.

To tease his wife, Ed LaPointe used to tell his children: "Your mother's family is proud of having come to the New World on the *Mayflower,* but when they arrived *my* family was standing on the shore, waiting for them." This wasn't exactly true because the Prescotts didn't come to New England until 1642, and the eastward migration of the Iroquois had only reached the Hudson River when they collided with the westward migration of the Whites. I later discovered that my grandfather's line about the White side of the family arriving on the *Mayflower* and the Indian side greeting them on the shore has been ascribed to Will Rogers; and that made sense because the wry, folksy Will Rogers, also a half-blood, was both Edmond LaPointe's favorite newspaper columnist and his favorite actor.

At the age of eighteen, the high-spirited Maud Prescott must have been very much in love to have married Edmond LaPointe against the wishes of her family, which not only refused to attend their wedding but had nothing further to do with either her or her children. The women of Fort Anne endorsed the Prescott family's behavior because, as they told one another in those tense whispers that adults naively believe are inaudible to children, there could only be one reason why a girl from a good family would marry a Catholic half-breed, and we all know what *that* is. The fact that Maud and Edmond's first child came, stillborn, a full year after their marriage did not stanch rumors of Maud's having married out of necessity. Fact and evidence being but feeble defenses against prejudice, the village women were able to say: "Well, all right, so maybe she wasn't 'that way' when they got married; maybe she just *thought* she was. But she wouldn't have thought so if the two of them hadn't been...well, you see what I mean."

Saturday was market day in Fort Anne, and it occasioned one of those splendidly eccentric New England traditions that made Yankee communities unique before the homogenizing effects of electronic mass communications. It was the custom for village women to hold open house between three in the afternoon and the fall of evening, when the wagons and buggies had to start back towards the farms. The signal that a house was 'receiving' was a lit oil lamp in the front window. Half the village women offered hospitality one week, half the next, and those whose turn it was to serve cookies and tea received those whose turn it was not, along with any passing farm people who might be glad for a chance to tie their wagons to the rail and rest their feet and bottoms for a while, letting their kids run the streets with the town brats while they sat in stuffy parlors whose only other functions were receiving preachers and laying out the dead. While sipping their tea and nibbling cookies, they would exchange succulent bits of gossip, grim prognostications about declining farm prices and public morals, and mutual assurances that the younger generation was far too pampered to ever develop into strong, useful, self-reliant citizens like—well, like themselves, though they shouldn't say it.

The first Saturday after Maud and Edmond returned from their two-day honeymoon in Montreal (Ed could not find a 'floater' to replace him for longer), Maud worked all morning baking the fancy cookies that were her only domestic glory, because before meeting Ed she had been determined never to marry, but instead to teach in some big city like New York or Albany and devote herself to the crusade for Woman Suffrage. A dozen brand-new cups and saucers and a tea pot were set up on the table, and a kettle was purring on the back of the coal stove when, at three o'clock, she lit an oil lamp in the window of their small house. She would have to receive the guests and well-wishers herself, because Ed could never leave the station until the northbound 7:53 had passed through.

When my grandfather got home a little after eight, he found Maud sitting in the gloom, the room lit only by the greeting lamp in the window. Not one cup of tea had been poured, not a cookie eaten, not a word of gossip exchanged. The 'fallen woman' had been ostracized by buggy after buggy that passed by, its occupants looking stiffly ahead. Maud was in tears. Tears of rage as much as tears of humiliation.

At a quarter after six the following Monday morning, my grandfather entered Henry & Francis Driscoll's General Store ('Hank 'n' Frank's Place') where the village men gathered around the pot-bellied stove in a start-of-the-week ritual. With Ed LaPointe's entrance, the conversation stumbled and dried up as men glanced at one another uneasily, but he greeted the gathering breezily and asked 'Mule' Milner, the village strong man who did odd jobs, how he was feeling that morning. Assuming that Ed LaPointe had a chore for him down at the station, Mule rose from his chair close to the stove and said he was feeling fit as a fid—Ed hit him so hard that his nose splatted, and Mule sprawled back into the laps of three townsmen.

"Don't get up, Mule," Ed warned. "I'll just have to put you down again."

Mule blinked, stunned and baffled. But he had the good sense not to stand up.

"Sorry I had to hit you," my grandfather said, passing him his handkerchief. "But you're the strongest man in town, and what I'm doing here is making a point. All right, you can get up now. Go over and have Doc Burns fix your nose, and put it on my bill. Come on, give me your hand. Up you come." After Mule had staggered down the front steps of the general store, Ed turned to the assembly. "Last Saturday my wife spent all morning baking cookies. And how many people came calling? Not one. Not a single one of you. Can you imagine how that hurt her feelings? Well, that's not going to happen again. Here's how things are going to be, gentlemen..." He told them that next Saturday there would be a lamp lit in their window, and his wife would be serving tea and cookies, and he expected every man in that store—and their wives!—to drop in for a cup of tea, a cookie or two, and a little pleasant conversation. He admitted that he couldn't make them do anything they didn't want to do. They were free citizens of a free country, and it was entirely up to them if they came calling or not. But Ed would drop in to the general store the following Monday morning, and if anyone there had not shown up in Maud's parlor—with his wife!—another man would have to bring his nose over to Doc Burns to get it fixed.

"Now, we all know that if you decide to take me on three or four against one, you're pretty sure to win. But it's a funny thing about those damned Indians. They just don't know when to quit. Sooner or later I'll meet you when you're on your own and you will get busted. You can believe that like you believe the sun will rise tomorrow. Well, gentlemen..." He took out his pocket watch. "...I've got to meet the 6:25. See you next Monday." And he left.

The following Saturday, Maud ran out of cookies and she had to refill the kettle several times. Most of her women visitors were tight-lipped and crisp-voiced, but the men praised her cookies volubly and begged her to give their wives her recipe.

In time, Maud earned the friendship and admiration of those younger village women who shared her sense of outrage that women were denied the right to vote and joined in her efforts to remedy that injustice. She and Ed had five live children before she died in 1918, a victim of the Spanish 'Flu that killed more people than the First World War. Ed LaPointe never remarried, and his grief never healed. He brought up his two sons and three daughters himself, and later he drained his modest savings to help them through the early years of the Great Depression, until he died in an automobile accident at the age of fifty-one. From time to time, chances for getting posted to better-paying stations came along, but he turned them down because he didn't want to leave Fort Anne, where his wife was buried and where, every Saturday evening from her death until his, he spent an hour sitting at her graveside, silently telling her how the kids were getting along, and what was happening in the village, and how much he missed her.

One bit of good news he was able to share with her was that women had finally won the vote.

This iconographic image of my grandfather sitting in the gathering evening beside the grave of his Maud took on a radiant significance within the families of his five children, symbolizing the tenderness of romantic marriage and the depth and durability of a great love. But as a man who has lived twenty years longer than my grandfather did, I discern something self-indulgent and damaging in his disproportionate grief at a time when his children needed all the attention and love he could give. A stronger, wiser or more sensitive man would have concealed most of his grief to prevent his children from feeling that he had loved Maud more than he could ever love any of them, which, in the self-immolating way of children, they would assume had something to do with their inadequacies, not their father's. The most affected by his selfish bereavement were my mother and his oldest daughter, Odette. He took Odette out of school at the age of fourteen to become the family's homemaker responsible not only for the cooking and cleaning, but for organizing her siblings' household chores. This removed her from the one-of-the-gang camaraderie of the children and put her into a no-woman's-land of responsibility without moral authority. Trapped by the praise of the entire town for her dutiful self-sacrifice, Odette continued to keep house for her father until she was nearly thirty, when she rebelled and left to enter the stream of life, thereafter maintaining only the flimsiest contact with the others, whom she identified with her lost youth. As though to rebuke my grandfather for taking her out of school where she had been a highly praised student, Odette worked hard to make up her lost education and eventually entered a normal college to train as a teacher. It was there that she met a man and married, starting her life as an adult woman at the age of thirty-three.

My mother's childhood was less obviously but more profoundly scarred by her mother's death. From the first, she had lacked the self-assurance that comes with having an established role within a family. As we know, the eldest child of each sex enjoys those character-building responsibilities and those first-through-the-gauntlet privileges that breed confidence and self-knowledge, just as the youngest benefits from greater freedom and the cosseting that engenders a sense of 'specialness'. But my mother was the third child in a family of five in which the eldest and youngest were boys, so she was the middle girl of a middle group of girls. Her elder sister was the responsible one; her younger sister was the cherished one; my mother was...the other one.

My grandfather's reaction to Maud's death did permanent damage to my mother's already fragile self-esteem. He asked his two unmarried sisters to take his 'middle girl' to live with them in Plattsburg, up on the Canadian border. He assured my mother that he would bring her back home as soon as he had 'worked things out'. She was the only child to leave the home; her older brother had quit school at sixteen and was contributing part of his earnings to the family; her younger brother was little more than a baby and had to be cared for by her older sister, the homemaker; and her younger sister's cute antics brought some sunlight into her father's life. My mother felt the pain of separation intensely, particularly as her maiden aunts had very little English, and she was expected to speak to them in French, of which she had only a smattering because her Yankee mother had insisted that theirs would be an English-speaking house because she knew that the only access to the unique American experience is through the English language. (A fact that fans of multi-cultural education still choose to ignore.)

My mother rebelled, refusing not only to speak French, but to understand the rules by which her aunts ordered their narrow, pious lives. She did, however, send monthly letters in French to her father, writing with a careful, blot-free hand. I have one of them on my desk at this moment, and the French is not only grammatically correct, but even elegant in the formulaic way of French epistles. I suspect that she copied letters written for her by her aunts. When she finally returned to her family a year later, everything in the running of the house and the daily routine had changed in her absence, duties and roles had been assigned, all the niches filled. An outsider in her own home, she sought recognition and significance by emulating her father, hoping to earn his approval. He pitched for the town baseball team and had its highest batting average throughout those years when Fort Anne was the terror of such centers of baseball excellence as Comstock, Truthville and Whitehall; so my mother became a tomboy and played short-stop for the youth club, the only girl on the team.

Over the years, Calvinist-Republican-Anglo-Saxon Fort Anne came to accept Catholic-Democrat-half-breed Edmond LaPointe, the man who knew more about them than their minister or their doctor because his position as station master meant that he knew of their every voyage, their every shipment of goods, their mail, their telegrams, and those great events of marriage, birth and death that gathered their extended families from up and down the railroad network, and he was never known to gossip or to break a confidence. In the view of the townsfolk, his life-long mourning for Maud mitigated, to a certain extent, his audacity in having married her in the first place. He was the outsider who overcame what they viewed as disadvantages of race, religion and culture, but who had, through hard work, earned the right to be considered a part of their village. It became idiomatic to speak of Ed LaPointe as a 'real success story'.

All her life, my mother yearned to be a success, too, and thereby earn her father's admiration and respect.

...Admiration and respect? Look at me! Ruby Lucile LaPointe, living on public charity! My mother would rage against the series of blows that had brought her low, until we knew the litany of misfortune by heart. First her husband deserted her, then the Depression swept over the country, drying up jobs, then her father died and she lost her last source of emotional and financial support, then her fragile lungs made it impossible for her to keep a steady job. The fact that she viewed even the Great Depression as a personal affront reveals the sense of grievance she nurtured all her life.

But she wasn't ready to give up. No, sir! She tightened her jaw against Fate and clung doggedly to her certitude that one of these days our ship would come in, and when it did, we'd be ready to board it, '...come hell and high water!'

> **Boo-Hoo...Two Sleepy People...Jeepers Creepers**
> **(where'd you get those peepers)...I Double Dare You...**
> **You Go to My Head...Thanks for the Memory...**

Her substitution of 'hell *and* high water' for 'hell *or* high water', the 'or' evoking Revelation's alternative eschatological cataclysms of Fire or Flood, led me into an error that persisted for years. I always envisioned an interfering she-devil named Helen Highwater who vented her wrath on people who were just trying to get along.

Another of Mother's life-long misapprehensions was her belief that the 'hoi polloi' were ritzy, snobbish folk. When she said the words she would push the tip of her nose up with her finger to illustrate the snootiness of these hoi polloi. I suspect this error was based on the similarity between 'hoi polloi' and 'hoity-toity'. In fact, the two derogations often appeared side by side in a rosary of epithets accusing someone of a real or imagined snub, as in '...and if that snooty, hoity-toity, hoi polloi bastard thinks that he...!' As is often the case with self-taught children who develop their vocabularies in cultural isolation, I later experienced the stinging embarrassment of misusing 'hoi polloi' and 'Helen Highwater' in public. Similarly, my Terpsichore had only three syllables, and my Penelope's last five letters were pronounced 'elope', as in 'to run away to marry'. My mortification when corrected on these occasions was all the hotter (and all the more deserved) because I had been parading my learning. It would be some time before I learned that 'the hoi polloi' was a tautology, and longer yet before I understood that to drop the 'the' was worse than tautological, it was pedantic.

Mother got idioms and adages wrong through mishearing or carelessness, but she also shared with most Americans the conviction that a person doesn't really have to be all that precise in speech (indeed, that there is something nitpicking and snooty in being so). So long as you're truly sincere about what you are saying, you can just throw sounds in the general direction of your notions, and your interlocutor will get the idea. But for all her liberal attitudes towards usage, one of her solecisms derived from an effort to avoid slack diction. When describing people who thought too highly of themselves (those ritzy hoi polloi bastards who stiffed her when she was working as a waitress, for example) she would accuse them of being 'highfaluting', the terminal 'g' scrupulously pronounced, as though it derived from the verb 'to falute', meaning something akin to 'to flaunt', and those who faluted broadly could be said to high-falute.

By the end of our second summer on North Pearl, my interest in unusual words and my eagerness to inflict them on others had earned me a place as one of the block's 'characters', those kids who possessed some special trait or ability. Some kids stood out because they were tough, some were envied because they were sickly and got to stay away from school a lot, some could run fast, one was famous for being amazingly dirty, another could almost rupture your ears with his piercing screams, one was called 'wormy', not because he had worms, but because he could eat them, to every onlooker's fascinated disgust, and I was known as the 'professor'...the smart one. This might have been a dangerous role to play because teachers tended to favor smart kids, but luckily I was also a clown and a wiseass, and that made my smartness less objectionable to my classmates. My wiseassery never made them envious of me because the ability to make subtle fun of a teacher was not considered nearly so desirable a social attribute as the ability to burp or fart loudly during a quiz, or a prayer.

Love Walked Right In...You Must Have Been a Beautiful Baby...Music, Maestro, Please... I've Got a Pocket Full of Dreams...

My dominant memory of our summers is the crushing heat. Unlike the lakeside village of my early childhood with its breezy summer days and cool nights, there was no relief from the oppressive heat waves of 1936 and 1938, two of the hottest ever recorded in Albany. Children suffered rashes and heat prostration, and some old people died of breathing problems. No one had electric fans, and air-conditioning was a thing of the future, except in a few movie houses, where it was concentrated in the lobby, so you could feel its effect upon entering and be attracted back out to the cool lobby during intermissions to buy candy or popcorn. The city's cement and brick absorbed heat all through the day and radiated it out into the street after dark, so the nights were as hot as the days. People who lived on upper floors where the heat was the worst allowed their kids to sleep out on fire escapes in nests of sweat-sodden pillows and sofa cushions, while the parents sat out on their stoops late into the night, fanning themselves with pieces of cardboard, and complaining sleepily about the heat. Every third or fourth day, a fireman would come and screw a spray nozzle onto a fire hydrant, then he'd open it with a big two-handed wrench so that little kids in their underwear could dash through the spray while bigger kids in sodden dresses or knickers struggled against the weight of the gush, striving to approach the hydrant, defying the pounding force of the water on their chests, then laughing helplessly as they were driven back, their feet slipping over the smooth, wet cobblestones. Even grown-up women would stand on the edges of the spray, smiling as they caught handfuls of cool iridescent mist in their palms and rubbed it over their arms and necks, receiving it like a blessing from God. Adolescent boys would yearn to strip down and rush in but, fearful of compromising their newly acquired reputations for being tough and cool, they were obliged to lean against the buildings with their hands in their pockets and look on, sneering. And sweating.

One scorching day when Anne-Marie and I were playing in the fire hydrant spray I looked up to see my mother dressed in the boyishly cut bathing suit of her flapper days, laughing as she fought her way towards the hydrant against the pounding force of the water, the only adult among the kids. It was like her to surrender to a caprice and come play with us, and I was proud of her youth and vivacity, but I was intensely aware of the brittle stares of other mothers sitting on their stoops, women who could never have squeezed into the swimsuits they had worn as teenagers, and who thought that those who revealed their bodies by doing so were little better than hussies. Swimsuits of my mother's era were made of thick wool knit so the water would drain quickly out, leaving the suit dry enough to provide some protection against cold Atlantic winds. When, breathless with laughter and the cold water, she stepped out of the stream and stood on the curb to watch Anne-Marie and me play, the water immediately drained out of her suit in a steady stream that fell from between her legs onto the cement, and one of the adolescent boys noticed this and nudged a friend to point it out. Look at her. Pissing on the sidewalk. I slipped away and went back into the house, the fun and relief of the fire hydrant spray ruined.

The 'difference' for which the neighbor ladies never forgave my mother expressed itself not only in a sense of dress that was lodged in her 'heyday', the 'Twenties, with the bell-bottom slacks and the close-fitting sweaters that revealed the existence of breasts, two distinct breasts with nipples, not the undefined shelf of wobbly flesh that other mothers had at their chests. There was also her boyish, rather choppy haircut that she did for herself in front of the bathroom mirror holding kitchen scissors in one hand and the wet strand of hair in the other.

And the way she was always polite to crazy Mrs Meehan, whom other women ignored broadly whenever they passed the cluster of houses that sheltered that incestuous clan. "It takes one to know one," the women would mutter under their breath when they saw Mrs Meehan running up to Mother to say hello. But the most unforgivably 'different' thing she did was to come out onto the street and play with my sister and me, just as though she were a kid. Kick-the-can, or Simon Says, or tag with a lamp post as 'home'. She would jump rope with Anne-Marie, or play the French-Canadian version of Ring-Around-the-Roses: *Rond, rond, macaron. Ta p'tite soeur est à la maison. Fais ceçi, fais cela, ah...ah...achoo!*

The block responded to Mother's difference by deciding that she was crazy. Not dangerous, and not as crazy as some, but a crazylady nonetheless. And that made me the son of a crazylady. As if I didn't have a sufficient burden of difference to bear on my own account.

But it was true that Mother was never quite in step with everyday realities. Everything that happened to her was heavily colored, either with portent or with promise. Her alternate moods of black depression and soaring elation converted minor setbacks into catastrophic disasters and occasional bits of good luck into spreading vistas of eternal promise, so she reeled from feeling crushed by the weight of her troubles to being treacherously deceived by false omens of good fortune.

She had been born with a zest for life, the resilience to overcome the rough moments, and the appetite to relish the pleasant ones. But a series of confidence-eroding events left her defensive, baffled, wounded and ready to wound in return.

The feelings my sister and I had for our mother were an uneasy blend of love, gratitude and apprehension. Our love was the unquestioned love of a child for his parent, the simple and comforting foundation for our daily lives. Our gratitude was for the way she unfailingly encouraged us and nourished our slightest glimmer of talent or gift, although we were sometimes uncomfortable with the expectations that accompanied that encouragement. Our apprehension had to do with her hair-trigger temper that lashed out at the least slight to her dignity. Those whose ethnic roots are grounds for popular derision become understandably touchy, and in bellicose compensation, they flaunt those ridiculed roots (as in: I'm a Martian and proud of it!). My mother boasted about being French and Indian. She viewed the first as the source of her innate good taste, and the second as making her dangerous to cross. Her French blood was really only rustic *habitant* Canadian, probably not racially French at all in origin, but either Nordic-Norman or Gaelic-Breton, like most of the early immigrants to Canada; but the war-like Indian was genuine enough.

This Can't Be Love...A-Tisket A-Tasket...
Falling in Love with Love...My Prayer...
I Can Dream, Can't I...

I first read about our Onondaga tribe one rainy autumn afternoon when I was cozily ensconced in a secret nest I had found in the architectural hodgepodge of the library at the corner of North Pearl and Clinton Avenue. Soon after our arrival in Albany my mother got library cards for the three of us, but I didn't find this library useful or attractive because I was issued a child's card that restricted me to a basement Children's Library that had cheery messages cut out of colored paper and pinned on the walls, and a corner for toddlers with little chairs and plenty of picture books for them to rip up and eat. For older kids, there were story books with salubrious moral parables, collections of things to do around the house on rainy days, and so-called Youth Books obviously written by middle-aged people who had had children described to them in considerable detail, but had never actually met one. I quickly used up the few good books, like Howard Pyle's splendid illustrated adventures, and I had just about given up on finding anything else of interest when, one long, rainy afternoon in autumn, I noticed a cast-iron spiral staircase in the corner most distant from the librarian's desk, and hidden from her by a ceiling-to-floor bookcase that blocked off access to the stairs. While the librarian sat at a table coloring in the letters of yet another poster, her mind focused on not running over the edge of the lines, I squeezed in behind the bookcase and noiselessly climbed the spiral stairs, inching up into a dusty, enticing darkness, until my outstretched hand discovered a door which I was sure must be locked, so I turned to go back down. But the devil told me to try the handle. It wasn't locked. I eased it open a crack and peeked out to find myself in a dark corner of a Victorian-Gothic room with oaken paneling and tall, narrow windows with stained glass depicting events in the history of Albany. It was the home of the De Witt Clinton Memorial Collection, bulging with bound manuscripts, diaries, records, personal memoranda; all rare, all arid, few read. For me, there was a rich rift of old books about the Indians of our state. Other than occasional staff meetings, the only use made of this room was to store trolleys of returned books that were left there until a librarian had time to re-shelve them. A book on one of these trolleys was in a kind of limbo: it had been checked in, but not yet put back into circulation, so it had dropped out of the library's retrieval system, and I could take such a book and keep it for weeks, eventually returning it to one of the trolleys when I was through with it. For three years I used the De Witt Clinton Room as a cozy hide-out. After selecting one of my personal books from where I stashed them behind a row of over-sized volumes on a lower shelf, I would scramble up into the deep niche of a Gothic stained-glass window where I was warmed by rising currents of air from an ornate radiator at my feet, and its ancient plumbing would alternate deep intestinal gurglings with long soulful sighs as I read by light diffused through colored glass. My most comforting memories of the years in Albany are the hours I spent reading in that hidden nest, dark and cool in summer, cozily warm in winter, but best when hard raindrops rattled on the stained glass behind me, and color rippled over the page of my book, while I lost myself in the story, safe, dry and warmed by my sighing, gurgling radiator.

I was installed in my reading niche one afternoon, playing hooky, as I often did after Miss Cox's death, when I first read about the Onondagas ('keepers-of-the-middle-lodge'), my grandfather's tribe, and therefore mine. I learned that from its central position within the five-nation Iroquois Federation the Onondagas acted as arbitrators in times of political discord. As befitted the tribe of Hiawatha, the Onondagas were also the Federation's story-tellers and weavers of myth. So, it was in my blood to be a story-teller and a weaver of myths! How about that? No wonder I lived such an intense secret life of story games in which I was pitted against Redcoats, Saracens, Cattle Rustlers and

Cardinal Richelieu's men, or, a couple of years later, the sneering Nazis and leering Japanese. This early belief that I was a born tale-weaver sustained me in my eventual life's work, telling stories like this one. There is a parallel between my becoming a writer and how men of another Iroquoian tribe, the Mohawks, became the builders of America's skyscrapers, able to work on naked steel girders at great heights without a trace of vertigo. Despite their cocky confidence and firmly held beliefs, there is no genetic basis for the 'natural balance' they claim to be born with, but their confidence gives them the ability to work high iron in wind and rain, protected from those lethal panic attacks that make the palms of lesser men sweat and their knees tremble. Mohawks have no vertigo because they *believe* they have no vertigo, just as I dare to face a pile of blank paper every day because I believe that I share the Onondagan aptitude for story-telling. This is one of those things that are dangerous to think about too long because if confidence sires ability out of daring, then what happens if a little crack appears in that confidence and doubt begins to seep through and spread and widen until you lose the belief that you can...whoa, there! Leave it alone. Don't pick at thoughts like that. They infect.

Whistle While You Work...Heart and Soul...
While a Cigarette Was Burning...
Flat Foot Floogie...Alexander's Ragtime Band...

I heard people talk about Adolph Hitler and Benito Mussolini, and we occasionally saw them in movie newsreels, but I never got the impression that anyone felt menaced by these comic figures, the one a strutting, pouting clown, the other a ranting, mechanical doll version of Charlie Chaplin. Then, in March of 1938, German soldiers marched into Austria, and within a few days that country was absorbed into the Third Reich. Newsreels showed Hitler arriving to declare Austria a province of the Reich, while Austrian children cheered and waved little flags with what looked like genuflecting crosses on them. Then we heard no more about Austria. Other events filled the news.

Mr Kane, who had relatives in Austria, was listening to short-wave broadcasts from Vienna the day the Germans marched in. He was not at all complacent about these events. He tried to explain them to me one evening on his side steps, mentioning people whose odd-sounding German names immediately slipped out of my memory (probably von Papen, Seyss-Inquart and Schuschnigg) and calling what had happened 'the *anschluss*', which I did remember because he repeated it several times and it had a strangely slippery sound. Seeing my confusion, he went into his living quarters behind the store, and came back with an atlas, which he opened to a page that showed central Europe. With his finger, he traced the eastern border of the new 'greater Germany' that included Austria, and he pointed out that it looked like the gaping jaws of a wolf. Then he tapped the western end of Czechoslovakia. "How would you like to be living between those jaws at this moment?" he asked. "There...in the Sudetenland."

Stairway to the Stars...Sunrise Serenade...Little Sir Echo...
My Prayer...Beer Barrel Polka...
Oh, Johnny, Oh, Johnny, Oh!...Three Little Fishies...

One manifestation of my mother's famous French-'n'-Indian pride was her refusal to accept that, poor though we were, her kids couldn't have what she called a 'decent Christmas', which meant receiving presents that were much too expensive for our budget, bought with money she earned working night shifts at restaurants through the Christmas season. She never seemed to be aware of how frightened my sister and I were that our family would be broken up by social workers who believed her ill health made her an unfit mother, all because she was stubbornly determined to give us presents as nice as other kids got...come Helen Highwater. I associate these 'decent Christmases' with my mother lying on the living room couch, coughing and fevered, while my sister and I opened presents, all the while dreading that she would end up in a hospital again, and we would be obliged to conceal the fact that she wasn't home from those social work people whose primary mission in life seemed to be to send us to some institution. Only once did they catch us and send us to an orphans' home. But that once was enough.

Our Christmas tree was always decorated in blue and silver because my mother considered garish splashes of color beneath the refined tastes she had inherited with her French blood (though what modifying effect her wild Iroquois roots might have had on that aesthetic reserve was never discussed). On the first Christmas after my birth, Mother cut snowflake shapes out of cardboard and pasted metallic blue wrapping paper on one side and tin foil on the other, creating the silver-and-blue motif that we would follow forever after. We added to these from year to year and put them, with the silver foil icicles we laboriously plucked off the tree before we threw it out, into a flat box at the top of our closet until the next Christmas. Throughout my childhood the blue-and-silver tree served as a symbol and proof of highly refined taste. My mother identified several other such peaks of excellence within creation: like the Northern Spy apple. She once pointed out some shiny examples of these superior fruit in the Washington Street Market where they were displayed in a perfect pyramid of sleeve-buffed globes. Another pinnacle of perfection was the delicate, golden, pink-hearted Talisman rose she showed me in a florist's showcase. Both of these she affirmed to be the finest examples of their species... all that a rose or an apple could ever hope to be...which was why we couldn't afford them. In the gustatory category, the most perfect things were understood to be T-bone steaks and the seedless centers of watermelon, to which I secretly added a delight I had experienced only once, in a movie house where I had splurged in madcap indulgence and bought a box of chewy licorice candy within a crunchy carapace. I promised myself that when our ship came in, my mother's days would be littered with blue-and-silver Christmas trees, Talisman roses, Northern Spy apples, T-bone steaks, seedless hearts of watermelon, and boxes of Good & Plenty...in short, all the really excellent things this life has to offer.

Most of our Christmas presents were clothing of the functional sort, but Mother always made sure that each of us got something splendid and totally unexpected—except, of course, that kids quickly learn the rules to life's game, so my sister and I always expected something unexpected, though we weren't so foolish as to actually hope for it, because we knew that there was nothing more likely to drive good luck away than hoping for it. But we never knew *which* unexpected thing to expect. One Christmas—the one that led to our spending two months in a grim Catholic orphanage while Mother teetered on the edge of life in a sanitarium—I got a toy microscope that let me see the ghastly things that inhabit mud puddles. I did well in science and math, so my mother decided that the surest way for me to bring our ship into port was by becoming a doctor. That Christmas my sister got a much-desired pouty-lipped doll with 'magic skin', whatever the hell *that* was.

Of course these gifts were reckless extravagances for a family that was never more than a couple of dollars and a few days away from hunger, but that's how poor people cope with being marooned in poverty while all around them flows the frothy stream of the consumer culture. When I hear middle-class people complain about the poor buying luxuries for their kids when they don't even have enough for groceries, I remember the lavish Christmases my mother gave us, even at the risk of breaking up the family. Prudence is a bourgeois virtue, because the rich have something worth saving. The poor splurge because they need desperately to make a colorful splash across the drab fabric of their lives. The hungry don't dream of brown rice and vegetables; they dream of cake.

**Over the Rainbow...Deep Purple...South of the Border...
All the Things You Are...And the Angels Sing...
Indian Summer...Wishing (will make it so)...**

Hunching over his short-wave radio late into the night, browsing the crackling ether in search of amateur broadcasters from Czechoslovakia and Poland to keep himself informed of the storm gathering over Europe, provided Mr Kane with escape from a wife who bullied him and derided him as a dreamer, a slacker and a luftmensch with no ambition. Actually, he had vast ambitions, but for mankind, not just for himself. His wife never tired of reminding him that she could have done better. A *lot* better. She'd had offers. Plenty! Before the Depression, Mr Kane had owned a small bookshop in New York City, where he spent more time discussing socialist ideas with like-minded droppers-in than he spent tending to business, so, lacking any savings to absorb the impact of the Wall Street collapse, he was quickly driven into bankruptcy. His wife's family had responded to her relentless nagging by setting him up in a cheap cornerstore a good distance up-state, not out of affection for

Mr Kane, whom they also considered an idler and a fool, but in order to get the formidable Mrs Kane off their backs. That was how the Kanes ended up on Pearl Street.

If Mr Kane was a daydreaming socialist romantic, his wife was a born capitalist entrepreneur. When hectoring her husband to be harder on customers who were neglectful about paying off their slates failed to improve their finances, she gave up on him and launched herself into gainful ventures, first as a cosmetologist and later as a clairvoyant. Soon after arriving on North Pearl Street she converted their living room behind the shop into a Thursday afternoon 'Beauty Salon' where she offered 'professional permanents by a trained beautician' to women of the neighborhood, whom she convinced that the newfangled home perms not only left one's hair too tight and springy but were, she felt obliged to inform them 'on the QT', scientifically proven to cause premature hair loss. Mrs Kane's 'professional' permanents were, in fact, amateur ones that she bought wholesale from a drugstore supplier, and her tonsorial training consisted of reading the instructions on the boxes. But no one could deny that she protected her clients from permanents that were unmanageably tight and springy, for Mrs Kane's hairdos were always slack, floppy, and short-lived because she allowed them to set for only half the time suggested by the instructions, reasoning that it would be foolhardy business practice to intentionally increase the time between permanents by obeying the instructions slavishly.

Her lack of training in the arcane intricacies of dying hair occasionally resulted in someone having to live with orange/pink hair for a month or so, but they continued to frequent her salon, largely because of the succulent gossip she retailed as a loss-leader. Most of this gossip was a product of Mrs Kane's fertile imagination and was only partially believed by the women who absorbed the juicy, often slightly naughty, tales, their eyes wide with wonder and their lips pursed with offended propriety. When the Depression got so bad that even her manufactured gossip didn't attract a sufficiently large clientele willing to risk bizarrely waved orange hair in return for being the first on the block to know of her neighbors' misdeeds, misfortunes and flaws, Mrs Kane restrung her mercantile bow: she announced that she had been the seventh daughter of a seventh daughter, born with a caul over her face, and therefore she possessed the ability to penetrate the mists of time, although she was obliged to follow the ancient traditions of her murky craft and demand that her palm be crossed with silver before she revealed what she saw in the bottom of a tea cup (tea cost a nickel a cup in her Beauty Salon cum Gypsy Tea Room). It wasn't that she was greedy. It was simply that if she broke the ancient tradition, she risked losing her rare gift. At first, the more cynical (and tightfisted) of Pearl Street's gossips doubted Mrs Kane's powers, but even they had to admit the amazing accuracy of the free character analysis that revealed her potential client's probity, goodness of heart and philosophic acceptance of being undervalued, underloved, and not often enough listened to and obeyed. Then an event occurred that converted all the ladies into fervent believers in Mrs Kane's Delphic gifts. While reading Mrs Donovan's leaves, Mrs Kane suddenly shuddered, closed her eyes and insisted on returning Mrs Donovan's quarter (the smallest coin that qualified as 'silver' when it came to crossing someone's palm). When asked what she had seen that gave her such a turn, she refused to say another word because...well, she mustn't say why. One month later to the minute (give or take a couple of days) Mrs Donovan's uncle fell off the loading dock of the Burgermeister brewery and would almost surely have hurt himself seriously if he had been sober. When this news was reported in the Gypsy Tea Room and Beauty Salon, a thrill ran down the spines of the clients, and each expressed the pious hope that Mrs Kane would not suddenly break off during *her* reading and refuse to reveal the dark things to come, thus exposing her to everyone's attention and sympathy.

One day I was buying a can of tomatoes for my mother, and Mr Kane was displaying his skill at manipulating the long-handled can-grabber, but the can slipped from the metal grips and smashed the glass top of the candy case, and Mrs Kane came roaring out of her Tea Room in back and tore into him. Grow up for once, why don't you! Always showing off! She wailed about how much that candy case had cost, even second hand! Where would they get the money for another one? Answer me that, why don't you? Answer me that! She grabbed him by his narrow shoulders and shook him so hard that his teeth clicked. Then she disappeared sobbing back into her Beauty Salon, leaving him standing there, smiling in a slack embarrassed way. Seeing an adult humiliated like that mortified me so much that for a couple of weeks I walked three blocks to shop at a different cornerstore so as to avoid having to look Mr Kane in the face after having witnessed his humiliation.

And to be honest there was another reason for not shopping at Mr Kane's: I was sort of worried about glass splinters in the candy. Surely Mrs Kane would have tried to save the candy and sell it. Oh, they would have sifted the glass out as carefully as they could, but still... I could feel my throat close on a painful needle of glass.

...Mr Kane's candy. Licorice Babies, a penny apiece, slick black on the outside, soft bituminous brown on the inside, and so sticky that there was a slight clicking sound when you pulled your teeth apart; Indian Corn, five-a-penny, orange at the base, white in the middle and red at the tip, no flavor other than a flowery sweetness, but kids were sure they could distinguish a hint of taste difference between the colors if the colors were carefully bitten off one by one and chewed on just the tips of your front teeth; Root Beer Barrels at two-a-penny were my personal favorites; the sugar-grit on the outside soon melted leaving them slick and hard and long-lasting, but dangerous to suck because deep holes with razor-sharp edges developed and they would lacerate your tongue if you were stupid enough to explore the hole with it...and you always were.

But if I had three pennies, it wasn't candy I bought at Mr Kane's, deliciously treacherous though those Root Beer Barrels were. My favorite things were the three-penny 'riffle books', little flimsily bound books about four times the size of a stamp and containing twenty or so pages with printing on one side and line drawings on the other. The print told of a simple event, like a farmer feeding his pigs. Then you turned the book over and riffled through the pages of line drawings and you saw, like an animated cartoon, the farmer fall into the sty and come up with a banana peel on his head. You talk about funny!

The illusion of motion created by the retention of image on the retina was a revelation to me. I had penetrated the mystery of how the movies actually moved. Years later, I would write scholarly articles and a book on film theory and linguistics, all flowing from the magic hours I spent riffling through Riffle Books. I slowly amassed a fair collection, and I would oblige my poor sister to sit through my 'movie shows' until her eyelids drooped with boredom.

**'Taint What You Do (it's the way whatcha do it)...
I'll Be Seeing You...The Umbrella Man...We'll Meet Again...**

For all of my mother's planning and care, our $7.27 sometimes ran out
before the week was over, and this was particularly hard if it coincided
with times when there were no dried potatoes and dried onions to be
had down at the Federal Surplus Commodities Corporation warehouse. We were obliged to buy more of our food on Mr Kane's slate,
which would put us in the hole, and it always took a couple of months
to work our way out, paying it off a dime here, fifteen cents there. During one such time my mother pretended not to be hungry so that my
sister and I could have bigger portions. But I refused to eat if she
wouldn't eat. She snapped that she was the head of this goddamned
family and I'd better goddamned well do what I was told. "The last
thing I need is sass from you, young man!" But I tightened my jaw and
refused to eat. She yelled and loudly slapped the table close to me—she
very seldom slapped us—then she suddenly broke down crying, overwhelmed by the injustice of it all. "All right!" I said. "I'll eat! *I'll eat!*"
And I stuffed the food down, swallowing tears of rage with it. Even
after I grew up, I never enjoyed dining out as a social event. I came to
include eating among the other basic biological functions I don't care
to perform in public.

The rage I felt wasn't directed against my mother, but I wasn't able
to tell her that because we were both too upset. It was rage at the injustices that are a necessary effect of capitalism, because wealth is meaningless without relative poverty. What joy is there in being rich if you
have to empty your own garbage cans, wash your own floors, pick your
own vegetables, mow your own lawns, die in your own wars? There
must be poor people against which the rich can measure their success.

**All the Things You Are...I Didn't Know What Time It Was...
This Can't Be Love...If I Didn't Care...**

Mr Kane had been following events on his short-wave radio and he
pointed out that the Czechs had, for obvious reasons, built their defensive fortifications on the German border. In allowing Hitler to take the
Sudetenland, England and France let him nip off the carefully constructed frontier defenses, and now nothing but a few wooden customs

gates stood between the Germans and Prague. In March of 1939, al-most exactly a year after what Mr Kane had called the Austrian *an-schluss*, Hitler entered Prague and declared Bohemia and Moravia 'protectorates', while agricultural Slovakia became a nominally inde-pendent state whose crops and livestock passed through the German market.

A month later Italy annexed Albania and I asked Mr Kane if this meant there was going to be a war. He sniffed and lifted his shoulders and palms. "*Going* to be a war? The war has already begun, but France and England cling to the belief that if they sit very still and whistle softly, the danger might pass over. But it won't pass over. Poland will be next. And after Poland—" Then, seeing in my troubled eyes how much the thought of a war distressed me, he waved a dismissive hand and said, "But who knows? Maybe I'm wrong. God knows I've been wrong before. Maybe Hitler's too worried about Russia to attack Poland."

Half the block came down with the chicken pox that damp, sunless April. The worst part was lying in bed recovering, my bones sore, my eyes stiff, my fingers yearning to scratch. Mother let me listen to the radio to distract me from the itching. I heard war correspondents broadcasting from Europe, their voices drenched with doom, and I felt helpless and vulnerable. What would happen to us if there was a war? Would war prevent our ship from coming in? Would it be torpedoed in the harbor?

MRS McGIVNEY'S
NICKEL

PANTING, MY lungs grasping for air after a desperate zigzag run down our back alley, I pressed back against the weathered siding of a disused stable dating from the horse-and-wagon era, and slowly...slowly...eased my eye around the corner to locate the snipers concealed in their bunkers at the far end of—Oh-oh! They've spotted me! Two near misses ripped slivers of wood from the stable just inches from my face! I drew back and hissed at my followers, "We'll make a dash for the shed. It's our only chance to stop the *anschluss!*"

I passed most of the summer vacation of 1939 incognito. It made me smile deep inside to realize that people seeing me walk down the street in last year's school knickers patched at knee and butt, worn-out sneakers with many-knotted laces, and no socks to cover my bruised shins, probably mistook me for just an ordinary kid, little suspecting that I was, in fact, the daring and resourceful leader of a team of battle-hardened mercenaries.

It was our assignment to defend North Pearl Street from the Germans who, having gobbled up Czechoslovakia, now set their sights on

Albany, which they planned to infiltrate by way of North Pearl. The U.S. Army and Navy Executive High Commander in Chief of Everything had called me to his secret underground office down in our basement coal bunker to explain that if North Pearl fell, Albany was doomed, and if Albany fell, what hope was there for America? So the fate of the Free World was in my hands and those of my loyal followers. Ranged against us were several thousand heartless, highly trained Nazi Strong Troopers dug in at the end of the alley.

My band of intrepid fighters were hand-picked from radio programs, except for Gabby Hayes, the toothless, bearded sidekick in innumerable grade-Z cowboy movies. They included Uncle Jim from the week-day radio adventure *Jack Armstrong, All-American Boy!*, which also supplied my admiring tomboy of a cousin, Gail, who mostly said, 'Wow!' or 'Whatever you say, chief.' Then there were Jack, Doc, and Reggie from *I Love a Mystery*. Since Reggie was British, I had to use my 'English accent' so he could understand my instructions. Finally there was Kato, my faithful valet, whom I borrowed from *The Green Hornet* without being exactly sure what a valet was, but if Kato was Britt Reid's 'faithful Japanese valet', he'd do for me.[18]

Each of my seven followers had a distinct personality and role: Gail was always astonished and admiring, Gabby was full of folksy wisdom and given to long strings of colorful curses, Reggie knew the correct way to do things, Jack and Doc were brave but headstrong and rash, Kato was faithful, and Uncle Jim always worried that I was taking on tasks harder than any one man could hope to accomplish. This mixed bag of disciples might fret about the risks I ran and occasionally let their hot heads carry them too far, but they were courageous and, what was more important, obedient, although they constantly got into trouble that called for quick reactions on my part. I was fond of them, God knows, but sometimes they tried my patience.

"Let's get to that shed!" I said. "It's our only chance to stop the *anschluss!*"

Uncle Jim exchanged a worried glance with Gabby Hayes who spluttered, "Goshdarn those dang-nabbed, lop-eared, low-down, pigeon-toed, no-'count..!" His outrage decayed into snarls and sniffs of impotent indignation. Gail looked at me, her eyes glowing with admiration, and Reggie nodded crisply in his stiff-upper-lip British way. I kept up a spitty covering fire with my Thompson submachine-gun stick as, one by one, my band dashed across the alley and dove for the shelter of the shed. Both Reggie and Doc got hit on their way across, and Kato, my faithful Japanese valet, had to drag them the rest of the way. Then it was my turn. After emptying my five-hundred-round magazine into the German trench-bunker-wall-fortification-thing, I scrabbled across the alley on all fours, getting a slug in one shoulder, another in my leg, another in my other shoulder, one in the stomach, and a scratch on my knee from a shard of broken bottle as I skidded into the shelter of the doorway—that one really hurt. I gathered my team around me. Clenching my teeth to conceal the pain, I drew a situation map on the ground with the map pointer, a stick that also served as a gun with an inexhaustible clip, a telescope that could read the enemy's plans at half a block, a radio that translated German into American, and dynamite that you lit with your snapped-up-thumb cigarette lighter and threw at the enemy, or rather, at the base of a huge rock outcropping that overhung the enemy's position and came crashing down on them, crushing them to a pulpy mass that your eyes flinched away from. I reminded my followers that sometimes war wasn't a pretty sight, but a soldier had to do what he had to do and that was that. Throwing your dynamite was a desperate last resort, considering the huge expenditure of war materiel the loss of this versatile stick constituted, but you usually had the remarkable good luck to find another such stick lying close to the body of a fallen—or crushed—Strong Trooper. (All right, so I misheard 'Storm Troopers' when Mr Kane was telling me about what was happening in Germany. Is that a crime? Jeez!)

I muttered continuously during my story games, because I had to play all the characters and do the sound effects as well. These games were always tense and emotional, so the volume of my muttering and the vigor of my gestures increased until, as sometimes happened, I would glance up and blanch to find someone looking at me. I would quickly convert the dramatic monologue into a song (with gestures) because, although talking to yourself is a sure sign that you're a nut, there is no shame attached to singing to yourself. But I never felt the ploy really worked, so I would wander away, furious with the eavesdropper for spoiling my game.

That summer afternoon in our back alley of derelict stables where people seldom went because there was no through passage, I was muttering in two voices as I questioned a snide German officer I'd managed to capture. Having ordered Doc to blindfold the German officer so he couldn't see the map I was scratching on the ground, I explained our desperate situation to my followers, muttering hard and gesturing passionately to convince them, but my attention was distracted by a sharp tapping sound. I looked around, but I couldn't see anybody, so I returned to explaining to my team that we had to stop those Germans from advancing another inch, even if it meant laying down our lives for our—

Again I was interrupted by the tap-tap-tap of metal against glass. I looked up and down the alley. Nothing. I was concentrating hard to keep my story game from dissolving when a movement at the edge of my peripheral vision caused me to lift my eyes, and there looking down at me was Mrs McGivney, one of our block's crazyladies, smiling in that vague way of hers. Immediately, my followers vanished, as did the four or five thousand Nazi Strong Troopers dug in at the far end of the alley, and I was left all alone: a leader of men suddenly shriveled into a skinny kid caught talking to himself.

The block's belief that Mrs McGivney was crazy was based on her peculiar shopping habits, her extreme shyness, and the long, old-fashioned dresses she always wore. She was never seen on the street except for quick trips across to Kane's cornerstore, always near to closing time. Even if other people were ahead of her, Mr Kane would serve her as soon as she came in, because she would slip away and not come back until the next evening rather than risk being noticed or, worse yet, spoken to. Respecting her timidity, Mr Kane never spoke to her. He would just smile and raise his eyebrows above his thick glasses, and she would quickly mutter off her shopping list, which he would fill, toppling cans from their high stacks with his can-grabber gizmo and catching them in his apron, or slicing cheese off the block with his hand-cranked machine, or scooping macaroni or rice from one of his tip-out bins and hissing it into a little paper sack on his scales, always bringing the weight up to just a bit more than he charged for. After filling her order, Mr Kane would tell Mrs McGivney the total cost as he marked it down in the dog-eared slate he kept under the counter. Mrs McGivney would take her sack and scurry back across the street to her apartment, never looking up for fear of catching someone's eye. Once a month, she came in with a check, which he cashed for her, subtracting the cost of her groceries. Everyone knew that Mrs McGivney received a small monthly government check for 'disability', which the street understood to mean because she was a nut, but Mr Kane once told me that in his opinion she was just painfully shy. Her reputation for insanity was, however, an element of received street-tradition and therefore impervious to evidence or reasoning. Even the modest check she got from the government was taken as proof, if any were needed, that she was insane. How else could a crazylady stay alive? She could hardly get a job—except maybe at a nut factory! And there was the suspicious way she would appear from time to time at her window giving onto the back alley, just looking down at the kids playing there, not bawling them out for making noise like any sane person would, or shouting at them for throwing stones that might put somebody's eye out. No, Mrs McGivney just smiled down on us sweetly—exactly like a crazylady would do.

And now there she was, standing at her window, smiling down at me after having scattered both my followers and my enemies to the distant recesses of my imagination.

She beckoned to me. Oh-oh. She'd never done that to any of the kids before. Although I was the only person in the alley, I made a broad mime of looking around to see who she could possibly mean before pointing at my chest, my eyebrows arched in operatic disbelief. She smiled and nodded. I lifted my palms and drew my head into my shoulders to say, but what did I do? She tapped the window again with a nickel—so *that's* how she'd made that sharp noise. She pointed to the coin, then to me, clearly meaning that she intended to give the nickel to me.[19] She beckoned again and made a big round gesture, which directed me to go to the end of the alley, around to our street, and to her apartment building. I really didn't want to go; my worst nightmares were about being pursued by crazy people. But I was a polite kid, so I went. Even the wildest and toughest of the kids on our block, several of whom ended up in prison and one on death row, would be accounted polite by today's standards. Then too, if there was a chance to earn a little money, I could hardly let it pass me by, considering that my mother regularly risked her health for just a few extra bucks. Resentful of losing my game and dreading my encounter with a crazylady, I left the alley...but not before rubbing out the map with my heel, so the Nazis couldn't discover my plans.

The staircase of 232 was dark because the hall windows meant to illuminate the stairs had been blocked up when the slum landlord divided the building into apartments and put a narrow bathroom into the front of each hall. Despite its darkness, I ascended the staircase with a sure step because 232 was in the same row as 238, where I lived, and therefore identical to it.

I tiptoed up to the fourth-floor landing and stood in the dark, uncertain. Maybe it would be best to sneak back down and out into the light and bustle of the street, but as I turned to go, the door to the back apartment opened and Mrs McGivney stood there, smiling.

"Would you mind going over to Mr Kane's for me?" she asked in a tiny, little-girl voice. "I'll give you a nickel." Her tone went up on the first syllable of 'nickel' in a kind of sing-song temptation.

"Well, I don't— All right, sure, I'll go." I was relieved that she only wanted me to do a chore for her, and not something...crazy.

She had a list already written out, and she said Mr Kane would put it on his slate.

When I returned with the small bag of groceries she was waiting at the head of the stairs and she gave me the nickel she had tapped the window with.

"Thanks." I put the nickel in my pocket and patted it to make sure it was there. The year before, I had lost a quarter. It must have fallen out of my pocket on my way to the Bond Bread bakery outlet to buy a week's worth of what was euphemistically called 'day old' bread. I retraced my steps again and again, hoping to find the quarter. But no luck. A whole quarter. Enough to buy five 'day old' loaves at the bakery.

"Just bring the bag in, would you please?"

I followed her in, and she took the bag and brought it into the kitchen, leaving me standing in the parlor, where there was a little round table with two glasses of milk on it, and four homemade sugar cookies on a decorated plate. The furniture was frilly and old-fashioned, and the room smelled of floor wax and recently baked sugar cookies. In the corner an old man sat facing the window and looking out through lace curtains that were filled with the setting sun. Actually, he wasn't looking out. His eyes were pointed towards the buildings across the alley, but I could tell he wasn't seeing anything. I said he was old, but the only old thing about him was a soft halo of fine white hair that held the sunlight filtering in through lace curtains. His face was unlined, his skin was tight, and he sat straight-backed in his chair, staring through the curtains out across the alley with an infinite calm in his unblinking pale blue eyes. Spooky.

Mrs McGivney returned from the kitchen and stood beside the little table, holding the back of her chair, waiting for me to sit down.

"Gee, thanks a lot, but I think maybe I'd better not—" But she smiled sadly at me, so I sat down. What else could I do?

There was a heavy linen napkin on each plate. Mrs McGivney took hers and put it on her lap, so I did the same, only mine slipped onto the floor. She smiled again and pointed her nose towards the plate of cookies, indicating that I should take one. I did. She took a tiny bite out of hers, and I tried to do the same, but two bits broke off, one falling onto the floor and the other getting stuck in the corner of my mouth so that I had to push it in with my finger, and I wished I were somewhere else—anywhere.

She smiled a little pursed smile that didn't show her teeth. "You live three doors up, don't you."

I nodded.

"And you're Mrs LaPointe's boy."

I nodded again, wondering how she knew, considering that she never talked to anyone.

"What's your name?"

"Luke. Well, it's really Jean-Luc, but only my mother calls me that. I like to be called just Luke."

"John-Luke. That's foreign, isn't it?"

"My mother's family is French Canadian. And part Indian."

"John-Luke's a nice name."

"Only my mother calls me Jean-Luc. Other people call me just Luke."

"I've noticed that you always play alone."

"Mostly, yeah."

"Why is that?"

"Why do I play alone?" I glanced past her towards the old man, wondering if we were supposed to pretend he wasn't there. "Well, I make up my own games, and other kids don't know the rules or the names of the people or...anything."

"And you read an awful lot, don't you."

How did she know that I read—? Then it hit me: I always cut through the alley on my way home from the library, not because it was the shortest way, but to avoid the little kids who, whenever they saw me with an armful of books, would chant 'pro-*fes*-sor, pro-*fes*-sor, pro-*fes*-sor', which was one of my street names. My other street name was 'Frenchy' because my name was even more French-sounding since my mother had reverted to her maiden name, LaPointe, but with a Mrs, so as to justify us kids I suppose.

"That's right, ma'am. I do read a lot. I get some of my games from books."

"Games?"

"Like Foreign Legion. Or Three Musketeers. But mostly I get them from radio programs."

"We don't have a radio," she said with neither complaint nor apology.

I had noticed this on my first glance around the room, and I wondered how anyone could live without a radio. So totally was my understanding of life linked to our old Emerson that I couldn't imagine not having *The Lone Ranger* or *The Whistler* or *I Love a Mystery* for excitement, or Jack Benny and Fred Allen and Amos 'n' Andy for laughter, or advice from Mr Anthony and *The Court of Last Resort* for insights into the human condition. My favorite moment of the day was turning on the radio when I got back from school, and feeling the delicious anticipation of those five or so seconds of hum while the tubes warmed up, then there was the deep satisfaction of a familiar voice announcing one of the kids' adventure programs that my mother let me listen to for an hour every afternoon before homework. Standing on one leg before the radio, my head down, eyes defocused, I was totally mesmerized by what I was hearing and seeing. Seeing, because for me the actions and settings that radio evoked were real and tangible. Splendid and enthralling, but somehow less *real*, were the worlds I glimpsed in books and movies. The life I lived on North Pearl Street was certainly not splendid, but neither was it real; just a grim limbo I would escape from someday. Until then, I found solace in radio, and in my story games.

"I'm afraid of them," Mrs McGivney said, offering me a second cookie, which I politely refused, then, because she continued to hold it out to me smiling, reluctantly took.

"You're afraid of radios?"

"Of everything electric," she admitted with a little smile of self-disparagement.

Only then did I notice that she didn't have electric lights. All the houses in our row still had their gas fixtures in place, but the gas had long ago been cut off except for kitchen stoves and hot-water heaters. In some rooms the gas pipes had been used as conduits for the electric wires, so naked bulbs dangled from fabric-wrapped wires that sprouted from the ceiling rosettes of former gas chandeliers. In our bathroom and kitchen the disused gas pipes had fancy wrought-iron keys, but you couldn't turn them because they'd been painted over so many times. But Mrs McGivney still had cut-glass gas lamps on her walls, with bright brass keys to turn them on.

"Mr McGivney loves the gaslight," she said. "He's always glad when it gets dark enough for me to turn it up." She smiled at the unmoving old man, her eyes aglow with affection.

I looked over at him, sitting there with his pale eyes directed out the window, his face expressionless, and I wondered how she could tell he liked the gaslight. Could he speak? Did he smile? And what was wrong with him anyway? Was he crazy or something?

I felt her eyes on me, so I quickly looked away.

"Mr McGivney is a hero," she said, as though that explained everything.

I nodded.

"My goodness! Do you know how long it's been since we've had a little boy come visit us?" she asked.

"No, ma'am." I didn't really care. What I wanted was an opening to tell her that I'd better be getting home.

"It's been a long, long time. Michael—that's my nephew?—he used to visit us sometimes. I don't think he much liked coming up here, but Ellen—my sister?—she used to make him come. And every time he came, I'd give him a sugar cookie. He loved my sugar cookies, not like another little boy I could mention."

"I like your sugar cookies, Mrs McGivney. I think they're...nice. *Real* nice. Well, I guess I'd better be going. My mother's been sick and—"

"Mr McGivney is a hero," she said again, clinging to her own line of thought and ignoring mine. I could tell she wanted to talk about him, but I was uncomfortable with the waxy-clean smell of the place, and with that smooth-faced old man staring out at nothing, so I told her that my mother would be wondering where I was, and I thanked her for the milk and cookies. She sighed and shrugged, then she opened the door for me, and I escaped down the dark staircase.

I sat on my stoop for a while before going into our apartment where I knew my mother would be lying in her sick bed, bored and wanting company after a long siege of lung trouble that had left her smelling of mustard plaster and Balm Bengué, smells that combined with the floor wax of Mrs McGivney's apartment to evoke memories of the orphanage that Anne-Marie and I had been put into the previous winter, a grim institution out in the country, surrounded by a high chain-link fence with barbed wire stretched along the top, located in wintry fields of corn stubble that seemed infinitely bleak to city kids. The first day, one of the Brothers took me aside and told me that I should pray every night for my mother's recovery and, that failing, for her soul. That night I alternately prayed and cried into my pillow, because it had never occurred to me that she might die, leaving Anne-Marie and me in that home forever.

We boys wore gray uniforms of a canvas-like material that was so stiff with starch that new kids were chafed at knee and elbow. We marched in silence to meals, classes and chapel, our lives punctuated by clamorous electric bells. We showered beneath jets of cold water and slept in cavernous unheated dormitories. The cold water and fresh air were supposed to 'harden us' against the rigors of life, but they only kept us in a permanent state of drippy noses, sore throats and earaches.

The first problem I met was going to the bathroom. There were urinals on the first floor and a long common trough in a shed beside the exercise field, but the only toilets were a bank of eight along the wall of the wash room at the end of the dormitory, and these not only lacked seats to mitigate the shock of cold porcelain but they were open to the view and the ridiculing comments of everyone, to the intense embarrassment of the boy uncomfortably perched and vulnerable. I used to wait until the small hours of the morning to slip into the deserted wash room and relieve myself. Fortunately, I was in the habit of being awake late into the night, but in the orphanage there was no street outside my window to absorb my interest, so I spent the time making up acronyms for memorizing names from history classes and lists from science and geography.

The dormitory rules were arbitrary and quixotic, and discipline was hierarchical, the older boys being in charge of the younger. This led to bullying and late-night punishments carried out in the shower room, where the offender was surrounded by a ring of older boys using sodden towels that hurt like hell but didn't leave bruises. The kid being punished stifled his cries because if the big boys got caught and punished for their illegal punishments, they would make his life a hell of secret punches, sneering taunts, and the torment of preference in that particular orphanage, Indian Burns, which consisted of grabbing a kid in a headlock and scrubbing his forehead or cheek with knuckles until the skin was raw and slippery with that clear fluid that becomes scab. These thin scabs identified their bearer as a victim and therefore fair game for further torment. Any passing bully could grab him and give him a few quick Indian Burns that would scrub off the scab and produce a new slippery rawness. Some kids always carried four or five of these blemishes on cheek and forehead that branded them as permanent victims and targets. Visitors from the social services identified these marks as impetigo and prescribed a bright blue medication, yet further marking and targeting. They didn't inspect the wounds closely for fear of catching impetigo.

Late one night when I had just finished going to the bathroom, four grinning older boys appeared at the doorway to the wash room, and the slack-lipped bully who was their leader told me that it was against the rules to go to the toilet late at night because that led to jacking off, which was a sin. He shrugged and sucked his teeth and said he guessed he'd just have to punish me, and he grabbed me and tried to give me an Indian Burn, but I responded with a rush of red rage that gave me the wiry strength to squirm out of his grasp and the next moment I had my fingers entwined in his hair and was banging his head on the tile floor until his eyes glazed over and he bit his tongue. His mouth filled with blood, and he was gagging and choking on it when his stunned buddies dragged me off him. They tended to him themselves, so he wouldn't 'get caught', and I returned to my cot in the darkened dormitory, my heart pounding with adrenaline, and with fear of reprisal, which was often threatened by word and gesture over the ensuing week. But nothing came of their threats, and they took out their anger on easier targets, the natural victims. In time I was able to relax, except in the chaos of the exercise yard where I felt in danger of being surrounded by enemies hidden in the screaming, madly romping throng.

But if social life at the orphanage was tense and menacing, the time spent in school was a blissful mitigation. For one thing, the classrooms were the only heated spaces, except for the infirmary. For another, while the Brothers were lax in protecting their charges from bullying, they took pride in their teaching, which was rigorous but caring. There were special classes for backward kids to help them catch up, and for those who did exceptionally well, there were accelerated classes with only five or six students. For the first time since Miss Cox I was not bored with schoolwork. One of the Brothers gave me an old grammar that had been published in 1898. I can still call up that book's smell of pleasing mustiness, and can feel the grainy greasiness of its worn fabric cover. I had always been fascinated by words, those little packets of sound that encased nuggets of meaning or feeling or attitude, like primitive insects in amber. That grammar book and those special accelerated classes in English helped my enjoyment of words to blossom into an interest in language: its structures, its shape; the machinery of grammar that binds words together, and the architecture of syntax that lets them spark meanings off one another like flint against steel.[20]

Inevitably, the favor I earned from certain of the Brothers because of my interest in language marked me as unforgivably 'different' in the eyes of the older boys, and this led to occasional tussles in meal queues or out in the anarchic exercise yard. Because of my involvement in these brief, covert and mostly silent skirmishes featuring elbows, knees and thumbs, and because I sometimes played the clown in class out of a pusillanimous desire to be one of the regular guys, I racked up more than my share of 'minutes', which were the general currency of punishment in the orphanage. The smallest unit of correction was five minutes. A Brother would give you a 'Five' for such venial transgressions as talking or fidgeting, or trying to sneak food out of the dining hall or failing to finish homework. Fighting always earned you at least a 'Ten', and a 'Fifteen' was the minimum for being cheeky or disrespectful. The heaviest penalty ever given for a single trespass was the two hours awarded, along with twenty smacks with the Paddle (which had holes drilled in it so it could move through the air faster), to a mentally deficient boy for masturbating in the shower in the presence of a score of other boys and the Brother in charge of our dormitory. The Brother could hardly believe his eyes as the oaf stood there, looking right at him, grinning as he performed his Onanesque outrage.

The Brother who assigned you so many minutes of punishment time would write your name and the duration of your penalty in one of the small notebooks they all carried in their breast pockets (close to their hearts). They snatched out their notebooks as an arresting detective might snatch out his handcuffs. Their penalties were communicated to Brother Bernard, who was in charge of the Glory Hole, the name given to our chapel during the half hour in the morning between breakfast and the first class, and the 'free hour' in the evening at the beginning of Quiet Time, when we were supposed to do our homework and assigned reading. Instead, you had to report to Brother Bernard, who always sat in the back row of the chapel, and tell him how much of your punishment you intended to work off, usually five or ten minutes at a time. He would take note of your intention in a ring notebook open on his knee, next to a large pocket watch, and you would sit in silence until his watch's minute hand reached the next numeral, then he would raise his hand and you could join the penitents kneeling on the stone step of the communion rail with their arms spread out wide, for your minutes had to be worked off kneeling straight up on the stone (No slouching there, Murphy!) with your arms straight out and your hands closed into heavy fists. And if, after five or ten minutes, your quivering arms started to lower (Arms, LaPointe! Arms!), there was only one warning about slumping posture or arms that were not straight out. Upon the second show of physical weakness or failure of will, Brother Bernard would say, 'Get out, Kennedy!' and you had to leave the Glory Hole without receiving a single minute's diminution of the time you owed. For this reason, it was wise not to try to work off too large a chunk of punishment in one go, a bitter lesson I learned during my first session in the Glory Hole where, after thirteen minutes of struggling to work off a quarter of an hour, my throbbing shoulder muscles weakened and I could no longer keep my quivering arms from drooping an inch or two. Brother Bernard's voice echoed from the back of the chapel 'Get out, LaPointe!' and I got no credit for the thirteen minutes of torment...well, about seven or eight minutes of torment. The first five minutes weren't all that bad.

Failure to work off your time and get your name out of the punishment book by the first of the month meant that you couldn't go into the exercise yard during recess. Instead, you had to sit in the library under the eyes of a Brother, but you couldn't read. Just sit there, silent. You also had to report to the library to sit in silence from noon to one-thirty each Sunday, thus missing out on Sunday dinner, which was the best meal of the week. In addition, you lost 'all privileges'. At first, I couldn't imagine what these elusive 'privileges' could be. I had come just after Christmas, so I didn't know that there was a party and presents and cake to celebrate the birth of Our Savior, or that amateur performers came from the city once a month to give us a Saturday evening 'concert' in which local church choirs sang at us, or a man-and-wife team did 'dramatic readings' of poems and bits of novels, or a man who owned several reels of film and a projector would show us flickering silent films of the explosion of the Hindenburg zeppelin, and a parade of men in old-fashioned uniforms and plumed hats passing the camera jerkily, and bottles on an assembly line spinning and rushing by as they were filled with some liquid. These opportunities for cranks to display their hobbies and for local hams to inflict their meager talents on a captive audience were the 'privileges' you lost if you failed to work off your minutes by the first of the month.

There was a handful of vicious fourteen- and fifteen-year-olds who were so deeply in debt to Brother Bernard that they didn't even try to catch up; they turned up every afternoon to do a minimal required 'five', and let it go at that. They never ate Sunday dinner, never had the privilege of watching some old gal strangle a handkerchief as she sang the 'Indian Love Song', in a wobbly soprano, never had a chance to run and shout in the exercise yard. These boys vented their pent-up energy and resentment late at night in the dormitories; they were the punishment teams.

Anne-Marie and I had been separated upon arrival at the orphanage; she was put in the care of nuns in the girls' wing where, only six years old and having no idea where I was, she cried herself to sleep every night and reverted to bed-wetting, for which she was both ridiculed and punished. She was picked on because she was pretty and vulnerable. Bigger girls yanked her around by her long blonde hair. One afternoon a couple of weeks after we arrived, I was in the tangled mass of boys that ran and hooted and screamed wildly during the pandemonium of our unmonitored exercise periods, when I thought I heard Anne-Marie's little voice within the chaos. I searched for her among the tight-packed shoal of blue-uniformed girls who used to watch the rampaging boys from their side of the high chain-link fence that separated us, but before I found her the bells rang and we had to run back inside and leave the exercise yard for the girls. I later learned that I had walked right past her while she vainly called my name. I hadn't heard her through the din of screaming kids, and I failed to recognize her because a nun had cropped her hair in an effort to save her from being tormented by envious girls. She cried all that night, devastated because I had walked right past her, and she might never see me again. But the next day I walked up and down my side of the fence until I found her, and we held fingers through a chain link while she sobbed with a mixture of relief and misery. She leaned against the fence, closed her eyes, and took long slow breaths, drawing in the smell of wool and of boy from my jacket as she slipped into that deep peace that was necessary to her well-being. And that's how we spent our exercise periods for the next six weeks, pressed against opposite sides of the chain-link fence, until the day we were called into the director's office and told that we were being sent home. Our mother was well again.

After we got home I learned that the social workers had decided Mother was not healthy enough to qualify as a 'fit parent', so we kids would remain at the orphanage until we were sixteen, old enough to get jobs. But Mother unleashed the formidable weapon of her French-'n'-Indian temper to browbeat the astonished social workers into letting us live together again. But next time...

To avoid there being a next time, when Mother got sick again and had to go into a hospital, Anne-Marie and I did everything we could to conceal the fact that we were at home alone. I washed our clothes in the bathtub, and Anne-Marie kept the house tidy, if not clean, and we shared the meal preparation, which relied heavily on potato soup and peanut butter sandwiches. When I was shopping at Mr Kane's, I would mention offhandedly that my mother had told me to get this or that, or that she was feeling just fine, thank you...anything to deceive any welfare spies that might be lurking around. Our deception gave me a chance to hone the dramatic skills I had developed by playing all the roles in my story games. When I left the apartment in the morning to walk Anne-Marie to her school before going on to mine, I would stop at the door of our apartment and loudly say something like, "What's that, Mom? All right, I'll take care of it. You just get well. I'll see you this afternoon!" Just in case there were welfare people hiding in the upstairs hall trying to find out if my mother was taking good care of us.

But soon Mother was back with us and life returned to its routine. From time to time, Anne-Marie would wake up crying from a recurrent nightmare that she was back in the orphanage pressed against the chain-link fence, calling my name, but I just walked away and she was left alone. Mother would take her into bed and assure her that everything would be all right. Don't worry. One of these days our ship will come in and carry us far, far away. When I was very young, I had envisioned Mother's metaphorical ship pulling in at one of the Hudson River piers and, dressed in matching sailor suits, the three of us would walk up the gangplank and never look back. It was a pleasant and comforting fantasy until one day when Mother was describing the splendid house we would live in when I became rich and famous because I had a high IQ and could invent things, I suddenly realized with an icy sinking in the pit of my stomach that *I* was the ship my mother was waiting for, and it was *my* task in life to rescue us from Pearl Street. The weight of this responsibility made me dizzy. I began to involve myself in my story games more intensely.

Evening had descended as I sat on our stoop daydreaming. With a start, I suddenly realized that Mother was still waiting for me to come home and put on the potato soup for supper. In the kitchen I dropped the nickel Mrs McGivney had given me into our Dream Bank, which was an empty box of Diamond kitchen matches we hid on the shelf under the real box of matches to baffle any thief that might come snooping around. The Dream Bank was money saved up from Mother's occasional part-time jobs and from my shoe-shining rounds of the bars and taverns on Friday nights. Only the occasional drunk or some guy trying to impress a woman ever wanted a shine, but sometimes someone would give me a nickel or even a dime to get rid of me. Like selling apples on the street corner, shining shoes during the Depression was a way of begging without a total surrender of dignity. The money in the Dream Bank was supposed to be for special things, fun things, like the movies we went to every second Thursday night, but more often than not, it was squandered on dull, soon-forgotten necessities.

That evening after the last of my radio programs, I willed myself back to reality and went to sit on the edge of my mother's bed to play two-handed 'honeymoon' pinochle with her, while my sister cut out and colored dresses for her paper dolls. To save the cost of new paperdoll books, my mother would buy one then trace and cut out the clothes, tabs and all, onto paper she gleaned by cutting open brown paper bags and ironing them flat. In this way, one paper doll book did the service of half a dozen, lasting until the cardboard dolls got too limp from handling to stand up. My sister would spend hours drawing her own designs on these blank dresses and coloring them in, then hanging them onto the cardboard dolls in a series of 'fittings', all the while twittering animatedly as she played both the dressmaker and the customer, usually a rich, spoiled, very demanding actress. Anne-Marie loved to create styles from what she saw in the movies or in back-dated magazines that percolated their way down to Pearl Street, but her games were burdened, and to some degree spoiled, by my mother's need to see everything as a way to get us off Pearl Street. That summer, Mother was sure that Anne-Marie would find success as a famous Hollywood costume designer, just as she viewed my bookishness as a sign that I would become a university professor and take us all to live in some nice college town up-state.

Or maybe a doctor. As my mother was often in and out of charity hospitals, I guess it's natural that her romantic ideal was The Doctor, just as her implacable enemy was The Nurse, particularly those snippy ones who were jealous of the interest the doctors took in her unique 'lung condition', which never did receive a specific name like bronchitis or emphysema or pleurisy. For a short time I wove and unraveled games in which I was a famous doctor who somehow managed to save the lives of rich patients without having to come into physical contact with them. Even in my games I was too squeamish to deal with people on the level of blood and pus and...other liquids.

I always felt relieved when the honor, and the onus, of bringing our ship into port was bestowed upon Anne-Marie, if not as a famous fashion designer, then as a dancer. Even as a little kid, Anne-Marie loved music and used to sing and dance to our Emerson. Some neighbor politely told my mother that she had talent and was 'a born professional, believe you me!' and overnight it was decided that she was just the girl to replace Shirley Temple, who, after all, couldn't remain young and cute forever, could she? The next day Mother put Anne-Marie's hair up in bouncy sausage curls like Shirley's (we called her by her first name now that we were all in show business). The sausage curls would help talent scouts from Hollywood to spot her, and the next thing you knew, we'd all be in sunny California where we would live, as my mother's defective ear for idiom put it, 'on the flat of the land.'

...As differs from the slippery slopes?

But for this dream to come true, Anne-Marie would have to take tap dancing lessons, and that was out of the question, because group classes cost a dollar fifty per session and she would need two a week, which would have been almost half of the $7.27 we received from the welfare people. So the Shirley Temple dream was put on the shelf for a while, and we went back to fantasizing about the things we would own and do when I became a rich diagnostician, famous for my unique non-liquid 'hands-off' technique.

While I was shuffling the pinochle cards, I mentioned that I had made a nickel doing Mrs McGivney's shopping for her.

"Mrs *McGivney?*" Anne-Marie asked, shuddering at the thought of getting close to a crazylady.

"How did you happen to run into Mrs McGivney?" my mother wondered, and I told her how I was playing in the back alley, and she got my attention by tapping on her window with the nickel.

"And you went up to her apartment?" Anne-Marie asked.

"Sure."

"You weren't afraid?"

"Nah."

"You didn't go *in*, did you?"

"Sure. She gave me a cookie."

"And you *ate* it?"

I asked Mother about Mrs McGivney, but she didn't know much: just that she had lived in that same house for as long as anybody could remember. "All alone in the world like she is, it's nice of you to run errands for her." Mother patted my hand. "You're a good boy, Jean-Luc." I had the feeling I was being pressured into visiting Mrs McGivney again. My mother had a great-hearted desire to help people, and when she couldn't manage it herself, she would volunteer me. But I never complained because, like she said, I was a good boy. A resentful good boy.

But the possibility of a new game began to take shape in my mind when Mother spoke of Mrs McGivney as being all alone in the world. "H'm...did you ever hear anyone talk about Mrs McGivney having a family?" I asked casually, as I dealt out the cards. "A husband, maybe?"

No, Mother had never heard anyone mention a Mr McGivney. "But I suppose that gossipy Mrs Kane has made up all sorts of stories about the poor old woman."

Shortly after we arrived on North Pearl, my mother got wind that over in her hairdressing salon cum tea room cum gossip shop Mrs Kane was telling stories about us, weaving them from the fertile threads of my mother's having no husband in residence, and being part

Indian, but with a blonde daughter who didn't look at all Indian, and a son who did. (Of course, we had the same father; it was just that different genes came to the surface.) Mother's French-'n'-Indian temper carried her, steaming, across the street and into Mr Kane's store. Anne-Marie and I watched from our front window for her re-emergence, our cringing neck muscles tense with worry about the outcome. She came out after about ten minutes with the air of a man rolling down his sleeves after taking someone to Fistcity, and I knew that we wouldn't be hearing any more about our origins again. The next time I went to the cornerstore, Mr Kane shook his head and blew out a long jet of breath. "She's got some temper, your mother," he said with reluctant admiration. I sheepishly admitted that she did.

"You never heard anyone talk about Mrs McGivney's husband, eh?" I asked my mother as I picked up my cards.

Mother said she was pretty sure Mrs McGivney was a widow, or maybe an old maid that people just called 'Mrs' out of courtesy.

So she *didn't* know about Mr McGivney! As I led out a middling trump, I mulled over the intriguing possibility that I might be the only person on the whole block who knew of his existence. With the part of my mind I didn't need to play cards, I developed a story game of Detective in which I helped radio's *Mr Keene, Tracer of Lost Persons,* track down the mysterious Mr McGivney, famous hero...of some sort. While I wondered if he had been a heroic policeman or a fire fighter or maybe he had saved a child from drowning in the Hudson, Anne-Marie sat on the floor, muttering complaints on behalf of her actress paper doll about how dull, dull, *dull* all the clothes in the shops were, then she gasped with astonished delight when Anne-Marie's latest 'creation' was revealed.

The next afternoon after helping Mother wring out the laundry in our tub and hang it up, I climbed over our back fence into the alley to play my new story game. Squatting in the doorway of a stable with a book on my knee and my back to Mrs McGivney's building, I pretended to be reading, but in reality I was keeping watch on the McGivneys' windows, looking over my shoulder through a small mirror I had borrowed from my mother's handbag and taped onto the inside cover of the book. But I could see nothing through the lace curtains.

My followers complained about being bored with this no-action game, but I reminded them that the stake-out was an important part of detective work. All right, so maybe it wasn't much fun! But it had to be done, and we were the ones chosen by Mr Keene, Tracer of Lost Persons to do it. They could quit if they wanted to, but me, I'd stay at my post until hell froze over, if that's what it took! I turned my face away and refused to listen to their apologies, until Uncle Jim and my faithful Japanese valet, Kato, pleaded with me to forgive them for complaining. But my admiring young niece, Gail, continued to whine about this being a dull game, so finally Tonto and I (sometimes I borrowed Tonto from the Lone Ranger, which was all right because I was part Indian) Tonto and I began a careful examination of the ground, using a magnifying stick to look for clues. We found what might have been part of a footprint, and there was a very interesting piece of broken glass, and a half-covered cat turd that Tonto said had been dropped since the last full moon, but that was all. Searching for Lost Heroes was beginning to lose its zest, and I was considering changing back to driving the Nazi Strong Troopers out of their bunkers with my blasting stick, when I heard three crisp clicks of metal on glass above me and I looked up to see Mrs McGivney smiling down from her window, holding up a nickel, and motioning for me to come up. At first I felt bad: it's pretty shoddy detective work when the suspect spots the stake-out; but then I realized that here was a chance to get into the suspect's apartment in the guise of a kid willing to run an errand, and do some undercover snooping around. I told my followers to wait for me there. I'd report back after I'd grilled the old dame.

If they got bored, they could blast Nazis.

Mrs McGivney met me at the top of the dark stairway and I followed her into the apartment, where her husband still sat at the window, looking out over the alley, his pale eyes vacant. She explained that she had forgotten to write 'pickle' on her list, and she knew that Mr McGivney would just love to have one of Mr Kane's big plump dill pickles.

I couldn't promise to get a big plump pickle, because Mr Kane always rolled up his shirtsleeve, reached into his barrel, and gave you the first pickle he touched. Even if it turned out to be a little one, he wouldn't drop it back into the brine and try again because, as he explained, he'd pretty soon be left with nothing but little pickles, so people would desert him and buy their pickles where they had a chance of getting a big one. When I returned with an average-sized pickle wrapped in white butcher paper I found the little table set up with napkins and fancy plates and sugar cookies and milk for two. I told Mrs McGivney that I really couldn't accept the nickel she was trying to press into my hand, not for fetching something that had only cost a nickel in the first place, but she pointed out that I had walked the same distance as if I'd been sent for a whole bagful of groceries and therefore I had earned the nickel; I said no, I couldn't take it, but she just stood there with her head cocked, giving me one of those ain't-I-the-cutest-thing glances out of the corners of her eyes, the kind of look Shirley Temple used when she wanted to get her way. Adults thought Shirley was just too adorable for words, with her dimples and her sideward glances, sticking out her lower lip in a pout and shaking her pudgy finger at people she thought were being naughty, but every red-blooded American boy yearned to kick her butt. Hard. In the end...all right, all right, I took the damned nickel. Jeez!

Those sugar cookies had something against me. They didn't get caught in the corner of my mouth this time, but I had just bitten one when Mrs McGivney asked me how my mother was, and when I tried to answer through the cookie I coughed and sprayed crumbs. Not much of a start for a slick detective.

I was curious to know what was wrong with Mr McGivney, but I didn't think I should ask straight out. So instead, I told her I'd have to be getting home before long because my mother was sick.

"Still? I'm so sorry to hear that."

"She's almost over it."

"Is she often ill, John-Luke?"

"Only my mother calls me John-Luke. Yes, she's sick pretty often. She's got weak lungs."

"And you take care of her?"

"My sister helps."

"What about your father?"

My mother hadn't mentioned my father since he failed to turn up with the green cake. But I knew that she thought of him sometimes because I once walked into her bedroom looking for something, and I found her sitting on the bed with photographs of the two of them strewn around her. Her eyes were damp and bruised-looking. I walked out, silent and embarrassed, as though I had seen her nude.

"I don't know anything about my father," I told Mrs McGivney.

"Oh, I...see. Well, the important thing is to always be a good boy and take care of your mother because you'll never have another."

"Ah-h...yes...well, that's certainly true." I wasn't getting anywhere in my investigation and I couldn't think of anything to ask without giving a hint that I was working for Mr Keene, trying to trace a Lost Hero. Mrs McGivney was no help; she seemed content just to sit there, smiling at me vaguely, her head tipped to one side. I glanced over at Mr McGivney, but he was still staring out the window. And I suddenly remembered a scary episode of *Lights Out* about zombies and the living dead.

I felt Mrs McGivney's eyes on me, so I turned to her and dredged my imagination for something to talk about so she wouldn't guess that I had been thinking her husband might be a zombie. "Ah...ah...what was your nephew's name again? You told me, but it slipped my mind."

"My nephew?"

"The one who used to visit you, but doesn't anymore?" Out of the corner of my eye, I watched Mr McGivney. I'd never seen anyone sit so still before. Even his eyelashes didn't move. I watched to see if he'd blink. He didn't. Was it possible not to blink? I looked at his neck, then his wrist, but I couldn't see any throbbing of a pulse. It was almost as if—

"He's dead," she said with a sigh.

"What?" Icy horror rippled down my spine.

"Michael. The nephew who used to visit us? He was killed in France. Poor boy."

Oh, the nephew. I took a deep breath and tried to think of a way to ease back into my interrogation, like smooth detectives do. So, let's see. If the nephew died in France during the Great War, then he hadn't visited them for about twenty years. "Don't you have any other relations?"

"No, no. My sister and I were the only children in my family, and she died shortly after her son. The Spanish 'Flu. The 'flu took my mother and father, too. They caught it caring for my sister." She seemed to think about this for a moment before adding, "Lots of people died of the Spanish 'Flu." She smiled a faint, sad smile. "My people are all gone, and Mr McGivney was an orphan, so, no, we don't have any relations." She shrugged, and sudden tears dampened her eyes. "No one at all."

"I'm sorry."

"Are you, John-Luke?" She looked at me with such intense gratitude that I felt nervous.

"Only my mother calls me— Look, Mrs McGivney, I really have to get home." I rose from the chair and went to the door. "Thanks for the cookie." Then I did something risky. I turned to Mr McGivney and said, "Good-bye, Mr McGivney."

"He can't hear you."

"Is he deaf?"

"No, no, he's not deaf." She opened the door for me. "Mr McGivney is a hero."

"Oh." I looked back at him. "I see. Well..." I left.

Uncle Jim, Gabby, Tonto, Jack, Doc and the rest were in the alley, anxiously awaiting my return. "Michael!" I whispered hoarsely out of the side of my mouth while gazing off into the distance so as not to tip off their presence to some onlooker. "Killed in the Great War. Write it down, and don't forget it!"

In the 'Thirties, the 1915–'18 war was called the Great War or just The War. It wasn't called the First World War until the advent of the Second World War, just as early films were not called 'silent films' until the advent of the talkie.

A week or so later, I was cutting through the back alley with an armful of books about birds. I no longer remember why I decided to bring Mother's ship in by becoming a rich, world-famous ornithologist, but I wouldn't be surprised if I had just stumbled across the word 'ornithologist' and taken a fancy to it. This was during a period when I shifted from one eventual profession to another, often on the basis of small clues to my destiny I found while reading the encyclopedia in the library or my three-volume *High School Subjects Self-Taught*. This idea of becoming an ornithologist lasted longer than most—maybe a week or two. I even began my first book, *Meet the Warbler*, which I wrote *as a book*, the sheets of paper folded in half and stapled together down the center crease so you could turn the pages and read my careful printing, which I justified by spreading or crowding the letters. The cardboard cover had a crayon drawing of a yellow warbler on it, and at the bottom: Written by Jean-Luc LaPointe, author. It was dedicated to 'my best friend, My Mother'. Working at the kitchen table, carefully wiping the tip of my nib on the edge of the ink bottle after each dip to avoid blots, I painstakingly produced half a dozen pages of this seminal study, scrupulously altering a word here and there from my single research source to avoid being a copycat. Then something went wrong; I don't remember what. Maybe I made a blot, or miscalculated the space necessary to fit a word in. At all events, my effort to erase the error made a smear, which my attempt to erase converted into a hole, so I abandoned the profession of ornithologist. I found this aborted scholarly effort many years later, when I was going through my mother's things after her death. She had underlined the dedication: To my best friend, My Mother.

I had stopped in the alley to shift books from one hip to the other when three sharp clicks on a window above made me look up. Mrs McGivney was gesturing for me to come up. I indicated the books I was carrying and tried to mime the complicated message that I had to bring them to the library before it closed. But she just smiled and tilted her head in that little-girl way of hers and beckoned me up, so I reluctantly returned the books to my apartment and went down the street, up her stoop, and up the staircase to the top floor.

Again the cookies and milk; again her wistful smiles, again Mr McGivney sitting perfectly still with the low evening sunlight caught in his fine white hair. But this time I was determined to uncover the facts about his heroism. I decided to try the double-bluff of a subtly deceptive direct approach. "Mrs McGivney, how did Mr McGivney become a hero?"

She seemed pleased that I was interested enough to ask. "Mr McGivney was a soldier. He fought the Spanish in Cuba."

Now we were getting somewhere! A war hero! I had read a short story about the Spanish–American War called 'Message to Garcia', but it wasn't a war that inspired novels and movies, like the Civil War and the Great War. "When was the Spanish–American War, Mrs McGivney?"

"He left to join his regiment the day after we were married. The Shamrock Regiment, it was. Most of the boys in the Shamrock Regiment came from New York City and only a few from up-state. He looked so grand and handsome in his uniform!"

"Yes, sure, but when *was* that?"

"I'll bet half the people on the block came to our wedding. It was up at Saint Joseph's. Do you know Saint Joseph's?"

Saint Joseph's was our block's parish church where I would eventually become an altar boy, but at that time my only religious distinction was my ability to get through the Stations of the Cross faster than any other kid on the street. None of us would have dared to skip a single word of the five Hail, Marys we said at each stage of the Passion, nor would we have failed to bow our heads at the word 'Jesus', but we saw nothing wrong in saying the prayers as fast as we could, rising from one Station while still muttering nowandatthehourofourdeathamen, then sliding into the next on our knees and beginning its string of Aves before we'd come to a complete stop. And we would never have dreamed of failing to genuflect as we crossed the central aisle to get to the second half of the Stations, but we sometimes did it so quickly that one kid sometimes got a bruised knee.

"So you got married at Saint Joseph's, eh?" I made a mental note of this. Where they got married didn't seem important, but you never know. In an investigation of this kind the smallest detail might turn out to be the key that unlocks the...

"We stood there at the altar, him in his uniform and me in my mother's wedding dress. It was all so beautiful. I was just nineteen, and Mr McGivney was twenty-three."

"And this was...*when*, exactly?"

"September. September weddings are good luck, you know."

"Yes, but *what year!*...Oh, I'm sorry. I mean, what year were you married, Mrs McGivney?"

"Eighteen ninety-eight. That's when our boys went to Cuba."

1898. Another century! But then—let's see—if she was nineteen in 1898, and this was 1939, that would make her about sixty. That was pretty old, sure, but not impossible. Still, it seemed strange to think that this old man had fought in the war *before* the Great War. The Great War had started when my mother was only about my age, for crying out loud.

"So he was wounded doing something brave in Cuba?" I asked.

"No, he wasn't wounded. I don't know exactly what happened. And, of course, he wasn't able to tell me, because he's..." She lifted her shoulders. "...well...like he is." After a moment, she continued in a distant voice, as though tenderly fingering the old memories. "I moved into this apartment right after seeing him off at Union Station. All the boys in uniform...a band playing...people waving and cheering. I made this little nest for Lawrence to come back to." She rose and started to walk around the room, touching things. "I ran up these curtains myself, and found furniture in second-hand stores, and my father helped me paint—he was a house painter by profession, you know—and I chose this paper for the parlor. Do you like the color? Ashes of Rose, they called it." She took a hairbrush from the sideboard and stood behind her husband, lightly brushing his white hair, while he sat bathed in the westering sun that filtered through the lace curtain. "I wrote to Lawrence every day, telling him how our apartment was coming along. He wrote every day too, but his letters used to come in clumps, nine or ten at a time. That's how the mail comes when a person's in the Army. In clumps. Then...then his letters stopped coming, and there was no word for a long time...more than a month." She lifted her brush and looked down upon his fine hair. "I was so worried...so frightened. I asked Mr O'Brien if he could find out why the letters weren't coming through. Mr O'Brien the mailman? Then this letter came from the government, and I was afraid to open it. Everybody on the block knew I had a government letter because Mr O'Brien told them. Mr O'Brien was..." Her voice drifted away and she stood there, frowning into the corner of the room.

"...Mr O'Brien was your mailman," I prompted.

"What? Oh, yes, that's right...our mailman. My mother and father came and asked what the news was. I told them I hadn't dared to open the letter. My father said I was acting silly. I might as well know one way or the other, and there was no point in putting it off. But I didn't want to know, not right at that moment. So my father said he'd open the letter for me, but I said no! No, Lawrence was my husband, and it was my duty to open the letter. ...When I was ready."

Tears stood in her pale blue eyes, and her voice had become tense and thin as she re-lived standing up to her domineering old-country father, probably for the first time ever, telling him that Lawrence was her husband and she would open the letter when she was ready.

She blinked back tears and looked across at me. "You know what? I believe that was the first time I ever said the word 'husband' aloud. I always called him Lawrence, of course. His friends called him Larry, but not me. I was his wife, so I always called him Lawrence. I wasn't used to saying his name aloud. We'd only been married four months, and I'd been busy fixing up our home, so I didn't see many people or have much chance to talk about my husband...my husband...husband." As she savored the word, she began brushing his hair again.

I sat watching her brush his hair while he gazed, empty-eyed, at the roofscape beyond his window. Then his flat, pale cheek trembled! His lips drew back in an unconscious rictus that revealed long yellow teeth, but the eyes remained dead.

A sharp breath caught in my throat. "Mrs McGivney...he just... he...!"

She nodded. "I know. He sometimes smiles when I brush his hair. Lawrence loves having his hair brushed."

Well, it didn't look like a smile to *me*. He looked like a man in terrible pain hissing out a silent scream through his teeth. Not daring to look away, I watched as, with a slight quiver, his cheeks relaxed, the grin collapsed, the teeth disappeared, and he was again looking out through the lace curtain, his eyes empty.

It was a couple of minutes before my heart stopped thudding in my chest. I wanted to get out of there, but a private investigator working for Mr Keene, Tracer of Lost Persons, doesn't turn tail and run. I drew a deep breath and said, "This...ah...this letter you got from the government. It said he was a hero, did it?"

"Yes, a hero."

"What had he done?"

"It was from his commanding officer—Captain Francis Murphy? He regretted having to tell me that Private Lawrence McGivney had contracted an illness in the performance of duty. He was in a military hospital and would soon be shipped home so he could get every care and comfort. I remember the exact words...every care and comfort. And that's what I've tried to give him. Captain Murphy went on to say that Private McGivney was a cheerful and willing soldier and that he was well liked by everybody in the regiment. Think of that! The whole regiment."

Being liked by everybody is fine, but it isn't quite the same thing as being a hero. But I didn't say anything.

And for a while Mrs McGivney didn't say anything either. She stood there brushing her husband's hair, a fond smile in her eyes as she seemed to re-read the letter from his captain in her mind. Then she blinked and focused on me. "You know what I'd bet? I'd bet dollars to doughnuts you'd like another cookie. Am I right?" She looked at me out of the sides of her eyes in that coy Shirley Temple way.

"No, thanks, I—"

But she shook her finger at me. "Now don't tell me you can't eat another cookie. A boy can always make space for another cookie."

As she went for the cookie jar on the counter I asked, "What was Mr McGivney sick with?"

"Brain fever," she said. "He ran this terribly high fever for days and days, lying in his bunk, sweating and shivering. The doctor at the veterans' hospital over in Troy—Doctor French?—he told us that most men would have died." She brought back one of her little decorated plates with a cookie on it and set it before me. She still had the hairbrush in her hand. The long white hairs entangled in its bristles made me shudder. "Doctor French said that Lawrence had fought a heroic battle against the fever, and survived!"

Oh. So *that* was the kind of hero he was.

"But..." She sighed. "The fever left him...well, like he is."

"And you've taken care of him ever since?"

She smiled. "I wash him and feed him and...everything. He likes it when I brush his hair. He doesn't say anything, but I can tell by the way he sometimes smiles."

So she had lived alone with him up here for more than forty years, feeding him and cleaning him and brushing his hair. Forty years. So long that the existence of Mr McGivney had dropped out of the collective memory of the block, which now thought of Mrs McGivney, when it thought of her at all, as a shy old spinster crazylady. But she thought of herself as the bride who had made a cozy nest for her soldier bridegroom.

I started to ask if she didn't get lonely, up here all day without anyone to talk—but a child's instinct for social peril stopped me short. Of course she got lonely! That's why I was sitting there, eating explosive cookies. That's why she gave me a whole nickel for buying a pickle. That's why she had given me a look of such intense gratitude the other day. I could sense the trap closing. I should never have asked her about her husband. Now that I knew how lonely she was, now that I'd seen tears in her eyes, I'd feel obliged to come whenever she tapped at her window with that nickel, and to sit with her and listen to her talk about how her husband liked it when she turned on the gaslight or brushed his hair. Another responsibility in my life. And sometimes when I dared to glance over, he'd be grinning his silent scream of a smile. Right then and there I decided I'd better stay out of the alley altogether for at least a week to get her used to not seeing me and depending on me.

It was during that week of weaning Mrs McGivney off me that my life lurched out of balance because a tube in our radio burnt out. A new one would cost a dollar and a quarter, and there wasn't enough money in the Dream Bank, so I had to go without the daily hour of those reality-blocking adventure programs that had become essential to my well-being. And this just when all the stories were at their most exciting and dangerous moments—or so it seemed to me.

Mother was furious because we'd only had the radio for three years. I reminded her that it had been second-hand—maybe fifth-hand—when we bought it, but she said we'd been robbed and she'd be goddamned if she was going to let them get away with it! She was sick and tired of everybody always taking advantage of her! Her French-'n'-Indian temper carried her out of her sick bed and down to the A-One Pawn Shop where we had bought the radio. I went with her, trying to calm her down all the way, but she stormed into the shop and slammed the radio down on the counter. I winced at the possibility of additional damage. The old pawnshop keeper came out from the back room. "Can

I help—oh, it's the lady who drives such hard bargains over radios. Help, I'm going to be robbed!"

I tried to be friendly. "Good afternoon, Mr A-One."

"And the boy with the sense of humor. Help, I'm going to be bored!"

I turned away, embarrassed by the scene I knew would follow. Mother told him that the tube had burnt out and she asked what he was going to do about it. He shrugged. "Lookit, lady, it's an old radio. Tubes burn out. That's life." Well, she wanted him to put in a new one and right now, because her boy was missing his programs! The pawn-broker said he'd end up in the poorhouse if he gave everybody tubes every time they burnt out, but here's what he could do. He could give us a new tube for a quarter down and a quarter a week until it was paid for. How was that? Mother took back the radio and said, "To hell with you, mister! This is the last time we do business with your sort!" And she stormed out. I smiled weakly at the man. He thrust out his lower lip and lifted both shoulders and palms in an ancient gesture of fatal-ism, and I had to run to catch up with my mother, who was steaming up the street towards home in a rage, muttering that she'd be god-damned if her boy would go without his radio programs because of a lousy buck and a quarter. She'd get a job in some goddamned hash-house to pay for the goddamned thing! I reminded her that she was still weak from her recent lung attack, but she said her kids had just as much right to listen to the radio as the kids of any snooty hoi polloi bastard that works in some bank! She knew how much the radio meant to me, and she'd get that tube if it killed her!

Then I got angry. So it would be my fault if she got sick and died and Anne-Marie and I ended up in the orphanage! I told her to forget the radio. I didn't want the radio! I was sick of the radio! I didn't care if I never heard a radio again! She told me to shut up! Shut up! Shut up! And I said I wouldn't shut up!...but I did, and we continued home, walking fast in the hot silence of rage.

When we slammed into our apartment, Anne-Marie knew things had gone badly. She shot me a scared look and begged Mother to go back to bed and rest so she wouldn't get sick again. Mother started on the 'I'll be goddamned if my kids...' routine, but I interrupted her, say-ing that she didn't have to worry about the damned tube anymore. I had a plan for getting the money. She asked what I had in mind, but I said it was a secret. With one of her sudden mood shifts, she took Anne-Marie onto her lap and started re-braiding her hair. I went into the bathroom and sat on the edge of the tub, the only place in our little apartment where I could be alone to think. I had succeeded in shutting Mother up by telling her I had a plan to get the money; now all I had to do was think up some sort of plan.

When I came back into our kitchen I had a plan...of sorts. Soon Mother was back in bed, braced up by pillows, and we were playing pinochle on the covers while Anne-Marie, dressmaker-to-the-stars, sat at the foot of the bed, murmuring soothing assurances to a movie actress who needed something really spectacular to wear to the Oscar Awards. Mother's rages were always brief. I think she knew how stomach-wrenching they were for us because afterwards she always tried to be lighthearted and fun. That night she told us about some of the wild stunts she had got up to when she was a kid, and Anne-Marie and I laughed harder than the stories deserved, because we were so relieved.

After Mother and Anne-Marie were asleep, I borrowed my sister's crayons and drew a sign on a piece of cardboard box. I was going into the transportation business in conjunction with a grocery that had just opened in a long-empty store two blocks down the street.

The spanking new red-and-gold sign above the grocery read: The Great Atlantic & Pacific Tea Company, a name that evoked books about the South Seas: cruel planters and vengeful natives, tall-masted sailing ships and sad-eyed captains who had gone to the East to forget. The new A&P was the product of a brief Depression-years experiment with small A&Ps that the company called 'neighborhood stores'. Their prices were only slightly lower than in cornerstores, but you were allowed to walk around and pick out your own cans and fruit and everything, which was a novelty at that time. Also, there were intriguing new foods, like maple syrup that came in a can shaped like a log cabin. You poured it out of the chimney and when it was empty you could use the cabin as a toy or a bank. And there were three kinds of coffee that they let you grind for yourself in machines, choosing between drip grind, percolator grind, and 'regular' (whatever that was). The newly ground coffee gave off so delicious an aroma that you closed your eyes and just breathed it in. The most expensive coffee was called Bokar, a name redolent of Africa so it was right that the bag should be black; the middle-priced one, Red Dot, came in a yellow bag with a red dot; we always bought the cheapest coffee, Eight O'Clock, which came in a red bag. I used to wonder if the Bokar could possibly taste as good as it smelled. But no coffee tastes as good as it smells: an apt metaphor for the gap between anticipation and realization. The new store's cheaper prices and wider selection attracted everyone for blocks around, but you couldn't charge things there so, in the end, Mr Kane's slate won out over the A&P's novelty and economy, and like other experimental 'neighborhood' A&Ps around the nation, it closed within the year.

The morning after our Emerson blew its tube, I was standing outside the miniature A&P with my sister's battered old cart and a cardboard sign with bold red crayon letters informing shoppers of my willingness to bring their groceries home for 5¢. That first day and the next, half a dozen old ladies used my services. I walked them home, pulling their bags of groceries in Anne-Marie's cart and chatting in the polite, cheerful way I thought likely to inspire them to tip me a couple of cents in addition to my nickel, but none did. Every one of those women lived blocks and blocks away from the A&P, and I had to lug their bags to apartments on the upper floors, leaving the cart in the first-floor hallway so nobody would steal it. I couldn't believe the rotten luck of every single one of my customers being an old woman who lived far from the A&P and on an upper story of her building, and each of them too cheap to give a friendly, smiling guy a tip. What were the odds? It took me a while to work out that this wasn't a matter of bad luck. Only women who were so poor they couldn't afford to tip would shop blocks away from their homes to save a few pennies; and only those who lived on the upper floors would be willing to part with a nickel to have their stuff carted home and carried up to their door. Still, after two days I had put thirty cents into the Dream Bank towards the tube, even if my sister did complain bitterly that I'd worn her red crayon down to a nub making my sign, so she couldn't make any red clothes for her paper dolls, just when red was all the rage, and her movie star customers were complaining that—

Oh, shut up, why don't you?

You shut up!

Copycat, eat my hat!

Oh, shut up!

No, *you* shut up!

(From the bedroom) *Both* of you shut up, for Christ's sake!

The third morning I arrived at the A&P bright and early to find another boy standing there with a wagon and sign—a bigger boy with a bigger wagon and a bigger sign. And he wasn't even from our block! Well, we had words. He said he had as much right as I did to be there because I didn't own the sidewalk, so just who the hell did I think I—

I got two solid shots in before he knew he was in a fight, then we really went to Fistcity, rolling around on the pavement, him mostly on top because he was bigger, but me getting in some pretty good face-shots from below. The manager of the A&P came out and snatched us around by our collars for a while, then he said that if we didn't behave ourselves he'd send for the cops. When I tried to explain that I had been there first, he told me that he'd seen me start the fight. Of course I started the fight! A smaller kid has to get his shots in first or he doesn't stand a chance! Jeez! But I promised not to fight any more, so this copycat interloper and I ended up standing on opposite sides of the store's door, glowering at each other until some old lady came out carrying groceries, then we'd try to out-smile and out-nice each other. I was at a disadvantage because my smile was sort of one-sided from a split lip. It was a scorcher of a day, and the time passed slowly standing there in the sun, especially since I got only one customer, and that only because this other kid was away on a delivery. I could read what was going on in the women's heads. They didn't like having to pick one kid and leave the other behind, so some of them carried their own bags home, and others chose this bigger kid because they didn't want to make a skinny little kid lug those bags all that distance. Yeah, sure! Give money to the big healthy kid, and let the skinny little one go without! That makes lots of sense, you stupid old...!

That night I walked home dragging the wagon behind me, too tired and disheartened to remember to avoid the shortcut through the back alley. I knew I should go straight home, but I wanted desperately to play some kind of story game for a little while because without my nightly dose of radio, there was no narrative narcotic to rinse away daily life and refresh my soul. Then too, I wasn't all that eager to arrive home with a split lip and only a nickel to show for a day's work. I was always better at playing the modest winner than the brave loser.

There was only one lamp post in the back alley, and its grainy light fell at an acute angle over the facades of abandoned stables, emphasizing textures and leaving pockets of felted shadow in entranceways...a perfect setting for scary games. I slipped into a space between a shed and a stable, one side of my face lit and the other in shadow, knowing how scary I must look as I whispered to my companion that there had to be a rational explanation for the case he called The Murders in the Back Alley. There just *had* to be! I wouldn't be a bit surprised to learn that Professor Moriarty had a hand in this, Watson. (A blend of clipped speech and Peter Lorre nasality did for my English accent.) I told the good doctor that the only way to discover the insane killer was for me to expose myself to the same dangers that those poor, bloody, axe-chopped, heads-ripped-off, faces-bashed-in women had met when they—

—I nearly pissed myself when that sharp tap-tap-tap on the window made my voice squeak and sent Dr. Watson vanishing into the darkness, leaving me to face the danger alone. I looked up to see Mrs McGivney beckoning to me, and her husband in the other window, both silhouetted by the soft gaslight of their parlor. I *knew* I should have gone straight home! Drawing a peeved sigh, I inserted a mental bookmark into my game so I could remember where I was, when I got back to it, and I trudged to the end of the alley, around past my own stoop where I stashed Anne-Marie's wagon in the hall, then down to 232, and up its stairs, the air getting thicker and hotter with every floor I climbed. It was really hot in the McGivney apartment so high up, close to the lead roof, and their gas lighting made it hotter yet. That was the only time in my life I experienced the effect of gaslight, which was softer than electric light and didn't seem to descend from the ornate gas fixtures on the wall, but rather to glow from within things and people, a golden radiance.

With an edge of grievance to her voice, Mrs McGivney asked where I'd been the last few days. I explained that our radio had blown a tube and I had been trying to earn money to replace it, but she made a tight little nasal sound, dismissing my excuse, so I rather curtly asked what it was she wanted me to do for her. It was late and Mr Kane's grocery was closed. But it turned out that she just wanted to give me a glass of milk and some of those cookies that 'all boys love so much'. I didn't tell her that this particular boy would rather be allowed to pursue his game than be dragged up there to spend time with a boring old lady and a zombie. Instead, I sat across from her and nibbled grumpily. But she just smiled at me, then looked over at her husband and sighed with satisfaction, as though everything was all right again, now that we were all back together.

I noticed that when she drank her milk she looked into the glass, like little kids do. And that's when it struck me that she was strangely young. She had white hair, sure, but her skin was smooth and her eyes bright. It was as if, living as she did on the edge of life, without hopes or fears, work or play, nothing had eroded and aged her, so she had remained eternally young and oddly...ghostlike.

As I left, she pressed a nickel into my hand. I protested that I hadn't done anything to earn it, but she just squeezed my hand closed around it, so I left thinking how nice people can be more trouble than mean ones, because you can't fight back against nice people.

I found my mother and sister sitting on our front stoop to get a breath of cool evening air, and I joined them. When Mother asked what had happened to my lip, I shrugged it off and changed the subject by telling them about the McGivneys. Mother was surprised to discover that there was a Mr McGivney, and Anne-Marie rubbed the goose bumps that rose on her arms at the thought of my sitting in the same room as a crazy man who just stared out the window all the time. I told her he wasn't crazy, only sort of...well, damaged, but she said that damaged people were just as scary as crazy ones, maybe even more, and she didn't care how many nickels they gave me. Mother said I shouldn't accept money unless I did some chore to earn it. It was like accepting handouts, and we LaPointes didn't do that. But she was glad I'd made some new friends, and she was sure I'd be a big help to these lonely old people. I almost told her that I resented being made to feel responsible for them, but I didn't. I was afraid she'd realize how often I felt the same resentment about being responsible for getting us off Pearl Street some day.

The next morning, there was a third boy outside the A&P, and he had a brand-new cart and a sign with professional-looking lettering that offered to carry groceries for 4¢. You could tell from his clothes that he wasn't poor, just a regular kid, lucky enough to have a new cart and somebody—probably a father—to help him paint his sign and to advise him about undercutting the competition. I could see right off that offering to carry the groceries for four cents was a smart scam because most of the women would give him a nickel, and wouldn't ask for their penny change back because that would make them seem stingy; so he would get the job by underbidding us, but he'd end up making as much as we did. I'll bet his father was a car salesman or a con man or a stock broker...one of those people who make their livings by selling the sizzle, rather than the steak. Well, I drew this new kid aside and explained that there wasn't enough business for two kids—forget three—and this had been my idea in the first place. Then I put on my most sincere expression and told him that I was very, very worried about him, and worried about how his mother would feel if he came home with no front teeth and his fancy wagon all kicked in and— But out of the corner of my eye I could see the manager watching me from within the store, so I just pointed at the middle of the rich kid's chest and skewered him with squinted-up eyes, which on my block meant 'You're standing real close to the edge, pal!' then I swaggered back to my battered old cart.

But he stayed, and I didn't get a single customer that day, bracketed as I was by a bigger competitor and a more attractive one. I stuck it out until the A&P closed that night. But I didn't bother to come back again. What was the use?

That Friday our weekly $7.27 welfare check came, so we were able to buy the tube, although it meant having potato soup every night that week and the next. That evening I stood in front of the Emerson in a state of deepest soul-comfort, my head bowed, my eyes half-closed, totally absorbed in the exciting adventures of Jack Armstrong, and the Green Hornet, and the Lone Ranger, Masked Rider of the Plains. The world was in its orbit again.

After my sister and I did the supper dishes, the three of us sat in the front room, listening to Friday night's run of mystery programs. We always turned off the lights and listened in the dark, with only the faint orange glow of the radio's dial because that made the stories deliciously spooky, such programs as *The Inner Sanctum* with its heavy door that creaked open and a darkly evil voice that said, "Good evening, friends." And there was *Lights Out, Suspense, The House of Mystery* and on Sunday nights at seven-thirty, *The Whistler*: "...who walks by night and knows many things. He knows strange tales hidden in the hearts of men and women who have stepped into the shadows. Yes, he knows the nameless terrors of which they dare not speak!" The Whistler's tales were told from a unique and effective narrative point of view: he spoke directly to the villain of the piece in a curling, feline voice with a little echo in it, as though he were the person's conscience, saying things like, "You thought you would get away with it, didn't you, James Townsend? You were so cunning, so careful. But you forgot just one thing..."[21]

It was a stifling August evening when I looked out our front window and saw Mr Kane out on his side steps, his head in his hands. I went across and sat silently beside him, wondering what could be wrong. After a few minutes, he said in a fatigued monotone, "The Russians. They've signed a nonaggression pact with Germany. You know what that means?"

I didn't.

"It means there's nothing to stop Hitler from taking Poland," he explained.

"Doesn't Poland have an army?"

"Yes, but Czechoslovakia had a better, more modern army than Poland's, and where did it get them?" His voice had a tone of leaden inevitability. Then I remembered that he had told me that both England and France had promised to attack Germany, if she attacked Poland. I reminded him of this.

"England and France guaranteed Czechoslovakia too."

"...Oh."

Mr Kane frowned at a patch of ground near his feet, and his jaw muscles worked as though he were chewing something tough. I understood that something vast and ominous was happening out there in the world, but there was nothing I could do about it, so after sitting in silence for a while, I got up and said I'd better be getting home. He nodded without looking at me, and I left. That night I sat on the edge of my bed, looking out onto the empty street, feeling that something terrible was on its way. I was confused and afraid, but I was also young and male, so I felt a prickle of excitement. War!

I awoke the next morning to the chilling realization that summer vacation was almost over and, what with trying to earn extra money and spending time up at the McGivneys', I hadn't gotten enough good out of it...sort of like a Popsicle that melts while you're obliged to talk politely to a nun, and you don't get to suck it white before it falls off the stick. Next year I would be ten, and I felt that advancing to a double-digit age signified the end of childhood, because, let's face it, once you get into two digits, you're there for the rest of your life. Everything was changing on me! I was growing up before I was finished with being a kid! And now a war was looming on the horizon. This would be my last summer before I had to give up my story games and start in earnest doing what I could to get my family off Pearl Street. And the summer was almost used up.

All right, I accepted that bringing my mother's damned ship into port was my job. But I couldn't take care of Mrs McGivney, too. I intended to play as hard as I could for the two weeks until school started, and this meant that I would need all my time for myself, for my games, for listening to the radio, for wandering the streets in search of mysteries and adventures. There just wouldn't be any time to sit around with the McGivneys.

I avoided the back alley for a week, during which I revisited one by one all the story games I had played since we came to North Pearl Street to imprint them upon my memory so I would never forget the exhilarating fun of them. That week I fought off Richelieu's swordsmen, ran cattle rustlers off the streets of Albany once and for all, blew up the planes of the Condor Legion to save Spain from the Fascists, and led an expedition to the Elephant Graveyard, where we almost lost Reggie and Kato to native black magic that sucked out their will to live so they could only be kept breathing by my passionate exhortations to fight, fight, fight. On Sunday, I changed into play clothes right after six o'clock mass and went off to spend the morning playing one of the best story games of all: Foreign Legion, in preparation for which I hadn't drunk anything after supper the night before. So I was good and thirsty by the time I had crossed Broadway towards the river, passed through Blacktown's tangle of still-sleeping streets, and scrambled over the high wooden fence of an abandoned brickyard where there were huge piles of sand and gravel. For the next two hours I staggered up and down the endless dunes, blinded by the glaring sun, suffering horribly from thirst made worse by the fact that I was weakened by half a dozen spear wounds inflicted by perfidious Arabs whom I had always treated well, unlike some of my brother Legionnaires. My throat parched, I muttered to myself that the pools of icy water I saw all around me were only mirages. Mustn't be fooled! Must...keep...going. I wanted nothing more than to give up the struggle and just lie down and let sweet death overwhelm me—but no! Must...keep...going! At the most distant corner of the brickyard, there was a stand pipe with a spigot by a watchman's hut, and it was part of the game to hold the vision of that cool, clear water in my mind as I crawled on my hands and knees over the piles of sand and gravel, dragging my wounded leg behind me (sometimes both wounded legs) but determined to carry the message from what was left of my decimated company besieged in our fly-blown outpost of Sidi-bel-Abbès to the colonel of the regiment stationed at our headquarters in the noisy, bustling city of Sidi-bel-Abbès. (All right, so I knew the name of only one desert city! Is that a crime? Jeez!) By taking the least direct path possible and weaving my painful, dazed way over the great central sand pile again and again, I managed to drag the game out to well past noon, by which time my lips were crusty and my tongue thick with thirst. When at last I arrived at the stand pipe, I put my head under it, ready for the blissful shock of its cool dousing gush, my fingers almost too weak to turn the rusty spigot. In a hoarse voice I cried out to Allah to give me strength. Give me strength! And I gave the spigot a desperate twist with the last of my fading energy—

—but no water came out. They'd cut off the water since last summer! Anything to spoil a guy's game!

By the time I got back to my block, I was *really* thirsty, so I cut through the back alley to get to my apartment as quickly as I could.

Three sharp clicks of a coin against the window above me—Oh no! And there she was, gesturing for me to come up. Nuts! Nuts! Double nuts!

But this time it would be different. As I trudged glumly up the dark stairs of 232 I decided on a plan to free myself of this lonely old lady and her loony husband once and for all: I would mope and be rude, so she wouldn't want my company any longer. But first—

"Could I please have a glass of water, Mrs McGivney?"

"Why, of course, John-Luke!"

I gulped it down, rather than sipping it slowly and savoring the life-saving sweetness of it, as I would have done in the dramatic last scene of the Foreign Legion game...if those idiots hadn't shut off the water!

"My goodness, you *were* thirsty. Want some more?"

"No, thank you." It was hard to remember to be rude.

"You're sure?"

Mrs McGivney sat across from me at the little table set for two. "Here, before I forget it." She placed a nickel beside my napkin.

"No, I don't want it," I said, pushing it back to her.

She cocked her head. "Don't try to tell me that a little boy can't find something to do with a nickel."

"No, my mother said I wasn't to take money from you unless I did an errand or something in return."

"Oh, I see. Well...I know what! You just put the nickel in your pocket." She pushed the nickel over to me.

"I don't want it." I pushed it back to her.

"No, you keep it until I think of something you can do for me." She pushed the nickel back to me.

I didn't touch it.

She held out the plate of cookies to me, and I lowered my head and stared at the table top. Finally she put one on my plate. I didn't look at it.

"Would you like to wash up, John-Luke?" she asked.

"Only my mother calls me that."

"What?"

"Only my mother calls me Jean-Luc!"

"Oh...I'm sorry, I didn't mean to..." She looked at me closely.

"Would you like to wash up? You look a little...dusty." She smiled sweetly.

I touched my forehead and felt the grit of the sand through which I had crawled all the way from Sidi-bel-Abbès to...Sidi-bel-Abbès. Having someone who wasn't my mother tell me my face was dirty was humiliating: something left over from the time two young, syrup-voiced social workers swooped down on our apartment to see if my mother was taking proper care of us. They asked Anne-Marie if any men had been sleeping at our house, and one of them made me stand in front of her while she checked my hair for nits. I was so outraged that I pulled my head away from her and told her to go to hell, and the two do-gooders made little popping sounds of surprise and indignation and said they'd never seen such a badly brought up child. After they left, Mother told me that I had to be polite to social workers or they'd write up a bad report, and the three of us would have to run away to avoid their taking us kids away from her. Oh sure! It was all right for *her* to lose her temper and give social workers hell, and get her way by ranting and raving, but I couldn't do it. Was that it?

I got up and went over to the McGivneys' kitchen sink. In the little mirror over it, I could see that my dirty face was streaked with rivulets of sweat. I was embarrassed, so I twisted the faucet on angrily, and the water came squirting out of a little flexible thing at the end of the spigot and splashed onto my pants, making it look as though I had pissed myself, then I was really embarrassed. To cover my discomfiture I quickly soaped up my hands and scrubbed my face hard, then I splashed water into my face, but I couldn't find anything to wipe it on, so I just stood there at the sink, dripping, the soap stinging my eyes, like some helpless thing. Like her husband, for crying out loud!

I felt her press a towel into my hand. I scrubbed my face dry and sat back in my chair, hard, very angry.

"You're not going to eat your cookie, John-Luke?"

"I don't want it."

"Suit yourself. But they're sugar cookies. Your favorites."

"Oatmeal cookies are my favorites. The kind my mother makes."

"...Oh." There was hurt in her voice. "I just thought you might be hungry."

"My mother feeds us real well."

"I didn't mean to suggest— I'm sure she does."

Actually, I was still thirsty enough to down that milk in two glugs, but I sat there in silence, frowning down at the embroidered tablecloth I supposed she had put on just for me.

She made a little sound in the back of her throat, then she said, "Poor boy. You're unhappy, aren't you."

"No. I'm just...awful busy." I meant, of course, with my games, trying to get my fill of fun before school started and I became two digits old and had to start looking for work and war broke out all over the world, but she took it a different way.

"Yes, I was talking to Mr Kane, and he told me how you do odd jobs to help your mother out. Shining shoes and all. She must be very proud to have a good boy like you."

I said nothing.

"I hope you don't mind if I ask, but..." She paused a second for permission, but then pressed on anyway. "Your father, John-Luke. Is he dead?"

I don't know what made me say it. A desire to shock her, I guess. "No, he's not dead. He's in prison." Not until many years later did I discover that I had unknowingly told her the truth.

She drew a quick breath. "Oh! Oh, I'm sorry. I didn't mean to pry, I was just—oh, that's too bad. You poor boy." She reached towards me, but I twisted away.

"No, we're proud of him! They put him in prison because he's a spy! They're going to hang him next month, but he doesn't care. He only regrets that he has but one life to give for his country!"

"Wh...what?"

"I'm going home!"

I started to rise, but before I could move, she stood up and hugged me, saying, "No, please don't go!"

I turned my head aside, so as not to have my nose buried in her bosom.

"You poor, poor boy. You've had such a lot of troubles and worries in your young life, haven't you? No wonder you're all worked up. But I know what will calm you and make you feel better." She opened a drawer and took out the brush that had white hairs trailing from the bristles, her crazy husband's hair, and she started towards me. I jumped up, snatched the door open, and plunged clattering down the stairs, the stair rail squeaking through my gripping hand.

On the first of September, the radio told us that Hitler had invaded Poland, whose courageous but useless cavalry melted before the German Blitzkrieg. Two days later, Great Britain and France declared war on Germany. It had begun, this new war, this Second World War.

By the Labor Day weekend that signaled the beginning of school, I had squeezed the last drops of adventure and danger out of that summer's game of single-handedly defending Pearl Street and, by extension, the world from Nazi invasion. As a sort of farewell tour, I was mopping up the last of the Storm Troopers (I had finally learned their real name) at the end of our back alley, where I had not been since the day I fled down Mrs McGivney's stairs to avoid the touch of that repulsive hair brush, the squeaking handrail rubbing the skin off the web between my thumb and forefinger and leaving a scab that took forever to heal because I kept popping it open by spreading my hand too widely: a child's curious fascination with pain.

Wounded though I was in both legs, one shoulder, and in the web between my thumb and first finger, I managed to crawl from the shelter of one stable doorway to the next, making the sound of ricocheting bullets by following a guttural *krookh* with a fading *cheeooo* through my teeth, as a Nazi machine gun kicked up the gravel at my feet and the tap-tap-tap sound of a coin against glass that...*what?* I almost glanced up, but I converted the glance into a frowning examination of the space around me, searching for snipers, because I didn't want her to know that I had heard her summons. Satisfied that there were no Nazi snipers on the rooftops, I made an intense mime of drawing a map on the ground. Again she tapped her three urgent taps, and I could imagine her looking down on me. I hunched more tightly over my map. She tapped again, but this time there were only two clicks, then she stopped short. That missing click told me she suddenly realized that I could hear her, and I was ignoring her on purpose. I kept my head down, knowing that if I looked up I would see her there, her eyes full of sadness and recrimination.

Miserable, and angry for being made to feel miserable, I pretended to see an enemy soldier down the alley. I shot at him with my finger then ran off in pursuit until I was out of Mrs McGivney's sight.

For a long while, I kept out of the back alley that had been the principal arena for my story games. A couple of times over the following year I caught a glimpse of Mrs McGivney scuttling across to Mr Kane's late in the evening, but I always avoided her. I never saw her hero husband again.

I am now considerably older than Mrs McGivney was when I first responded to the rap of her nickel against the window. For many years I have lived as far away in space, time and culture from Pearl Street as one can get this side of death. And yet, on those nights when the black butterflies of remorse flutter through a sleepless *nuit blanche*, I still sometimes hear that broken-off summons, those two clicks followed by a recriminating silence; and my throat tightens with shame as I remember the lonely old woman who I didn't have time for because I was too busy trying to save myself.

Night Thoughts

Infinity gave me a lot of trouble. So did Time. And God.

I could define these words, but I didn't really possess them, not in the way I possessed 'house' or 'hate' or 'red'. "Infinity has neither beginning nor end." I understood that in the sense that I knew what each of the words meant, but it was one of those slippery concepts that I could grasp, but not hold, and the harder I grasped, the quicker they would fly away...like trying to pick up a greased marble with chopsticks.

Late at night I would struggle with these awkward abstractions until I ended in a kind of intellectual vertigo that made me hug my pillow for comfort.

Take Time, for instance. I envisioned 'Now' as a bright instant of time racing forward from the Future into the Past, but the Past never grew longer by accumulating the constant flow of moments Now deposited into it, nor did the Future get any shorter for all the bits of Now that Time tore from it, because both Past and Future were infinite, and one cannot imagine infinity plus a bit, or minus a bit. Even that fleeting spark of Now is elusive, because as you pronounced the N, the W is still in the Future, and when you get to the W, the N is already in the Past, never to be seen again.[22]

In the end, I found respite from doubt and confusion by adding Infinity and Time and God to an ever-growing list of notions that were beyond my comprehension. I comforted myself with the assumption that I might come to understand them some day or, if not, that I would learn to accept that there were three categories of things out there: those I understood, those I would someday understand, and those I would never fully understand.[23]

. . . .

I was born in 1930 when Hoover was president and Prohibition was still in force, so all the years of my life had been nineteen-thirty-something. But one afternoon as I was walking home from school I saw the date 1940 on a billboard advertising forthcoming models of Ford cars. I stopped and frowned at the number with a sense of foreboding. That 40 seemed ominous, a number that not only looked strange, but felt awkward in your mouth when you said it. *Fooorrrtee.* No, no, that was all wrong. Years ought to be 1935 or 1939 because that 3 was a nice round, safe, smooth, stable number. Who knew what harm this brash, unreliable 4 would bring, with its sharply protruding elbow and its precarious one-legged stance?

My misgivings about this new decade were confirmed when, by the end of 1939, Germany and the Soviet Union had divided Poland between them, and the Russians had gobbled up Estonia, Latvia and Lithuania. Then Stalin attacked Finland, whose small but fierce army fought the vast Russian war machine to a standstill through the winter. The courage and daring of the Finns was in stark contrast to the inactivity on Germany's western front, where England dithered and France cowered behind the Maginot Line, frozen with incertitude, wincing at phantoms. Mr Kane said that Hitler could have been stopped back in March of 1938, when he marched into Austria. At that time, his army had consisted of fifty-four divisions as against the thirty-plus divisions of Czechoslovakia, France's fifty-five divisions, and Poland's thirty. Even discounting chronically unprepared Britain, Hitler would have been outnumbered by more than two to one, and both the tactics and the machinery of his later vaunted Blitzkrieg were so untested, so unreliable that when he marched into Austria to receive the acclamation of the people, more than seventy percent of his mechanized infantry broke down and were obliged to continue to Vienna on foot. But by the winter of 1940, the Czechs and Poles were out of the game, and Germany was ready for war, both in materiel and morale, while the English lacked the first, and the French the latter.

Despite Mr Kane's gloomy predictions, there was reason to hope that we might not be swept up into a terrible European war after all. During Roosevelt's campaign against Wendell Willkie, when the only real issue was that FDR was running for a third term against all precedent and tradition, he had assured us, "Your boys are not going to be sent into any foreign wars." I can still hear the drawled, syllable-and-a-half Groton pronunciation of 'your' and 'war', an accent America had come to trust as the sound of truth.

But Mr Kane believed it was our duty to get involved in the European war as soon as possible because of the things the Nazis were doing, not only to Jews, but to Gypsies, Communists, the mentally deficient, and homosexuals. He knew about the Warsaw ghettoes because, hunched over his receiver late one night, he had intercepted a desperate Morse code message from a courageous short-wave enthusiast in Warsaw, a man who used what may have been his last moments to broadcast.

During the Christmas vacation that began in the last of the comfortable 1930s and ended in the first of the ominous-sounding 1940s, my mother ragged and pestered the principal of Our Lady of Angels school into letting me transfer in mid-year, then she took me out of P.S. 5 where I was making low grades and always getting into trouble. Mother, who had a gift for explaining away every fault or flaw in her children, put it another way: she said she wanted to send me to a Catholic school where my energies, abilities and talents had a better chance of being recognized. It is true that more was expected of us at Our Lady of Angels, and its greater discipline produced an atmosphere more conducive to learning. Those stunningly plain, no-nonsense nuns nurtured their brighter students while they dealt efficiently with the mediocre and gently with the backward, but they did not tolerate those who disrupted the calm of the classroom, neither the recalcitrant dummies nor the precocious show-offs. Those tough old birds would swoop down on the wings of their starched wimples and snatch a trouble-maker around with dexterity and style that was a wonder to watch, and if the boy fought back or continued his disruptive ways, they would simply kick him out of school and let the public system deal with him.

Our Lady of Angels was seventeen blocks up the Lexington Avenue hill, steep blocks on sleepy mornings, and long cold windy blocks in winter, when I walked against the prevailing westerly winds that seemed to gain momentum as they swept downhill towards the river. Parochial school started half an hour earlier than public school and continued for half an hour longer in the afternoon (although we got Holy Days of Obligation off), and we had at least twice as much homework, but that didn't trouble me much. I could dash off the repetitive arithmetic problems or list the principal export products of the Belgian Congo or diagram compound sentences between my radio-listening hour and supper, and I would do the reading assignments at night, after Mother and Anne-Marie were asleep and before I began the nightly reading, mostly history and novels, that had become habitual to me, and remains so to this day. I enjoyed displaying my quickness at the blackboard in Math class, and I soon discovered that my knowledge of history was broader than that of the diligent, slightly baffled nun who taught the subject and who reacted to my occasional corrections or amplifications by lowering my grade on the basis of 'attitude in class'.

There were two categories of tedium-stunned students in every classroom: the slow kids who had so completely lost their grip on things that the teacher's instructions were meaningless clumps of sound, and the quick kids who got the idea somewhere in the middle of the teacher's first sentence, and whose minds were beaten into a pulpy stupor by the endless repetitions and illustrations necessary to bring the first glimmers of comprehension to the rest of the class. Early on, I learned to sit with my eyes on the teacher, my face set in an expression of rapt attention, while my mind was light-years away, totally engrossed in some internal game. I felt safe from being called on because kids who didn't know the answers seldom looked the teacher in the eye, fearing that to do so was to invite undesirable attention. Instead, they would frown into their textbooks and pretend to be thinking so hard that it would be a pity to disturb them with questions. But teachers were on to this ploy (probably having used it themselves when they were kids) so the safest way to avoid being called on was to appear to know the answer and to be eager to produce it aloud. But occasionally I got caught out.

One afternoon I was sitting at the back of a social studies class taught by a nun who had kept me late one day to tell me that she enjoyed the essays I wrote for her, and to say that she was sorry I was sometimes bored in her class, but she had to make sure the average student understood the work. My eyes were locked on this teacher's with the eager expression of a boy who knows the answer and is inwardly squirming for a chance to demonstrate his cleverness, while, in fact, my mind was off in some distant galaxy...and I'll be damned if she didn't call on *me!*

I stood beside my desk as we were required to do when our names were called, and after a moment of trying to remember what she had been rattling on about, and not coming up with anything, I said in an earnest voice tinged with wonder, "I don't know the answer, sister. I thought I did, but I don't. I honestly don't. It was right on the tip of my tongue, but..." and kids around me grinned with pleasure at watching me string the nun along. I continued with my protestations of baffled regret until the sister interrupted me with, "All right, Luke. You can sit down." But I wouldn't be thwarted in my need to explain the astonishing phenomenon of being unable to produce an answer that I knew perfectly well, but for some reason just couldn't bring up from the depths of my—"All *right*, Luke. That will do!" My eyes filled with injury I slowly sat down, muttering plaintively, "I can't understand it. I knew it just a minute ago, but somehow it's—"

"Be quiet, Luke!"

"Yes, sister. It's just that I can't—"

"I don't want to hear another word from you!"

"Whatever you say, sister."

"Shut up!"

"Yes, sister." (This last muttered softly, so as to sneak in the 'last touch'.)

By this time, the class was sputtering with pent-up laughter, and for the rest of the hour the teacher's wounded eyes accused me of being a traitor in her eternal battle against mediocrity, but such occasional demonstrations of caste solidarity kept me from being thought of as a lick-spittle apple-polisher. Instead, the kids just thought I was a nut.

But playing to the gallery didn't keep me in the good graces of the bullies. I still had to go to Fistcity from time to time.

. . . .

Unlike P.S. 5, I wasn't the only smart kid at Our Lady of Angels. There was a handful of bright, hard-working Jewish kids whose families paid to get them better educations than were available in the public schools. I envied those Jewish kids because when we had to take catechism they could sit in the library and do their homework, or just read books. And not only did they get out of school on Holy Days of Obligation without the morning-ruining burden of having to go to mass, but they didn't have to come to school on their own holidays, and during Lent they weren't obliged to make the stations of the cross twice each school day. It wasn't fair! Of course, these privileges had to be considered in light of the fact that they were sure to go to hell in the end. But even granting this harsh final reckoning, I wasn't at all sure they had the worst of the bargain, particularly as we Catholic kids were repeatedly assured that no matter how many rosaries we said, how fervently we made the stations of the cross or how many delicious things we gave up for Lent, there was always the risk of sudden death. Street wisdom held that being run over by a truck was as common an end for sinful kids as it was for those who didn't change their underwear regularly, and if death befell us before we had expunged our mortal sins, we'd go rocketing down to hell along with the Jewish kids, clear shorts or not. This, at least, was my understanding of the matter, one that was shared by the majority of kids who went to Our Lady of Angels school.

I brought this matter up during a catechism class given by my old antagonist, the intense young priest with pink-rimmed eyes, terminal acne, and little patience with those who asked awkward questions. I asked how it could be that failure to obey any of the ten commandments would put your soul in danger of an eternity in hell. Surely some of these rules were more important than others, and some mortal sins were more...ah...mortal than others. It just couldn't be as bad to steal something or to bear false witness as it was to kill someone. Would you really be shot straight down to hell for having coveted something that belonged to your neighbor? Come on! And how did adultery, which was defined as sexual concourse of a married person with someone who was not his or her spouse, somehow get expanded to include just about every fleshly act, word or thought? Instead of answering this last question, the priest condemned the smutty and titillating practice of looking up dirty words in dictionaries and encyclopedias. (So even the *word* adultery was a dirty thing? And this priest found looking up such things 'titillating', did he?) On the wall over the priest's head was a hand-tinted photograph of the new pope, Pius XII. I could see that the pope was trying to smile benevolently, but his ascetic features and thin lips were not designed for smiling, and the eyes behind those round metal-framed glasses had an icy piscine glaze. That frozen smile and those pink rouged cheeks were somehow more forbidding than a righteous scowl would have been.

After our earlier encounters, the young priest avoided the nuisance of my questions by ignoring my raised hand, so I passed the time in catechism class by repeating some word the priest had said over and over in my mind until the meaning was ground out of it and it became just a pulp of sound, or by working out the total number of tiles in the ceiling by counting the ones down and the ones across, multiplying them in my mind, then estimating the tiles lost when a supply cupboard had been built in the corner, and subtracting these from...

"...maybe young LaPointe thinks he can find the answer written on the ceiling," the priest said in his most scathing tone. "Or is he looking to heaven for guidance?" Some of the girls obligingly giggled.

My mind scrabbled for a fragment of what the priest had been saying before I drifted off...but I drew a blank, so I just grabbed the first thing that came to mind. "I was thinking over what you said about transubstantiation, Father."

"I wasn't talking about transubstantiation."

"Ah-h...yes. That's true, but I'm still thinking about it from back when you explained it to us the other day."

"...And?" His tone was cautious, like a man poking a stick at a snake.

"Well...I don't have any problem accepting that the wine and the wafer are the body and blood of Christ—"

"That's good of you."

"But it's still a wafer. Right?"

He frowned and his eyes narrowed. "What do you mean, '...it's still a wafer'?"

"I mean, even though the communion wafer has become the body of Christ, it's still bread, right?"

"Wrong. Once consecrated, the Eucharist is the body of Christ."

"Yes, I know. I accept that on faith. But it's still bread, right? I mean, it looks like bread and tastes like bread, so it's still—"

"No, no. The communion bread becomes the very body of Christ."

"I'm not contradicting you, Father. What you say is all right with me. I know that the wafer is a symbol of—"

"Not a symbol! That's where you're wrong. It's not a symbol. It is the actual body of Christ! Can't you get that through your head?"

"I realize that we accept the host as the body of—"

"It's not a matter of what we *accept*. The bread *is* the body of Christ! Therein lies the miracle! Why can't you understand that?"

"I *do* understand, Father, but—"

"Get out."

"Father?"

"Leave the room. Go stand in the hall."

I collected my books and went to the door, muttering.

"What was that you said?" the priest demanded.

"Nothing."

"Don't give me that. You said something."

"I said, 'But it's still bread.'"

"Out! Out! Out!"

I went into the empty hallway and nursed my sense of injustice. I hadn't been trying to bait or annoy the priest, and I had no intellectual antagonism to the idea of transubstantiation. I accepted the miracle in all its poetic and symbolic significance. I was only insisting that we all keep a little grip on reality here. It was, after all, a bread wafer, and I refused to pretend either that I was stupid or that I had been conned.

Years later, when I read about the recanting Galileo leaving the chamber of the Inquisition muttering '...*eppur si muove*', I had to smile at the comic strip parody acted out between a rattled young priest and a wiseassed kid.

I decided not to seek any further clarification of theological quandaries. Instead, I gnawed on these doubts late at night. The first of these conundrums was the one that every child has pondered at one time or another: how can God be benevolent and all-powerful, and yet there be so much pain and injustice in the world? I dismissed the glib answer the catechism priest had offered: that God allowed evil and injustice to exist in order to test our faith. If God is omniscient, He knows in advance which of us will pass the test and which will fail, so of what use is the test? It's not as though we had a chance to improve on our destiny. No, it would not be benevolent of God to test us, when He knew what the outcome of that test would be; it would be cruel and pointless.

Then, late one stormy night, I came up with a way to slip between the horns of the dilemma that God is benevolent and omnipotent yet the world is full of suffering, evil and injustice. I could account for this seeming contradiction by assuming that God was indeed benevolent and omnipotent, but also...insane.

That was too spooky to dwell on, so I let this dilemma fall into the growing category of things that were beyond my comprehension, like my newly discovered ability to lift certain sounds out of the background stew of sounds that is 'silence' in a big city, then let them drop back in. From the mantelpiece above the blocked-up fireplace our cheap alarm clock ticked with a loose, scratchy sound that had long ago been enfolded into the ambience of our apartment. As long as my attention was absorbed by what I was reading or thinking about, I was unaware of the ticking, but if something broke my concentration, the sound of that clock would return to my ear, only to be enveloped again by the sounds of silence when my attention drifted away from it. Once

I discovered this phenomenon, I would play with it, pulling the sound of the clock out of the background 'silence', then letting it fall back in.

I kept the clock on the mantel rather than on my bedside table so that I would have to get out of my warm bed and stagger across the room to kill the nerve-shredding racket of its alarm. By then I was sufficiently awake to get dressed and go on my paper route. In winter I had to get up half an hour earlier and go to the basement to shake down and feed the monstrous old boiler, carrying half-shovelfuls of coal back and forth from bunker to furnace. After the boiler was stoked, I got the bottle of milk out of the orange crate nailed to the side of the back window and set it on the kitchen table to warm up a little while I was in the bathroom. The frozen milk would have expanded, lifting a column of 'ice cream' that wore a flat bottle-top hat. I would splash water into my face and brush my teeth with Dr. Lyon's Tooth Powder, which always made the milk taste funny. When we ran out of Dr. Lyon's, we would sprinkle a little baking soda and salt into our palms and brush our teeth with that. Baking soda also made the milk taste funny. I sat at the kitchen table, numbly eating the breakfast my loyal mother had made for me, either hot oatmeal or one of her dense pancakes made with powdered eggs. Then I would put on my jacket, a knitted toque that I could pull down over my ears, a scarf and my finger-nipping galoshes, and I would step out into the dark of the street and set off on the long up-hill trudge to the newspaper broker's basement den where, together with a dozen other bleary-eyed newsies, I folded my papers and put them into my shoulder bag. Then I would slog around my route, into strange-smelling apartment houses, up stairs and down, ending up back at my house to drop off my bag and begin the long walk up the Lexington Avenue hill to be at school by the eight-thirty bell.

After each snowfall, car wheels churned the sooty slush into grooves and crests which froze over night into sharp peaks and ankle-twisting channels that I would stumble over as I crossed the street carrying my heavy canvas paper-bag, my head down against the wind that stung tears out of my eyes. I was clumsy in galoshes that were always too big in the hope that we could make them last two seasons, but they never did because the sharp peaks of frozen sludge cut them until they leaked, so we would have to buy another pair...another of those grand plans that have only one flaw: they don't work. By the time I finished my round, cars would have mashed the sludge into new shapes, which would freeze with the next night's cold so I could slip and trip over a new arctic gutterscape the next morning, and swear bitterly as I gathered up my scattered papers.

I had been lucky to get a paper route when I was still a couple of years under the legal age. The newspaper broker couldn't find anyone who wanted the route because it was in the slums where the few people who could afford newspapers were thinly spread, which meant there was a lot of walking between deliveries. Also, it was often hard to make the slum customers pay up at the end of the week. But I was willing to take it on because we needed the extra income. After 1939, when war in Europe brought work to factories and farms producing the war materiel and food we supplied to England, the upturn in our economy had its inevitable inflationary effect on prices, so the purchasing power of our weekly seven dollars and twenty-seven cents diminished.

· · · · · · · · · ·

I was nine years old when I experienced one of those terrible moments that haunt your nightmares for the rest of your life. Somewhere along the twenty-two blocks between the FSCC warehouse and home, I lost the 'two children' card that gave us access to surplus food, and although I walked back and forth over my trail, my eyes scything the sidewalk from edge to edge until it was too dark to see, I couldn't find it. It took three weeks for the welfare officials to accept that we weren't trying to gyp the system and to issue us a new card...three pretty thin weeks. From then on, I always carried the card in the foot of my sock, and it always smelled of tennis shoe.

The loss of that Federal Surplus Commodities Corporation card led to my running away from home. It wasn't until the next morning that I got up the courage to confess that I had lost it, and my mother, already at her wits' end because both Anne-Marie and I had needed shoes in the same month, reacted with panic and accusation. How were we to get through the month? What in Christ's name had I been daydreaming about *this* time? She thought she'd brought me up with a little sense of responsibility, for God's sake!

Having already passed a night chastening myself for my stupidity,

I reacted to her hysteria with hysteria of my own. Give a guy a break! If I'm so damned irresponsible, why don't you drag the wagon down there and pick up the crap yourself?

She gave me a slap, and I stormed out of the house.

But I soon came back, shame-faced. I found my sister sitting out on the hall stairs, playing intensely with her paper dolls. She looked up at me, silently begging me to make peace with our mother.

I found Mother crying in that silent, son-lacerating way of hers. She asked me how she was going to feed us children for the next week. I put my arm around her and muttered something about how we'd find a way, just...but she shook my arm off.

So I stormed out again! This time slamming the door. My sister clutched at my leg as I passed, but I pulled away and rushed down the stoop and across the street. I turned towards the river, furiously driving my heels onto the pavement as my vision swam with self-pity. I was determined to run away and this time never come back. Never. Muttering to myself, gnawing on my grievance, I passed through the freight yards and followed the tracks north, then I climbed over the barriers and started to cross over to Rensselaer on a dangerous but seldom-used single-track railroad bridge. About halfway across I stopped and looked back to see how far I had come, and I saw two men back on the Albany side waving their arms and shouting at me. I ignored them and continued on, assuring my balance by keeping one hand in contact with the rough wooden railing along the downstream side, as I carefully stepped on the center of each creosoted tie, not letting my eyes focus through the gaps down to the roiling surface of the Hudson far below. What if I fell into the river and drowned? That would show her! I was sick of it! Sick and tired of being responsible for everything! Was it my fault she married a bum? I thought I felt an approaching train vibrating the girders underfoot, and I turned to look behind me. But no train came.

I got across the bridge and picked my way through the Rensselaer freight yards, then I cut through town and headed east. I was in open country with fields and a few scrawny cows when the first plump raindrops splatted dark on the dusty road. Fine! Now I'll get pneumonia and die! Like Miss Cox. That would teach her.

I was soaked through and rain was running down my collar by the time I reached a scattering of houses at a crossroads called Snyders Corners, where I cowered in a bus shelter improvised from rusty advertising signs. I shivered as diagonal rods of rain drilled on the Beechnut Tobacco sign that served as a roof. After a long time spent conjuring up vindictive scenarios in which I was ill or lost and Mother was suffering remorse for having treated me so badly, I became aware that the sound of rain on the roof had stopped and the wind had fallen to a sigh. It was twilight, and dense banks of sodden, low-hanging clouds made it dark enough for the people of Snyders Corners to light their kerosene lamps. And it was at this moment, in this unlikely place, and for no reason I can account for, that I experienced what I suppose people mean when they talk about the mystic. It had something to do with the sudden silence after the long, isolating, narcotizing din of rain on sheet metal, and something to do with the darkening sky so close overhead, and with the golden light of kerosene lamps glowing in the windows of those simple clapboard houses. I suddenly felt that I was otherwise and elsewhere...someone who was not quite me, experiencing the moment from somewhere that was not quite here, a witness more than a participant in an epiphanous revelation, and I knew...knew with a certainty beyond the rational...that I was destined to be a drifter. I sat in that bus shelter, shivering, alone, anonymous, no longer connected to anything, unable to hurt or disappoint anyone. And it felt so good!

Adrift. A drifter. Not responsible for anything or anyone. I knew that someday I would leave home, and once I got away I would never, never...

But for now, I decided to go back. I could afford to be magnanimous now that I knew I would someday hit the road and be free. I hadn't forgiven my mother for pushing me away, but I didn't want to cause her further anguish. And my sister was probably worried about me. And anyway...I was hungry.

A moonless night had fallen by the time I threaded my way through Rensselaer's deserted freight yard. Crossing the railroad bridge at night as the Hudson seethed and purled below was a slower and more daunting business than crossing it by daylight. To assure my balance in the disorientating dark, I kept my hand on the weathered, splintery wooden railing and I felt for the center of each railroad tie with my foot before putting my weight on it. About a quarter of the way across, I felt a slight quiver underfoot. I looked back and saw the distant headlight of a freight train piercing the river mist as it made a slow, creaking turn towards the bridge. I froze.

I'd better go back before—no, no, I'll rush forward and—no, wait, maybe I'd better...Too late!

The engine was already on the bridge, its sides nearly scraping the wooden railings. I hurried on, trying to out-run it, but my foot slipped off the rain-slick ties and my leg went up to the knee into the gap between, barking my shin. The bridge began to vibrate. With a yelp of panic I yanked my leg back out, giving my shin a second painful scrape. A quick glance back at the train. The cone of light was so bright that when I held up my hand to shield my eyes I could see finger bones, like an X ray. I waved my arms and shouted, but the roar and hiss of the engine, the squeal of the wheels and the groaning of the bridge absorbed my voice. No whistle...the engineer hadn't seen me. The bridge throbbed and shuddered. My heart pounding, I clambered over the railing and stood out on the ends of the ties, clinging to the handrail, my butt out over the river, and I turned my face away as the metal-screeching, steam-hissing engine passed inches from my knuckles. My eyes were squeezed shut but the powerful light filled my head with bright orange. Gasping for breath, I gripped the railing with all my might as the chaos of noise, vibration and hot metal passed so close that it stirred my hair. I knew that I was clinging to the railing too hard, using up my strength. I should ease my grip a little...but I couldn't! I was afraid that the slightest relaxation would drop me into the river. After an eternal five seconds of clamor-roar-squeal-clash in my face and panic screaming within my head, the engine passed, and the freight cars rattled and creaked close to my fingers, which continued to clutch so hard that the fingertips were splayed flat. When the freight cars finally passed I opened my eyes to see the little red light on the caboose receding into a swirl of steam and smoke. My knees buckled with relief—and that sent a fresh tingle of fright into my testicles. I climbed back over the railing very carefully, because it would be just my rotten luck to slip and fall into the river *after* the train passed!

For a long time I sat on the end of a tie, completely drained, my arms wrapped around a tacky creosote spar, my legs dangling over the abyss.

It was late when I eased open the door of our apartment and slipped in. My sister was already in bed, and my mother was sitting in the kitchen over a cold cup of coffee. I stood in the kitchen door; she lifted her head and looked at me with battered eyes.

"I found a place out of the rain," I said.

She reached out and felt my corduroy knickers. "You're wet to the bone. You're going to have a fever for sure. You better take a hot bath. I'll heat up some soup."

When I undressed, my socks stuck to the congealing gouges on my shin, making me flinch and snort. I said only that I'd fallen down, and without further question Mother gently cleaned the wounds then dabbed them with iodine, which stung and made me suck air through my teeth.

I soaked in the tub with my knees up to keep my shins dry. She sat on the toilet lid and looked down on me sadly. "You're your father's son, all right. Nine years old, and you've already run away from me twice."

"*Twice?*"

"The first time you were just three. You took your brand new red trike with you and left it somewhere. We never found it."

"Oh...yes. I forgot about that. But I didn't run away this time."

Her eyes widened. "What do you mean?"

She needed to believe I hadn't deserted her, as my father had. "Jeez, you didn't think I'd run out on you, did you? I wouldn't do that. Never. Oh, sure, I was mad, but I only wanted to get away and think things out. But then it started to rain, and I had to stay in this bus place until the rain stopped, and by then it was dark, so I...But I always meant to come back."

"You'd never run out on me? Is that the truth, Jean-Luc? Cross your heart?"

"And hope to die, Mom."

. . . .

During the '30s and '40s, most urban Americans went to the movies at least once a week, even though this meant an outlay of from twenty-five to fifty cents for adults (not counting popcorn or candy) and between a dime and fifteen cents for children. With only a few exceptions, my paper route provided the two dimes required for Anne-Marie and me to attend the weekly triple-feature kids' matinee offered by the Grand Theater on the corner of North Pearl Street and Clinton Avenue where the atmosphere tightened with joyful anticipation as the theater filled with noisy, restive kids laughing, whistling through their fingers, calling across aisles to one another, throwing paper wads, clattering their chair seats. Those rich enough to buy candy made much show of noisily unwrapping bars and opening popcorn boxes, while near-nubile girls found it necessary to go up the aisle from their front-row seats, walking quickly, always in twos, their heads down to show how desperately they hoped they weren't being *noticed*, then returning to their seats, where they clutched one another and rolled their eyes and twisted with embarrassment at the thought that *you-know-who* might have been looking at them...but soon finding another urgent reason to go out to the lobby, even if it did involve running the distressing gauntlet of gawking *boys*...who in fact never paid the slightest attention to them.

Just as the chaos and confusion reached a frenetic pitch, the theater would darken, and the kids would cheer to the rising notes of a steam-organ version of 'The Merry-Go-Round Broke Down' that introduced the first of two or three cartoons. A final scuttling for seats, and the kids' triple-feature was on. This usually involved a C-grade western by Monogram or Republic, with such stalwarts as Hoot Gibson, Whip Wilson, Lash LaRue, Ken Maynard, or the Three Mesquiteers, a trio of cowboys who rode out of the mesquite-covered prairie to help the weak and foil the bad guys. One of these Mesquiteers was the rangy young John Wayne, who had a clumsy, faintly effeminate walk that he would later convert into the ursine burlesque of feline grace that became a trademark. The western was followed either by a scary film about vampires or werewolves or mummies, or a B detective film featuring The Saint, or Boston Blackie, or Charlie Chan (with his wise-cracking all-American number-one son), then there would be a knock-about comedy, the kids' favorite being a new comic team that appeared a couple of years before the war: Abbott and Costello. Interspersed among the features were a *March of Time*, a weekly newsreel and an adventure serial each episode of which ended with the hero locked in a room with a lit stick of dynamite, or being crushed as a mine caved in or clinging by his fingernails to the rim of a cliff above a raging river (whence the term 'cliff-hanger'), then we'd have a travelogue narrated by some fruity-voiced man and shot in a cheap color stock that was mostly brown and blue, and then at least two comic shorts like *Behind the Eightball* or the Ritz Brothers or Laurel and Hardy (the most under-rated comics of the sound era, just as the Marx Brothers are the most over-rated).[24] After the Saturday Special's six-hour assault on your senses, you would stagger, blinking, out into the drab, insipid real world (still sinfully sunlit in summer), your eyes blurry, your ears buzzing, your knees stiff, your butt numb, but your soul effervescent with adventure and your spirit strengthened by personal experiences of peril and courage.

My sister and I saw movies of a very different sort on the first and third Thursdays of each month when our mother brought us to Dish Night at the Paramount Theater, a hole-in-the-wall neighborhood movie house that smelled of dust and bug spray. The management tried to bolster receipts on these slow nights by offering dishes at the door and a double feature: a family comedy followed by what my mother called 'drama films', in which broad-shouldered heroines wearing thick lipstick drew cigarette smoke far down into their lungs then exhaled it through mouth and nose simultaneously as they slogged their way through an hour and a half of histrionic athletics, standing with their hands on their hips and snapping sassy lines to bland, baffled men. Pencil-thin eyebrows arched, nostrils flaring, lips compressed, eyes flashing, they indulged in towering rages, or wept torrents, or bravely fought back their tears...and sometimes all three within ten minutes. Characterized by high-contrast 'hatchet' lighting and expressionistic camera angles, these drama films relied heavily on background music so volcanic that half of the string section risked getting violin elbow in their efforts to support the performances of Bette Davis, Barbara Stanwyck, Joan Crawford or the relative newcomer, Susan Hayward, all of whom viewed their craft as an essentially quantitative affair and sought to satisfy their emotionally undernourished fans by loading each gesture, each glance, each word with tons and tons of 'acting'.[25]

These high-calorie feasts of passion left a boy of ten feeling that love was a dark and dangerous business.

Bette Davis and Joan Crawford were my mother's favorite actresses, and she identified with the roles they played: strong women done in by weak and duplicitous men but standing against the world. Photographs of Mother when she was a Charleston champion reveal that she looked something like Joan Crawford, who, towards the end of the silent era, had played Charleston-mad I-don't-care girls.

With the first blush of puberty, girls who had been happy enough with the raucous chaos of a kids' matinee suddenly developed, as a kind of secondary sexual trait, a taste for the bathetic involutions of drama films and the emotional gymnastics of the actresses who played in them, while boys of the same age displayed a healthy shallowness of spirit and aesthetic judgment that made them prefer westerns, gangster films, historical adventures (which we called sword-fighting movies) and, after 1942, war films in which actors like John Wayne, having managed to stay out of the real war, shot, bombed and bayoneted two or three thousand Nazi or Nip extras per film.

Although my mother loved her drama films and my sister was fascinated by the costumes, it was the lure of a door prize of free dishes that justified our indulgence. We had enough dishes for our needs, but nothing matched, and it was Mother's plan to collect a service for four, just in case we had a guest to dinner, though we couldn't imagine who this might be. The acquisition of these dishes helped to salve her conscience about spending money on movies once every two weeks. She estimated it would take two and a half years to collect the full set, but it didn't work out that way because sometimes they gave dishes to kids and other times only to those who had adult tickets, and they never seemed to have the bigger pieces, like dinner plates or serving dishes, so we ended up with three soup bowls and half a dozen salad plates. I found one of those milky green glass soup bowls among Mother's things when she died more than forty years later and three thousand miles from Pearl Street.

On Dish Thursdays, Anne-Marie and I had to finish our homework early while Mother made a quick supper of potato soup and bean sandwiches, then the three of us would walk up Clinton Avenue to the theater where, in addition to the films, the free dishes, and the usual bouquet of newsreels and short subjects, there would be either Screeno (a projected version of bingo, but we never won the free passes that were the prizes) or an amateur talent show emcee'd by the theater manager, who would dress up in a bright red jacket and crack jokes that we'd all heard on Jack Benny or Bob Hope earlier that week. Mother used to fantasize that one of these days Anne-Marie would dance in that talent show, and she'd bring the house down with applause, and the next thing you know, talent scouts from Paramount studios—it *was* a Paramount Theater, after all, wasn't it?—would come knocking at our door, and there she'd be! Our ship! Standing at the dock!

This semi-monthly outing cost us a quarter for Mother's ticket and ten cents for each of us kids. Forty-five cents was a significant chunk of our budget, so we never bought candy or popcorn, but if the movies had been particularly long and Anne-Marie was sleepy when we got out at nearly midnight, or if it was snowing or raining, we sometimes spent an extra fifteen cents for the three of us to ride the trolley back down the Clinton Avenue hill, and get off just after the trolley's metal-screeching turn at Pearl Street. A total of sixty cents spent in just one night! Without my paper route, that extravagance would have been unthinkable.

During our long, late-night walks home from the Paramount Theater with Anne-Marie plodding along between Mother and me, half-asleep on her feet, I could usually get Mother to tell stories about her youth in Fort Anne, where her energy and competitive spirit brought her such success at boys' games and sports that she was known to the tish-tish-ing townswomen as 'that LaPointe girl', a reckless hoyden who could out-run, out-climb, out-shout and out-brag any boy in the village. I loved hearing about the outrageous pranks her gang used to play on Halloween: the live snake she once tossed into a passing roadster full of college boys up from Albany, who scrambled out doors and windows before the car came to a full stop in a ditch; how, late one night, one of her 'gang' surreptitiously moved an abusive drunk's privy back a yard, so that its hole was in front of its door; the shovelful of fresh horse manure they put on an old grouch's front porch, then covered it with newspaper which they lit before knocking on his door and running away, and when he came out, he automatically tried to stamp the fire out only to discover...God *damn* those kids!

Inquisitive and quick-minded, Mother had led her class in the annual statewide Regent Examinations, and her father talked of her becoming the first of his family to earn that sure passport to success and economic security, a high school diploma. But during the summer of her sixteenth year she suddenly became aware of boys as boys, and outlandish clothes became a vital form of self-expression. She tried lipstick for the first time and learned to strum a banjo/ukulele at evening sing-alongs down on the platform of her father's train station, where the town's young people gathered to watch the late train pass on its way from Montreal to New York City, and to sing the popular tunes that adults despised for both their listless 'crooning' and their dangerous messages of saucy independence. To her surprise and pleasure, she discovered that the fashion ideal had shifted from the ample, pigeon-breasted Gibson Girl to her own trim tomboy figure which, together with her zest for life, constituted ideal attributes for a girl of the Charleston era. She exchanged her role as a competitor and a buddy of the town's boys for the unsure but exciting role of a desirable hellion with stockings rolled down to below the knee. Her desire to dive into the foaming currents of life caused her to quit school, leave her home town and take a job in a textile factory in Hudson Falls, where she spent most of her wages on the flimsy fashions she could wear to such advantage as she ran with a fun-hungry gang in roadsters with rumble seats, and entered dance marathons to the challenge-and-response patterns of ragtime, or danced romantic 'slows' to the suggestive croon of Russ Colombo or the nasal mewl of Rudy Vallee, both of whom would be eclipsed in her affections when sound came to the movies and millions of American women fell under the spell of Maurice Chevalier's irresistibly pendulous lower lip. This was Mother's golden age, her heyday. She got into a shouting match with a suggestive foreman at the cotton mill (that French-'n'-Indian temper of hers), so she quit to become a waitress in a roadhouse frequented by hooch-runners bringing whiskey down from Canada. She also met laughing, carefree college boys who were working through their summer vacations and spending most of their nights singing, strumming their banjos and ukuleles, and drinking hooch from pocket flasks. Life was bright and gay and good, and she was at the very center of it.

Then, at the age of twenty, she met and instantly fell in love with my father, who came from that sophisticated metropolis, Philadelphia, and who had an alluring whiff of the bad and the dangerous about him because he worked with rum-runners, played cards with criminals, and possessed the con man's facile charm. He had the thick, slicked-down hair and the arch profile of a model for Troy shirt collars, and he fulfilled those twin lofty ideals of the 'Twenties Woman: he was a good dresser and a great dancer. Most wonderful of all, this exciting paragon preferred her to all the other girls. He thought she was special!

They married, but after two days of honeymoon, he met some men who had a good thing going in Florida seaside property and could use a slick talker as a front man, so he left, explaining that he'd only be away for a week at most. A week passed, then two, then a month. And suddenly he dropped out of sight, and she had to return to her people and seek work locally.

But she couldn't believe she'd been abandoned. There must be some mistake. She made up stories about what might have happened to prevent his return. Several months passed and she was noticeably pregnant before she could accept that she had been deserted. She plunged into bitterness, hurt and disappointment. Didn't anyone love and want her? Not even her father, who had sent her away to live with her aunts after her mother died? It must be her fault in some way. What was wrong with her? It was in this state of self-doubt and self-loathing that she gave birth to me, and she attached all her love and hopes for the future to a baby boy who would never abandon her and always love her. As a little girl, my mother had dreamed of becoming a success in life because 'that would show them all'. And if she couldn't do it herself because some irresponsible man had abandoned her, then her boy would go out into the world, capture success and recognition, and bring it home for them to share. Together, they'd show them!

Mother's stories about the things she had gotten up to as a wild hoyden in Fort Anne would be punctuated every fifteen minutes by the passage of a rattling, clanging, glittering block of glass and light, the Clinton Avenue trolley car with its motorman in front working his foot bell and accelerator lever, and the conductor in back, responsible for collecting fares and keeping the contact wheel on the wire, both wearing black uniforms and visored caps with wicker sides to ventilate their heads. At that late hour, there was only a handful of half-asleep passengers. A moment of brilliance and noise, and the ground-shaking trolley had passed and was going down the dark street towards its union with Pearl Street at the bottom of the hill, taking its light and animation with it. If Anne-Marie was particularly sleepy, we would consider taking the next trolley, but we usually rejected the idea as a shameful waste of money because a ride down the entire Clinton Avenue hill only cost a nickel, so it seemed prodigal to spend a nickel to go only halfway down. We would continue on, Anne-Marie's feet numbly slapping on the pavement as she walked between us, eyes closed, half-asleep, relying on us to guide her.

Mother's favorite story was the one of how she trained all through the fall and winter of her fourteenth year to compete in the annual long-distance race down the frozen Champlain Canal to Fort Edward. This skating competition was held at night, when the temperature was lowest and the ice most stable. With the crack of the starter's gun, she broke into the lead, then, bent low over her skates, her hands clasped behind her back, she sped over the black ice between banks of ghost-gray snow, chasing a ripple of reflected moonlight down the ice, as the uneven surface beneath her skates made her feet thrum, and the wind stung tears from her eyes. The long, rhythmic click-hiss, click-hiss of the Patented Tubular Racer Skates her father bought her especially for the contest; the shouts and laughter of her competitors fading behind her as she began to outdistance them; the bonfires farm children built along the way to greet the racers with cups of hot chocolate, but Mother passed by and skated on, intent on victory, until she crossed the line scratched on the ice at Fort Edward a full fifteen minutes before her closest competitor. She described that race through the frigid moonlit night with such intensity that the details of her triumph are frozen into my memory, as though I had been there, as though it had been mine; this victory made her famous for a whole winter. Her feat was even mentioned in the Glens Falls paper. She was someone, a success!

The story of her great race and the one about my grandfather forcing those stuffy ladies to sip afternoon tea with his young wife were the ones I most often asked my mother to re-tell as we walked back home after Dish Night at the Paramount.

It began to snow as we were returning from the movies late one winter night, large lazily tumbling flakes that Anne-Marie and I tried to catch on our tongues. The last Clinton Avenue trolley clanged and rattled past us, snow swirling around it like the white particles in a 'snowstorm' paperweight. When we got home, Pearl Street was deserted and strangely silent in the muffling snowfall. We climbed our stoop, and I looked back down the street and saw our tracks on the new-fallen snow, three sets of footprints stretching down the sidewalk to a pool of streetlight and disappearing into the darkness beyond, and already the snow was filling our footsteps in. I felt sure there was something portentous in this vision, something symbolic and oceanic. A woman and two children had passed through the storm and the darkness. Seeking what? Fleeing what?[26]

. . . .

Nothing so stimulated my imagination as a raging storm late at night...sudden lightning and sky-shredding claps of thunder so close together that I gasped again in mid-gasp. I felt safe with my Hudson Bay blanket around my shoulders as I watched Nature rage out in the street, although there was always a tinge of guilt at being snug and dry while down-and-outers pressed into doorways with newspapers stuffed under their shirts for warmth. Silver streaks of rain hatched through the cone of light from our streetlamp, and plump raindrops exploded on the cobblestones until swirling, frothing water gurgled up through the gutter grill, sheeted across the sidewalk and ran down basement steps to flood coal bunkers and leave them dank and smelly.

Autumn windstorms sharpened my senses but dazzled them at the same time, as if electricity and friction caused me to read fast and think in a hectic, scattered rush. Lots of thinking, little thought. And when the night wind moaned around the corners of buildings, wuthered in basement wells, fluted through chimney pots, and sucked at the loose panes of my window, rattling them in their crumbling putty, I would turn newfound words in my mind, particularly windy-sounding words like 'vicarious' and 'ethereal', or I would grapple with big ideas like Free Will and Sin...especially sin. Has any word ever been so yeasty as 'sin'? I would weave sounds and unravel meanings while the rain danced on the cobbles and the wind sucked at my window.

Baffling thoughts on blustery, wind-dazed nights.

· · · · · · · · ·

I was staring out into the street one night, empty-minded, coasting, when my attention was snagged by a drunk having trouble negotiating the cracks in the pavement. While looking back over his shoulder swearing at the crack that had tripped him up, he stepped off the high curb on our side of the street and lurched across to the streetlamp, which he embraced just in time to save himself from falling on his face. It was Old Joe Meehan, tyrant of the Meehan tribe.

Sometimes at night there would be a sudden shout or a scream from within the Meehan warren, and ten or twelve of them would come pouring down their stoops into the street, arguing, snarling, fighting: human magma ejected by the heat of some internecine friction, probably over those breeding rights and sexual tangles that were the constant subject of the block's indignant but riveting gossip. I sometimes found my imagination wandering to what sorts of things those Meehans got up to. I knew it was shameful and sinful and ugly and foul and all that...but it was also intriguing for a ten-year-old boy. Not that I wanted to *do* anything. No, no, I just...well...wondered.

Sometimes the Meehan warren contained as few as twenty people, sometimes twice that many. Births, runaways, imprisonments, desertions, hospitalizations, deaths, benders, and simply getting lost for a few weeks kept the population variable, so no one knew exactly how many Meehans there were at any given time, but the number slowly and continually grew because, whatever their other moral defects might be, the Meehans were good Catholics who scrupulously abjured birth control.

From the mailman the block learned that the Meehans received six weekly welfare checks, one for each 'family'. In addition, they got five dollars per adult from the ward heeler whenever there was an election of any kind, a gift from the O'Conner Gang to make sure that the Democratic Party continued to enjoy the full support of the Meehans. There was always a riotous party over at the Meehans' on election nights, one that inevitably ended with random couplings and a great tangled fistfight in which some Meehans would gang up on others and try to throw them out onto the street. Finally the police would arrive and there would be a fight between the police and the suddenly re-united Meehans, nightsticks on the one side, iron rods, chains, and gravel-filled socks on the other. Some Meehans always ended up in the slammer after election night, and others ended up pregnant.

I have to confess that my mother also sold her vote at each election for five dollars from our perspiring, derby-hatted ward heeler, but she refused to feel guilty about it because we needed every cent we could get our hands on. And anyway, she was devoted to Roosevelt, who she felt understood her problems on a personal level and would never let her down, a feeling shared by most of the poor, so she would have voted the Democratic ticket anyway. She justified her vote-selling by claiming to have gypped the ward heeler out of his five dollars—and let that be a lesson to the vote-buying bastard!

I was passing the mouth of our alley on my way home from the library late one evening, and I was startled by a voice. "Hey, you! Professor! Come here!" It was Patrick Meehan. Oh-oh.

Patrick Meehan and I had never exchanged a word, and that was just fine with me. Patrick was seventeen, and he was big and tough and stupid. He had earned his reputation as the meanest kid on the block by beating up any boy or man who fooled with his simple-minded sister, Brigid. And not just beating them up, but pounding them until they had to go to the emergency room of the hospital. Patrick could only see out of one eye; the other was sunken and had a milky membrane over it ever since it had been poked with a stick during a fight with two kids who had used Brigid. The two kids ended up in the hospital, and Patrick went back into reform school for six months.

So you can see why his shout of, "Hey, you! Professor! Come here!" brought me to a standstill at the mouth of the alley. I considered hotfooting it to the safety of my apartment, but I would have to go back out onto the street sooner or later, so the best thing to do was to face the music.

"Come here!"

I walked up the alley, my knees watery. "Hey, what's up, Patrick? How's it going?"

"Lookit, professor, your...mother...she's..." he started. But he had difficulty dragging words out of the thick tangle of his thoughts.

"What about her?" My voice was stronger. I wasn't going to take any crap about my mother, even from Patrick. But it seemed unfair to get beaten up by him when I'd never had anything to do with Brigid. Well...all right...maybe I had sat up a few nights, looking across at the Meehan warren, wondering what sort of...things...might be going on over there, but you wouldn't beat a kid up for that. ...Would you?

"She's nice."

"What?"

"Your mother, she's nice. She's nice to my mother. Always says hello and stuff. So she's all right by me, your mother."

"Ah...good."

"I just wanted to tell ya."

"Well...fine. I'm glad you told me. I...ah...well, I guess I better get along."

"Yeah, you go ahead. But tell your mother she's okay by me."

"I'll do that. See you around, Patrick."

"See ya 'round, professor."

When I got home I passed on Patrick Meehan's compliments to Mother, and she seemed pleased.

"He sounds like a nice boy."

I stared at her, unbelieving. "No, Mother, Patrick Meehan is not a nice boy."

"Oh, really?"

"No, he has this little problem. He hurts people, and one of these days he's going to kill someone."

"Oh, I doubt that."

I just shook my head. How could anyone living on North Pearl Street be so far out of contact with the brutal facts of life?

. . . .

After fighting through the winter, 'courageous little Finland', as radio commentators always called her, finally surrendered to the Russians in March of 1940, that ominous-sounding year whose arrival I had dreaded. In April Germany occupied Denmark and swept up through the Norwegian ports. News broadcasts reported that German submarines were sinking many of the British ships carrying American goods to England. Then on May 10, after the months of inexplicable inactivity of the 'Phony War', the German army launched a lightning assault through the Netherlands into France, outflanking the totally useless Maginot Line.[27]

By the end of June 1940, most of France was occupied, and the southern part had become a neutral, collaborating state with Marshal Pétain at its head and Vichy as its capital.[28] A cross-channel invasion of England seemed imminent, but throughout July History held her breath as Germany digested the huge territories it had gobbled up, and England, the only enemy left, struggled to make up for decades of un-preparedness and years of appeasement. It was not until August that the Luftwaffe began massive bombing raids in an attempt to soften Britain up for invasion.

In America, the 1940 harvest of popular songs was so rich and var-ied that few of them remained long on the Hit Parade before they were crowded off by newcomers swarming in behind them.[29] Some of these songs came from the Big Bands, others from Broadway musicals or films, which also resurrected a few oldies. They were the songs you could hear at night, playing quietly from radios within apartments... quietly, not out of consideration for neighbors, but because our Irish believed that it cost more electricity to play a radio loudly. The summer sky above our jagged roofscape didn't darken until after eight o'clock, and streetlife on North Pearl extended late into the night; kids bawled and brawled as adults sprawled around the stoops listening to music from radios put out on window ledges, the women in faded cotton housedresses lifting their chins to let the evening breeze cool their moist necks; men in sticky undershirts sucked at quart bottles of ale, only rarely deigning to enter the women's conversation, and then only

to tell their wives that if they didn't know what the hell they were talking about they should shut up, then going on to abuse the goddamned
New Deal, the goddamned welfare system, or today's goddamned kids,
the first for trying to force men into slave labor with the WPA, the second for being run by a tightfisted bunch of fancy-talking stuck-up college guys who, when it came right down to it, didn't know shit from
Shinola, and the third for not showing proper respect for their elders.
And it's all that Eleanor Roosevelt's fault! A woman shouldn't stick her
nose in where it wasn't wanted!

Hot and airless though it was in our apartment by the end of a
sweltering day, my mother wouldn't sit out on our stoop for a breath of
evening air because she didn't want to have anything to do with 'these
people' who had been slum-dwellers for generations, unlike us, who
were only on Pearl Street because the Depression had ambushed us.
She maintained that it was dangerous to consort with people who
didn't come up to your standards of cleanliness, honesty, and self-
respect because 'You can't tell a flock of birds by its feathers'. (Another
of my mother's addled adages: in this case, perhaps the result of a high-
velocity collision between 'you can't tell a book by its cover' and 'birds
of a feather flock together'.) Instead, after our evening programs were
over, she would click the radio off and say, "Let's get out of this dump!"
and she'd take Anne-Marie and me for a walk downtown, where flashing signs in rippling patterns of small lightbulbs or in the newer bent
neon tubes (how do they bend light like that?) spilled colors over the
faces of the crowd, and we could smell the rich baritone aroma of
chocolate from the open door of the Fanny Farmer shop as we passed
on our way from store to store, window-shopping and fantasizing
about all the fine things we'd own and all the interesting things we'd do
when we got out of Albany. Sometimes we'd meet the Peanut Man on
the street in front of the Planters Peanut Shop, a sandwich-board man
wearing a huge peanut with a top hat and monocle and thin black-clad
legs sticking out the bottom. He offered passers-by free spoonfuls of
freshly roasted salted peanuts. The three of us would queue up for our
samples, and sometimes Anne-Marie, who had reached an age at
which she was fully aware of the charm of her long blonde hair and
large innocent blue eyes, would go back for a second spoonful, although we knew you were supposed to take only one. I envied her

brass, but I never dared to try for seconds for myself. A refusal would have been so humiliating that I would have done or said something rash and yet more humiliating.

By the time we had threaded our way home through quiet side streets it would be after ten o'clock, and Mother and Anne-Marie would go to bed, but I would sit in the dark, watching the street, my window open the couple of inches its warped frame would allow to catch the breeze. On a typical summer night, a knot of teenaged boys would have gathered next to the cornerstore on the strip of hard-packed waste ground that Mr Kane sardonically called 'his garden'.

Girls who had just that summer disdained hopscotch and jump-rope as kids' stuff would detach themselves from the giggling gaggle that by ancient tradition collected two stoops down from the corner-store, and they would stroll up past the boys on the corner, always in protective twos. Pretending to be lost in earnest conversation, a pair of girls (usually a prettier, more confident, more developed one and her shyer, plainer, fatter friend who got vicarious thrills from her desirable friend's love life) would run the gauntlet of ogling, wisecracking boys, the shy one gripping her friend's hand as they hurried by. Once they reached the corner, there was nothing to do but undergo the indignity of being looked at, evaluated and commented on again as they returned to the knot of girls clustered around the stoop. The brassy one would sometimes engage the boys in racy single-entendre badinage, then upon returning, she would recount her encounter to breathlessly ad-miring friends.

"...so he goes: How about it? So I go: How about what? And he goes: You know what. So I put on my ritzy voice and I go: I beg your pardon I'm sure, but I certainly do not know to what you are referring to. Why don't you inform me of it, if you're so smart. (Oh, hon, you *didn't!*) I did so. And I turn my nose up and start to walk away, but he grabs me by the arm, so I go: Don't handle the merchandise until it's paid for. (Oh, hon, you *didn't!*) Well that stops him cold, so he goes: How much? And I come right back: More than you'll ever have! (You *didn't!*) I did so. And he goes: Come on, give a guy a break. So I go: I'll have my cousin break your arm, that's the only break I'll give you. So his pals laugh at him, and I walk away. (Oh, *hon!* You *didn't!*)

Listening to the explicit lyrics of this primitive mating chant through my open window, I was repelled by the banality and stupidity of it all, for I was a crisp-minded eleven-year-old while these salivating canines nosing one another's crotches were teenagers...worlds, entire cultures, infinities beneath me. There was one thing I was absolutely sure of: when I was a year or two older, nothing in the world would make me behave in that undignified way, sniffing around girls like a dog. I was, of course, wrong.[30]

I was not spared the baffling onset of testosterone madness, for within six months of the night I sat at the window, eavesdropping on that girl's neo-nubile prattle and feeling superior to her crude mating rituals, I fell victim to the nameless urges and surges of desire. I was eleven years old when I first fell in love, a hesitant, secret love untainted by desire. Well, no desire that I recognized as such. Well...not at first, anyway. She was, after all, a nun.

Love on Pearl Street

(or: Brigid Meehan's Left Breast)

Although I was only eleven when I first fell in love, I was not totally unequipped to grapple with the mysteries of that glorious affliction of heart and groin. Not only did I know where babies came from and how they got there, I even had inklings of the nature of romantic love.

First, the babies and the ballistics. I already knew the fundamental mechanics of copulation because my remarkably modern mother believed it was healthiest to respond as honestly as she could to questions posed by me or my sister. I listened soberly, and with growing incredulity, to her frank description of human love-making. I couldn't believe it. Why would two sane people want to do that...especially people who claimed to like each other? Responding to my doubts and my basic squeamishness, my mother went to some lengths to assure me that love-making was a pleasurable thing, indeed the most sublime act that two people in love could share. I remained dubious. Why should I believe love-making was all that sublime and beautiful when Nature herself held so dim a view of the act that She obliged us to perform it with our pissing gear? If body space was so tight that Nature had to double up on functions, why didn't She have us smell with our fingertips or hear with our elbows—anything to save some special part of the body for the performance of this sublime act? (Perhaps the belly button, which seemed to have no very urgent function assigned to it.) Something wasn't right here. Either my mother was wrong about the loftiness of love-making, or Nature was playing a cruel joke.

In addition to my mother's explanations, with their odd blend of medical terms like 'tube', 'egg' and 'channel' and romantic words like 'love', 'tenderness' and 'caress', I had other sources for appreciating the physical aspects of human relations. There were, for instance, Miss LaMonte's solid thighs and ample breasts.

A couple of months after I got my paper route, Mother decided that the best way to 'invest' the extra money that began to accumulate in our matchbox Dream Bank was to start Anne-Marie's tap-dancing lessons.

"It would be a dying shame if some Hollywood talent scout passed your sister up because she didn't know how to tap dance. You know what they say: Opportunity only knocks on wood!"

Well, I couldn't argue with that, although the only reason there were a few dollars in the Dream Bank was that Mother had been having a run of good health for the last few months. What if she broke down when our savings were all gone?

Anne-Marie took tap-dancing lessons in the basement studio of the LaMonte Dance Academy (Tap, Acrobatic, Ballet and Latin American—Hula a Specialty) where lines of panting little girls shuffle-ball-change-ball-change-ball-change'd their hearts out, their curls bouncing to the rhythm of an upright piano pounded by a hoarse-voiced old woman who squinted through threads of smoke rising from an eternal cigarette in the corner of her mouth: Miss LaMonte's mother. The dance routines always ended with little curtseys and broad smiles, as the girls pointed their forefingers up under their dimpled chins, for they were all preparing themselves to step into Shirley Temple's tap shoes, should anything untoward happen to America's little sweetheart, God forbid. Group lessons cost a dollar and a half, and Anne-Marie took them two times a week, which absorbed most of what my paper route took in. When Miss LaMonte decided that my sister's exceptional talent deserved an additional semi-private lesson each Friday evening, the total rose to five dollars a week. But my mother had faith in Anne-Marie's artistic gifts and in her own boundless determination. To supplement my paper route, she got fairly regular fill-in work at a chop house on lower State Street (on the QT, of course, so the welfare people didn't reduce our allowance). Buying Anne-Marie's tap shoes might have presented an insurmountable problem, but Miss LaMonte had an arrangement with the owner of a shoe store down on South Street whose sign was a splendid example of first-generation Jewish commercial rhetoric: Classy Shoes, Inc. We could buy the tap shoes on time, a quarter a week, the same terms as those under which we had bought our Emerson. In fact, the A-One Pawn Shop was only a couple of doors down from Classy Shoes, Inc.

I accompanied my mother to the monthly recitals intended to showcase the talents of the dancers and to give them a chance to get used to 'working an audience'. Miss LaMonte always danced a final solo number to inspire by example. We would sit on bentwood chairs among other admiring mothers and a scattering of awkward, reluctant brothers with wet-down hair and tight ties the narrow ends of which always ended up longer than the wide. Miss LaMonte was loud, glittering, energetic and very blonde (but this was acceptable in one who had received 'professional New York legitimate stage training'), and her ample breasts sloshed within the stiffened cups of her low-cut dancing costume. She admitted to being 'no chicken' but her legs were still good! she would laughingly assure the mothers, slapping her muscular thigh and stunning them with a huge smile, her painted lips bigger than her mouth. I'm sure the mothers had no idea of the role Miss LaMonte's slapped thigh and tidal breasts played in the fledgling fantasies of the wet-haired, tight-tied brothers, who stiffened on their bentwood chairs when she made her post-recital round of the mothers, bending over each one in turn to give a few words of praise and encouragement (with a breast nearly in the brother's face!). The boy would stare straight ahead, riveting his eyes on Miss LaMonte's perspiring neck, never letting them drop to her breasts, not because he didn't want to look at them, but because he didn't want to be seen looking at them. And often a boy whose mother had just been visited by Miss LaMonte's breasts would catch the eye of another boy, and the message 'Jeez!' would pass as both boys swallowed and drew deep breaths. Miss LaMonte assured each mother in turn that her daughter had 'star quality', which gave her a good chance of making it, provided that she kept on with her lessons and, of course, that she got 'the breaks'. Not wanting to raise any false hopes, Miss LaMonte frankly admitted that you couldn't make it in show business without 'the breaks', no matter how gifted your teacher was. After the recital, the mothers would gather out on the sidewalk, hollowly complimenting the efforts of other mothers' awkward offspring, and assuring one another that Miss LaMonte knew talent when she saw it, believe you me! Then we would walk home, my sister's glittering, hand-made costume covered by a long, second-hand winter coat. She was allowed to wear her costume and make-up until she got home, just in case a talent scout happened to pass by. After all, that was the way most of the Hollywood stars had been discovered, wasn't it?

Apart from some puzzling and anatomically improbable drawings on the walls of public toilets, I learned little about sex on the street because kids in the 'Thirties were reticent and puritanical in comparison to children of today.[31] But information of a decidedly unreliable sort could be had by hanging around the older boys who used to loiter in the mouth of our back alley, awaiting the two girls from our block who had reputations for being willing to 'do it'.

One of Pearl Street's two 'fast' girls was Kathleen Gogarty, a fifteen-year-old with dead eyes lost in folds of fat, a granular complexion, and a limp-knee'd, flat-footed waddle that made her seem half crippled, although the real problem was that she wasn't strong enough to move her weight gracefully. She would walk homeward from Our Lady of Angels down the steep sidewalk of the Livingston Avenue hill, her books digging into her belly, her feet slapping on the pavement, her flesh jiggling within a too-tight navy blue uniform. Street lore insisted that Kathleen Gogarty would do it for a Baby Ruth bar or a bottle of Dr Pepper, but you had to be quick as she'd only give you the couple of minutes it took to consume her bribe because her mother would beat her if she got back from school late. I have no idea why that particular

brand of candy bar or that particular soft drink was understood to possess the power to undermine Kathleen's morality and prudence, nor do
I remember any of the boys bragging that he had actually ever done it
in the allotted two minutes, or explaining how he had managed it while
she was drinking a Dr Pepper, but street lore is a resilient strain of
truth, capable of shrugging off any assault from logic, probability or
observation. As she neared the mouth of the alley, a couple of boys
would push one of their gang out in front of them and say, "Hey, Kathleen! Look who's got a Baby Ruth for you!" The other boys would snig-
ger while the chosen lover struggled, his heels slipping on the slimy
cobbles as he tried to get back into the safe anonymity of the pack, all
the while making gagging sounds as if his refined sexual taste revolted
at the prospect of having to do it to 'fat old gravel-faced Gogarty'.
Kathleen would not complain or try to push past the blocking boys.
She would just stand there in bovine patience, her fat-squeezed eyes
looking dully ahead, until the boys got tired of razzing her, then she
would continue her way down the street, her feet slapping on the pavement, her body heaving and jiggling.

The other girl on our block who was understood to be willing was
Brigid Meehan. Unlike Kathleen, Brigid really would do it because she
was simple-minded and biddable. Although she would soon be sixteen
and out of school, she sat at the back of Sister Agnes-Joseph's fourth-
grade class, cramped in a desk much too small for her. Sister Agnes-
Joseph got all the 'difficult' kids because of her unique blend of
maternal sympathy and prison-guard toughness. She was gentle and
understanding with the backward ones, but disruptive, unruly boys
learned to fear the edge of her ruler across their knuckles and to respect
her ability to defend herself in a one-on-one tussle by slamming the
kid against the cloakroom wall until he was dazed and docile. Sister
Agnes-Joseph possessed the indwelling power of a Force of Nature. I
have seen a whole playground of rampaging kids fall silent as she
passed through on her way to the chapel. Shouts would fade in a
minor-key Doppler decay, wild runners would stumble to a sedate
walk, jump ropes would swing limp, and balls would bounce away un-
attended as she walked by, a calm half-smile on her lips, her eyes beneath the starched wings of her head-dress glinting quick darts of
intimidating benevolence left and right.

Brigid always walked home alone because, being in the fourth grade, she got out of school half an hour earlier than other girls of her age. As she descended Livingston Avenue from Ten Broeck, wearing the yellow knitted toque that she wore summer and winter, the boys would begin their ritual catcalls and whistles and wise-mouthed suggestions. Although they knew she would do anything she was asked to do (she had once been knocked down by a passing brewery wagon when a boy told her to step out in front of it), they usually let her go on her way because they were afraid of her brother, Patrick. They knew that if anything happened to her, Patrick would come looking for the boy, and the prospect of being hunted down by a tough, determined, one-eyed dummy was a powerful anaphrodisiac.

I was always uncomfortable because Brigid's mother was the woman with whom my mother had, against my better judgment, struck up a friendly relationship, exchanging 'good afternoons' whenever they met. And also because I had had a...well, let's call it an experience...with Brigid. This, despite Patrick's tendency to beat to a pulp anyone who fooled with his sister.

One hot evening a few days after my eleventh birthday, Brigid came knocking on our door in a tearful panic. She explained in an urgent yet stumbling way that her mother was 'stuck', and all the grown-up Meehans were drunk, and her brother Patrick was still in the Reformatory, and she didn't know what to do! She begged my mother to come and help her. I followed along, unwilling to let any mother of mine go over there alone. When we got to the foul-smelling Meehan warren we found Mrs Meehan in her kitchen, one hand on the gas tap of the stove and the other on the handle of the back door. She was 'stuck', unable to release either one. Added to the kitchen's boiled-cabbage-and-urine smell was the sickly sweet smell of gas because in their efforts to pry their mother's hand off the gas tap the kids had repeatedly turned the gas on. To turn it off again they'd had to twist hand and all. Now two of them were clinging to their mother's arm, trying to tear her hand off the door knob. Crucified between door knob and gas tap, Mrs Meehan was sobbing that it wasn't her fault! She was trying to let go! But she couldn't! She just couldn't! My mother, always calm and efficient in an emergency, ordered the swarm of little kids out of the kitchen. Out! Out! Then she sat with me and Brigid at the kitchen table and began talking to us quietly about how grown-up Brigid was getting to be, and how it was so hot at night that it was hard to sleep—anything that came into her mind. I played along, chipping in when I could. Brigid didn't contribute; she just sat there with her eyes lowered to the greasy oilcloth, her old knitted yellow toque down to her eyebrows. In time, Mrs Meehan's sobbing tapered off and her white-knuckled grip on the door handle slowly relaxed. My mother was telling us about one summer up in Lake George Village when the weather was so hot that...

Out of the corner of my eye I saw Mrs Meehan turn the gas on again. I was about to cry out a warning when she calmly struck a match with her other, now liberated, hand, and lit the metal nipples. "Would you like a cup of coffee, Missus?" she asked. Mother said Yes, she would love a cup of coffee, and Mrs Meehan slid the percolator over the stiff blue jets of flame...and that was it. She was all right again. Brigid sighed with relief and left the room, and her mother sat down in the chair she vacated and began talking about the heat. I couldn't help looking at the wide shiny red welt across her palm where, the day we arrived on Pearl Street, she had held on to a hot iron frying pan, unable to release it until Old Joe Meehan kicked it out of her hand.

While Mother and Mrs Meehan were drinking their coffee, I slipped out into the front hallway to get away from the olfactory cock-tail of grease, garbage, cabbage, gas and pee that was making me queasy. The hallway was dark and spookily alien, so I decided to await Mother out on the stoop, but I was startled by a voice from the depths of the shadow. "Luke?"

"...Brigid?"

"Come here, Luke."

I stepped toward the voice, sliding my feet so as not to trip and stretching out my hand to keep from bumping into anything. She took my hand, turned it over and laid something on my palm. It was warm and oozy-soft and silky smooth; it felt like nothing I knew. I moved my hand slightly, and the dense liquid interior shifted, like tepid mercury in a silken pouch. I caught my breath and my senses slithered at the re-alization that lying on my palm was Brigid Meehan's left breast, which I held, the nipple towards my wrist, as though I were offering it to some god of Forbidden Things. It was so soft, so smooth that it seemed to flow into the spaces between my fingers like fine sand. I gently put my thumb over the nipple, petal-soft within its thin, silken erectile crust, even more liquid-centered than the breast, even more mysterious, more exciting. I stood in that dark hallway, my breath short and my pulse pounding in my ears, but I knew that this breast had not been offered to me out of desire; it was a gesture of gratitude for our having come over to help her mother. Brigid was offering what she knew all boys and men wanted.

But even as my senses were being transported by the thralldom of that breast on my palm, an icy thought penetrated my bewildered bliss: What if her brother, Patrick, suddenly appeared and found me holding his sister's breast? That dead eye with its white veil would pierce me to the heart as his fists clenched in anticipation of pounding my face to jelly. What would I say to him? Could I possibly bluff my way through? "Hey, Patrick, how's it going? Long time no see. Say, I'll bet this looks funny to you, but the truth is...well, I was just...ah...holding your sister's breast. You know, giving her a hand? So! What do you say, Patrick? How were things in the Reformatory?"

Standing in the dark hallway, simultaneously luxuriating in the sensation of that breast on my palm and dreading getting my face pounded to jelly, was like absorbing alternate doses of Spanish fly and saltpeter. But I didn't know how to take my hand away without seeming to reject her gift. For a confused instant, I considered kissing it good-bye, and my senses reeled at the anticipation of that warm satiny skin on my lips, that nipple brushing my lips...but Brigid lifted her breast out of my palm. From the rustle of clothing I assumed she put it back under her blouse, and I knew I would never touch that breast again. Without a word, I walked down the hallway and out onto the stoop, where a cluster of Meehans was strewn over the steps, sucking beers and snarling at their communal kids. I felt strangely adrift; my mind couldn't span the contrast between this real place populated by drunken Meehans and squalling kids and that magic place in the dark, only a few feet behind me, where I had experienced the ardent alchemy of Brigid Meehan's left breast.[32]

The moment when Brigid Meehan laid her breast on my palm in that dark, cabbage-and-piss-smelling hallway was the dawn of my manhood, and her breast became an indelible and universal metaphor for desire. I would often let my imagination finger the whole tactile gamut of that awakening like a pious convert to hedonism telling the beads of a sensory rosary, lingering over each sensation. And I always felt a blend of tenderness and shame when I thought about her, tenderness because of the confused pleasure she had given me, and shame because I knew it was wrong to have anything sexual to do with a girl who was simple-minded.

When we got home from Mrs Meehan's kitchen, I wondered aloud why Mrs Meehan couldn't let go of things. Mother said she didn't know, but maybe the poor thing had lost too many things in her life: lost all her dreams and hopes, lost the family she had before she ended up in the nuthouse where one of the Meehans found her, lost two babies who died...of neglect, according to street lore. Maybe after losing so much, Mrs Meehan just couldn't let anything else get out of her grasp. I nodded, impressed by my mother's insight, but puzzled. Despite the glib explanations with which movie psychologists 'cured' a guilt-laden heroine's problems, I couldn't accept that the human condition could be reduced to such literal plots and simple symbols. It would be many years before I read the facile generalizations that make Freud better literature than science.

So, when I first encountered love at the age of eleven, my understanding of its physical aspects was a compound of my mother's clear clinical explanations, drawings on public toilet walls, Miss LaMonte's firm thighs and sloshing breasts, what the older boys on the block did—or claimed to have done—with Kathleen Gogarty for the price of a Dr Pepper, and above all, the stimulating but troubling effect of Brigid Meehan's silky left breast melting on my palm. A disturbing stew, and a tangy one.

In addition to my partial and confused understanding of the meatier aspects of love, I also had some notions of love's more heroic manifestations. The principal of these was the inspirational beacon of my grandfather's undying love for his Maud, whose grave he had visited every Saturday evening of his life. And there was Mrs McGivney's self-sacrificing love for her war hero husband. I still saw Mrs McGivney occasionally, scuttling across the street to

Mr Kane's. I spoke to her once, hoping she had forgiven me for deserting her, but she frowned and drew back, as though she didn't recognize me.

Along with these instances drawn from life, I found examples of romantic love in movies and radio dramas. In the hard-breathing 'drama films' my mother enjoyed, the quest for love was a high-voltage matter loaded with urgent need, perfidy and suffering. There was also a lot of sin involved, and guilt, and recrimination, and denunciation, and pleading, and denial, and retribution, and vengeance, the whole emotional stew served up with great dollops of unabashed over-acting. All a bit frantic and messy for a boy of eleven.

Lighter romantic films, on the other hand, made love seem like a game...but a game that I would not be likely to win, because the narrative conventions were against people of my sort. Hollywood idiom made it inevitable that the guy who was the zany, fast-talking female star's boyfriend at the beginning of the film (a polite young man, well-spoken and bookish) was not the person she would end up with; just as the intelligent, refined gal who began with the male star was not the woman whom Fate and the brothers Warner had destined for Clark Gable. The moral to be deduced from this was that bookish, considerate men never get desirable girls; just as educated, independent-minded girls never end up with the really desirable men. The stars of the film would usually meet through some silly accident that made them both angry, and they would spat and shout at each other through a series of unlikely complications, often declaring that they wouldn't marry the other one, no, not if she/he were the last person on earth! Deduced moral? Two people who don't like each other and who have totally incompatible beliefs, aspirations and backgrounds are sure to end up together forever.

But it wasn't from the movies that I garnered the greater part of my understanding of romantic love; it was from the radio. My mother's favorite weekly radio-theater was *First Nighter*, which began with the buzz of an expectant audience in a theater as the voice of an usher said, "Right this way, Mister First Nighter. Two seats on the aisle, center section." Then the curtain would go up to a riffle of applause and the play would begin. All *First Nighter* stories were romances with the basic MLG structure of boy-meets-girl, boy-loses-girl, boy-gets-girl.

The commercials came in the interstices between these structural slabs, the first batch of ads just after the couple broke up, and the second just before they got together again...two moments that the sponsors considered so suspenseful that the listener wouldn't be able to step away from the radio for fear of missing the resolution.[33] My mother also listened to *Grand Central Station,* which opened with an excited announcer describing a train's approach to the outskirts of New York City, flashing past rows of tenements, plunging into the dark tunnel leading to the depot, then coming to a stop with a screech of train brakes and a hiss of steam at 'Gra-a-and Central Sta-a-ation! Crossroads of a million private lives!' Each of the love stories began or ended in Grand Central Station, and they too were simple MLG tales in which the couple always broke up through some silly misunderstanding that would make my mother furious because nothing seemed more tragic to her than two people who were meant for each other, passing each other by 'like ships in the night': the first poetic simile I remember her making. (Perhaps because she had, for once, got it right. An instance of anti-chance.)

I also learned quite a bit about the nature of romantic love from soap operas, which operated on the principle that life was a long uphill struggle characterized by work, woe, worry and misfortune...then things suddenly got a lot worse. I listened to soap operas only when my mother had a bout of lung trouble and I had to care for her. While she was devoted to certain soap operas, she dismissed others as mindless trash, but I could never discover what fine measuring instrument she used to distinguish the one from the other.[34]

It was common for soaps to open with the announcer posing the program's essential question. *Our Gal Sunday* asked if a girl from a little mining town in Colorado could find happiness as the wife of a wealthy and titled Englishman. *Mary Noble, Backstage Wife* wondered if a woman could find contentment married to the matinee idol of a million other women. And *The Romance of Helen Trent* asked if a woman could find love after thirty-five.

To all of these questions, a heartless boy of eleven responded: Who cares?

So, like my understanding of physical love, my youthful notions of romantic love were compounded of many elements, no small part of which came from Dish Night movies and radio soap operas. Armed with these lofty ideals and my own sordid ones, I entered into my first romance, my eternal love for Sister Mary-Theresa, a relationship that was complicated by the fact that we both had official roles within the church.

My becoming an altar boy had nothing to do with piety, or even belief, for that matter. I was a Catholic for the same reason I was left-handed, because I had been born that way. Neither conviction nor spirituality nor a desire for personal salvation played any role in the matter. My common sense, what I had read about Darwinism, and above all my natural inclination towards the rational and away from the authoritarian and the superstitious combined to make me assign much of what was taught in catechism about miracles and the mysteries of the Church to the category of more or less well-intentioned myth.[35]

As an altar boy I was captivated by the theatricality of the mass and I enjoyed playing my role in it, up there on the stage, wearing a fancy costume. The ritual, the incense, the poetry, the pageantry attracted me so much that, in the course of considering one future occupation after another as a means of taking Mother out of the slums, the idea of becoming a priest briefly passed through my mind, although I couldn't quite see how the priesthood with its vows of poverty could bring in enough money. Well, maybe I'd become a radio priest with a large following to whom I would sell specially blessed medals and phials of holy water. I confess that the fact that priests are obliged to live in priest houses, separated from their mothers, was not without its attraction. Then too, priests were admired and their opinions were sought, and I was pretty sure that I could learn to accept my congregation's respect, even a certain amount of veneration, without damaging the humility they all admired so much in me.

But all thoughts of the priesthood as a vocation were swept away by that watershed moment when Brigid Meehan's warm, silken left breast lay on my palm.

My mother's attitude towards the Church was typical of her uncompromising, black-or-white view of the world, and of her tendency to maintain life-long grudges, a propensity that kept her many self-inflicted wounds from healing. In this case, her grudge was against

God. I was reading in bed one night when I heard her crying softly in her bedroom. This happened very seldom, and only when she was in the blackest depression. For a while I just lay there, pretending I didn't hear her. Finally, I got up and went into the kitchen, where I lit the popping gas ring and put on the percolator. I knew the sounds of my moving around in the kitchen would bring her out of her bedroom and into the bathroom, where she would bathe her face in cold water, then come to sit with me. This had become our tacit ritual when she had a bad case of the blues and needed to talk to someone...me. I was putting the ground coffee into the top section of the percolator when she came into the kitchen and sat at the table. I didn't say anything, I just set out her cup and opened a can of evaporated milk—always a tricky business because evaporated milk cans had no rims, so the can opener could easily slip off and stab your hand when you smacked it to punch a hole. I heard her sniff behind me but I didn't turn around. I gave her time to pull herself together, because she hated anyone seeing her cry. When the coffee bubbled brown in the glass top of the percolator, I poured out her cup and put it in front of her (I didn't drink coffee at that age), then I sat at the table across from her, my eyes lowered to the oilcloth.

After a while she began speaking in mid-thought...mid-complaint... as she often did in these rare late-night confessionals. She told me how, one night shortly after my father had left her penniless with a toddler and a new baby to support, she had broken down and sobbed for hours and hours. She didn't know what to do, which way to turn. Her father had all he could do to help feed and shelter her brothers and sisters and their families, as he was the only one in the family whom the Depression had left with a job. She couldn't ask him to do more for her than he was already doing, and that wasn't enough to keep us going.

Well, that night she felt so low, so blue, that she considered suicide. She went so far as to run hot water into the sink and get out a straight razor...the razor my father had left behind that morning when he left to 'look for work'. She stood at the bathroom sink, not daring to look into the mirror for fear of what she'd find in her eyes. But in the end, she couldn't do it. She couldn't leave her children alone in the world. Desperate, she went out into the backyard and knelt in the snow, and for the first time since she had been obliged to attend interminable high masses by her pious aunts in Plattsburg, she prayed. She asked God to help her...to help her children.

She returned to the house and was trying to get some sleep, when suddenly she sat up in bed with the full-blown plan. She would go to live with her father in their old house in Fort Anne. He was all alone, now that her older sister had left to start a life of her own. Mother would keep house for him, and we would be his family. She would finally be the necessary and preferred daughter, making her father's life comfortable, and at the same time providing a home for Anne-Marie and me. The perfect solution! Everything was going to work out. God had heard her prayers and had shown her the way.

Two weeks later, her father died in a road accident.

So that was God's answer to her prayers, was it? All right. All right! From that day on, she never entered a church again and never allowed a priest or a nun into her house. But in her stubborn way, she didn't forsake her belief in the existence of God; instead she carried a lifelong grudge against Him. And if it was true that when you die you pass before God in judgment...well, she'd give him a piece of her French-'n'-Indian mind, believe me you! And if God sent her to hell for it...well, that was all right too! She didn't care!

At this point, she began to cry again. Angry tears at the injustice of it all. I kept my eyes on the oilcloth. After a while, she wiped her cheeks with the back of her hand, finished her coffee, and said, "You don't mind me telling you things like this, do you? I sometimes need to get them off my chest."

I shook my head.

"You're the only one I can talk to. My good right hand."

She hugged me and returned to her bedroom, and soon she was asleep. I rinsed out the cup, put the evaporated milk into the icebox, tapped the coffee grounds out into the bucket we used as a garbage pail, and went back to my bed, where I lay, listening to the faint sounds of the street and to the old building creaking and settling.

Despite her grudge against God, Mother insisted that Anne-Marie and I go to church regularly, and she was pleased when I became an altar boy. After all, the fight was between her and Him. He had no right to take it out on her kids.

At the age of eleven I hadn't yet had any sexual experience. Few kids had in that more innocent, more romantic era. But as though to compensate for our lack of experience with evil, the Church had extended the definition of sin beyond deeds, into the shadowy realms of word and thought, and this extension dropped the net of sin over me. While I was completely innocent in deed and nearly so in word, my lively imagination often dragged me into the mires of sin-by-thought, and ultimately beyond the mires of sin, all the way to the inescapable morass of sacrilege. And with a nun, too.

Such adjectives as 'young' and 'pretty' do not rush to mind when trying to describe the nuns at Our Lady of Angels, women whom God had designed for functional rather than decorative purposes; but Sister Mary-Theresa was the least old and homely of those devoted brides of Christ who, beneath their starched wide-winged wimples that hid their hair and made their faces look peeled and vulnerable, sailed in whispering gowns, sweetly smiling and iron-willed, down the halls, through the playgrounds and across the lives of generation after generation of school children. Towards the middle of my second year with Sister Mary-Theresa I wrote for her, unbidden, a sixteen-page paper on the forms and functions of the adverb, which puzzled her at least as much as it impressed her.[36] In addition, I was a whiz at the high-speed verbal parsing that she considered to be one of life's loftier accomplishments. You might think that these accomplishments were enough to make me the star of her class and living proof that hers could be a noble and rewarding profession. I certainly thought so. And she did occasionally compliment my weekly essays for their 'creativity'. Unfortunately, my spelling was also creative, and when it came to penmanship, I was hopeless. I forgave these failings in myself because I held both spelling and handwriting to be trivial matters, but Sister Mary-Theresa considered them every bit as important as love of language, a rich vocabulary and correct grammar. In her eyes, my orthographic and calligraphic lapses were not only pedagogical, but moral as well, for she believed that bad spelling was a manifestation of sloth, and sloppy penmanship a sure indicator of weak character. Hence, the row of A's on my report card were broken by C's for English, C's that were the average of a roughly equal number of F's for cramped, messy writing and quixotic spelling and A's for such of my work as she could manage to make out.

We wrote with straight nibs that we dipped into glass inkwells set in round holes at the top of our desks. I was totally and unalterably left-handed (willfully so, my early teachers had claimed) so the only way I could avoid passing the heel of my hand over my still-wet writing was to turn the paper sidewards and write from above, guiding the pen with my fingertips, rather than moving my whole arm on the cushion of the forearm, as the Palmer Method required. This accounted for my cramped writing. The blobs and blots that seeded my work came from the tendency of the nib to splay because I held the pen so tightly that the side of my finger had a permanent dent. The splayed point would dig into the paper and leave a blot, and when I lifted the buried pen point from the paper, I would get a little spray of ink dots across the page. I resented being marked down for penmanship so much that I often let my inkwell run low, so that the bits of ink-sodden fuzz and grunge at the bottom would end up on my paper, adding to the patterns of blots and sprays that personalized my writing. In addition, there wasn't a smooth spot on my deeply scarred desktop, so each essay contained at least one messy puncture. Although I felt that she gave such peccadilloes unjust weight in estimating my total grade, I wanted desperately to please Sister Mary-Theresa (to impress her, really) so I would try my hardest to write without blobs and scratch-outs. During the strained silence of the weekly in-class essays, she would float down the aisles on her head-wings of immaculate white, looking down at our efforts. I was always intensely aware of her approach because her long dark blue robes would whisper against the desks, and when she leaned over my desk the chalk-laden air was enriched by whiffs of freshly baked bread and yellow bar soap...the smell of nun...a medley of aromas that filled me with nameless longing.

She never scolded me for the blots, the cramped writing, the punctures, the creative cacography, but her little sigh before moving on to the more commonly gifted students stung me to the heart.

Given my repeated failures to earn Sister Mary-Theresa's praise, I was surprised by her appearance in a dream one night during Christmas vacation, a dream that had a confused but seemingly anodyne narrative, but from which I awoke with my heart pounding, my stomach cramped from tension, and the troubling, irrational image of Brigid

Meehan's breast beneath Sister Mary-Theresa's starched bib. I dreamed about her the next night, and the next. And pretty soon these dreams settled into a regular little narrative. I would be writing, and her hand would touch mine to guide it. Then we would slowly rise into the air together...something to do with the wings of her wimple...and we would float along bathed in the perfume of bread and yellow soap...our faces would come closer and closer until our cheeks touched beneath the shelter of her wide wings...

...And I would wake up with fragments of the dream still clinging to my consciousness together with confused tactile memories of Brigid Meehan's breast. I couldn't work out what Brigid Meehan had to do with Sister Mary-Theresa. And why was it so comforting, so pleasurable to float along, our cheeks touching as we wafted through the clouds?

One afternoon, Sister Mary-Theresa asked me to stay to help her with the blackboard. Both excited and anxious about what this might lead to (...rising into the air together?...a weightless ballet through scented clouds?...) I brought the erasers out onto the fire escape and clapped up a storm of chalk dust while she wiped the blackboards with a damp rag. When I returned, she said in a suspiciously offhand tone that Sister Angelica, my mathematics teacher, had mentioned that I often worked problems in my head while other kids slogged through them on paper. I explained that Sister Angelica was wrong; I didn't work the problems out. The answers just seemed obvious. But I wasn't really very interested in math. I just couldn't make myself care how long it took Farmer Jones to meet Farmer Brown if they were driving towards each other at different speeds, and one took a lunch break while the other got a flat tire. She asked where I had picked up the uncommon words I used, and how I happened to know the names of the various geological eras, and the rulers of France, and things like that, and finally she got around to asking if I had ever had my IQ tested. (So that was what this staying after class was all about. Nothing to do with weightless ballets and Fels Naphtha. Nuts.) I described the tests I had taken for Miss Cox when I was seven, and she said she would like to have me tested again, if I didn't mind.

So a few weeks later I spent most of an afternoon taking a battery of tests down in the school library, sitting beneath the hand-tinted photograph of a painfully smiling Pope Pius. The results were not revealed to me, but she asked if I would be willing to spend an extra hour after school each day, improving my writing and spelling. I was glad she wanted to give me special help, and I was secretly excited about the idea of spending time alone with her.

Winter came, and by the time the four-thirty bell emptied the school of students, the evening sky gravid with snow was already beginning to draw in around Sister Mary-Theresa and me, alone in her classroom. I would move up to a front-row desk and work at whatever she had assigned, while she sat at her desk in front of me, correcting papers or reading. Every once in a while, she would rise and come to bend over me to see how I was getting along, and I would breathe in the nun-scent of bread and soap, and my concentration would skid. But my spelling improved rapidly. Once I learned a couple of rhyming rules like '*i* before *e* except after *c* or when sounded like *a*, as in neighbor and weigh', the rest was simple memorization, which rote drudgery I was willing to do to earn her praise, although I secretly considered spelling to be a pretty arbitrary business—as indeed it is in English. But while my spelling became more conventional, her efforts to improve my handwriting were thwarted by the total inability of any left-handed person to write with a dip nib using the Palmer Method.

One day, after the rest of the class had clattered out of the cloakroom and down the hall, and I had moved up to the front row and opened my writing tablet, Sister Mary-Theresa beckoned to me with her forefinger. There on her desk was a tubular object wrapped in a piece (*i* before *e*) of flowered wallpaper. It was a fountain pen with a little silver lever on the side that you worked to suck up ink from a bottle. It wasn't new, but it was very fine nonetheless. And there was a second present, a bottle of blue-black ink. The bottle had a 'patented hexagonal design', that made it possible to stand it at a forty-five-degree angle so you could dip your nib in and suck up a load of ink when the bottle was nearly empty. That bottle's clever design was my first encounter with modern communications technology. I had never written with a fountain pen before, and while I still had to turn the paper sidewards and keep my hand above the line of writing to avoid smearing the wet ink, the fountain pen's rounded nib glided smoothly over the paper without the point digging in and making splats, and I could guide it easily, without gripping it so tightly that it dented my index finger. Sister Mary-Theresa gave me an exercise to write out, and when she leaned over my shoulder to compare my new work with something I had written the day before (I felt her warm breath stirring my hair, and I closed my eyes and breathed in that sublime essence-of-nun), she said that my writing, if not beautiful, was at least decipherable, save for a big blot where I had fiddled with the pen, wondering how far you could lift this little lever without causing the ink to—oops...not quite that far, I guess.

That night Sister Mary-Theresa appeared in my dreams, smiling down on me, the radiant whiteness of her winged head-dress blurring her features, like an over-exposed photograph. I was lofted towards her until our cheeks touched beneath the wings of her wimple, then she gripped my pen and we floated through space. When I awoke with a great erection—well, as great as I could manage at the age of eleven—I was deeply troubled...yet happy. What the hell was going on here?

It was a rainy afternoon in early spring when Sister Mary-Theresa asked me why I didn't work harder to make good grades when I had so much ability. I knew she was referring to civics class, where I did not agree with my teacher that we should accept poverty as a 'trial' given to us by God to test and strengthen our faith. On my next report card she graded me down for 'bad attitude'. I explained to Sister Mary-Theresa that grades didn't really matter because I wouldn't be staying in school past the age of sixteen, when I would have to get a job to help my family. And anyway, I had the feeling that I would make my way in the world, if I made it at all, by doing something outside the conventional professions and jobs. Inventing things, maybe. Or entertaining people. Something like that. But she was wrong to think I didn't care about grades. On the contrary, I liked doing well on tests. It was a kind of game, and I liked winning.

"I see," she said. Then, in what I had come to recognize as her too offhand voice, she asked if I had ever thought about praying for help with tests. I felt uncomfortable that the idea of prayer had come up between us. I didn't want to think of us as nun-and-kid, but rather as teacher-and-inventor/comedian...or even as man-and-woman. But she went on to say that scholars often prayed to Saint Thomas Aquinas, and youngsters can pray to Saint Nicholas, patron saint of children, or to Saint Rose of Lima for good luck. When I added that maybe the dumber kids in our class should pray to Jude, patron saint of lost causes, she frowned. "That was an unkind thing to say, Luke." Then she told me that she'd once had personal experience of the positive power of prayer.[37] When she was training to become a teacher, she had been worried about a test she hadn't studied properly for, so she prayed hard to Saint Rose of Lima, and she did just fine. I suggested that her confidence in prayer may have kept her from the panic that often chokes people faced with important tests. She smiled and said, yes, she supposed that working from within could be *one* of the ways God answers your prayers. I admired her fast footwork. If she had been born a man, she could have been a Jesuit.

After this first casual mention of the power of prayer, Sister Mary-Theresa began slipping little comments on faith and belief into our afternoon work sessions, and the material she gave me to copy out was no longer taken from a penmanship book, with its awkward sentences contorted by the effort to use all the letters in the alphabet. Instead, the little paragraphs I was assigned to copy out were about boys who didn't know what they wanted to do with their lives until somebody, often a wise old priest, advised them to pray for guidance. Then something happened to show them that they had a calling. Maybe it was God's will that they become...

...She was trying to draw me into the service of God!

At first I resented her oblique slyness, but soon I found myself working up story games about becoming a priest and working in the slums with kids who accepted me because I was tough and street-wise. I would win the kids' admiration and confidence by beating them at ledgey, the way some Spencer Tracy might.

When I walked down Pearl Street, inwardly playing the priest role and smiling and nodding left and right, kindness and forgiveness in my eyes, I got some pretty strange return stares from other kids, but I persisted in the story game, imagining that the old ladies behind their curtains were looking out at Father Luke and Sister Mary-Theresa walking together, spreading love and charity around the neighborhood. The old dears would nudge one another and say: Look at that fine couple, off on their rounds of good works. They would never imagine that every night the young priest and the nun met in the privacy of his dreams, where their faces drew closer and closer together beneath her winged head-dress and she held his pen firmly as he...No, it was better that the admiring old ladies didn't know about all that. It might shake their faith.

But by the end of the week the priest games dried up for lack of fresh material, and I began rehearsing the moment when I would tell Sister Mary-Theresa of my love for her. I took my models from the women's films my mother dragged us to every other Thursday night. After trying out variants of their avowal scenes for a week, muttering both my lines and Sister Mary-Theresa's responses, I decided that I would wait until our after-school session was over and it was time for me to go home. I would open the door, then turn back and say: "Oh, by the way, Sister Mary-Theresa?" She'd look up from grading her papers and say: "Yes, Luke?" And I'd say in a gentle, grave voice: "Oh, nothing. It's just that...well, I love you." And I'd turn and leave, closing the door behind me. She'd sit there at her desk, stunned, overwhelmed, speechless, nonplused...or maybe she'd rush to the door and open it, but I'd already have disappeared into the swirling mists, so she'd close the door and, like women do in movies and nowhere else, she'd press the door closed with her butt and lean back against it, a dreamy smile on her lips as she envisioned our glowing future as man and nun confronting a suspicious world.

By the time my baffling, never-quite-innocent dreams of Sister Mary-Theresa brought me to daydreaming about revealing my feelings for her, she and I had been co-workers in the spiritual vineyard for nearly a year, ever since I joined the corps of altar boys at Saint Joseph's.

As soon as my training was over I found myself dragooned into serving the ill-attended six-o'clock low mass, a task the older altar boys avoided because Father Looney, the old priest who said these low-status masses, was notoriously crotchety and eccentric. (And don't imagine that his name escaped comment in the vestry.)

Saint Joseph's was only four blocks from our apartment, but despite its being on the edge of the slums it was an important church with a large, fairly prosperous congregation. In the 1870s priests from Ireland managed to supplicate, bully, threaten and shame the faithful into paying for the vast, echoing neo-Gothic cavern of Vermont granite that was Saint Joseph's, located in the southern end of the thirty-square-block area then known as Irishtown. Over the years, most of the Irish prospered and assimilated into the American ethno-cultural salad. They dispersed west and north, away from the river and the docks, leaving behind a handful of feckless bog Irish marooned on North Pearl Street. This is how Albany's 'Irish church' ended up in what most of its adherents considered a tawdry part of town. But still they came to hear the soft, curling accents of our priests, who continued to be supplied from Ireland.

The ladies of Saint Joseph's Altar Society were locked in pious competition with those of nearby Saint Anthony's, where Italians went because its priests could shrive and console in Italian, a great comfort to the older women who could not help feeling there must be some advantage in praying and receiving blessings in the Pope's (and presumably God's) native language. The kids of my block thought the Italian kids were lucky to have Saint Anthony of Padua as their special advocate because he was the patron saint of Lost Things and kids are forever losing or mislaying things and so have special need for his gifts of location and recovery. I never really believed in all that hokum, but once, just as a test, I shot off a quick prayer to Saint Anthony on the occasion of losing a nickel through a hole in my pocket. Although I didn't immediately find my nickel, I did come across three pennies over that summer (one flattened by the wheels of a trolley car), and this suggested that there might be some value in praying to Saint Anthony...about a fifty-percent value, assuming that a flattened penny is worth half of a normal one. So the Italians' Saint Anthony interceded usefully on behalf of people who had suffered losses, while our Saint Joseph championed more mundane groups: fathers, carpenters and cuckolds—although in reaching out to protect this last constituency, Saint Joseph reveals a refreshingly wry view of his relation to his eldest son.

As a gesture of sisterly solidarity, the Altar Societies of Saint

Joseph's and Saint Anthony's exchanged visits once each year. These included attending a high mass followed by triangular sandwiches with the crusts cut off and tea (which the Italian ladies didn't like) or coffee (which the Irish ladies mistrusted). These visits provided opportunities to score points in their on-going competition, which was fought out over the number and thickness of candles, the invention and abundance of floral decoration, the richness of fabric and fineness of stitching on the vestments, the volume of song, the lavishness of display, and the general cleanliness, glitter, polish and shine. Determined to be fair ('giving the devil his due' was how they saw it), the women of Saint Joseph's conceded that Italians had a certain innate decorative flair (a euphemism for their Mediterranean penchant for the garish and the gaudy). But Saint Joseph's could also pull off an impressive display on High Holy Days: forests of glittering candles; procession vestments of green, red and gold silk; swirls of dense incense tumbling over the edge of a swinging thurible; walls of sound erected by the organ whose bass notes were so low that they vibrated your bench and buzzed in your testicles as the massed voices of the Women's Chorus, the Men's Chorus and the Children's Chorus of Our Lady of Angels drenched the congregation with thick, luscious sound. High mass would be served by as many as four of the priests for whom our widows and spinsters nourished feelings that were largely, if not exclusively, maternal. These smiling, smooth-voiced priests were served by half a dozen stars of the corps of altar boys, mostly older lads who were seriously considering The Calling.

Father Looney was not smiling and smooth-voiced. An irritated frown was the expression into which his brow collapsed when he relaxed, and the papery cackle of his worn-out voice was better suited to reprimanding than to guidance and consolation. And his lone helper was unlikely to be 'called' to a vocation and, even if he had been, was unlikely to answer. The bleary-eyed early-morning masses that gruff old Father Looney and I ran were a down-market, off-the-rack version of those up-lifting spectacles that were the pride of Saint Joseph's and, our ladies felt sure, the secret envy of Saint Anthony's.

Father Looney with his scowling face and his unforgiving eyes behind steel-rimmed glasses was the parish's doyen. Over eighty years old and by turns vague, eccentric and prickly, he should have been retired years earlier, but as a zealous young priest at the turn of the century, Father Looney had taken upon himself the task of raising the money for all the church's stained glass; and no one, not even the bishop, had the courage to tell him that he could no longer serve in the church he had so richly illuminated. Instead, they restricted him to one early morning low mass each Sunday, with its small catchment from the seedy southeast edge of the parish: a handful of shelter-seeking bums and a scant score of pious old women, none of whom were ever seen by the grandees who attended high mass, that glittering ninety-minute feast for eye, ear, heart and spirit.

Father Looney was notorious for his tendency to divert his sermons from the text for the day onto his pet peeve: those evil children who played baseball in the street outside his church, their foul balls a constant threat to his precious windows. By the end of each sermon he would be hanging over the front of the lectern, his round eyeglasses askew and flashing as he assured the congregation in his broad west-of-Ireland brogue that putting the church's stained glass into jeopardy by playing ball in the street was a *sin*! Wanton destruction of God's house, that's what it was! Theft, pure and simple! It was stealing from God every bit as much as if you pulled out a gun and stuck the Baby Jesus up in some back alley! And don't you imagine for a minute that God doesn't see what you're up to. He sees! He knows!

The old women in front pews would shift their eyes nervously, and the bums at the back would turn up their collars and pull in their chins.

We were a team, Father Looney and I. I viewed myself as the smooth, nearly invisible facilitator of Father Looney's star turn...something like the black-clad puppet handlers of Bunrako. But I also relished my solo time, when all eyes were on me, or so I hoped. While Father Looney was in the sacristy, tugging his vestments on with impatient grunts, I would enter alone and genuflect as I passed before the tabernacle lamp. I always genuflected very deeply, bringing my nose to my knee, and holding the posture for a long moment to let its significance sink in for any onlookers. Then I would take up the long wood-and-brass candle lighter/snuffer, light its wick from one of the squat votive candles that flickered within red glass and, moving as gracefully as I could, I would touch my flame to each of the six candles that were our meager allotment. I always moved my wick away from the candle as soon as the flame caught, because I had noticed from out front that it never looked as though the candle was alight just at first, so I could create the near-miracle of candles seeming to light by themselves in the wake of my snuffer's passage. I would then return to the sacristy to give Father Looney's vestments a quick glance, because he was careless and often got things on crooked or wrongly tucked in and I, his theatrical dresser, would have to pull them around straight while he snorted and complained, after which I would assume my most severe and pious mien and follow him in to begin the service.

When I shook the little silver bell as Father Looney elevated the Eucharist, I tried to make the movement invisible, hoping that some of the celebrants might think the tinkle of the bell was a magic accompaniment to the miracle of transubstantiation. Father Looney was always impatient to get away as soon as mass was over, so he never stood outside the entrance, harvesting compliments and bestowing blessings. I would follow him to the sacristy, take his stole and chasuble and carefully fold them into his locker, then undo his rope girdle and hang it up. He insisted on grunting his own flailing, arthritic way out of his alb with a grumpy irritation that threatened to rip the seams. As he sat back, breathing heavily after his struggle, I took off my own starched surplice, so that I was in the all-black stage-hand's cassock when I returned to the altar to snuff out the candles, which I did in a new rhythm, the efficient motions of the workman cleaning up after a job well done. As I lifted the cup of the snuffer from each candle in turn, a thread of silvery smoke would wriggle up and vanish into the darkness above. I discovered that moving the candle wand away quickly after snuffing out a candle would drag the thread of smoke after it, crumpled and twisting, and the moment of miracles was over for another week.

For me, the smell of just-snuffed candles will always be the scent of sanctity...of mystery...of faith...of century upon century of secret fears and hopes whispered into the darkness.[38]

I liked the evocative sound of old-fashioned holy days like Quinquagesima Sunday, the Epiphany of the Magi, Pentecost and Childermas. When I came across the character Quasimodo in Hugo's *Notre Dame de Paris,* I thought I was probably the only kid in Albany to know that the hunchback's name came from the Quasimodo Sunday introit that begins, *Quasi modo geniti infantes:* "As newborn babes..."

For me, Eastertide ran from Quinquagesima, the Sunday before Lent, to Quasimodo, the Sunday after Easter, not because the season actually included those two bookends, but because I liked the sound of them.

I shall never forget Quinquagesima Sunday, 1941, for it was during that early mass that it suddenly dawned on me that I was guilty of sacrilege, for which my soul deserved all the torments of hell. And that's the kind of thing likely to cling to one's memory.

Among the pious old women who attended those six o'clock Sunday masses were two spinster sisters who always sat in the front pew because among the many afflictions God had sent to test their faith, they were hard of hearing. The poor dears also suffered from Parkinson's disease, so throughout Father Looney's tirade about evil baseballs and vulnerable church windows their heads would shake in what, if their eyebrows were lowered, might be interpreted as frowning disbelief that children could be so irresponsible or, with raised eyebrows, might be frightened denial of any personal complicity in this outrageous vandalism.

Each Sunday, after pouring first the wine then the water into Father Looney's chalice and watching him take the blood of Christ on behalf of the congregation, I would be the first to receive the communion wafer. Father Looney suffered from bouts of palsy that made his hand tremble uncontrollably, causing his nicotine-yellow fingernail to click against my front teeth as he gave me the wafer. It is the altar boy's responsibility to protect the incarnate body of Our Lord from the desecration of falling onto the church floor by catching it on a golden paten, should it slip from the priest's fingers in its passage to the communicants' mouths. I took this awesome duty very seriously as I accompanied the palsied Father Looney along the communion rail, particularly when we came to the two sisters with Parkinson's. Fearing a slip, I would grip the handle of the paten so tensely that my hand trembled, and with priest, communicants and altar boy all shaking, each in a different plane and at a different tempo, it was truly a miracle that the transubstantiated body of Christ didn't end up in the dust.

At the end of the mass Father Looney would turn to the congregation and chant, *Dominus Vobiscum,* and I would answer for the people, *Et cum spiritu tuo.* Finally back in the vestry, I would draw a deep breath of relief that the host had once again made it through communion without desecration.

For some time I had been sorely troubled by my dreams about Sister Mary-Theresa: the two of us floating on the lift of her wimple wings, she gripping my pen. I just *knew* this was sin. It had to be. It was too pleasurable not to be. Oh, not sin by deed or by word, maybe, but certainly sin by thought, because I couldn't help amplifying the details of our night flights in my imagination after I woke with an erection and sat at my window on the street, thinking about her, about us, about what she and I might someday...no, I mustn't think about that! But it wasn't until the Friday before Ash Wednesday, as I was walking home from school after my private lesson with Sister Mary-Theresa, that it suddenly occurred to me that during mass the following Sunday, Quinquagesima Sunday, I would be taking communion there before the congregation, while my soul was besmirched with the unconfessed sin of...well, I guess it would be grouped under Thou Shalt Not Commit Adultery.

Adultery. And not yet twelve years old. Jeez.

I decided to confess everything. I knew I'd feel better when this sin was off my soul. That Saturday evening I stayed home, listening to the radio, until it was almost time for the priests to leave their confessionals. There was ignoble method in waiting until the last minute, for I had decided that although I had no option but to confess my disgusting sins-of-thought, I would wait until the priest was eager to leave the confessional for tea at the priest house. That way I might get away with slipping my adultery in amongst my other sins and just sort of gliding over it without the priest really noticing. But, absorbed in the spooky radio mystery I was listening to, I dallied too long, so I had to run all the way to Saint Joseph's, and by the time I came clattering through the church door only one confessional still had its candle burning, and the last sinner was just returning to her pew and beginning to recite her penance.

I slipped into the confessional and breathlessly ran through blessmefatherforIhavesinned, then I whispered to the shadow beyond the perforated screen that I was sorry to keep him so late, and I quickly told him that it had been a week since my last confession and that during that time I had sinned twice against the Fourth Commandment in that I had disobeyed my mother, and a couple of times against the Sixth Commandment, and once against the Eighth Commandment in that I—

"The Sixth Commandment?" the priest interrupted me. "You're telling me that you committed adultery, Jean-Luc?"

The blood drained from my face. Father Looney never did stints in the confessional, not since there had been complaints about his quixotic notions of the relative gravity of various sins (playing baseball without a thought for church windows being ranked with apostasy, heresy and a taste for black masses). I guess they pressed him into service because of the rush for Easter absolution. Father Looney had, of course, recognized my voice.

"Let's hear about this adultery of yours," he said impatiently.

"Ah...Well, Father, it wasn't exactly adultery, it was more like... something else. But...ah...all sexual sins are grouped under the Sixth Commandment, so I guess—"

"I don't need you to tell me what commandment sexual sins are grouped under, boy. Now, just what was the nature of this sexual sin of yours?"

"I didn't sin in deed, Father. It was sin of thought."

"And what sort of thoughts were they that you entertained?"

Entertained? Could I tell Father Looney that his altar boy had been fantasizing about making love with a nun? No, of course not.

"Is it playing with yourself you've been doing, Jean-Luc?" Father Looney prompted, eager for his slippers and tea.

"No, Father. I...ah...well...I never did it before." I automatically fell back on a device I often used with authority figures: avoiding a downright lie by couching an irrelevant truth in terms that would cause them to draw a false conclusion. In this case, I said that I had never done it before, which was true. If he chose to extrapolate from my phrasing that I was admitting doing it now, was that my fault? I never thought out these sleight-of-mind ploys in advance; they just came naturally. My con-man genes, I guess.

"Now that wasn't so hard to confess, was it? The sin of Onan is a serious matter, but at least you didn't lure some poor girl into evil ways.

Tell me, Jean-Luc. Do you ever play baseball in the street outside the church?"

"Oh, no, Father, never!" I said in a wounded tone.

"No, no, I didn't think so. But there are those who do! Vandals, they are! Little heathens that don't care how much..."

When his tirade against fenestraclasts came to its muttering, tooth-grinding end, Father Looney told me to make a good Act of Contrition, and he gave me a milder penance than I had anticipated, just a little bouquet of Hail, Marys and a few Our Fathers. Masturbation was obviously a venial matter compared to breaking church windows.

As I walked home I told myself that I had been guilty of lying to a priest in the confessional, and therefore my absolution was invalid. But what choice did I have? Confess that I had dirty thoughts about a *nun?* I could never have made him understand that my thoughts weren't actually bad. Just mysterious and...well, loving. Sort of.

It wasn't until I was serving mass the following morning at six o'clock, and Father Looney's trembling fingers were lifting the wafer out of the chalice to place it on my tongue, that it suddenly occurred to me that I was about to take the sacred body of Christ into the unclean tabernacle of my body, knowing perfectly well that I was in a state of sin! This was worse than sin; this was sacrilege. But what could I do? Could I refuse the host, there in front of the congregation of gawking old ladies and hawking bums? For a second I considered tucking up my robe and running out of the church to avoid the eternal damnation that is the sure and just punishment for sacrilege, but Father Looney was holding the wafer out, frowning with impatience, so I opened my mouth and took it.

But I didn't swallow.

I followed Father Looney along the communion rail, holding the paten beneath the chins of the old women while the damning wafer melted against the roof of my mouth, and the heads of the spinster sisters shook in helpless pity for a soul forever lost.

My sacrilege had an unanticipated consequence: Sister Mary-Theresa never again visited my dreams to offer her cheek to mine as we levitated beneath the canopy of her wide-winged head-dress. I guess the sin of lust was scared out of me. And perhaps this was just as well because my sessions with Sister Mary-Theresa came to an end a couple of weeks later when she told me that she thought my spelling and penmanship had made sufficient progress that it was no longer necessary for us to spend an hour together after school every afternoon. Obviously she had given up on me as priest material, probably after talking to the young priest who taught the catechism classes.

I wasn't the only one visited by romance in 1941. My mother found a man who loved her. A cowboy.

A Cowboy Called Ben

I N THE fall of 1940 a powerfully built but hastily assembled man
from out West rented one of the low-ceilinged rooms on the top
floor of our building, rooms that were usually occupied by drifters
passing through, or by old men, lonely, furtive and seldom seen on the
street, many of whom moved out late at night to dodge paying their
rent, and a few died in their rooms. They were rented 'semi-furnished',
meaning a bed of sorts, a wobbly table, one or two chairs and usually
one other piece of anonymous, functionless furniture that somebody
had put in one of these top-floor rooms to be rid of it: a hall mirror,
perhaps, or an umbrella stand, or a Victorian what-not cabinet with
missing shelves and jammed drawers. The block didn't pay much attention to the transients who lived in top-floor rooms because they
weren't really part of our society, but this new young man from the
West, whom everyone called Ben (but whose last name no one knew)
turned out to be a more permanent resident. He got a job on the loading dock of the brewery, where he worked hard and kept to himself.

But the men of our block were suspicious of him when they discovered something about him that, in their view, was strange, even unnatural: Ben didn't drink. He never pinched the odd quart bottle of ale and drank it out behind the boiler room, like the other loaders did. Easy-to-steal beer was a perquisite for the Pearl Street men who did two- or three-month stints on the loading dock before getting fired for loafing or for bad-mouthing the boss. Work on the loading dock was 'casual', meaning that you got paid cash-in-hand at the end of each working day and no records were kept. The work was hard and the pay low, but the Welfare couldn't check up on you and dock your ADC payment because you were making money on the side.

In addition to his suspicious abstemiousness, Ben was an object of curiosity and conjecture because of his Sunday suit. He worked six days a week, doing as much overtime as he could get. On his way back from the brewery each evening he bought something at Mr Kane's that he could heat up on his gas ring for supper, so no one saw anything of him except on Sundays when he would emerge at about ten in the morning, freshly bathed and shaved and wearing a double-breasted suit of that hairy, acid-green material you saw nowhere but in South Street's 'barrel shops' that hung suits, trousers, dresses and coats from rope lines out in front of the store, watched over by a merchant who didn't bother to rise from his kitchen chair tipped back against the door frame when a customer was sniffing around, and whose only gesture towards salesmanship was a shrug and an ironic 'it's you, lady, believe me' or a factual 'you ain't going to find cheaper'. These establishments were called barrel shops because in the past hogshead barrels had been provided so people could change their clothing with a modicum of modesty, but by the time we lived in Albany the barrels had been replaced by small canvas-walled cubicles at the back of the shop. There were three such shops in a row, all displaying similar merchandise and run by men who could have been brothers. Perhaps they were. The clothing was bright, even garish, in keeping with the widely held tenet that the poor have a natural proclivity for the riotous and the gaudy. When Ben appeared at the top of our stoop every Sunday morning, his acid-green suit would have caused comment in itself, but he added dissonant elements that lent his ensemble a slapstick note. His suit was capped off by a wide-brimmed, pearl-gray Stetson, and he wore a pair of ornately tooled cowboy boots. He would stand for a moment at the top of the stoop looking shyly proud of his Sunday best, then he would descend and walk south on Pearl Street towards downtown, his broad shoulders tight within a suit jacket with a long back flap that made him look as though he were two-thirds torso and only one-third stubby legs. His upper body rocked and his shoulders dipped with each step; his fists were jammed deep into his pockets, bulging them out; and one trouser leg, if not both, was always hung up on the top of a cowboy boot. There was something ungainly about his walk, too, as though he had to re-mind himself to swing his right arm as he stepped out with his left leg, and he didn't always get that just right.

He wouldn't return until after dark. If anyone was out on the stoop, he would greet them in passing by touching the brim of his Stetson with two fingers, but he never said a word.

One Sunday morning during a glorious October Indian summer we were sitting out on the front steps to catch a little of that ephemeral sunshine, when Ben appeared at the top of the stoop. After his usual moment of showing himself with shy pride, he walked down past us, careful to leave lots of space, touched the brim of his Stetson as he passed Mother, and went down the street with his lurching walk. My mother looked after him and shook her head helplessly. "Poor guy. Not what you'd call graceful. From behind, he looks like two dogs fighting in a gunnysack. And that suit!" I couldn't help thinking of her bright blue 'Bette Davis' outfit that could be seen—perhaps even heard—from a block away. "Now, your father...he wouldn't have been caught dead in a suit like that."

Anne-Marie and I exchanged glances. Except for the night she was mired so deeply in the blues that she broke down and wept, this was the first time she had mentioned our father since she had snatched down the green crepe paper chain he had hung around our kitchen. Her voice oddly softened by memory, Mother went on to say that, irre-sponsible bastard though he was, you had to hand it to him on one count: he was a classy dresser. Always looked like he'd just stepped out of a bandbox. You felt proud to be in his company. All the women said he was a classy dresser. And a good dancer, too.

She turned to me. "You're going to be a classy dresser too, Jean-Luc. You've got a lot of your father's strut."

In one way I wasn't surprised that Mother saw some similarities between me and my father: over the years, my role had slowly shifted from that of son to that of helper and confidant. The money my paper route contributed to our income was even more important now that Lend-Lease had opened new markets for American farm products, and this reduced the agricultural excess available down at the surplus food warehouse. I guess it was partly because of Mother's dependence on the money from my paper route and partly because she couldn't have taken on tending the furnace and cleaning the halls without me to share the work and to take it over when she was ill, that I found myself promoted to the management level of our family. Problems were discussed and plans for the future made between Mother and me after Anne-Marie was asleep. These plans usually involved my leaving school and getting a job at the age of sixteen, when I would be dropped from the Welfare roles, but we still clung to our old daydream of my becoming a university professor in some small college up-state, or a doctor specializing in some non-contact, bloodless, pus-less, puke-less, piss-less branch of medicine, although just how I was going to get into medical school after leaving school at sixteen was not exactly clear.

We had returned to the front stoop after supper to enjoy the last of the Indian summer sun when Ben came back up the street, fists crammed into pockets, open suit jacket swinging behind, one trouser leg hooked up on a cowboy boot. He touched the brim of his Stetson to Mother, carefully stepped over Anne-Marie who was dozing with her head in Mother's lap, and disappeared into the building. Mother looked after him and shook her head again over his total lack of dress sense. This must have returned her thoughts to my father because after a silence she asked, "Jean-Luc? Do you feel bad about not having a father?"

I didn't answer, just shrugged and pushed out my lower lip. Like most kids, I was uncomfortable when my mother assumed a serious tone and I knew that if I said the wrong thing I might offend her or make whatever was troubling her worse. We had recently had to stop Anne-Marie's tap-dancing lessons 'for the time being', and Mother had grimly predicted that it would be just our rotten luck if the Hollywood talent scouts descended on Miss LaMonte's studio when Anne-Marie wasn't there to be discovered.

"I know that Anne-Marie misses having a father," Mother said, caressing my sister's sleeping face. "She needs someone to do things for her, someone to cheer her on. Oh, I know you go to her recitals and all, but a brother isn't a father. Fathers are special to girls, like mothers are to boys." She slipped her fingers into my hair. "...my good right hand."

Oh-oh, it's good right hand time again. And I immediately felt ashamed of this disloyal thought. I stood up and rubbed my upper arms like I was getting cold, and we all went inside.

I first spoke to Ben late one evening about a month later. The year's first snow had fallen, a slushy snow gray with soot that everyone tracked into the hallway and up the stairs, where it melted into the dents and cracks of the ancient linoleum. Mrs Hanrahan had come down from her fourth-floor rear apartment to scratch on our door (she scratched on doors, rather than knocked) and complain that the halls ought to be mopped right now, so someone didn't slip and break a hip.

About an hour later I had worked my way up to the top floor with the mop and bucket. I had long nourished a fantasy about having one of those top-floor rooms all to myself someday. I fantasized coming home to my own private nest from some office job I would land when I left school at sixteen. Maybe a job on a newspaper, since I was already in the newspaper business...if only at the delivery end. I would start out as a copy boy, and somehow that would lead to my stumbling upon a major 'scoop', which quickly made me a valued reporter, which developed into my having my name over a column in which I told everybody what I thought about everything, and this, of course, led to my writing books in the same vein, which soon made me a rich and famous author...and there she is, ladies and gentlemen, docked outside our window, all her flags fluttering in the breeze. Our ship! Yeowzah, yeowzah, yeowzah!

I recognized that to dream about having a little room of my own indicated a desire to get away from my mother, but I didn't see much harm to it. It was, after all, only a daydream. And I'd be in the same building, so if she got sick or anything went wrong, I could be down there in a flash to help her wring out the wash or to apply mustard plasters. Once I had the room, I would nick books out of the library (mostly encyclopedias and atlases with big, highly detailed maps) that I would keep in a bookcase along the wall, and from these I would learn all the useful things I wrote in my newspaper column and books. Above all, I'd have a radio all my own, one that received short-wave broadcasts from all over the world so I'd know about everything, like Mr. Kane did.

I was mentally furnishing my room and my future life as I mopped the top hallway, working by feel in the dark (the lightbulb had burned out), when I heard music from the room that belonged to Cowboy Ben. He was plucking some instrument, picking out what sounded like a Mexican melody. I stopped mopping so as not to disturb him, and I stood in the dark hall, listening. The plucking stopped and his door was snatched open. "What do you think you're...! Oh, it's you. How's it going, ol' buddy?"

"I was just mopping the floor," I said. "I'm sorry if the noise disturbed you."

He smiled. "It wasn't the noise. It was the sudden silence when you stopped mopping that disturbed me."

I knew exactly what he meant, but I thought I was the only one who 'heard' things like sudden silences or 'saw' things like nobody being where there ought to be somebody. I never gave this sense of negative perception a name, but I had always felt it.

"It's nice...I mean...your, ah..."

"It's called a mandolin. Come on in."

I followed him in. "It's a kind of guitar, isn't it?"

"No, not really. Guitars are mostly for chording and rhythm. You carry a melody on a mandolin. See how it's double-strung?" He held out the instrument, but I couldn't see much with the only light coming from behind him. "You pluck between the two strings to sustain a note and you...well, fact is, I'm just learning myself. I bought a book on how to play the mandolin after I found this thing in a hockshop in St. Louis."

The table behind him was strewn with manuals and complicated schematics that I would later discover were for radio receivers. He had recently taken up amateur short-wave radio as a hobby. That's where he went on his Sunday outings, to a ham radio club where people sat around and talked about sideboards and superheterodynes and stuff like that. I wonder what his fellow radio hams thought about the cowboy boots, the Stetson and the green suit.

I was interested in the complicated-looking schematics, and I could tell that he was hungry for conversation by the way he had volunteered information about his mandolin; but I still had a couple of pages of penmanship to do for Sister Mary-Theresa in my best imitation of her round Palmer hand, using the fountain pen she had given me, so I told him that I had to be getting back downstairs. He said, "Okay. See you around, ol' buddy," and closed his door behind me.

. . . .

In November Mussolini invaded Greece, but his incompetent generals and half-hearted troops soon got tangled in the mountains and came to grief. That same month, Hungary, Romania and Slovakia joined the Axis, as Bulgaria would do four months later.[39]

The winter of 1940–41 was long and cold. I would arrive at school with chapped cheeks and frozen ears after rushing through my predawn paper route then climbing back up the Livingston Avenue hill to Our Lady of Angels school, where the over-heated classrooms and unchallenging schoolwork soon lulled me into dozing and daydreaming. I filled the time imprisoned at my desk with story games, a new favorite being the development of an 'unbreakable' code that I intended to offer to the American army and navy because everyone was saying that war with Germany was inevitable, although the Irish on our block said they'd be goddamned if they'd fight alongside the English.

In the evening, I sat with my mother and Anne-Marie in front of our Emerson, listening to hissing short-wave broadcasts by Edward R. Murrow from London. We could hear the *crump* of bombs dropping in the background, and we knew that the blitz was happening right then. At that very moment! It was America's first experience with war as a live media event, and it was impressive. And chilling, too.[40]

. . . .

I only saw Ben occasionally over the months when I was weaving my delightful, if sinful, love fantasies involving Sister Mary-Theresa, but when we happened to pass in the hall or on the street, he would always say, "How's it going there, partner?" which sounded cowboy enough to please me.

That early slushy snow was followed by one of the coldest winters on record. The Hudson froze over, and two boys from Troy were drowned when they tried to walk across and fell through the thin center ice. (Who but a kid from Troy would try a stupid stunt like that, I ask you?) It was after midnight and I was reading in my daybed, my Hudson Bay blanket around me, when I noticed that double cones of mist came from my nose when I breathed out. The room had grown cold. Something must be wrong with the old boiler...again. Since heat was included in the price of rent, everyone in the building complained if the radiators weren't hissing and thumping with hot water from September 15 to March 15, regardless of the weather. Every winter morning before setting off on my paper route, I had to shake down the ashes then carefully pile a little coal on the remaining embers, then when the smoke from the pile thickened and caught with a little puff, I would put on a few more lumps of coal, and when they in turn caught, a full load that would last until noon. Sometimes I would find that the fire had gone out during the night, and I'd have to start a fresh one using broken-up orange crates for kindling. This always took more time than I had allotted for morning chores and made me late for my paper round, which in turn made me late for school. Most frustrating were those times when a big fused clinker would get caught in the grating while I was shaking down the ashes, and I would have to throw my body weight against the shaker handle in an effort to break the clinker up, often bruising my shoulder on the iron bar. I was obliged to open the fire door and bang around in the embers and ashes with the shaker handle to break up the clinker, raising clouds of ash and smoke and inevitably putting out the last lingering embers while getting myself filthy with ash and coal dust, then having to start the fire from scratch, and being late for school yet again, Goddamnit to hell! ('Jeez' had, by this time, been relegated to those childhood years when I had been innocent enough to imagine that God didn't know it was a euphemistic variant of Jesus.)

For a while I lay there breathing out jets of mist, hoping the fur-

nace would start working again of its own volition. But it wasn't long
before Mrs Hanrahan up in fourth-floor rear expressed her displeasure
by banging her radiator with her slipper, waking up the rest of the
apartment house on the jungle telegraph of our pipes. Mother came
staggering out of the bedroom she shared with Anne-Marie, tying her
robe about her, but when we got down to the boiler room and turned
on the naked overhead bulb we found that the fire was burning just
fine, and there was pressure in the system...too much pressure, in fact!
Steam was escaping from the safety petcock in a screaming jet! We
fumbled around, trying this and that, touching hot things and snapping our fingers to keep the burn from hurting, but all to no avail! And
Mrs Hanrahan kept up her angry Morse of complaint until my
mother's short-fused temper snapped and she went charging up five
flights of stairs to engage in a shouting match through Mrs Hanrahan's
door, which the old lady didn't dare open because Mother's French-'n'-
Indian rages were well known on the block. While this was going on, I
rushed up to our apartment, filled a bucket with water from our tub
and brought it slopping down the narrow, unlit basement stairs to fling
it into the roaring mouth of the furnace because the needle on the
boiler gauge had pegged at the top of the red danger area, and I was
sure it would blow up at any moment. I emptied the bucket into the
fire but it had no effect on the roaring flames. (Oh, sure! But the damn
fire would go out just like *that* in the mornings, when I was trying to
revive it!) I dashed back up the stairs for more water. Even in these
dangerous circumstances when I feared the boiler would blow up in my
face, and even though my teeth were chattering because my pajamas
were drenched with slopped water, I couldn't help making a story game
of it, muttering to my frightened comrades, telling them that we must
save this military base from sabotage by the dirty Storm Troopers. You
can imagine my embarrassment when, making my way down the dark
stairs with a second brimful, slopping bucket of water as I issued orders
and encouragement to my followers and growled defiant threats to the
Nazis lurking down in the coal bunker, I ran into someone in the passage. No possibility here of converting my theatrical muttering into
song, so I tried profanity. The stranger was Ben, who had come down
from his top-floor room. He took my bucket and preceded me down to

the basement, where he looked over the situation with an amused calm that won my instant admiration. (Indeed, calm amusement became the principal idiom of my manner as leader of my band for the next few games.) While Mother's angry voice filtered down from five floors up, blending with the inhaling roar of the fire within the open furnace door and the angry hiss of the steam from the petcock, Ben felt his way along the pipes until he came to an especially hot area, over which he poured the bucket of water in a slow even flow until, suddenly, there was a loud clank in the pipes, followed by a drop of the needle towards the safe green area and a sighing decrease in the force of the steam jetting from the petcock. Ben threw a couple of shovels of coal into the boiler, kicked the door closed and handed the bucket back to me.

"Well, I guess that's got her whipped," he said. "Some sort of vapor lock, I reckon."

I nodded gravely. Yup, that was probably it. Some sort of vapor lock. But we had her whipped. Oh sure, we were tired and wet and cold, but we'd done it, this cowboy and I. The Storm Troopers were beaten. We'd licked 'em fair 'n' square. Vapor lock.

I changed pajamas and went back to my daybed to read until I fell asleep, but from back in the kitchen I could hear the quiet voices of my mother and Ben talking over cups of coffee. A little later, a loud clank snatched me out of a doze during which I had been reading through closed eyelids—slowly, perhaps, and not absolutely clearly, but reading nonetheless. The clank was Mrs Hanrahan getting in a last wrathful word by banging on the pipes. I heard my mother threaten to go up those stairs and give that old nut a piece of her mind, but Ben's soft western burr joshed her out of her anger, saying that probably the only thing keeping the poor old biddy alive was the hate and frustrations she gnawed on like an old dog worrying a bone. That evocative image of the toothless old dog 'worrying' a bone carried me into sleep.

The following Sunday, Anne-Marie and I came home from a movie Ben had treated us to, and walked in to find him kissing our mother. All four of us blushed. But that night, as we sat around the kitchen table playing hearts (Mother and me against Ben and Anne-Marie because I was the best card player and Mother loved to win), we talked about all sorts of things. I could see that the adults didn't intend to explain anything about their feelings for each other, and that was just fine with me because I didn't want to hear about it. When it comes to making a child cringe and shudder, the idea of parents being in love comes second only to envisioning them *making* love.

I guess I had been right about Ben's being lonely and hungry for conversation, because during the next few evenings around our kitchen table, he responded to Anne-Marie's and my frank curiosity by telling us great stories about the years he had been on the drift after running away from an orphanage at the age of thirteen. Because he was what he called 'well-grown', he had been able to find work as a fisherman in Alaska at the age of fourteen, and later he worked as a harvest hand through the South and Midwest, as a gandy-dancer on the Great Northern Railroad up along the Canadian border, as a mechanic in the wildcat oil fields of Texas, in general construction in New England, and most interesting to me, as a cowboy in Wyoming for two years. I had the typical urban kid's image of the cowboy: Gene Autry or Roy Rogers singing as he rode into town, followed by the Sons of the Pioneers or the Riders of the Purple Sage playing their guitars from the saddle and singing in close harmony, all dressed in fancy cowboy suits with bright buttons and dangling fringe.

Before we met him, my family had shared the block's view that Ben's ridiculous Sunday get-up qualified him as 'a weird one', but when we learned that his tooled two-tone boots and his Stetson were not just quirky affectations, but came from his time as a cowboy, Anne-Marie and I were able to overlook his sartorial peculiarities, even if Mother was not. Everything else about him seemed admirable. He was kind and polite; he knew lots of jokes and hundreds of folk songs; he had a powerful sense of justice and fair play; and although almost entirely self-taught, his curiosity and his native intelligence had equipped him with most of the building skills, from carpentry and masonry to roofing, electricity and plumbing, as well as an intimate understanding of internal combustion motors. In addition, he had a vast store of odd bits of lore including a buff's hair-splitting knowledge of Civil War minutia, the ability to rattle off all the sails on a clipper-rigged schooner, the names of the presidents and vice presidents in order, and the capitals and nicknames of all forty-eight states. He was at that moment teaching himself what he believed was the coming field of employment: electronics, and he was able to pick out tunes on the Italian mandolin. All fascinating stuff for an admiring boy, but I couldn't help wondering why a man as intelligent and knowledgeable as Ben was doing brute-work on the loading dock of a brewery.

Within a week, he was eating his suppers with us, and soon after that he was also coming down to have his morning coffee with Mother before going to work, and paying her for his board. When he began coming back from the brewery at lunchtime for a sandwich and a cup of soup, the women of our block sniffed and raised their eyebrows about the goings-on over at 238.

"If I said it once, I said it a thousand times: for all her airs, that Canuck ain't no better than she ought to be."

It was no coincidence that Ben's arrival in our lives put an end to the periodic flights from my mother that began when I ran away on my tricycle at the age of three, and included that night I ended up hanging off a railroad bridge while an engine passed inches from my face. All in all, I ran away eight or nine times.

...Well, I didn't actually run away... When things got too bad I used to escape into a story game *about* running away from home. This involved days of preparation. I planned to leave on a Sunday, right after mass, and I made up plausible stories about chores I had promised to do up at the priest house, jobs that would involve working all day and well into the evening. This would keep my mother from contacting the police until after nightfall, by which time I would be miles away from Albany. I intended to walk and hitchhike west, living by my wits. I would travel from one little lake to the next because I knew from living in Lake George that rich people had lake cottages that stood empty most of the time. I'd be able to sneak in and out of them and no one would ever know. There would be a few cans of food in the larders that the owners wouldn't miss, and of course, being by a lake, I could always supplement my diet with fresh fish...once I learned how to fish, that is.

At the library I pored over the road maps and worked out my route west along the Mohawk Valley. I chose secondary roads to avoid getting picked up by the state police, and I listed the small towns where I could stay overnight after getting my supper in a warm, cheerful little house in return for whitewashing a back fence for a kind-hearted woman with a name like Aunt Polly. Once I got to Lake Erie everything would be fine. I'd stow away on a lake freighter and the next thing you know I'd be in Canada or Minnesota, where I'd find someone who needed a smart kid to help him with his business, and I'd make money to send home, and sooner or later I'd make a big killing and become rich enough to get my family off Pearl Street.

Part of my preparation involved stashing away, bit by bit, the emergency food I might need on the road: pieces of dark toast for my 'hardtack' and a glutinous mixture made of oatmeal, mashed up dried apple and whatever else I could find, dampened with water and pressed into a washed-out tin can. This was the 'pemmican' of my 'iron rations'. (I had gone through a period of masochistic fascination with the privations of polar exploration.)

But the days of careful planning needed to effect my break-out always sufficed for me to get over feeling wounded by whatever sharp word or criticism had made me want to run away in the first place, so in the end I would decide I really couldn't leave my mother and sister, and I would confirm this acceptance of my obligations by the ceremony bringing my iron rations into the back alley and eating them...stuffing them down, that is, because the toast was by then explosively dry and my versions of pemmican were always vile-tasting and slimy. Despite my native squeamishness I was usually able to dispose of the evidence of my perfidious plan to leave my family in the lurch by swallowing the filthy stuff, thus punishing myself for even considering running out on them. But sometimes it was just so foul that I had to leave it out in the back alley, where some other kid needing iron rations might be glad to find it.

It would be misleading to give the impression that I found the responsibility for getting my mother and sister out of North Pearl Street so burdensome that I sat up every night planning to run away and free myself. In fact, the hours I spent looking out onto the street were, for the most part, pleasant and restful. I would sit on the edge of my bed or kneel by the window, drifting through daydreams, making up narratives, or slowly turning some concept in the fingers of my mind until drowsiness overwhelmed me. Only occasionally, when the pressures became too great, would I slip into the balm and refuge of what I called The Other Place...a mystic internal locale to which I enjoyed privileged access.[41] But when money was particularly tight, or Mother was ill for a long time, or deep in the blues that crushed the joy out of her, tension would sneak up on me as I sat at the window, until I realized that my jaw muscles were sore from standing out like ropes as I ground my teeth with the dread that I would never be able to accomplish the task of bringing our damned ship in. I simply didn't know what to do! It was at these times that I found comfort in planning to run away from home. Not often. Maybe twice a year or so. But I never did carry out the escape game that served as an emotional release valve, and after Ben arrived I no longer felt the need to run away because I had found someone on whom I could off-load responsibility for my mother's happiness.

Over the months that followed I learned more about Ben, some of it troubling. I learned why he didn't drink...or, rather, that he did drink, but only rarely and with considerable risk. Mother talked him into taking his acid-green suit down to the barrel-shop and trading it in on a looser-fitting mud-colored three-piece suit. To initiate it they both dressed up and went out for a beer at the Corner Tavern down on Quackenbush Street, where I used to drop in with my shoe-shine box on Friday nights. They got back pretty early, and Ben didn't seem drunk or even especially exhilarated, but the next day he got into a bitter argument with the foreman in the brewery and the upshot was that he got fired. It wasn't long before he found another job, digging sewer lines in the nearby town of Watervliet, but it paid less and it was cold, wet work. Mother made sandwiches for his lunch pail and a thermos of hot soup, but he missed coming home to her every noon so they could have an hour together without us kids around. Ben confessed to Mother (and she thought it was necessary to take me aside and tell me 'on the QT') that drinking that beer at the Corner Tavern had been a big mistake. He swore to her that he drank very seldom, so he certainly wasn't an alcoholic or anything like that, but this wasn't the first time that he had taken a few drinks, and then had done something stupid that cost him his job, or his money, or a friend. He couldn't understand it. Above all, he couldn't understand why he took a drink in the first place, considering the disastrous effect it almost always had on him. It wasn't that he got drunk—not unsteady or morose or maudlin or aggressive; he didn't drink enough for that. The effect drinking had on Ben was to make him do something stupid or self-harming, a loss of judgment that usually didn't occur until the day after he had drunk a couple of beers. He had promised himself a hundred times that he would never touch a glass of beer again, but he always did. He claimed that he sort of forgot the consequences. Forgot! Now *that's* nuts. He wondered if maybe his father, whom he had never known, had been an alcoholic or a nutcase or something like that.

He told Mother that he had first noticed this weakness when, at the age of sixteen, he had lied about his age and enlisted in the Navy. After surviving those boot-camp routines and fatigues that are designed to crush the last traces of individualism, he took his first liberty from the Great Lakes Naval Training Station with some other boots. During his twelve hours of freedom in Milwaukee he drank a couple of shots of whisky...just showing off, playing it for grown up. The next day, although he had nothing against the Navy, he climbed over a fence and kept going until he was in Seattle. From that time on, Ben had drifted from one low-paid, casual job to another, never daring to seek regular employment because he feared that the Navy was looking for him and if they found him, they would put him into prison for desertion. This accounted for all the crappy jobs taken over the years by a man who possessed a powerful work ethic and the gifts of intelligence and initiative that should have brought him better-paid work. It also accounted for his drifting from place to place across the country, keeping on the move because he feared that 'they' were looking for him.

Even in that winter of 1940–41, when unemployment was beginning to loosen its stranglehold as industry expanded to serve America's Lend-Lease Program for equipping England to fight the Germans, Ben never sought the higher-paying work his native abilities merited, because such work would oblige him to reveal his Social Security number, through which the Navy could find him. He limited himself to doing mindless stoop-labor at places that paid him cash-in-hand at the end of each week and no questions asked.

I resented Mother's taking me into her confidence about Ben's peculiar problems with alcohol, because there was nothing I could do about it other than worry. But I still enjoyed his company, his rich cache of stories, and his wry, earthy view of human nature. Because he was quick-minded enough to have picked up the essentials of half a dozen building trades by working as a casual helper, he viewed all claims of privilege based upon 'experience' to be smoke screens thrown up by those who feared competition. He said that most men who brag of having ten years' experience on the job have really only had a week's experience repeated 520 times. He believed that any bright person can do anything these 'craftsmen' can do; the only 'experience' he needs is learning the language of the trade and having access to the specialized tools; all the rest is down to brains, motivation and the ability to generalize from particulars. When a lamp needed repair Ben would let me help him. He began by explaining the general principles of electrical flow, personifying an electron as 'this negatively charged yahoo who comes high-tailin' it down a wire so fast that his friction heats up the filaments and makes them glow.' Having sketched in the principles involved, he would do the specific job in hand, repairing a short in a wire, for instance, explaining everything as he did it, step by step, then he would undo his work and let me do it, patiently accepting the fact that my clumsiness and inexperience would cause any job to take three times as long with my help as it would have taken without it. Finally, he would generalize what we had done and show how the same theory and the same methods would apply to other problems with electrical things that didn't work.[42]

I liked the rubbery flexibility of Ben's battered face. His roughhouse life had left him with a broken nose and puffy brows, but he had remained an optimist at core, and he knew hundreds of folksy similes, some of which were pretty blue and drew my mother's prudish disapproval, like 'being as frustrated as a one-armed paper-hanger', or working as hard 'as a one-legged man in an ass-kicking contest' or saying that something unpopular 'went over like a fart in a diving bell'. I also appreciated his well-developed sense of the absurd. He and I would sometimes join forces in chasing some idea to its reductio ad absurdum, usually to my mother's frowning annoyance because she found the absurd baffling and irritating (perhaps irritating because baffling). I recall one evening when Ben was telling stories about hobos he had met while riding the rails. He described one of them as being ugly... so-o *ugly* that all his ugliness wouldn't fit on his face, so he had to carry some of it around with him in a paper bag. I instantly jumped into the stream of his absurdity, suggesting that some day this hobo might meet a woman who was beautiful...so-o *beautiful* that all her beauty wouldn't fit on her face so she had to carry some of *it* around in a paper bag. And if, for some reason, this ugly hobo decided to pour the excess ugliness out of his bag into hers—

Ben immediately caught on and continued, "...there would be a loud snap, crackle and pop, and when they looked into her bag...it would be empty!"

"Exactly!" I said, slapping the table with delight.

Mother blinked. "I don't get it. Why was the bag empty?"

"Because," I explained, "his ugliness had canceled out her beauty, leaving nothing behind!"

"Maybe there was a gray powder of ordinary looks left behind," Ben suggested.

"No," I said. "If his ugliness had *blended* with her beauty, they might have produced ordinary looks; but they didn't blend, they *neutralized* one another!"

"You're right, partner. There wouldn't have been anything left in the bag. In fact, the vacuum created by the sudden neutralization would have sucked that bag together so tight that it wouldn't have been a bag any longer, just a double-thickness piece of paper."

Mother sniffed and said she just didn't see the point of all this nonsense, and Ben winked at me and told her with great seriousness that she was absolutely right, there was no sense to it. Then he admonished me for wasting time on ridiculous ideas that didn't have any sense to them, and I said I was sorry and I would never, ever do it again, and Ben said, "And make sure you don't!"

Although Ben didn't possess any of the social and physical graces that my mother had found so attractive in my father (on the few occasions that I saw Ben run, his arms and legs had the every-which-a-way chaos of a startled herd), and although his habits of speech were too scatological and salty for her, she appreciated his essential kindness and his native sense of fair play. But she was not proud to be seen in his company. In short, except for his bizarre and troubling reaction to alcohol, Ben possessed all those solid qualities that parents look for in a husband for their daughter, but few of those decorative ones the daughter seeks on her own behalf.

The five dollars a week that he paid Mother for his meals was enough for her to put a little into the Dream Bank, and that made her feel more secure than she had for years. By Easter, Ben had become a member of our family even to the extent of joining in the ritual of sitting in the dark to listen to the Friday night mystery programs on our Emerson. Anne-Marie was comfortable with him, and she was more sensitive than I about Mother's ambiguous feelings towards him. One Saturday when we were walking home from a movie we had been sent to so the adults could be alone together, she confided to me that she thought Ben liked Mother more than Mother liked Ben, and she hoped Mother didn't 'break Ben's heart'. I wrinkled my nose at the soap-opera phrasing, but I knew what she meant.

· · · · · · · · · ·

Summer vacation was half over when my mother received a letter from her cousin, Lorna, who lived in a small quarrying town on the Vermont border. Lorna and Mother had been very close when they were teenagers, closer than Mother had been to either of her sisters, with whom she had felt she had to compete for her father's love. The two cousins won all the cups on offer for dancing the Charleston together, but the 'Deadly Dancing Duo', as they styled themselves, broke up when Lorna met Tonio, a lazy, handsome bully who had a newspaper/magazine/candy shop that was also a numbers outlet. Right from the first, my mother and Tonio didn't hit it off, and when he made a play for her while dating her cousin, she told Lorna that she was too good for him, and she ought to drop him like a hot tomato. When Lorna got pregnant, Mother offered to help pay for an abortion, because anything would be better than living her life with a man like that. There was no abortion and Lorna and Tonio got married, but she miscarried a month after the wedding, and something must have gone wrong because she never got pregnant again. Tonio never quite lost the suspicion that he had been somehow tricked into this marriage.

Tonio saw to it that the two cousins didn't see much of each other over the years that followed, but when Mother married my father, the whole family got together for the wedding, where my grandfather didn't bother to hide his low estimation of the strutting Tonio, who wore black silk ties and fedoras with wide snap brims in imitation of George Raft, whom he resembled. When Tonio bragged about his contacts among the 'smart boys' from Glens Falls and Troy, there were words between him and my grandfather that ended with Tonio dragging Lorna away from the reception, and Mother always felt that her favorite cousin's failure to stay at the reception had jinxed her marriage.

After my father deserted us for the second time, we had been obliged to live with Lorna and Tonio for a couple of months while Mother looked for a job. But the presence of Anne-Marie and me in their childless home caused friction. 'Uncle' Tonio (Mother had us call them aunt and uncle out of affection for Lorna) took a particular dislike to me. He looked on my bookishness as a personal affront because he had flunked out of school. But he'd shown them all by buying his newspaper/magazine/candy shop with a loan from 'the boys down in Troy', the boys he ran numbers for. Uncle Tonio found my habit of muttering to myself in the course of my story games particularly irritating. "You wanna know what that kid is? I'll tell you what he is. He's crazy, that's what he is. A crazy kid with big words running out his mouth, that's all he is." One day I responded sassily to something he said, and he cuffed me on the back of the head. Mother's F-'n'-I temper flashed, and there was a shouting match, with Mother calling Tonio a cheap numbers flunky and Tonio responding that it was no wonder her husband had dumped her, with her constant carping and bitching. My mother said at least my father hadn't knocked up some romantic kid to make her marry him, and the next thing you know, the two cousins were going a few rounds, picking at the scab of an old sore concerning the Charleston cups they had won when they were dancing together. They both wanted to know where those cups were now. You tell me! I don't have them! Well, *I* certainly don't have them! Well, *somebody's* got them! Well, not me! And it all ended up in shouts and tears and slamming doors.

An hour later, I found Anne-Marie sitting on the cellar stairs, rocking herself, her eyes fixed on the darkness below. Although she was not yet two, strife and tension upset her deeply, obliging her to withdraw into herself in search of a peaceful place to be. I sat beside her until she became aware of my presence and stopped rocking herself. For a time, she just sat there, breathing in and out evenly, then she rose and went out into the backyard. I knew from experience that she would have to be alone for a while before she was able to be with people again.

The following morning, Mother, Anne-Marie and I were on a bus for Lake George Village, where she managed to find a job before the money in her purse ran out.

About a year later, when my father wrote to her out of the blue asking us to join him in Albany so we could pick up the threads of our life together, Mother had to swallow her pride and contact Lorna to ask if Tonio could help us move our few possessions to Albany. Grudgingly, yet triumphantly, he drove over to Lake George Village in his old truck, loaded it up with our stuff, crammed the three of us into the front seat beside him, and brought us to North Pearl Street, all without saying more than half a dozen words, and most of these grumbled under his breath. Mother never forgave him for just dumping us on the sidewalk and driving away, and the two cousins had not communicated since. Mother had been hurt by her long separation from Lorna—not that she ever thought their falling out was *her* fault in any way! No, sir! And she'd be goddamned if she'd be the first to apologize, believe me you!

Aunt Lorna's unexpected letter invited me to come to Granville that summer and spend the month of July with them. Mother read this as a gesture of reconciliation, an oblique request for forgiveness on Lorna's part, if not on Tonio's, and she was willing to meet her part way. She asked me what I thought about the idea of spending July in Granville.

"Well...I don't know..."

"It might do you good to get out of the city for a while. I'll do the paper route for you."

"Yes, but..."

"And you won't be bored. Lorna says that Tonio says there's plenty for a boy to do around there."

"Yeah...well..."

And it was settled. I was going to have a nice vacation, like it or lunk it.

. . . .

In April Hitler came to the assistance of the Italians who had been beaten to a standstill by Greek partisans. Germany invaded Greece and Yugoslavia, both of which were overrun by the end of the month. On the radio, solemn-voiced commentators explained that Hitler had dared to attack Yugoslavia because the Russo-German Nonaggression Pact assured him that the Soviets would not intervene on the side of their fellow Slavs. Now the Axis dominated all of Europe except for six countries: Switzerland and Sweden, which enjoyed a profitable neutrality, Spain and Portugal, which were ruled by fascist dictators whose neutrality was distinctly pro-German, and Ireland, whose neutrality was distinctly anti-English.

England stood alone.

That June, Hitler renounced his Nonaggression Pact with the Russians and launched a surprise invasion, his armored units penetrating deep into Soviet territory as all opposition seemed to melt before the invincible German tanks.

When I asked Mr Kane about this out on his side steps, I was surprised that he seemed less gloomy than he had been of late, despite the news broadcasts telling us day after day how much farther the Germans had thrust into Russia. "He's made a mistake," Mr Kane said, looking down at the hard-packed sooty earth of his 'garden' with narrowed eyes, as though he were peering into the future. "Hitler has made Napoleon's mistake. He'll be conquered by the vast distances, and by the weather. The versts and snow. Russia's ancient weapons. Like Napoleon, Hitler will be beaten by General Winter."

Nothing brought the reality of the distant European war to us so personally as the popular songs we followed on the weekly *Your Lucky Strike Hit Parade*. As early as 1939, many people had been touched by the resilience and courage evinced in 'We'll Meet Again', a song that we knew, not in its original stiff-upper-lip British version by Vera Lynn, but in the smooth, easy-listening version made popular by the Ink Spots.[43] As the war came closer, three popular songs in particular revealed the state of things in Europe: 'White Cliffs of Dover', 'My Sister and I', and 'The Last Time I Saw Paris'.

．．．．．．．．．

July came, and I had the adventure of traveling alone on the bus to Granville, changing buses at Glens Falls. But by the time I had passed three days in Aunt Lorna and Uncle Tonio's house, my most ardent desire was to be back on North Pearl Street. I felt out of place in the silent, childless house that Aunt Lorna kept immaculately tidy: a nervous cleanliness that seemed unnatural to me. It turned out that Uncle Tonio's 'plenty for a boy to do' began with mowing his lawn. Then he suggested that I go around the town asking people if they wanted their lawns mowed. 'Make a little money for yourself. It's better than taking hand-outs from the welfare.'

In Granville, as elsewhere in America, mowing the lawn and shoveling the snow were the man's major contribution to household chores, and he did both with more fuss and gadgetry than was necessary, so my only potential customers were old women living on their own. But Granville had lots of old women on their own because it was a quarry town, and slate quarrying is dangerous work that tends to skew populations towards a preponderance of widows. I walked around town knocking on doors and offering to do their lawns using their own lawn mowers, all of which turned out to be heavy antiques that hadn't been oiled in years and had never felt the harsh caress of a sharpener's stone. The going rate for a lawn was fifteen cents, and to save money the old women let their grass go until it was at least three inches high, so mowing it was really hard work. By the time I had slogged my way through the first lawn, I had a row of puffy blisters on each palm and the web of each thumb was raw and weeping. I was able to take only short bites in the long grass before it jammed the reel and obliged me to back off to get a run at the next short bite, throwing all my weight against the wooden handle of the mower with each short surge. My first lawn took all morning, then when I knocked on the door to collect my fifteen cents, the lady called my attention to my failure to trim around the edges and borders, and to rake up the grass and pile it neatly in back, and did I really intend to put that lawn mower away without cleaning it first? Would I treat my own mower that way? Mowers cost money, you know, and money doesn't grow on trees.

It took from after breakfast until lunch to do a lawn, then most of the afternoon to do a second one, if I was lucky enough to find another customer. The backs of my calves and the nape of my neck got so sunburned that I could only sleep on my stomach; and the blisters I got that first day burst again with every job and never got a proper chance to callous over.

Most of the old ladies I mowed for were so demanding and tight-fisted that I was surprised when one customer, a gaunt woman with the gimlet eye and the razor-thin lips of a storybook witch, gave me a glass of Kool-Aid and a nickel tip in addition to my fifteen cents. My very next client was a sweet old dear with a vague smile and pale blue eyes. When I finished her lawn she dumped fifteen pennies into my palm and, with a twinkle in her faded eyes, she asked, "Would you like a dime?" Assuming she was offering a tip, I said, thanks, that's very nice of you, so she took back the pennies and gave me a dime, all the while smiling and winking at me in an impish way that made it impossible for me to complain without seeming disrespectful and greedy. I'd been conned by an old lady! I'd made a nickel extra on the hag's lawn, then lost a nickel on the sweet old lady's anti-tip.

Throughout my 'vacation' I never made more than thirty cents a day, but I worked every day it didn't rain, except Sundays because Tonio said he'd be damned if any kid staying with him was going to take the Lord's day in vain. When I told him it was the Lord's name one took in vain, not His day, he muttered something about my being a wise-mouth, just like my mother...and crazy too, always talking to myself!

One day I was pushing a dull mower over a big corner lawn for a crabbed old woman who watched me from behind her curtains, as though I was going to steal her grass or something. The overgrown lawn was full of hidden twigs the previous day's storm had brought down from the trees, and these kept jamming the cutting blade, stopping the mower short and wrenching my wrists. It was miserable work: the air was heavy and muggy, sweat stung my eyes, my shoulders smarted where the old sunburn had peeled off leaving sensitive new skin, and the old blisters on my palms had broken and were weeping stickily. I was about halfway through when I heard a sound like ten thousand strips of bacon frying in a huge pan. This sound came sweeping down the street towards me, and before I could run for cover, the heaviest hailstorm I've ever known was ripping leaves off the trees, hissing into the grass, white ice pebbles bouncing up waist high. Gasping for breath and being stung by a thousand needles, I managed to get the mower back into the lady's shed, then I dashed to her porch and shouted through the screen door over the din that I'd come back to finish when the storm stopped, and I ran off. By the time I got back to Aunt Lorna's the hail had changed into a cold sleety rain and I was drenched and sneezing, so she put me into bed with a hot water bottle.

I was in bed for three days with a feverish summer cold. By the time I was well enough to sit out on the porch, it was only a couple of days before my return to Pearl Street. But first I had to finish the lawn I had partly done when that monster hailstorm came in. The half I had already mowed had grown a little while I was sick in bed, and the old battle-ax made me mow the whole lawn because she wasn't going to pay good money for a lawn that was uneven. The mowing was slow and difficult not only because the fever had left me weak but because the hail had knocked down a lot more twigs from her trees, and these jammed the mower even more often than before. It took me all day, and when I finished the woman gave me a glass of buttermilk as a cheapskate sort of tip. I've always hated buttermilk, but I drank it to spite her. It wasn't until I was walking back to Aunt Lorna's that I wondered if that had been stupid. What if it had been a glass of spit? Would I have drunk that to spite her, too?

By the end of my vacation in Granville I had cut forty-seven lawns and earned, according to my pocket notebook, seven dollars and five cents, minus the twenty-five cents I squandered over the month on five Royal Crown Colas, which I bought after particularly exhausting lawns had left me with a raging thirst, too good a thirst to waste on water, so I bought a Royal Crown Cola (the biggest nickel bottle you could get) and I brought it home to my room, where I drank it slowly, savoring each sip from one of Tonio's comic shot glasses that had on it a woman in a skin-tight dress bending over to tie her shoe, with the inscription 'bottoms up!' So my net earnings, after returning the last bottle for its two-cent deposit, were six dollars and eighty-two cents, including a Canadian dime that one of those sweet old ladies had slipped me.

The last night before going home, I was sitting at my uncle's kitchen table, listening to him brag about how some smart guys he knew made big money by buying up vacant factories and shops, insuring them to the hilt and then...whadda you know? They suddenly burned down! Tough luck! And he knew a couple of card sharks from Troy who cleaned suckers out slicker 'n shit. They'd let the sucker win for a while, then...whadda you know? His luck suddenly turns sour and he ends up stripped to the bone. And if the sucker complains...? Well, you don't complain about *these* guys. They got friends, and their friends got ways...you get what I mean? (He winked.) Then Tonio asked what I was going to do with all the money I'd made while I was having a vacation at his expense, and I told him I was thinking of buying something nice for my mother. I'd never had enough money before for a really nice present for her. He nodded. "That's good. That's a good boy." Then he screwed up his eyes and looked up at the ceiling as though he were examining it for cracks. "Hey, I got it!" he cried. "T'maidas!"

"Tomatoes?" I asked.

He explained that the best thing I could possibly buy for my mom would be something the whole family could enjoy, because that way she'd feel good knowing we kids were getting decent food for a change. I started to object to the suggestion that my mother didn't provide us with good food, but Uncle Tonio waved that aside with an impatient gesture and told me that six dollars and eighty cents wouldn't buy shit these days. I said that was just fine with me, because shit wasn't among the things I'd been considering, but he pressed on, saying that a quart can of tomatoes cost twenty-five cents in the store, and that was for just ordinary store-bought crap! But he knew where I could get three dozen quarts of high-quality home-canned tomatoes for seven bucks, which would be a saving of...well, about...well, quite a bit. "About six cents a can," I calculated off the top of my head, which I knew would infuriate him. Then I reminded him that I didn't have seven bucks, but he waved that objection away grandly. "What the hell. I'll make up the difference myself."

I knew this oaf thought he was conning me, but still...it *was* cheaper than store-bought tomatoes, and my mother had often praised the vegetables her mother used to can every summer. A box of home-canned tomatoes might be just the present for her. It would certainly be a surprise. And if she wanted to, she could buy herself something nice with the money she saved on the tomatoes she wouldn't have to buy all next year.

The next morning the three of us piled into Tonio's brand-new car after loading up three twelve-quart boxes of Mason jars containing tomatoes Lorna had put up the year before. At the last minute, Tonio had decided to drive me home rather than put out the money for my bus ticket. It had been intended that I pay my own way back home, but now all my money was in tomato futures. And anyway, it would give him a chance to show his car off to my mother, proof that Lorna hadn't done so badly in marrying him after all. I asked if we shouldn't telephone to Mr Kane's store and ask him to tell my mother I wouldn't be on the bus, but Tonio said that would be a stupid waste of money because we'd get there long before the bus.

After getting lost twice because Tonio's 'short cuts' tangled us in mazes of country lanes where he raged at his wife for not keeping her eye on the map...the least she could do, for Chrissake!...it was late afternoon before we got to Albany. We came in from the north through run-down neighborhoods, and for the last several blocks Tonio peered uneasily left and right with the expression of someone who has rolled back a rock and found disconcerting life forms under it. In fact, everything seemed a lot dirtier and more tawdry than I remembered. Flocks of screaming kids with runny noses and blue-daubed impetigo sores on their scalps; cracked windows repaired with peeling paper tape, broken ones replaced by cardboard or plywood; battered garbage cans on the curb; unshaven men in sweaty undershirts loitering on stoops; adolescent boys blocking the street with their games of stick ball, drawing back to the curb with sassy languor to let us by only after making us wait until the inning was over, and then giving Tonio churlish stares as he negotiated his way through the narrow opening they granted us; a fire hydrant spraying kids who had been suffering through a heat spell, but making Tonio wince at the water marks it made on his car's polish...summer on North Pearl Street.

Tonio pulled up at the high curb in front of 238, having decided that he'd better park close to our front window so he could keep an eye on his car. When he opened the door, it banged against the high curb and he swore between his teeth, then he squeezed out and bent over the blemish, which he tenderly tried to heal with spit on his finger, as though it were a scratched knee. Tonio got the tomatoes out of the trunk, and I led the way up the stoop and into our front hall, which smelled of leaking gas, rotting wood, mildew, crumbling plaster, eons of soaked-in steam from root vegetables, Lysol, roach powder and rat shit behind the baseboards...the whole bouquet of poverty, an olfactory background that I had become inured to over the years, but which I could smell again now after a month away had made my nose sensitive again. I was embarrassed on behalf of Pearl Street. Aunt Lorna, an obsessive house-cleaner, walked down the hall towards our door with her hands pressed flat against her hips so her new linen suit wouldn't brush the walls.

I knocked for the first and only time on our door, just in case Mother and Ben were...whatever. Mother opened it with a huge greeting smile that collapsed when she saw her cousin and Tonio behind me. She had expected me to come hours earlier, and she and Anne-Marie had made a welcome-home party while Ben awaited my arrival down at the bus station.

"How's the gal?" Tonio greeted as he pushed past his wife and me to disburden himself of the boxes of tomatoes. "Still skinny as a rail, I see! Me, I like mine with a little padding on 'em." He patted Lorna's hip. "But there's guys who like 'em skinny. The closer to the bone, the sweeter the meat, they say! And Anne-Marie! Hey, I haven't seen you since you were only *that* high! You've turned into a real looker!"

"Hello, Lorna," Mother said flatly. "I wasn't expecting you."

Lorna started to explain that they had decided at the last moment to—

But Mother cut her off with: "You might as well come in." I knew from her tone that she could feel her cousin's abhorrence of Pearl Street and she resented it. I glanced at Anne-Marie, who made big eyes, telling me she too felt the radiating antipathy and was apprehensive.

To celebrate my return Mother had baked an apple pie, which I had proclaimed to be my favorite back when we could get dried apples from the surplus warehouse, but blueberry was my real favorite. Tonio insisted on being able to keep an eye on his car out front, so we gathered in the front room, rather than the kitchen, our guests in the old wicker armchairs that twisted and squeaked when you sat in them. One of the predacious broken canes immediately clawed at Lorna's new linen suit and tore a little triangular rip that she assured Mother didn't matter...was hardly noticeable, really and truly, don't worry about it...but she couldn't help fingering the rip ruefully. Mother, Anne-Marie and I lined up on the edge of my daybed like birds on a telephone wire, all awkwardly balancing the pie and drinks on our knees or putting them on the floor because my bedside table was filled to toppling with books. Lorna made a couple of hopeful rushes at conversation that my mother's monosyllabic replies quashed. Time moved at a glacial pace.

Ben returned from the bus station, hot and frustrated. He had waited while three buses arrived from the north, but I was not among the passengers, so he gave up and came home. There were awkward introductions and Ben ended up perched on the ledge of the open window, his cup of coffee and pie plate on the sill beside him, while Lorna tried not to look at his tooled cowboy boots and the big Stetson he forgot to take off until Mother reminded him. In standing up to put his hat on the mantel, he knocked his pie and coffee off the sill and dishes shattered on the pavement below.

Ben excused himself, shaking his head at his awkwardness and admitting in his soft western burr that he's always been as clumsy as a one-armed man trying to wipe himself with waxed paper. Both Mother and Lorna stiffened.

"So, tell me...ah...Ben, is it?" Tonio began, playing the role of the protective brother-in-law. "I hear you're a cowboy or something, is that right?"

"I've been lots of things. I rode fence for a while in Wyoming, so I guess that makes me a cowboy."

"If you say so." Tonio half rose from his wicker chair as a pair of neighborhood boys stopped beside his car to look it over. He was about to tap on the window and gesture them to move on—which would have been a serious mistake—when they drifted away on their own, so he settled back into the squeaking chair. "And so, what are you? I mean...are you a friend or a neighbor, or what?"

"I live up on the top floor."

"That's handy."

"Handy?" Ben's face darkened. "What do you mean, handy?"

"Oh, I'm not suggesting anything. It's just that..."

To deflect the contentious path of this conversation, Lorna said quickly, "You know, hon, I'd just *love* another cup of coffee. And that apple pie...it's *just* like your mother's." As Mother wasn't looking at her, she turned to Anne-Marie. "Your grandmother always made her pies from two or three kinds of apples, one for sweetness, another for flavor, one that mushed up quickly, another to give texture. One of the apples she used was Northern Spy. I don't remember the names of the others. Do you remember them, hon? If I'm not mistaken, they used to be your favorites...those Northern Spies?" She directed this last at my mother, seeking her help in smoothing things over. Mother didn't help.

Lorna laid her hand on Tonio's sleeve. "I think we'd better be going. I hate to eat and run, but I'm afraid of these roads by night, and it's already nearly—"

"Wait a minute!" Tonio said. "I don't need no bum's rush. I wasn't accusing nobody or nothing. I was just asking."

"Maybe it's best not to ask," Ben advised.

Tonio rose and snatched down his celluloid cuffs in a brisk gesture, muttering, "...we give the kid a free vacation...get him out of this hole for a couple of weeks, and what thanks do we get?"

Lorna turned to Mother. "Look, honey, I'll write soon. It'd be a sin for you and me not to stay in touch."

"You can write," Mother said, ceding little.

"Come on, Tonio," Lorna said, already at the door.

As they passed down the hall, I could hear Tonio assuring his wife that for two cents, he'd show that phony cowboy a thing or two!

When they got to his car, Lorna turned to wave good-bye, but Tonio started to drive off while Lorna was still settling down, so she flopped back in the seat, and the car stalled because in his anger he had forgotten to take the hand brake off, so he gave the steering wheel a terrible smack with his fist. Then, the veins standing out on his forehead, his teeth clenched, he very slowly, very carefully released the hand brake, started up again and crept away from the curb...then he stamped on the gas and squealed away down the street, having to veer sharply to miss an absent-minded old lady crossing to Kane's Grocery...Mrs McGivney.

The air in our apartment crackled with the static of anger for a minute or two, then Ben shook his head and chuckled. "That Tonio must of been hiding behind the door when they were passing out the friendly. But your cousin's nice. I like her."

"She's a doormat."

"Well...it's her life, honey."

Mother shrugged, neither convinced nor mollified. Ben asked Anne-Marie if she'd help him pick up the broken dishes down on the sidewalk. Glad to escape the spiky atmosphere, she got the dust pan and broom and they left together.

"Sorry," I said after a short silence.

"Sorry about what?" Mother asked.

"That I didn't call Mr Kane and let you know I wasn't coming by bus."

"What's done is done. So, what's in the boxes Tonio left?"

"It's a present for you. Not from him. From me. Open it and see."

She smiled. "Always thinking of your mother. My good right hand." She opened the lid of the top box. "What's this?" She lifted out a Mason jar.

I told her I had planned to get her something nice with the money I made mowing lawns, but I hadn't made enough for anything really nice, so I...

"Tomatoes?"

"Yes. Home canned. Aunt Lorna put them up."

"And they *sold* them to you?"

"Yes. I got them for what I had earned from cutting lawns, six dollars and eighty cents for thirty-six quarts. That's less than twenty cents a—"

"Six dollars and eighty cents for her tomatoes? Tonio's idea, I'll bet." Mother let the Mason jar drop back into the box with a clunk. The three boxes of quart jars stood on the table for the rest of that afternoon then were stored on top of the wardrobe in her bedroom where they remained, unused, until we moved away from North Pearl years later, when they were thrown out. I knew that in her involute way my mother was punishing her cousin and her husband by not accepting their tomatoes. She didn't realize that the uneaten tomatoes were a constant reproach to me.

I felt like an ass to have let Tonio con me, and I resolved to make up for it by giving her something really splendid for Christmas.

When Ben and Anne-Marie returned from cleaning up the broken dishes, I could tell that my sister was bursting with a secret. Ben exchanged a look with Mother, who smiled almost bashfully, then he asked me to come into the kitchen; he had something to tell me.

The four of us sat at the table with the quarter of an apple pie left over from my welcome-home party in the middle of the oilcloth. Mother and Anne-Marie watched me to see how I would take the news as Ben told me that he and Mother intended to get married. Then he would be our dad. How'd that be?

How would that be?

Ben was offering to assume my responsibility for Mother!

How would that be? *I was free!* But of course I didn't let myself express this disloyal joy. I pulled a thoughtful frown and asked when they were planning to get married.

"As soon as your mother can get a divorce."

Mother explained that in New York a woman seeking a divorce on the grounds of desertion—the only grounds available in her case—wasn't considered well and truly 'deserted' until seven years passed without her receiving a word from her vanished husband. It had been almost five and a half years since my father failed to show up with his green cake, so the soonest she and Ben could marry would be the spring of 1943.

Born worrier that I was, and possessed of a unique gift for finding the gray cloud at the center of every silver lining, I immediately realized that if we got another letter out of the blue from my father—and this had happened twice before—then all bets were off; there could be no divorce on the grounds of desertion. When I could repress this anxious thought, I felt a mixture of joy and guilt at the prospect of their marriage. Joy because I liked Ben and admired his gentle Western, can-do masculinity; and guilt because I was shifting my burden to him. I felt like a rat, and like something worse than a rat for thinking of my Mother as a burden, when she never thought of us kids that way. But then...they were grown-ups, and that's what grown-ups were for: taking care of kids.

Overnight our lives became brighter. With Ben we had plans, hopes, a future.

Our ship had come in: the SS *Ben!*

. . . .

The summer of 1941 came to an end, and I returned to Our Lady of Angels where I occasionally met Sister Mary-Theresa in the halls. Once she told me that Sister Mary-Joseph, my social studies teacher, had described me as the best student she had ever had, despite the disturbing communist views I advanced in every essay question. In defense, I explained that Sister Mary-Joseph didn't know the difference between a socialist and a communist. "She's nice enough, but you have to admit that she's not the brightest bride in Christ's chaste harem." (A phrase I had worked up while doodling at the back of Sister Mary-Joseph's class.) She compressed her lips and looked at me reprovingly over the tops of the glasses she had recently begun wearing. I smiled. Then she smiled too, then shook her head in admonition...of both of us. As we stood there in the window bay, I was aware of her characteristic aroma of yellow bar soap and starch. From the first, I had associated the smell of starch that followed her with the delicious aroma of fresh bread. Now I knew it was only the starch that stiffened the wings of her wimple. Wearing glasses, she seemed more teacherly, less womanly. The flames of my pre-adolescent desire had cooled and I was seeing her with cruelly honest eyes, seeing her as she was, an imperfect thing. I felt a little sorry for myself. As you see, I was becoming a young male.

While chatting one evening, Mother and Ben hatched the idea of someday building a nice little tourist camp somewhere in the West... Wyoming, maybe. Typically, they soon elevated this casual fantasy into a grand life-plan, a dream upon which their future happiness would depend. Ben would build snug little tourist cabins out of varnished logs, beginning with just six units and adding more as the tourist camp prospered through word of mouth, which would spread the news of its down-home charm and reasonable prices. Throughout that autumn they spent almost every evening at the kitchen table, weaving and embroidering this dream, trying to make it real by sheer force of wanting it so much. They drew sketches of the little log cabins surrounding a 'frontier-style' cafe-cum-office-cum-general store with living quarters for the four of us above. They furnished and equipped the cabins and the cafe down to the smallest detail from the Montgomery Ward catalogue which, like most Americans of the era, they called the Monkey Ward Dream Book, choosing furniture, blankets, curtains, cutlery, dishes, wall art, bathroom equipment—even the seeds and bulbs for the little flower gardens that would lend each cabin its special cachet: Pansy Cabin, Marigold Cabin, Tulip Cabin...that sort of thing. Choosing specific things and making long detailed lists lent the heft of reality to their dreams. Mother always chose the 'Best' line from the catalogue's options of Good, Better and Best, because, she explained, quality goods are the least expensive in the long run. And anyway, she'd had it up to here with shrimping and saving and making do with cheap trash. Ben would build everything with his own hands, the cabins, the fencing, the general store-cum-cafe, even the rustic archway entrance from which would hang a sign with a Double-R-Bar brand burnt into it. (Ben was known to his cowboy friends as 'Red', and my mother's name was Ruby.) Ben would also run a small herd of high-value breeding stock on the side; while Mother, with her experience as a waitress, would operate the cafe year-round, so between them they would bring in some income even during the off-season. Well-off guests from the

East seeking a real Western experience would come swarming in, eager to stay in a clean, authentic, ranch-style, log-cabin tourist camp run by such honest, friendly people. Mother and Ben filled a notebook with things they would need, together with their catalogue numbers and prices, all carefully totaled up.

I used to sit with them at the kitchen table, tossing in occasional ideas and enjoying the atmosphere of eager, hopeful planning for our future. But Anne-Marie would often slip away to the back bedroom to read or design fashions for her demanding paper-doll movie stars. She fell asleep early and was hard to waken in the morning, a sure sign that she was troubled. One Sunday evening after a long planning session at the kitchen table, Mother and Ben decided to take a walk to get the cricks out of their backs. I went into the kitchen for a glass of water and found Anne-Marie sitting there, looking glumly at the Montgomery Ward catalogue lying open to a page of pots and pans they had been selecting for the cafe's kitchen.

As I ran the water to get it cool, I glanced over and noticed that Anne-Marie's eyes were brimming with tears.

"What's the matter?"

She shook her head, not daring to speak because her tears were too close to the surface.

"You've been down in the dumps lately. Are you sick?"

She turned her face away.

Always embarrassed and uncertain of what to do when she was in a fragile mood, I drank my water and went back to the book I was reading in my daybed. I was absorbed in it when I felt her presence behind me in the doorway.

"...what about me?" she said, her voice wobbly.

I set down my book. "What *about* you?"

"I want to dance. Or be a costume designer, maybe."

"And?"

"That used to be what we *all* wanted. But now..." Her voice caught, and she had to clear her throat to go on. "We never talk about my dancing any more. Now it's always these tourist cabins, and how Mom will run the cafe and pick out the decorations, and how Ben will build everything and have cows and all, and how you'll have smart ideas and keep the books and all...but what about me?"

"There's lots of things you can do. You can help Mom, and...plenty of things."

"Make the beds and wait on table?"

It hadn't occurred to me that this new phantom ship of ours had no place in the crew for an all-singing, all-dancing costume designer to the stars, nor had I been aware of how much Anne-Marie felt left out. Brothers are like that. They love, but they're dense and self-concerned.

"Don't worry about it," I said with the breezy confidence of the un-threatened. "You'll be able to take dancing lessons out there."

"In the middle of Wyoming? How often do talent scouts check out tourist camps when they're looking for new movie stars?" She blinked, and a tear ran down each of her cheeks.

I reached out and took her hand. "Oh, we'll get away, you and me. Just you wait and see. One of these days, I'll get away to some college and become a scientist, and you'll get to California and end up..."

But she was shaking her head fatalistically. "I have a feeling I'll never get away. *You'll* get away, sure. But not me."

"I wouldn't leave you behind."

"Yes, you will." She said this without rancor, a simple statement of fact. "One of these days, you'll just up and run away."

"I never would!"

She looked at me levelly for a moment. "Yes, you will. You'll run away."

And I knew she was right. One of these days, I would just walk away.

I squeezed her hand to say I was sorry, but she pulled away and left for her bedroom, where Mother would find her in that comatose sleep she fell into when she needed to find peace.

Their dream of those Double-R-Bar Ranch Cabins in Wyoming would be the first of many Ships-Coming-In that Mother and Ben would conceive, plan, and even venture into over the years, all of which would fail for lack of realistic analysis and adequate resources—doomed Titanics, every one.

Thanks to Ben's generosity, and maybe his sensitivity for Anne-Marie's feelings of being left out, she was soon taking tap-dancing lessons again, and even a brother had to admit she was getting prettier every month. With her pleasing singing voice, outgoing personality, and the thick, long blonde hair that Mother tormented with a curling iron until it was a mass of sausage curls, she was sure to replace Shirley Temple, when the time came. And, as Mother never tired of reminding us, Shirley couldn't stay young forever. Anne-Marie made rapid progress and soon was chosen by Miss LaMonte to appear with her at smokers, men's clubs and occasional wedding suppers. For each of these night performances, Anne-Marie earned a hypothetical three dollars which Miss LaMonte applied to her lessons. But still Anne-Marie always went vacant-eyed and elsewhere-minded when Mother and Ben talked about their tourist camp. Her dreams and fantasies were all about backstage excitement and flashing marquees and audiences buzzing with anticipation, none of which were consonant with plans to bury the family in some quaint roadside place out in the infinite spaces of the high chaparral.

An old hand at escapist story games, I recognized this Tourist-Camp-in-the-West for what it was: an analgesic fantasy; and I was worried when Mother and Ben behaved as though it was not only real, but practical, indeed all but inevitable. I intuitively knew better. The only place things worked out that way was in the movies.

. . . .

The year 1941 had been a busy and fraught time for me. I had become acquainted with Brigid Meehan's left breast and fallen in love with Sister Mary-Theresa; circumstances had trapped me into the sacrilege of taking the transubstantiated body of Christ into a sinful mouth; the summer had brought me my first vacation, an experience I never wanted to repeat; and in the fall I had learned that Ben was going to become my stepfather. And through it all, Hitler's war was a storm growling on the eastern horizon.

And 1941 wasn't through with me yet, for on December 7th the Japanese Empire declared war on North Pearl Street.

North Pearl Street
Goes to War

STASHING AWAY a dime here and a nickel there, by Thanksgiving of 1941 I had managed to save enough from my paper route to buy my mother a really nice Christmas present to make up for the three boxes of Mason jars full of tomatoes which still sat on top of her wardrobe in silent accusation. This present had to fulfill two criteria: it must be truly splendid and glorious, and it must cost less than five dollars. To be able to pounce when I found the perfect thing, I carried the five dollars I had saved up in my shoe whenever I was wandering around the city, as I did often, now that I had relegated to 'kids' stuff' the complex story games that had occupied so much of my free time when I was younger.

One Saturday afternoon I was peering into one of the 'Aladdin's Cave' junk shops that had sprung up in previously abandoned stores along South Street. The windows had been soaped over on the inside, then the soap had been rubbed off in small rectangles and circles randomly placed here and there so the passerby could peek in and see what was on offer...a clever device for attracting the curious. There was a sign above the door bearing the disarmingly frank statement: We Buy Junk/We Sell Antiques. Craning my neck to look through one of the cleared circles at the used goods, factory seconds and odd lots of un-sold merchandise, I spied something interesting among the things piled higgledy-piggledy on rough plywood tables: an open cigar box containing a dozen or so of the 'riffle books' I had begun collecting several years before. These palm-sized books had simple stories, usu-ally something corny, like Betty Boop telling some ogling guy that he could go jump in the lake, and when you turned the booklet over and riffled the pages with your thumb, you saw the man jump into a lake with a big splash of exclamation points! As far as I could tell from my oblique view, none of the riffle books in the cigar box was a duplicate of any in my collection, so I went in to see if I could afford to buy one or two of them. The place was filled with junk of all descriptions, the ejecta of a hundred attics and closets. At first it seemed that there was no one around to serve customers, then an old guy with mussed-up hair sat up from a cot where he had been napping between two over-burdened tables, and he asked what he could show me. I said I was just looking around, and he said, "Be my guest, kid. Looking is free. Steal-ing, on the other hand, is not free. It is a crime. Breaking stuff is not a crime, but it's a mistake, because you got to pay for anything you break."

Feigning brief interest in this and that, I slowly made my way to-wards the cigar box with the riffle books. Feeling the man's eye on me, I walked right past the cigar box and examined a frayed old silk fan very closely. Then I frowned and blinked as though baffled, and I asked, "What are those things there?"

"What things?" the man asked, coming over.

"Those...gee, I don't know what to call them. They look like little books, or something." I pushed them around with the tip of my finger. "What are these called?"

"I don't know. But you flick through them like this and—you see? They move! Just like the movies."

I tried one. "H'm. Not a very long movie."

"You could flick slow."

"Yeah, I guess you could." I dropped the booklet into its box and moved on, pretending to examine other things while my interior focus remained on those riffle books, particularly the one about a scantily-clad hillbilly girl and an ogling traveling salesman. With studied disinterest, I opened another box and—would you believe it?—I was staring at the perfect Christmas present for my mother! It was an ornate tea service of six cups with little saucers and plates, and an intricately decorated teapot with a bamboo handle. The price tag was in letters...some sort of code so the shopkeeper could screw you out of as much as he thought you would stand for.

"How much is this going for?" I asked.

"More than you got."

"You don't know that, mister. For all you know I could be a rich kid dressed up in old clothes so I can jew you down on the price of your stuff." On the streets we used the verb 'to jew' for 'to haggle' without intending any hurt and, in those crusty, insensitive days, without the slightest realization that it could be offensive. But the shopkeeper didn't rankle at my usage although, like all the shopkeepers in this part of town, his accent and idiom were purest first-generation shtetl, despite his evident facility with language and love of word-play.

"I suppose you *could* be a rich kid come slumming," he said. "But then, I could be an eccentric Rothschild amusing myself with a little hobby."

"Well then...between us rich guys, how much are these used plates and stuff?"

"As a special offer from one very rich person to another, I could let you have that set of one-hundred-percent fine oriental porcelain for...say...five ninety-nine. A steal at twice the price."

A beautiful tea set for six bucks! I just knew that Mother would love the raised decorations of little flowers and birds that were, although I was not then equipped to recognize it, typical of shoddy/gaudy oriental export ware designed for the barbaric taste of westerners. Then too, my mother never drank tea. Only the Irish drank tea. But this set was so intricate, so colorful, so chock-full of things to look at. I could see Mother, Anne-Marie, Ben and me sitting around the kitchen table, drinking tea in little sips so we didn't empty the delicate cups too fast. Very hoi polloi indeed.

"Six bucks!" I exclaimed with staggered disbelief. "Six bucks for some old crockery? Do I look like I just jumped off a freight train from Hickville?"

"This set of original, one-of-a-kind, top-quality bone china was hand-made to sell at twelve dollars—"

"Twelve dollars?"

"—but a customer broke one of the saucers, and that's why I'm willing to practically give it away."

I hadn't noticed that one of the saucers was missing. I counted and found it was true, and this greatly reduced the appeal of the set for me because Mother would immediately spot what I had not. She had a quick eye for imperfection. But as I started to walk away the shop-keeper told me that I could use one of the small plates as a saucer, which is what they customarily did in the Orient where this set had been made by a family of artisans who had been in the pottery line for five, maybe six hundred generations, some even longer. Who can tell with Orientals? "And look at it this way. With six cups, five saucers, six little plates and a two-piece teapot (including the lid, which you've got to have if you want to keep the tea hot), that makes nineteen pieces of genuine top-quality hand-wrought bone china for under six dollars... and what does that come to?

"About thirty cents a piece," I said.

"A steal! In fact, there ought to be a law to protect me from myself."

I told him I didn't have six dollars to spend—

"That must be a big come-down for a rich kid like you."

—but I would think about it and maybe come back.

"Okay, you think about it, kid. But don't think too long. There was a man in here just this morning...a collector of rare top-quality bone china...and he was interested. Very, very interested."

I walked to the door and opened it...then I turned back. "What about four-fifty?"

"You took the trouble to change into old clothes and come all the way down here from your mansion just to rob me?"

"Four-sixty. That's all I've got."

"That's not all you got, kid. You also got plenty of chutzpah. But...tell you what. I'll let it go for five-fifty. Who could ask better?"

"Four ninety-nine...oh, and throw in those stupid little books for good measure."

"Never!"

"And that tray the dishes are on, too."

"Are you crazy? That tray is worth fifteen maybe twenty bucks all by itself!"

"All right, forget the tray. Now you're fifteen maybe twenty bucks ahead. Just put the china in one of those boxes with wood shavings and all, and wrap it in nice paper. It's a present."

"You know what you are? You're a very nasty little kid, that's what."

I took off my shoe and unpeeled the five sweat-moist dollar bills from the insole, then I took the seven cents I had in my pocket and placed the tennis-shoe-smelling bills, the buffalo nickel, and the two Lincoln pennies on the top of the glass display case. "There. Five dollars and seven cents. That's everything I've got. My last penny."

"I couldn't possibly do it, kid."

I sighed and picked up the pennies...then the nickel...then one of the dollar bills, which I folded carefully and put back into my pocket... then the next...then the next...then the—

I walked down the street with two packages, the tea set tied up in elegant oriental wrapping paper and the cigar box with its eleven riffle books, my chest effervescent with anticipation of my mother's delight on Christmas day, when she set eyes on that fancy tea service.

· · · · · · · · ·

It was evening of a crisp Sunday in early December, and I was alone in the apartment because Mother, Ben and Anne-Marie had gone downtown to see the display of Christmas decorations in the store windows. I was standing in front of the Emerson, staring at the floor with defocused eyes, totally engrossed in one of my favorite radio programs, *The Great Gildersleeve*, which was a spin-off from *Fibber McGee and Molly*. In this episode Gildersleeve and his niece and nephew were in the train station to meet Gildersleeve's aunt, a stern, overbearing woman. When the nephew, LeRoy, wondered what the aunt was like, Gildersleeve said, "Have you ever seen the battleship Idaho in a bad storm?" "No." "Well, just wait until she gets off." The studio audience laughed dutifully. This moment only came back to me later, when the irony of the reference to a battleship became apparent. The punchline of a joke was about to be delivered when an announcer broke in to say:

We interrupt this program for a special bulletin: Tokyo, Monday, December 8.[44] Japan went to war against the United States and Great Britain today with air and sea attacks against Hawaii, followed by a formal declaration of hostilities. Japanese Imperial headquarters announced at 6 a.m.—that's 4 p.m. Sunday, eastern standard time—that a state of war existed among these nations in the western Pacific as of dawn. Shortly afterwards it was announced that naval operations are progressing off Hawaii and that at least one Japanese aircraft carrier is in action against Pearl Harbor, the American naval base in the islands.
We return you now to *The Great Gildersleeve.*

We rejoined the interrupted program just as the studio audience let out a burst of laughter following a joke that we of the radio audience had missed. I remember thinking there was something ominous in the coincidence of *Pearl* Harbor and *Pearl* Street, but while I was considering the baleful implications of this, the announcer broke in again with his urgent, amateurish voice:

We interrupt the program to bring reports on the Panama radio. According to the Panama radio, a Jap aircraft carrier was sunk off Honolulu. I repeat, a Jap aircraft carrier has been sunk off Honolulu according to Panama radio.
We return you now to Hollywood.

This turned out to be untrue. The Japanese suffered no losses in the attack that sunk or damaged most of the major ships of our Pacific fleet, save for the three active aircraft carriers which, by sheer luck, happened to be out on manœuvers. *The Great Gildersleeve* continued in an eerie, maniacal way because the program had been recorded with a live audience, and broadcast at better listening times for the various time zones; therefore neither the wise-cracking cast nor the laughing audience was aware that reports of cataclysm and catastrophe were being interjected into their innocent exuberance.

During the final advertising pitch from *The Great Gildersleeve*'s sponsor, Kraft Parkay margarine, it occurred to me that the outbreak of war was sure to produce a big 'extra!' edition for newsboys to hawk in the streets.

I grabbed my jacket and ran out of the house and all the way up to the squalid little basement office of my newspaper broker, where half a dozen newsies had already gathered, awaiting the arrival of the 'extra!' edition, which in fact was only the regular middle section of the Sunday paper encased in a one-sheet wrapper carrying a bold banner headline—WAR!—and such meager details of the Pearl Harbor attack as were available, together with archival pictures of Hawaii, soldiers, airplanes, and anything else that might be useful filler. The winter evening was closing in when the extras arrived on a truck, and we newsies grabbed as many as we could carry and ran down the Clinton Avenue hill towards the commercial downtown, shouting: Extra! Extra! Japanese Attack Hawaiian Islands! Reeeed aaal-abahdit!

In search of a hot corner to hawk my papers, I headed for downtown where people would be gawking at the Christmas lights and doing some window-shopping, the only kind of shopping you could do on Sunday in those days. Unfortunately, other newsies had the same idea, so there were four of us at the intersection of State and Pearl, one on each corner, stamping our feet to keep out the cold and bawling out: Extra! Extra! Sneak Attack on Hawaiian Islands! Ships Sunk! *Reeeed aaal-abahdit!* I was in mid-*aaal-abahdit* when I looked up to see Anne-Marie standing in front of me, her face lit by flashing red and green Christmas lights. She was grinning at my histrionic efforts, and Mother and Ben were in the crowd behind her, he in his new mud-colored suit and without either the Stetson or the fancy cowboy boots, for Mother was 'civilizing' him. I gave them a free paper and turned away to continue hawking, trying to out-shout the competition.[45]

When I got home that night with my sack still half full of unsold extras, I found Mother and Ben sitting before our Emerson, hoping to learn something about the extent of damage and loss of life at Pearl Harbor. Soon running out of fresh information because the government was concealing from the enemy the shocking extent of our losses, and from America their criminal lack of preparation in the face of frequent and clear indications of Japanese intent; the networks repeated the terse scraps they were fed by the Department of the Navy. These were interspersed by patriotic songs and Sousa marches. Ordinary programming was suspended, and this more than anything made the world seem very strange indeed. Ben told me that he had heard on the street that all of Japan's aircraft carriers had been torpedoed and sent to the bottom while they were trying to enter the Panama Canal on their way to attack New York City. Over the following week, embroidered variants of the wishful-thinking 'Panama bulletin' I had first heard during *The Great Gildersleeve* would percolate through the rumor mill, slowly metamorphosing from hot news of total victory to dire reports of absolute defeat before they finally dried up and blew away, the forgotten ashes of folk hokum.

Anne-Marie was in the back bedroom, muttering to her paper dolls, assuring them there was nothing to worry about, this war wouldn't last long. Mother forgot all about supper until after ten that night, when she heated up some tomato soup and made grilled cheese sandwiches... not real cheese but Velveeta, that vaguely cheese-like substance that we inflicted on ourselves in those pre-gastronomic days, when Americans still put Miracle Whip on salads and ate desserts constructed from cubes of different-colored Jell-O topped by a squirt of a sweetened petroleum substitute for whipped cream.[46] Long after Ben had gone up to his room and Mother to her bedroom where Anne-Marie crawled into bed with her for solace, I sat in the dark, watching the street and worrying about war, and invasion, and death, and what all this would mean for our plans to get out of Pearl Street.

The next day, Monday, Ben went downtown to enlist in the army, but the enlistment offices were packed with men eager to kick Japan's butt and afraid they wouldn't get into the scrap before it was over because—well, come on! How long could a bunch of bow-legged, slant-eyed midgets withstand the power of...?[47]

The line stretched down the street and around the corner, and police went up and down the queue telling men there was no chance of enlisting today, so why not go home and come back later? Ben decided to try again on Tuesday, and this gave him time to consider what might happen if the army discovered that he had deserted from the navy when he was only sixteen. But when he returned to sign up, the recruiting offices were so hungry for bullet-blocking meat that they didn't look very carefully into a man's past.

In those early days of the war, the Selective Service System was so overwhelmed by men eager to fight for their country that the system couldn't immediately absorb them, so after he signed up Ben was told to go home and await orders. These didn't come until two weeks later, instructing him to take a train for Fort Dix, New Jersey, on January 2 (car and seat numbers given). So Ben passed Christmas with us after all and was a witness to Mother's reaction to my gift of the ornate tea service.

You might assume that Christmas celebrations were forced and flavorless that year because so many of the block's men were waiting to be called up, but quite the opposite was true. There was an almost desperate festivity on North Pearl Street that Christmas of 1941, and people were uncommonly solicitous of one another.

Ben appeared at our door on Christmas Eve bearing a lush, soft-bristled tree quite unlike the spindly, prickly runts that were sold on street corners. The tree was freshly cut and still bleeding sap, so we didn't ask where it came from, but it was so tall that he had to cut several inches off the bottom which, unfortunately, cost the tree some of its lushness and balance, but the ever-resourceful Ben cut branches from the stub and trimmed their ends into points, then he drilled holes here and there in the main trunk and socketed the extra branches in tightly, producing a tree that was the plumpest and fullest we had ever seen.

Ben had been putting a little money aside every week against unexpected emergencies, but he decided to splurge it all on Christmas, assuming that the United States Army would be attending to his needs for the foreseeable future. So our harvest of presents that Christmas was the richest ever. Everyone but me got toiletries of one kind or another. In addition to the 'Original Hollywood Child-Star Make-Up Kit' that Anne-Marie had been hinting about for months, she received from Ben something she hadn't dared even mention because she knew we couldn't afford them: dancing shoes with 'jingle taps' like Miss LaMonte's: loose taps that made half again as much noise as normal ones. She had those shoes on in a flash and was shuffle-ball-change/ball-change/ball-changing all over the place.

Ben gave me two presents that brought me years of pleasure. The first was his slide rule and a well-thumbed book of logarithms. The second and greater gift was spending all Christmas afternoon teaching me how to use the slide rule. Unlike electronic calculators, a slide rule requires adroit manipulation, predictive thinking, and the ability to conceive of numbers in terms of their multiples, their powers of ten, and their logarithms, and hold these in one's head while working at the answer. I found it all spellbinding, and for a couple of weeks I felt sure I was destined to become a rich and famous mathematician.

Anne-Marie and I had pooled our Christmas money, as we did every year, to buy Mother a pre-packaged set of her favorite toiletries, Evening in Paris, which was surprisingly affordable considering that it contained half a dozen expensive-looking bottles and boxes in deep blue like our Christmas lights. Mother must have read somewhere that Evening in Paris was 'common' (not at all the sort of thing the ritzy hoi polloi would use), but she led us to believe it was her favorite brand because it made a splendid many-packaged gift that was inexpensive yet fun to select and give. I guessed this when I was disposing of her possessions after her death and I found three boxed assortments of blue-bottled Evening in Paris cologne and blue-wrapped soap and blue-boxed bath powder that she had never used, but had saved because they were gifts from her children.

I gave Anne-Marie three presents, two she had asked for and one that was a total surprise. The anticipated two were illustrated biographies of her favorite movie stars, Shirley Temple and Deanna Durban. Each book came with a signed photograph of the star 'suitable for framing'. She unwrapped her surprise present to find a cigar box. She had done a pretty good job of feigning surprise at the movie-star books, but she frowned with genuine puzzlement as she opened the cigar box and plucked out one of the second-hand riffle books which she held out between her thumb and forefinger like something she would as soon not come into contact with. "What's *this?* It's not me who's nuts about riffle books. It's *you.*"

My eyes widened in astonishment. "Well, I'll be darned! Maybe you're right. Maybe Santa sent them to you by mistake. Pass them over."

"Rat."

"Pardon me?"

"You heard me."

Ben surprised Mother with an engagement ring in his birthstone, an opal. She told him with what she believed was admirable frankness that she had never liked opals because they brought bad luck, but Ben said this was true only if you bought them for yourself. Given opals carry no such curse. I could tell that Mother only half believed this, and I was embarrassed by the way she didn't bother to conceal her disappointment.

Mother, Anne-Marie and I had pooled our ideas and money to buy Ben a genuine imitation leather travel bag with places for men's toiletries, so he would have them handy in the army. The most fun was filling the travel bag with products that were advertised on the radio: a bar of Ivory soap ('99.44% pure...It floats!'), a double-edged safety razor (with genuine Gillette blue-blades for a smoother shave, after shave, after shave, after shave!), a small bottle of Brylcreem ('a liddle-dab'll-do-ya'), a jar of Mum ('Even your best friends won't tell you.'), and a tube of Ipana toothpaste ('...for the smile of beauty.').

Out of the corner of my eye, I could see Mother's attention drift again and again to the large package behind all the others, the one wrapped in mysterious oriental paper. She had a suspicion that it was for her and was itching to know what it was, but she didn't want to seem eager. Back before I began to make money with my paper route, she had always pretended that she didn't like to receive presents. She admitted that she didn't know why she didn't like presents, but that's the way she was. I knew, of course, that this was a lie to cover for spending all our money on gifts for Anne-Marie and me.

Slyly pleased that she was consumed with curiosity, and anticipating her delight when she opened it, I dragged the moment out. It wasn't until this last present had sat alone under the tree for a quarter of an hour that she said in an offhand tone suggesting she had just noticed it, "Say, what the hell is that back there? The thing wrapped in the funny paper?"

I told her I had no idea. "Something from Santa Claus, I guess. Why don't we just leave it there and maybe open it after dinner...if we want to."

We exchanged glances and she smiled. "All right, all right! I guess I might as well take a peek at it."

She unwrapped it with tantalizing slowness, carefully folding up

the ornate oriental paper before lifting off the lid. When she set eyes
on the cobalt-blue teapot encrusted with raised figures of birds and
flowers she sighed with pleasure. One by one, she took out the cups
and saucers and plates and arranged them before her on the table.

"I know you don't drink tea, but..." I shrugged.

"That doesn't matter. I'll just set them out so I can look at them.
You know how I love fine things. It's my French blood. And these are
so pretty and delica..." She had picked up one of the small plates and
was reading the bottom. Her expression froze. She looked at me.
"Made in *Japan?*"

"Yeah, well..." Ben intervened. "The Japanese are known for their
beauti..."

"They're known for sneak attacks that kill American boys, that's
what they're known for!" Mother said. "Jean-Luc...how could you?
What in God's name were you thinking of?"

"I didn't know it was made in Japan! I bought it more than a month
ago! Long before Pearl Harbor!"

"That's no excuse!"

"What do you mean, it's no excuse? Of *course* it's an excuse!"

"Don't raise your voice to me, young man."

"I'm not raising my voice. It's just that—"

"And don't contradict me! You take this Japanese crap away and do
whatever you want with it. Me, I never want to set eyes on it again!
No one's going to accuse me of keeping Jap stuff in my house, believe
me you!"

"It's believe you me."

"What?!"

"It's not believe me you! Believe you me! You always, *always* say it
wrong!"

"What are you talking about?"

"I'm talking about how you get lots of things wrong! It's embarrassing and stupid."

"Are you saying your mother is embarrassing?"

"Sometimes, yes!"

"Well...I like that!"

"You don't have to like it, Mom! Just accept it."

"Like it or lunk it, eh? Is that what you're saying?"

"Lump it, Mom."

"What?"

"*Lump* it. No one says *lunk* it!"

"What are you talking about? Everyone says like it or lunk it. Don't they, Anne-Marie?"

"I'm reading my Deanna Durban book."

"And anyway, what's all that got to do with giving your own mother Japanese crap for Christmas? Answer me that, Mister Know-It-All!"

"Nothing! It doesn't have anything to do with it. And I'm getting out of here!" I stormed out into the hall and down the stoop into the street, where I stood in my shirtsleeves with my back against the building, protected from the worst of the snowfall but taking grim pleasure in the big, lazy snowflakes that collected on my eyelashes. Maybe I'd get sick and die. That would teach her. After a couple of minutes Ben came out, also without a jacket, and stood beside me, his back against the wall, his hands in his pockets, looking out through the falling snow onto the empty street. We didn't speak.

After a while he cleared his throat and said, "Your Mom...she's crying in her bedroom."

I shrugged.

"Look, Luke, I'm sorry she took on that way. She shouldn't have done that. But you understand, don't you? I mean, what with the war and all...and me having to go away and fight. Naturally, she's..." It was his turn to shrug.

After a long silence, I complained to the snowfall before us, "I get sick and tired of that French-and-Indian temper of hers! It spoils everything. Oh, I know she loves us kids and all. And she works until she's sick to give us presents. She's a great giver. She's always giving. But when it comes to receiving, she's crap!"

"You don't have to tell me, partner. She wasn't all that hot on my ring."

"Yeah, I'm sorry about that."

"But she's a great gal, your mom. Brave and strong and lots of fun and all that stuff. Nobody's perfect. You've got to take the rough with the smooth." He chuckled. "I didn't think anyone but me noticed those funny things she says. Like 'believe me you'."

"How about 'put that in your hat and smoke it'? Have you heard that one?"

He laughed. "No, it's a new one on me. Hey, I'm getting colder than...there's a saying about the balls of a brass monkey, but your mom wouldn't like it. What do you say you and me go back inside? I'll show you how to work that slide rule."

"All right."

We were working at the kitchen table, our heads close together over the book of logarithms, when Mother came in and silently began to make coffee in the percolator. Her eyes were damp and red. Ben pushed my knee with his, and I got up and put my arms around her. "Sorry, Mom. I should have checked to see where those things came from."

"It's not your fault, son. The man who sold them to you should have told you."

When, later that evening, it occurred to me to look for it, I couldn't find the tea set anywhere. It wasn't until a month or so later that I happened upon it on the top shelf of her wardrobe, back in the excelsior-filled box that she had carefully re-wrapped in its decorative Japanese rice paper with little autumn leaves pressed into it. I knew that like the Mason jars of tomatoes, those cups would never be used in our house.

Night came and we turned off the lights except for the little blue-and-white Christmas tree bulbs that reflected a million times in strands of tinsel. Ben picked out tunes on his mandolin, and we all sang along. Mostly old songs, sad ones like 'My Buddy' and 'Sonny Boy' and 'That Old Gang of Mine' which suggested 'Those Wedding Bells Are Breaking Up That Old Gang of Mine', and that led us to 'And Let the Rest of the World Go By' and 'Me and My Shadow' and 'Maybe'. These old songs of friendship, love and loss were followed by a recent Hit Parade number that blended contemporary history with nostalgia for times past, 'The Last Time I Saw Paris', and we ended up singing hits from 1941, the year that would be history in just a week...the last year of peace.[48] It was very late and we were all a little hoarse by the time we finally went to bed, Mother and Anne-Marie into our back bedroom,

Ben up the stairs to his top-floor room. I sat up for a couple of hours, watching the snow that slanted down close to our window, the flakes tinted by the blue lights of that splendid Christmas tree.

Despite the tea service fiasco and my spat with Mother, the memory of the four of us sitting in the front room, Mother and Ben in the squeaking rattan chairs that had come with the apartment, Anne-Marie and I sprawled at opposite ends of my daybed, singing together softly in the dim blue-and-white light, remains for me after more than sixty years an iconographic image of Christmas, a moment rendered poignant by the unspoken knowledge that Ben and so many men and boys from our block were going off into danger, and might not come back. In fact, several didn't.

* * * * * * * * *

We all went down to Union Station to see Ben off to Fort Dix. Impressed by the fact that Ben was studying radio design on his own and was proficient at Morse code, and by the high scores he had made on the basic tests, the enlistment officer had designated him for the Signal Corps, where Ben hoped to learn things he could use to get a better job when the war was over. He regretted that he and Mother had to wait two years before they could marry, because if they were married Mother would be entitled to widow's benefits if something happened to him. But he wanted to take care of us as best he could, so he had brought Mother downtown and set up a joint bank account into which he intended to send a portion of his pay in the form of what were called 'allotment checks'. He told Mother to use some of this money to continue Anne-Marie's dancing lessons, but the bulk was to be saved as a nest egg to start the Double-R-Bar Tourist Cabins in Wyoming just as soon as this war was over, which would surely be by next Christmas because how long could a ranting maniac with a Charlie Chaplin mustache and a bunch of near-sighted Japs hold out against an aroused America?

We had all dressed up in our finest to see him off, and we had cups of hot chocolate in the crowded station cafeteria while we waited for his name to be called over the loudspeaker...the first time we had eaten out since our arrival in Albany. And the last time too, Mother declared, at these prices! Ben found their song, the 1940 hit 'Only Forever', on the jukebox. He put in a nickel to play it, and Mother squeezed his hand under the table. Silent tears filled Anne-Marie's eyes. We stood on the platform in a dense pack of friends, family and lovers, all of us waving good-bye as the train pulled out with hissing jets of steam that billowed up into the platform lights. Men hung out train windows, waving as the train slipped into the dark tunnel, the edge of its shadow chopping off one waving soldier after another. Then the three of us walked back to North Pearl Street through a fresh snow that covered the sooty slush, making everything look clean and beautiful.

That night I sat up for a time, working out problems with the slide rule Ben had taught me to use, then I lifted my eyes from my work and numbly watched the street through a muffling curtain of snow. Everything was so quiet and still. The three of us were alone again...just as though Ben had never come into our lives. And suddenly I got a scary idea: what if there never had been a Ben, with his plans to take care of Mother for the rest of her life? What if I had made him up, like I made up so many characters for my story games? Made him up because I so much wanted someone to relieve me of responsibility for her future. How could I find out without the risk of everybody finding out that I had gone crazy? If I asked about him tomorrow and he didn't exist, they'd all know I was a nutter. No, I'd just have to wait for someone to mention his name...then I'd be safe. *Am* I crazy? I don't *feel* crazy. But then, crazy people don't feel crazy...because they're crazy!

But the next morning, Mother announced that she had decided not to touch a penny of Ben's allotment money. "Not a penny! When he comes back, I want to see the surprise on his face when he sees how much we've saved up for Wyoming!"

Yeah, I thought to myself, that's a great idea, but what about Anne-Marie's dancing lessons? Prices for everything had jumped up a notch as soon as war was declared, but our welfare income had remained the same. And we had come to depend on the extra dollars Ben gave us for his meals. It was obvious that we would need an additional source of money, and it was equally evident that it was up to me to find it. But where?

Frankly, I was beginning to tire of hearing about that 'place in

Wyoming', tired of pinning our hopes on so flimsy a fantasy. I felt that hope was a dangerous thing because it made you vulnerable to disappointment. Ben had made Mother's nose wrinkle with an earthy adage describing those who waste their time hoping and dreaming: 'Like the fella said: Hope in one hand and shit in the other, and see which fills up first'.

In the end, through the good offices of Mr Kane I got a second paper route to pay for Anne-Marie's tap lessons without touching Ben's allotment money. A newspaper broker used to bring Mr Kane a handful of Sunday papers for his customers, and one Sunday he mentioned that he was looking for a kid from the neighborhood to deliver papers, and Mr Kane recommended me. So now I had two paper routes, one for the *Times-Union* and another for the *Knickerbocker News*. Technically, I was still under the legal age to have a paper route, and it was against the rules for the same kid to deliver the two rival papers, but this broker, a slimy Dickensian gnome with mossy teeth and a taste for boys, routinely hired kids too young to have paper routes legally, reasoning that they wouldn't dare complain when he cheated them. But he was having trouble finding anyone to take a route in our neighborhood, where people who could afford a daily paper were so few and far between that seventy-five papers, the average for a five-block route, covered a twelve-block area. This meant that the kid had to walk more than twice as far and climb twice as many staircases to deliver the standard number of papers. Another thing that made my neighborhood unpopular with paperboys was the great number of deadbeats, some just because they were cheap, but most because they were poor. This made collecting hard and sometimes perilous, because frustration and shame could turn a drunken man into a bully when he was asked to cough up a quarter for his week's five papers.

Between the two paper routes, I carried a daily average of a hundred and fifty papers, which obliged me to start an hour earlier than the other newsies and to make two trips up to the brokers' because I couldn't carry a hundred fifty papers at one go. This and the exceptional length of my route meant that now I had to respond to our sadistic alarm clock at four-thirty every weekday morning in order to get to school on time. And four-thirty was suddenly earlier and darker and colder when, in February of 1942, all clocks in the United States went one hour ahead of standard time to save on fuel by reducing the need for lighting in the evenings. This 'Standard War Time' (in summer we changed to double daylight savings time) continued until September of 1945. So those were war time years in the literal sense.

Mother did everything she could to help me. Except when her lungs betrayed her, she never failed to get up and make my breakfast and, on rainy or snowy mornings, to make sure I wore my galoshes and was muffled up to the ears. And she always said, 'God bless you, son' when I left to go out into the dark and the cold. Which is a little odd, considering how she felt about God.

The newspaper business in the Albany of my day did not favor the newsie, who paid his broker four cents per paper and charged his customers five, so in theory he made a penny for every paper he delivered. For me, that would have been about a buck fifty a day, or seven fifty a week, more than we got from welfare and enough to pay for Anne-Marie's tap lessons and still save some for big emergencies or little pleasures. But the paperboy paid for his papers in advance, so when a customer stiffed him, it wasn't just his penny profit that the kid lost, it was also the four cents he'd paid for each paper. One deadbeat running behind for several weeks before either dropping his subscription or being cut off by the paperboy would reduce your takings by twenty-five cents a week. Because so many of the people on my paper routes were either poor or stingy, I never had fewer than a dozen deadbeats in any given week, and this cut my seven and a half dollars in half. While most of the customers eventually paid up to keep me from cutting them off, a fair percentage of them were old hands at the scam of quitting their subscription, then starting a new one the next day, and the paperboy was obliged by the circulation office to accept this 'new' customer. And why not? After all, the newspaper company wasn't losing any money, and the broker was still getting his four cents per paper. Only the newsie was out of pocket.[49]

I did well to make three fifty a week from eighteen hours of pre-dawn delivering in all weathers, and an additional tense four or five hours each Saturday, when I went around the route making my collections. I could have made a little more if I had been quick to cut my losses before the deadbeats got very far behind, but both crippling compassion and crippling hope kept me from cutting them off as soon as they stopped paying. An instance of crippling compassion would be the old people for whom the arrival of their paper was the only incident in a lonely day, and their only contact with the world beyond their door. An example of crippling hope would be when a customer already owed me for a month, and I knew that once I dropped him that money was lost forever, so I would con myself into believing that maybe, just maybe, he might pay up and I'd have an extra dollar and a quarter to drop into the Dream Bank. This hope caused me to extend his credit for one more week...then one more week...then just one more...until finally he'd move away or drop his subscription and leave me flat. The other situation that trapped me into compassionate losses was when the woman (it was usually the woman with a crying, squirming baby that you had to deal with, while the husband kept out of sight) wept when you threatened to stop delivering the paper, saying that her husband needed the want ads to look for work. What would they do if they didn't have a paper? I swear that word of my vulnerability on this ground must have spread among my customers, because I heard that tale so often. I knew, of course, that it was true in only a few cases. But which ones?

Mrs Hanrahan, who lived in my own building, was typical of the bad customer. She complained that her papers came late, or weren't delivered at all, or were dirty, or had already been opened and read by some phantom paper-snooper, and on these grounds she would refuse to pay her bill. I twice cut her from my list, but both times she immediately subscribed again, and I was obliged to deliver to her, even though she never, never, never paid up. And if I simply refused to drop off her paper, she would be served by one of the paper broker's 'favorites' and I would be charged ten cents for each paper.

If I came down with a bad cold and couldn't do my route, the broker would send out one of his pets to cover it, and I would have to pay that kid ten cents a paper, no matter how much or little I collected that week; so my Mother used to bundle up and deliver my papers for me, taking twice as long as I did because she didn't know the route, and costing us money on complaints for late papers, but at least we didn't lose the paper route. There were two occasions when both of us were ill at the same time, me having caught her cold while caring for her, and this brought us to the edge of financial disaster, but still Mother steadfastly refused to touch Ben's allotment savings.

The purchasing power of our weekly $7.27 continued to dwindle because OPA price freezes slowed, but could not prevent, wartime inflation. And yet Mother stuck pugnaciously to her decision to save Ben's allotments for their tourist cabins. The only money she would draw from their joint account was to pay for her divorce, which came through early in 1943. She reasoned that the divorce was as much for Ben as it was for her.

For the first two months after Ben enlisted Mother got regular letters which she read to herself with a soft, elsewhere look in her eyes that was strangely, but pleasantly, inconsistent with the cocky, flash-tempered mixed-blood I knew. When Ben came back on a three-day embarkation pass, Anne-Marie and I were proud to be seen with him in his uniform with two stripes on his sleeve. With his knowledge of radio, he had scored the highest of his radio class and was made corporal almost immediately. I still have a photograph of the three of us together, the slightly overexposed streetscape of Pearl Street's stoops receding diagonally behind us. I remember Mother taking this snapshot with her old billows Kodak, looking down into the viewer and moving back and forth to get the composition right. The embarkation leave was quickly over and we saw Ben off on his train. There followed a silence of several weeks that had us all worried until, one morning, we received a bundle of V-mail letters with words and addresses inked out. It seemed remarkable to me that Ben (a sergeant already) was in England, the England of Robin Hood and Sherlock Holmes, the place Edward R. Murrow's voice came from, the frying crackle of short-wave lending realism and immediacy to his savory baritone descriptions of the blitz he was watching from a rooftop, bombs and ack-ack fire audible in the background.

Nightly news broadcasts brought the nation to a standstill. Energetic children slowed to a hushed tip-toe at exactly six o'clock when their families clustered around radios to learn how the war was going; men in barbershops stopped wisecracking and frowned importantly at the radio in solemn silence; women decorating church basements stepped down from their ladders and listened, strands of crepe paper dangling from senseless fingers, everyone tense and vulnerable lest they hear something dreadful. After the newscasts came commentaries by men whose voices had become identified with the truth and with sympathetic concern: the didactic H. V. Kaltenborn;[50] the atonic, unflappable Elmer Davis; the quaintly named Raymond Gram Swing; the plummy elocutionist, Lowell Thomas; the jabbering scandal-huckster, Walter Winchell; and the lugubrious doom-herald, Gabriel Heatter. But the most widely admired was Edward R. Murrow, who in later years would confirm his reputation as the nation's most trusted journalist with his public demolition of that rabble-rousing national embarrassment, Senator Joseph McCarthy.

· · · · · · · · ·

Spring came, then summer, and we were back in school when Ben's letters told us he was being shipped out of England—he didn't know his destination. Mother wrote to him on the kitchen table almost every evening after supper, while Anne-Marie and I did the dishes and sang Hit Parade top tunes. The most immediate effect of the war on popular music was a vogue for peppy marches like 'American Patrol', played in a Big-Band swing version. And there were pitch songs like 'Any Bonds Today?' which sought to sell Americans on the idea of paying for the war. Later the Hit Parade offered dramatic, wartime action songs like 'Comin' In on a Wing and a Prayer' and 'Praise the Lord and Pass the Ammunition' in which an Army chaplain mans a gun to kill the enemy...a spooky idea upon reflection, but I don't recall thinking so at the time. Anne-Marie's favorite for some months was the romantic 'He Wears a Pair of Silver Wings', and I got sardonic pleasure out of singing 'Johnny Got a Zero', the story of a dumb kid who had made bad grades in school, but who turned out to have a gift for shooting down Japanese pilots and was therefore praiseworthy...also spooky.[51]

Hits of that first year of the war reflected the departing soldier's worry lest the girl back home not remain faithful, such 1942 Hit Parade songs as 'Somebody Else Is Taking My Place' and the heartfelt entreaty, 'Don't Sit Under the Apple Tree (with anyone else but me)'. Presumably 'sitting under the apple tree' was a euphemism.

Representing the girls at home, female band singers stepped up to the microphone and protested their innocence: 'I Don't Want to Walk Without You' which is why I 'Don't Get Around Much Any More'; but perhaps the real reason they didn't get around much was that the men back home were 'Either Too Young or Too Old'.

The boys overseas enjoined their girls to be faithful, but an entrenched double standard allowed them to admit that 'I Left My Heart at the Stage Door Canteen' and that 'Johnny Doughboy Found a Rose in Ireland'. (Obviously a song from the early months of the war, when the faceless soldier was still called by his First World War sobriquet, not yet having become a Government-Issued 'G.I.')

In 1944–45, as the war approached its end, the guy-over-there would promise 'I'll Be Home for Christmas' and warn his sweetheart that 'It's Been a Long, Long Time'. The gal-at-home responded by pledging 'I'll Walk Alone' and assuring him that although she was 'A Little on the Lonely Side' she would have 'No Love, No Nothin'' until her baby came home. She declared that for good girls like her 'Saturday Night Is the Loneliest Night of the Week'. My sister's favorite of these assurances of Penelopean constancy was 'I'm Making Believe' in which the girl says that until her dreams come true she'll kiss her pillow, making believe it's you. Anne-Marie thought that gesture so poignant! So touching! So sweet! I sometimes had to step out into the back area for a little fresh air.

It wasn't only popular song lyrics that went to war; radio programs also rolled up their sleeves and joined the fight. In a *Fibber McGee and Molly* broadcast made just after the December 7 attack, both Fibber and Molly made cracks about the physical appearance of the Japanese, and about Hitler not being a functioning male. These strained jokes must have been inserted into the script at the last minute, leaving no room for Fibber to open his famous closet door—one of the few episodes from the house at 79 Wistful Vista not to include this classic sound-effects gag.

Even the soothing, even-tempered Vic and Sade, who lived in 'the little house half-way up the next block', had nasty racial things to say about the Japanese. Overnight, cowboy Gene Autry became Sergeant Gene Autry (though he continued to serve his country from his 'Flying A' broadcast studio); and Kate Smith's yeasty singing of 'God Bless

America' instantly made her 'America's Sweetheart', which the gals in her radio audience didn't much mind, as Miss Smith's corpulence rendered her unthreatening.

The war touched even kids' action programs. The Green Hornet's faithful Japanese valet, Kato, suddenly became his faithful *Filipino* valet. And I remember the evening a gang of cattle rustlers on *Red Ryder* turned out to be Nazis trying to sap our soldiers' strength by denying them good red American beef, a nasty underhanded plot that Red Ryder and his pals discovered while hiding in an echoey cave to spy on a newcomer in town, a smooth-talking dude who claimed to be a botanist combing the western hills in search of wild plants. The rustlers came riding into the cave and the 'scientist' relaxed his guard sufficiently to let his German accent slip out as he led them in a shout of 'Heil Hitler!' which all the kids listening accepted as just the sort of thing your typical evil smooth-talking Nazi scientist involved in cattle rustling would shout in an echoey cave the minute he thought he couldn't be overheard. But I had known that this Nazi botanist/rustler would turn out to be the bad guy from the minute I heard him asking Red directions at the beginning of the program. He used long words and he spoke with careful pronunciation, and it was a given of the Western genre, both on the radio and in the movies (it's interesting that one was 'on' the radio but 'in' the movies) that anyone who used long words or spoke with precise diction was a bad'un.[52]

The Hollywood sausage factory ground out a string of war films featuring a Whitman's Sampler of the 'all-American platoon': one Scandinavian farm boy, simple, honest, wholesome, trusting...and inevitably the first to get it; one intense Italian who dreams of his mama's cooking and tells us how proud his papa had been to see him in uniform; one spoiled rich Anglo-Saxon guy who is either hardened into manhood by the crucible of danger, or revealed to be a sniveling coward; one 'other race' (Latin Americans often substituted for Negroes...they were safer); one educated 'professor' type who learns that when the chips are down, the earthy, common sense of your average uncultured Joe Blow is more valuable (and oddly 'wiser') than all this world's book learning; one ladykiller who brags about his romantic conquests, but in truth is lonely and has never known a woman's touch;

one mouthy comic from Brooklyn who will be the last to get it, dying with a wisecrack on his lips, his death enraging the tough, demanding (but deeply caring) officer played by the star of the film, who then snatches up an inexhaustible weapon and slays several thousand Nazis or Japs in an orgy of retribution while the audience cheers him on.[53]

This was war waged in and by the media. War as it touched us on North Pearl Street was felt mostly in shortages and rationing. We were issued books of red stamps for meat and blue stamps for canned food. Such things as canned spinach or lima beans were never rationed (the things one liked least, of course). You got change from ten-point stamps in little one-point coinlike disks made from matte-finished Bakelite, red disks for meat, blue for other things. And there were special stamps in the back of your blue stamp book for sugar, lard and oleo. Butter, too, I suppose, but no one on Pearl Street ever bought butter. Food rationing had little effect on my family's shopping, as we always ran out of money long before we ran out of ration stamps. Some of the poor used to sell their unused ration stamps to richer people. We were visited one afternoon by a sleazy middleman who was combing the slums, offering to buy ration stamps. Mother told him that one of our family was overseas in the army, and she'd be goddamned if she was going to help hoarders, war profiteers and slimy pigs like him to make money out of the war, so get the hell out of here!

Gasoline was also rationed, most cars having minimal-allowance 'A' stickers on their windscreens. But the shortage of gasoline demanded no sacrifice from North Pearl Street; nobody owned a car.[54]

It was not long before people started hanging service banners in their windows: a blue star for each member of the family in the armed forces, a silver one if he'd been wounded, and gold if he'd been killed. There was only one gold star on North Pearl Street. The oldest Brannon boy had run away to join the navy a couple of years before war broke out, and had died when his ship, the *Arizona*, sunk in Pearl Harbor. Just a week before the attack Mrs Brannon had received a present from her son, a silken pillow with hula girls embroidered on it and the words 'Aloha from Honolulu'. She wept every time she saw it, so the Brannon kids told her to put it away until she felt better, but she said she felt better when she was crying.

My mother hung a service banner with a blue star in our front window for Ben, and when she heard that Mrs Hanrahan had complained that we didn't have a right to hang a banner because Ben wasn't really a member of our family, she stormed upstairs to confront her, telling her that Ben was an orphan and we were the only family he had. And Ben was over there defending her constitutional right to be a pain in the ass, with her constant sniping and complaining! So put *that* in your hat and smoke it!

I was coming back from the library by the shortcut through the back alley, when I caught a glimpse of Mr McGivney sitting up there behind his lace curtain, looking sightlessly out over the roofscape; and it occurred to me that maybe Mrs McGivney should hang out a service banner to honor her husband's service to the country, even if it was two wars ago. Her banner should have a silver star because he had been wounded...in his mind anyway. But she probably didn't even know the country was at war, having neither a radio nor the electricity to run it. The chances were that the complications of rationing were managed for her by Mr Kane, who kept the ration books of several of the block's old people in a drawer under his counter and tore out the stamps as they were required. People who didn't like Mr Kane—mostly those who had run up a big slate with him and now avoided his shop out of shame and out of anger at being made to feel ashamed, or the women of Mrs Kane's circle who took her at her word when she declared that her husband was a hopeless dreamer, hence a failure—these people whispered that he used those ration cards to supply a city-wide black-market operation. And when his defenders said that they'd never seen anything fishy going on over there, his detractors would nod and say: Of course you don't *see* anything! They're sly, these people. Nor was this the only instance of a lack of evidence being used as corroboration of an accusation against Mr Kane. When one of his customers died, it was his custom to send a note of condolence to the family and to include in it a bill for the outstanding slate with 'paid in full' written across the top. If you imagine that this kindness endeared Mr Kane to North Pearl's collective heart, you are not reckoning with the subtleties and depths of prejudice. His humane gesture was taken as evidence that he had been criminally over-charging us for years. How else would he be rich enough to be able to write off ten or fifteen dollars just like that? And if he thinks we're going to bow and be grateful for being squeezed out of our money...well, forget it!

One evening shortly after the first Thanksgiving of the war, Mrs McGivney came across to Mr Kane's cornerstore just before he closed up. Following his custom, Mr Kane asked the last-minute customers if they wouldn't mind, and he went to the end of the counter to greet Mrs McGivney and ask what she needed today. She spoke so quietly that he had to bend his head close to hear. "What's that?" he asked. She repeated what she had said in a whisper, her eyes lowered as though she were telling him something intimate and shameful. He patted her shoulder and drew her gently through the door that led to the living quarters behind the store, so she could sit in the room Mrs Kane used as a Beauty Shop/Tea Salon. He said a few words to his wife, who offered Mrs McGivney a cup of tea, impatiently anticipating the moment when she would be able to retail her news to the neighborhood.

Mr Kane returned to his shop, took a nickel out of the till, looked up a number in the telephone directory and dialed. He turned his back on the waiting customers who pretended to be examining the air for defects while their ears strained to overhear what Mr Kane was saying with his hand curled over the speaking cup.

About a quarter of an hour later, an ambulance came down the street and stopped in front of the McGivneys' apartment house. Two men in green uniforms brought a stretcher up the stoop and disappeared into the building. The entire street had by now found reason to sit out on their stoops, or to stand around on the sidewalk, just having a breath of nice cold air this fine brisk evening. The men in green came back out wearing gauze masks and carrying Mr McGivney's body down the steps. He was tied onto the stretcher, a sheet covering his face, but not his bare toes with their thick yellow nails. Mrs McGivney stood with Mr Kane at the foot of the steps and watched them slide the stretcher into their ambulance, then drive off. She waved uncertainly after the departing vehicle, then Mr Kane brought her back across the street to stay with them for a day or two, until the public health men had come to fumigate and air out her apartment.

This was the first most people on the block knew of Mr McGivney's existence, and some of them felt personally affronted that they had been kept in the dark all those years. When word spread that someone had overheard one of the public health men say that the old guy must have been dead for quite a while, a shudder went up and down the block, and for a time there were rumors that the authorities were going to send Mrs McGivney to Poughkeepsie. The idiom throughout the Hudson River Valley for being put into an insane asylum was being 'sent to Poughkeepsie', a reference to this town's large establishment for people with mental problems.[55]

But Mrs McGivney didn't go to Poughkeepsie. By the end of the week she was back in her apartment. A few weeks later, close to Christmas, I was coming through the back alley late one evening and I glanced up. My heart almost stopped when I saw Mr McGivney in his usual place behind the lace curtains, his silhouette dimly halo'd by nacreous gaslight. I gasped. But how...? No, wait a minute. It wasn't Mr McGivney; it was his wife. She was sitting in his straight-backed chair, looking out just like he used to. Had she taken over his responsibility for keeping an eye on the alley? Did she sometimes brush her hair with his brush?

I wondered why anyone would spend time looking out at a deserted alley. What was the point? Then I thought about myself sitting on the edge of my daybed late into every night with my Hudson Bay around my shoulders, looking out at the empty street. Watching what? Expecting what? Fearing what?

Over the next couple of weeks, people on the block often glanced up uneasily towards Mrs McGivney's floor as they passed 232, and they would pull their necks into their collars and shudder. The superstitious Irish of North Pearl Street did not want to be reminded of Death, nor were they comforted when Mrs Kane (the seventh daughter of a seventh daughter, born with a caul over her face) assured her gossip clique that bad things always come in threes. And sure enough...

Old Joe Meehan, who was mate, father, grandfather, brother, uncle or several of the above to everyone in that inbred tangle, hadn't been seen on the street for a while, and the rumor was that he was lying on a mattress somewhere in the Meehan warren, sick and abandoned. It was after midnight and I was dozing at my window when suddenly a door across the street burst open and slammed against the side of the building with enough force to shatter its window. Old Joe came lurching

down the stoop wearing dirty, slack-knee'd longjohns and a red knitted
cap with a tassel. He was barefoot, and his toes looked like crooked
claws. He staggered down the deserted street and stood on the edge of
a cone of light from the streetlamp, the tassel of his cap swinging before his eye, one foot rooted in place, the other shifting back and forth
to keep his balance as he glared angrily up into the starless city sky. He
reached a long bony arm up into the shaft of light and shook his
fist. "Screw ya!" he croaked. "You hear what I'm sayin'? This is Joseph
Michael Meehan saying: Screw ya! And screw all the angels and
archangels too, while you're at it!" He stumbled over to the gutter and
sat down heavily on the curb, his elbows on his knees and his palms
pressed into his eye sockets. Lights came on in a nearby apartment and
a head peeked through curtains, but no one had any intention of getting mixed up in a Meehan brawl, especially a brawl between Old Joe
and God. When I looked back, Old Joe had slumped over and was
lying on his side with his butt overhanging the gutter, his knees up to
his chest and his cheek on his palm, like a kid. Two of the Meehan men
came out and tried to pick him up, but they couldn't, not because he re-
sisted, but because he was so limp that his body kept slumping through
their arms and folding up between their legs. With his trap-door
longjohns and his tasseled cap, Old Joe was a figure of slapstick comedy, a Mack Sennett gag. A sad one.

I watched until the ambulance came and collected the body about
an hour later. The next day, people who passed would glance angrily
from Mrs McGivney's windows across to the Meehans', annoyed to be
reminded of Death a second time. Our block worried about death the
way richer neighborhoods worried about burglars and vandals and
child snatchers. Pearl Street's children were already in the hands of
street forces; we had nothing to interest burglars; and anything worth
vandalizing we had already vandalized ourselves. All we had was our
lives, and therefore we worried a lot about death. Death had visited our
block twice now, and everyone remembered Mrs Kane's prediction that
bad luck always comes in threes, so they held their breaths until Mrs
Kane was told by a women who had her tea leaves read regularly (just
in case) that her aunt in Cohose had slipped in her bathroom and
bruised her knee badly. "There it is!" Mrs Kane pronounced triumphantly. "What did I tell you? The third fatality!" When one of the

women had the temerity to mention that Cohose was a long way from Pearl Street, and that a bruised knee, even a badly bruised one, didn't really qualify as a fatality, Mrs Kane shook her head ruefully and reminded her that Fate doesn't always conform to human expectations. If it did, what need would people have for someone who was born with a caul over her face and therefore had the gift of being able to see the future in the bottom of a teacup?

· · · · · · · · · ·

In addition to the service banners hanging in our windows, the ration stamps and disks cluttering up the bottom of handbags, and the new steel pennies that replaced copper ones in 1943 because copper was needed in wartime production, the war brought us those scrap-metal drives to which kids contributed by breaking into scrap yards and stealing stuff they had previously contributed, and contributing it again. The war also made itself felt in 'shortages' that caused us to save waste paper and used cooking fat, and to flatten tin cans, until trucks came around to collect them. Because the rubber plantations of southeast Asia were in Japanese hands, it was impossible to buy a new tire for a bike or a wagon unless you 'knew somebody'; and silk stockings had disappeared from the shops because silk was needed for parachutes, so young women shaved their legs closely, dyed them a light tan, and got a girlfriend to draw lines up the back of their calves to simulate the seams of stockings. Entrepreneurs quickly rushed into the market with expensive 'silk stocking' dyes and 'Seams Real' marker pencils specifically designed for this patriotic purpose, but the thrifty young women of North Pearl Street made do with diluted iodine or walnut oil for dye and eyebrow pencils for the seam line.

Lucky Strike cigarettes wrung every drop of advertising advantage out of their new white package by claiming that the green dye they had previously used had been requisitioned for the war effort. "Lucky Strike Green Goes to War!" declared the radio announcers in strident, courageous voices, as though the tobacco company was sacrificing itself to rid the world of the Nazi scourge, and so our boys might come back safe and well.[56]

Despite her worries about Ben and the pressure of wartime inflation that tightened our budget with every passing week, Mother still managed to be fun. Sometimes she would push the furniture to the edges of the middle room and show us the Charleston, the Varsity Drag, the Bunny Hug, the Turkey Trot or the Castle Walk.[57] She was a natural performer who blossomed under appreciation and applause. She taught Anne-Marie how to do the Jackson Strut, which they would perform together, side by side, with me as the clapping, whistling audience.[58]

After the early panic, patriotism, paranoia and profiteering passed, America accepted war as the natural state of things with surprising equanimity. In my routine of school, homework, the paper route and radio-listening there was little time for the story games that had sustained my early years on North Pearl, and I assumed that I had outgrown the need for them. Without these games, I had the long Saturday afternoons free after I returned, tight-stomached, from often confrontational and never totally successful collection rounds. I often spent Saturday afternoons watching movies at the Strand Theater, because I had worked out how to sneak in through a second-balcony fire door. This involved slipping down a narrow, slimy alley clogged with dented garbage cans to the back of the theater, where, unseen, I would scale its brick wall, which had a decorative recessed course every two feet and was therefore suitable to my felonious purposes. I would work my long, dicey way up to the third-story level, blowing and panting with effort and fear, but maintaining purchase on the gritty brick with just my fingertips and the tips of my tennis shoes, careful not to look down lest the view of the ground far below chill my stomach and make my hands go weak. When I reached the level of a big cantilevered iron fire escape I paused to build up the courage (actually it was more desperation than courage) to release my trembling fingertip grip on the edge of the brick and grasp the bottom step of the fire escape, which I would 'ride' back down to the level of the alley, always careful to keep it from banging on the cement and alerting ushers whose sole purpose in life was to deny me the enjoyment and enlightenment of the movies just because I didn't have the money for a ticket. Now the dangerous part was over and the tricky part began. I would slowly mount the fire escape to the point at which my weight was insufficient to hold it down against the counterweights that normally kept it up out of the reach of

larcenous brats trying to sneak into the movies. As the stairs started
rising, I would inch back down to control the speed of ascent, ultimately finding a balance point at which I could make them rise slowly
and silently by shifting my weight back and forth. When finally I managed to coax the fire escape back up in place without clanging hard
against the wall and warning the ushers within, I began the third phase
of the complex *Rififi* heist film machinations I went through every Saturday to save fifteen cents. With the twelve-inch ruler I had taped to
my leg, I tripped the latch of the heavy metal door which had no outside handle, because it was a press-bar fire door. Taking several deep
breaths to ready myself, I would snatch the door open, enter the
curtained-off exit niche of the second balcony, then close the door
quickly/softly behind me, hoping that the flash of daylight around the
edges of the curtain hadn't alerted ushers down on the first floor; but
they had their hands full with the mob of chattering, whistling, hoot-
ing, foot-stamping kids impatiently awaiting the beginning of the
show. The balconies were always empty and roped off during these afternoon performances because...well, what theater manager in his right
mind would let a street kid sit in the front row of a balcony with a
paper cup of soda in his hand and a sea of vulnerable heads beneath
him? I accomplished the move from the empty second balcony to the
anonymity of the crowded orchestra by first going down to the mezza-
nine where the toilets were. When the coast was clear, I would slip into
the men's room, where I would stand at the trough with my pecker out,
looking down at the sodden cigarette butts until a couple of kids came
in together, then I would mime shaking off and I'd wash my hands
carefully, wasting time until they were through and I could descend
with them, smiling and asking them questions about the movies we
were going to see, so it looked to the ever-vigilant ushers like we were
all chums together.

When I didn't go to the movies on Saturday afternoon because it
was raining or snowing and the brick wall was too slippery and dangerous, or because something was playing that I didn't care to see, like
a romantic film, or a musical, or anything by Disney, I would spend
my afternoon in the library. At the age of twelve, I received an adult
card that permitted me to take out anything I pleased; but I missed the

adventure of sneaking up the iron spiral staircase from the basement children's library to my cozy niche above the gurgling Gothic radiator where I had sat in the light of the stained-glass window and read books I had nicked from the return carts. One rainy afternoon after I had my adult card I thought about how pleasant it used to be, reading in that warm niche while rain running down the windows caused rivulets of colored shadow to ripple over my page, so I brought a book to my old nest in the hope of recapturing the zest of those stolen hours, but I couldn't concentrate because I was afraid that someone might find me there, and I would look like an ass, hiding away to read what I had every right to check out and read, now that I had an adult card. I guess it's true that you can't go home again. Each moment has its place in the flow of time, then the moment passes, and if you reach back for it, you come up with a handful of dust.

· · · · · · · · ·

Ben's appearance on the scene had let me ease myself out of the center of our tight little family. Except for routine responsibilities like my paper route and household chores, I was free to drift on the edges of my mother's life, and she didn't seem to miss me. But after Ben was shipped overseas, she began to slip into 'the blues' more often and more deeply than before she met him. Almost every evening she would sit at the kitchen table after supper, writing to him, while Anne-Marie and I did the supper dishes. She always used V-Mail, those one-page letters that folded up to become their own envelope and didn't require a stamp if addressed to someone in the armed forces, and she made up for the lack of space by writing in a small, tight hand that must have cramped and crispened what she said.

The winter of 1942–43 came early, cold and hard, the first heavy snows falling in mid-November. Restrictions on coal meant that I had to bank the furnace at nine o'clock every night, and the building became chilly enough that you could see your breath by the time I went down to the basement to stoke it up again the next morning at four-thirty, before starting my paper round. As the first year of the war came to its end, the excitement and newness faded into grim routine, and people began to wonder how long these shortages and high prices would last. The regular stream of Ben's letters from England suddenly stopped, and Mother became preoccupied and tetchy. Then the radio announced the landing of American forces on the shores of French colonial North Africa, and she felt sure Ben was among them. She confessed to me that she had a premonition that something terrible had happened to him. She could feel it in her bones. It turned out she was right.

It was the first Saturday in December, almost the anniversary of Pearl Harbor, when the mailman knocked on our door because the chubby packet of V-mail letters he had for us wouldn't fit into our mailbox. Ben was indeed in North Africa. He had written every day while he waited in communicative quarantine to sail from England with the invasion force, and twice a day during the long, slow, dull, but tense voyage as his convoy skirted the Iberian peninsula, rendezvous'd with the convoy originating in the United States, passed through the Straits of Gibraltar, then lay at anchor off the coast of Algeria. All these letters had been found in his kit and returned to him in the hospital after he was wounded during the landing at Oran. To this bundle of letters he had added another, scribbling on the outside of its envelope 'read this first'. This note told her that he was recovering from a flesh wound in his side (wounded by a *French* bullet, he underlined bitterly) but he was being well taken care of. In fact, he was at that moment sitting in the forecourt of a French resort hotel that had been converted into a field hospital overlooking the sparkling Mediterranean. Oh...by the way...he was officially a hero, having received a Purple Heart. Oh, and another thing. Mother would have to change the way she addressed his letters, now that he had made staff sergeant. He ended by saying that considering his lofty rank and his status as a hero, he expected one hell-of-a-lot of respect when he got home, and maybe even a little obedience...just kidding. Ha-ha!

We were all relieved that Ben was all right, but from that time on Mother seemed to flinch inside whenever someone knocked at our door, as though she were expecting bad news. Ben's long silence, then his wound had put an end to her feeling that their future out West was certain and inevitable.

Sometimes at night, when Anne-Marie was asleep and I was reading, Mother would come in and sit on the edge of my daybed and ask what my book was about, or what I was studying in school, and I knew she was down in the dumps and needed company, so I would suggest a late-night game of honeymoon pinochle, which was really what she had come in for. She always protested that I needed my sleep, what with having to get up early in the morning to start the boiler and do my paper round, and she would only agree to a game when I insisted that I was feeling tense and maybe a game or two would help me get to sleep. We would go into the kitchen which we could warm up by lighting one of the gas burners. She would make hot chocolate if we had the milk, and we would play at the kitchen table. I must have inherited some of my blood father's card-playing genes because I had long ago become much better at pinochle than she, but I contrived to let her win most of the time. I would absent-mindedly fail to meld part of what I had, or I would weaken my playing hand by sloughing the highest card I could without winning the trick. I was afraid that she might catch me letting her win, but she was always too exhilarated by her narrow victories to notice, especially when, after over-bidding, she managed to save herself by taking good fat tricks towards the end of the hand, snapping her winning cards down on mine with gusto. Because she took such pleasure in winning, I didn't mind losing, but it always seemed that as soon as I decided to lose, the ironic Gods of Chance would send me the greatest hands of my life, so it was not only a crying shame to lose, but difficult too.

Playing cards was not our only home entertainment. There was also the radio, and endless games of 'twenty questions', and at night as we did the supper dishes, Anne-Marie and I would challenge each other to 'Name That Tune'. One of us would hum or whistle a couple bars and the other had to guess the song. Anne-Marie knew more popular music than I did, but my memory for lyrics was infallible. I knew the words to all the hits of the 1941–42 season.[59]

Another game we played was called One Hundred Dollars! (Anne-Marie and I agreed that the exclamation mark was part of the name). Each of us was allotted a fictional hundred dollars to spend on anything in the Montgomery Ward catalogue. We each had a strip of brown bag paper and a pencil to make our list, and at the end we voted on who had made the best buys. (Anyone who had more than two dollars left over automatically lost.) Anne-Marie usually bought clothes

for herself together with bits of fringe and ruffle and ribbon to person-
alize the generic styles, but she always remembered to get at least one
present for Mother and one for me, which was something neither
Mother nor I ever thought of. Mother bought things for the house,
mostly sensible, but occasionally decorative, like three wrought-iron
fish in diminishing sizes that she could hang on the tiled wall of our
future bathroom in Wyoming to give it 'that decorator touch'. I usually
bought things I thought I might be able to make money with: tools for
use as a hired handyman, or paintbrushes, a ladder and white bib overalls with a white cap to equip myself as a freelance house painter.

While Anne-Marie and I compared lists, defending our choices
while ridiculing the other person's, my mother would mend our socks
and clothes using the wooden egg with a screw-in handle. That old
hickory egg was the only memento she had of her mother. Some of her
darning was so extensive that it amounted to re-weaving, just to make
worn-through knickerbockers last another month or two. I had seen a
war movie at the Grand in which Germans tossed 'potato masher' hand
grenades at French partisans, and it occurred to me that my mother's
darning egg would make a perfect German hand grenade, so the next
day I snuck (that was the past participle in Pearl Street usage) it from
her sewing box and hurled it with devastating effect at nests of Nazis
from one end of our back alley to the other. But the darning egg got
dented and scuffed up (war is not without its costs) and I didn't dare
return it to her sewing box before I had scraped up enough money to
buy some sandpaper to remove the scars of combat and some varnish to
return it to as good as new. In the meantime, I continued to use the
darning egg in its martial capacity. One afternoon as I was walking past
a parked dump truck, my imagination suddenly sparked and I flattened
myself against the brick wall, lobbed my hand grenade into the back of
the tank the duplicitous Nazis had camouflaged as a dump truck, then
threw myself on the pavement to avoid the shrapnel, and while I was
lying there with my arms over my head, the goddamned tank drove off!
Taking my mother's darning egg with it.

That very night—wouldn't you know it?—she suggested that we
play One Hundred Dollars! while she did her darning. I was unable to
deflect her to pinochle, so I sat there, drawing up my list with a frown

of total concentration as she pawed around in the bottom of her sewing basket with growing irritation, muttering that she couldn't seem to find her darning egg. "H'm," I hummed, with a 'How-about-that?' inflection. She asked if I had seen it. Asked *me*. Not Anne-Marie, no, only me. As though everything was always my fault. I didn't lie to her. I almost never lied to my mother, but I was adept at the misleading non-lie. When she asked if I had done something with her darning egg I said, "Me?" (Just a matter of clarification, not a lie.) Then I sighed, put my list of purchases aside, and said, "All right, all right, I'll help you find it!" And I went around the house, looking under beds and in drawers, from which actions my mother may perhaps have drawn the conclusion that I hadn't taken it, but I never actually lied to her. Indeed, I gave her reason to be proud of my ingenuity when I unscrewed the lightbulb from a lamp and told her to try using that until her darning egg showed up. It worked perfectly, and for the rest of her life, my mother darned with a burnt-out lightbulb, although she would occasionally raise her eyes from her work and wonder what on earth ever became of her mother's hickory darning egg.

· · · · · · · · ·

That June, a few days after the school year staggered to its dreary end, I became thirteen years old. A teenager? Me, who had always scorned the mooning, mawkish ways of teenagers like radio's chicken-voiced Henry Aldrich? Me, a teenager! But wait, I didn't want to be a teenager. I wasn't through being a kid, yet.

Later that summer, the Allies landed in Sicily, and we all worried about Ben when, once again, the flow of his letters stopped for nearly three weeks. Then we got a V-mail from a hospital in Palermo. The letter was short, and Ben's handwriting was shaky, but he made a joke about how he seemed always to be standing just where some bullet hankered to be. For all the jocular tone, Mother felt sure that this new wound was more serious than the one he got in North Africa, and she was tense and edgy for a couple of weeks, until she received a letter in which Ben said he was out of the hospital and loafing around in a recuperation center. Oh, and he'd received his second Purple Heart, along with an increase in rank to technical sergeant. "If this war goes on long enough, I'll end up a general!" Mother talked about changing the service banner in our window from a blue star to a silver one in recognition of Ben's wounds, but she never got around to it. At the time I thought her indifference had something to do with a long letter that came a few days later in which Ben confessed that he was no longer a technical sergeant. He had been broken back to private. Along with some buddies at the recuperation center, he had gone into town to celebrate with a couple of beers...only a couple, honest...but the next day he passed a lieutenant without saluting, and when the newly commissioned shavetail rebuked him, Ben unleashed a spate of abuse and rage that he didn't realize had built up within him. Mother had been proud of the way Ben had risen so quickly through the ranks and she was vexed to have to write 'Private' on her V-mail letters.

Ben's loss of rank didn't matter a bit to me, but I sensed ominous potential in his strange, self-destructive kind of alcoholism.

. . . .

My mother and I were playing honeymoon pinochle at the kitchen table. She and Anne-Marie had gone to bed a couple of hours earlier, and I was reading in my daybed when she came padding in and asked if I was ready to face the licking I had coming to me for winning our last game...by pure, blind luck! Our habitual challenge routine involved this sort of lippy banter, but I could hardly tell her that I'd rather stay in my cozy bed with my book because I felt she wanted to get something off her chest. "Any time you feel lucky, Mother o' mine," I said, climbing out of bed and draping the Hudson Bay over my shoulders. "But I warn you that you're in for another humiliation."

"That'll be a hot day in hell," she said.

I sighed, but let it go.

Partway through the first hand, she mentioned offhandedly that her divorce had come through.

"Really? When?"

"A couple of weeks ago."

"A couple of weeks? But...why didn't you say something?"

She shrugged. No other answer.

"Well anyway," I said, "that's great news!" For the past six months,

I had been haunted by fantasies of coming home after school and finding my father sitting at the kitchen table, swigging down green soda and smiling slyly because he knew that we wouldn't be able to divorce him for abandoning us...not for another seven years at least. I considered killing him and hiding the body somewhere. How to hide him was an engrossing problem, and I occupied some of the boring time in class working up inventive solutions, like drying him out like a mummy then dressing him in Indian clothes and putting him in the glass-case diorama of Iroquois life in the Natural History Museum. "So, you and Ben are free to get married whenever you like."

"Except that he's on the other side of the ocean, fighting this damned war."

My trouble-hunting imagination instantly shifted from my father showing up to ruin the divorce to the possibility that Ben might not come back, having been killed in battle, or become infatuated with some foreign woman, or hit on the head by a falling roof tile and wandering around Europe, a victim of the amnesia: a plot gimmick that was making the rounds of the soap operas at that time.

I was counting up points when she spoke as though giving voice to a thought she had begun in silence, "...it gave me a funny feeling, seeing that word written down in black and white: 'Desertion'. That's what it said under 'plaintiff's grounds for seeking divorce'. Desertion seems such a...I don't know...such a cruel way to say it. I mean, Ray didn't really 'desert' us."

"Oh no? What would you call it?"

"Well, he...I don't know. He can't stay put. It just isn't in his nature."

"H'm."

"I somehow can't get used to the idea that I'm a divorced woman. I can't believe I'm no longer married to your father. He was the first man I ever..." She shrugged and shook her head.

The game wasn't over, but I didn't shuffle because she obviously wasn't interested in playing.

"All the time I was waiting for the divorce to become final...all those months...I had this funny feeling that any minute Ray would open the door and toss his hat in like he used to do. He'd wait to see

if I was going to throw his hat back at him, and if it didn't come sailing back out, he'd come in with that crooked grin of his and...He
was a charmer, your father. Oh, sure, he's no good and irresponsible
and all that, but he was a charmer. You've got to give him that. And
a woman was proud to be seen on his arm. Great dresser. Smooth
talker."

"He's a con man, Mom."

"He never thought of himself as a con man."

"What did he think he was?"

"A dream-merchant." She smiled to herself and repeated, "That's
what he told me one night. A dream-merchant. He didn't con people,
he sold them dreams." She compressed her lips and shook her head.
"I guess there's no love like your first love."

"And what about Ben?"

"Oh, I love Ben. I really do. But...in a different way."

"What if Ray were to come through that door right now? What
would you do?"

She looked at me for a long moment. Then lifted her shoulders.

"Mom, you're not marrying Ben just because of Anne-Marie and
me, are you?"

"No! What an idea! Definitely not."

"You're sure?"

She nodded, then was silent.

"Have you written telling Ben that your final papers came through?"

"Not yet."

"Why not?"

"No special reason. Come on. Deal, why don't you."

"Because it's your deal."

As I picked up my cards (one of the secret 'edges' I gave my mother
so she could win now and then was not to arrange the cards in my
hand; I would just hold them in the order in which I had picked them
up), I wondered what Mother would do if my father did come back
into our lives, even now, after the divorce had been granted. I had an
instinct that it would be something foolish. And I wondered what Ben
would do. He was younger than Mother, so I wondered if maybe he was
seeking a mother to make up for having been raised in an orphanage.

If he was, he was making a big mistake. Even I was more her pal and burden-sharer than her child, and I'd been born to her.

For some time after she went back to bed, I sat looking out at the street and wondering if she and Ben had any chance of being happy together. It was like one of those questions the soap opera announcers used to pose in their richest, fruitiest voices...Can a deserted woman trying to bring up two children in a slum find happiness as the wife of a younger man who is neither a great dresser nor a smooth talker, and who does himself harm every time he takes a couple of drinks? Tune in next week.

· · · · · · · · ·

We emptied the Dream Bank to put together a Christmas package for Ben containing things he wouldn't be able to find overseas. He once told us that he loved pickled pig's feet (you can imagine how that made Anne-Marie shudder), so we looked all over town, but the only ones we found came in glass jars, and we knew from disastrous experience that no matter how carefully it was packed and padded, a glass jar wouldn't survive the rough handling of APO mail. We managed to find a can of the corn syrup that Ben preferred to maple syrup, which Anne-Marie and I thought was *really* strange. Maybe it had to do with his being born in Missouri, while we were Northeasterners. And we sent him a box of Bull Durham in those little sacks with yellow drawstrings because, although the tobacco industry provided servicemen with 'free' (meaning government-subsidized) cigarettes that would assure the cigarette company thousands of new addicted customers when the war was over, Ben couldn't get the roll-your-own 'makings' he preferred. In a used-book shop I found a collection of Western stories written before the turn of the century by Owen Wister and illustrated by Frederic Remington.[60] But what he probably appreciated most was a special year-end songbook that contained all the hits of 1943.[61] Before putting it into the box, Anne-Marie, Mother and I sang our way through it, and the sentimental ones dampened Mother's eyes.

On her way back from mailing off Ben's Christmas package, my mother stopped off at Kane's cornerstore and when she got home there was a small tin of cinnamon among her groceries and an extra loaf of day-old bread. She almost never bought spices other than salt and pepper because they were expensive and not essential to a healthful diet, but this cinnamon had caught her eye and reminded her of winter nights during her childhood when she and her sisters used to sneak down from their shared bedroom to make cinnamon toast as a forbidden late-night feast, so she bought some for Anne-Marie and me, and to hell with the cost! For the next few weeks, through the heavy snows of Christmas and New Year's and well into the leaden cold of February, she made cinnamon toast for the three of us each night before bed. She would spread toast with margarine and sprinkle a mixture of sugar and cinnamon over it, then put it back under the gas grill (we didn't have a toaster as such) until the sugar and margarine bubbled and formed a candied crust. I relished the feeling in my mouth of slippery melted margarine between the crusty cinnamon sugar and the crisp toast. The little tin of cinnamon ran out, and we didn't squander money on a second one, but it was a splendid treat while it lasted.

·········

I occasionally saw Mrs McGivney scuttling over to Mr Kane's, as timid and furtive as ever. She always seemed slightly baffled, as though her mind were sort of...'windblown' is the most accurate word I can think of. Her old-fashioned dresses were often misbuttoned, and wisps of hair escaped from the amber combs she used to keep it in place. I tried to speak to her a couple of times, just a friendly word to cheer her up, but her eyes would graze mine with a wincing glance and she'd scurry away, leaving behind that faintly cheddar smell of old women. I was sorry that I hadn't gone to see her after Mr McGivney died. It wouldn't have hurt me to sit up there for half an hour or so every once in a while, eating a sugar cookie and listening to her tell me how much all the other soldiers had liked her husband when he was down in Cuba. Maybe if she had someone to talk to once in a while she wouldn't have become so...windblown. But remembering that she now sat in her husband's straight-backed chair, looking out over the back alley through her lace curtains, just like he used to, sent shivers up my spine, so I always put off going to visit her.

When I stepped out onto our stoop one Sunday afternoon in the

summer of 1943, I immediately knew something was afoot. There was
that faint but legible spoor of trouble that street people can sense...like
when the police are in the neighborhood, or there is violence in the
wind. Sometimes it's not signs you read, but the absence of signs, like
an unaccountable silence, or kids who should be playing, but are not.
Word had spread through the block, and all the gossips had found reason to be out on their stoops. One woman came out with a broom as
though to sweep the steps, and a moment later Mrs Hanrahan appeared, also carrying a broom and obviously piqued that this busybody
had not only copied her excuse for being on her stoop, but had had the
cheek to copy it first. Some people! Kids abandoned their games and
clustered in silent twos or threes against the walls between stoops,
itchily impatient to return to play but cowed by the spreading aura of
anticipation. Two little girls clung to the metal railing around a sunken
basement and swung back and forth, hanging straight-elbowed from
their stretched arms, covetously eyeing a freshly chalked hopscotch
pattern, their young bodies hungry for activity, but hindered by the
gravity of the moment. A white car with something written on its door
was parked down the street outside Mrs McGivney's building. Women
chatted desultorily as though unaware of the chilling portents, but
their corner-of-the-eye attention never left Mrs McGivney's front
door. I walked over to the next stoop and asked, "What's happening?"
of a woman who had decided to darn her kids' socks in the good daylight of her stoop.

"They're taking her away, poor thing," she whispered, tipping her
head towards Mrs McGivney's, but not looking that way because she
didn't want to be thought of as some kind of snoop.

"Taking who away?"

"Men in white. From the nuthouse. They're up there with a nurse."

I crossed the street to Mr Kane's cornerstore, and he told me that
Mrs McGivney had been getting more and more vague over the last
few weeks, and he got worried when she didn't come to do her shopping for a week, so he made an anonymous call to the Social Services
people, asking them to look in on her. One of the young social workers
had come. (You could recognize them by their eager faces and the
enameled smiles they bestowed on children, while their bodies stiffened in dread of physical contact.) The social worker had gone up to

Mrs McGivney's apartment, only to reappear on the stoop a few minutes later and look up and down the street until she spotted the white
enameled metal plaque with its dark blue bell that announced the presence of a Bell pay telephone in Mr. Kane's store. She crossed and
placed her call, speaking quickly and quietly with her lips close to the
mouthpiece (which she had first wiped with her handkerchief), then
she left. Half an hour later, the white car arrived.

I went back out into the street where the curiosity was so intense
you could taste it, like ozone before a thunderstorm, but despite their
curiosity, no one was sitting on the stoops on either side of Mrs Mc-
Givney's building where they could have had a good view of the show.
And I knew why. An article of folk-dogma of North Pearl was that it
was dangerous to get too close to 'people from Poughkeepsie'. Those
funny-farm goons might just grab you, too, while they were at it. Save
themselves a trip! I decided to cross over and sit on Mrs McGivney's
stoop. Maybe when they brought her down she wouldn't feel so frightened if there was someone she knew close at hand, someone who
would smile at her and say a pleasant word, maybe touch her hand.

The front door opened and they came down, first a nurse and a
young orderly, then an older, chubby orderly who had Mrs McGivney's
elbow cupped in his palm in a gallant, protective way as he walked
slowly beside her, leaning close as though eager not to miss a word of
what she was telling him. I scooted over to let them pass me, and Mrs
McGivney's urine-smelling dress brushed my shoulder. She wasn't
even aware that I was there as she animatedly explained to the orderly,
"...then his commanding officer—Captain Francis Murphy?—well, he
wrote to say that Private McGivney had been a cheerful and willing
soldier and that he was well liked by everybody in the regiment. Everybody in the whole regiment!"

"Gosh, imagine that," the orderly said, helping her into the official
car. "Liked by everybody in the regiment, was he? I'll be darned."

They drove away, and we never saw Mrs McGivney again.

. . . .

Wool-gathering and dozing in the classroom must have supplied
some of my need for sleep and dreaming, because I seldom got
more than five hours of normal sleep. It was always after midnight

when I gave up looking out on the empty street where misty light fell from the widely spaced streetlamps, leaving patches of dense shadow between. Someone walking down the street late at night would emerge out of the darkness, his shadow dim and long behind him. As he approached the lamp post, his shadow would shorten, then as he passed under the streetlight, it would swing beneath him and lead him out of the pool of light, lengthening until both man and shadow were absorbed into the next slab of shadow.

I had a front-row seat for those nights when the police came to break up street fights. The prowl cars seldom came during the day because most street fights were fueled by drinking, which didn't get going until nightfall. When a prowl car came, I would move back into the shadows of my room so I was invisible to anyone outside, and I would watch the rotating red light atop the prowl cars rake brick walls and sweep over the cobbles. Twice the police came when someone broke into Kane's Grocery, and Mrs Kane put her head out her window and screamed in short earsplitting blasts like a mechanical alarm, as the befuddled thieves ran away. And once the police came shortly before dawn because an old tramp had gone off his nut and was breaking the basement windows along the street, kicking them in with his bare feet. When I went out to start my paper route at dawn the next morning, I found his bloody footprints on the pavement.

One night I was startled out of a consoling reverie by the noisy arrival of two prowl cars. Cops piled out with much bluster and slamming of car doors. They had come to arrest Patrick Meehan because he had badly beaten up a boy who had taken his sister, Brigid, up the back alley. Four of them dragged the writhing, snarling Patrick out onto the stoop where, furious because he had punched a couple of them, they beat him with their nightsticks until he lay unmoving on the pavement. Then they folded him into the back seat of one of the prowl cars. Brigid and her mother rushed out to plead with them not to take Patrick away. The cops tried to make Mrs Meehan let go of the car's door handle so they could drive off, but she couldn't let go. Unaware of her compulsive inability to release things, they thought she was just being obstructive, so one of them hit her knuckles with his stick and she howled with pain, but still didn't let go, so they drove off slowly, thinking that would break her grip, but she held on, and they dragged her along the street for a distance before finally her hand came off the handle and she lay in the street sobbing, her knees scuffed and bleeding.

The prowl cars left and the street was empty again, except for the growling, cursing knot of Meehans around their stoops. Down the street, Mrs Meehan sat on the curb, her skirt up to her hips, her shoulders heaving with silent sobs as she bent forward and gingerly touched her tongue to her scraped knees. Young Joe Meehan, who had taken over the leadership of the clan when Old Joe died, led Brigid up the stoop and into the house, drawing her along by her slack arm. I felt sure he intended to use her, now that her brother would be safely out of the way for a while.

· · · · · · · · · ·

Sacrifice and Courage were constant motifs in war movies and in radio dramas, and everyone talked about how our boys in the service were getting along, and wondered when we were going to open a second front in Europe to take the pressure off the Russians. But at the same time, people were beginning to express irritation about rationing and shortages. For the first time since Pearl Harbor they talked about what they were going to do 'after the war'. So the war had stopped being an eternal condition of life and was already beginning to loosen its grip on us, preparatory to slipping into history.

Mother and Ben's bank account grew with his monthly allotment checks and its accruing interest, and I sometimes found myself half-believing in their tourist cabins out in Wyoming when the war was over. I accompanied Mother to the bank when she had to sign something, and for the first time I experienced the cool marble, dark wood, and glistening brass of a temple of capitalism. It would be more than twenty years before I found myself in a bank again. Most people from North Pearl Street, or any other slum in America, went through their entire lives without ever seeing the inside of a bank, just as they never learned to drive or went on vacation. Banks, automobiles, holidays, these were for rich people.

After being sent back to England to recover from his second

wound, Ben was assigned to instructing in a Signal Corps school, where he worked his way back up to sergeant. His letters never failed to ask how Anne-Marie was getting on with her dancing lessons, and if I was still the star pupil in school. Well, no, in fact. I had given up trying to excel in the classroom because there was no point in it. If things went wrong between Mother and Ben, I would have to get a job at sixteen anyway, so why bother?

Although I didn't do much schoolwork that year, I devoted a couple of hours each night and many Saturday afternoons to translating *Poil de Carotte* into English, one of those Herculean tasks that you accomplish because you don't know it's supposed to be impossible. I had found the book on a cart of foreign-language holdings, along with a French–English dictionary and a dog-eared first-year French grammar. I spent hours in my window niche above the sighing, gurgling radiator, working out baffling passages as though I were breaking enemy codes, and this appealed to the role-playing boy in me. Considering that I undertook this task with no preparation other than a careful study of the thirty-two-page "Introduction to French" in my *High School Subjects Self-Taught*, it is probably just as well that I didn't mind whole paragraphs remaining intriguingly ambiguous...a quality I ascribed to French literature in general.

. . . .

"We interrupt this program to..."

It was June 6, 1944, and the Allies were landing on the beaches of Normandy. Mother couldn't sleep that night, sure that Ben was involved in the invasion, despite his repeated assurances that the wounds he had received in North Africa and Sicily would keep him in England and out of combat. We played honeymoon pinochle into the small hours, talking about the place in Wyoming and all the things we'd do when Ben came back. I made her laugh a couple of times by letting her win then pretending to be angry that she'd beaten me by just one or two tricks, but it wasn't until a week later when we received a V-mail letter from England postmarked later than D-Day that she really believed that Ben was safe. A weight was lifted from me, too. I wanted nothing more than for them to marry and be happy and to-gether forever and ever, leaving me free to go do something on my own. Even after her divorce came through I could never quite rid my-self of the fear that I might get home from school one of these days, and there my father would be, drinking lime soda and eating green cake, and Mother would be all aglow. She'd tell me that she had de-cided to give him one more chance, and they'd ask me to write Ben and explain. (You're so good at words, son.) Then, of course, Ray would run off again, and Mother would collapse into depression and bitterness, and I'd have to take care of her for the rest of her life. And mine.

The morning after the announcement of the Normandy landings, the front page of the newspaper had a map of the Cotentin peninsula with little American, British and Canadian flags indicating the assault beaches: Utah, Omaha, Gold, Juno and Sword. I cut the map out and taped it on the wall beside our radio, so I could follow events as they were broadcast. Although the news reporters were confident in tone, there didn't seem to be much advance from the beachheads in those first days. We were not told of the terrible losses our troops took on Bloody Omaha beach, nor did we know how close they came to being thrown back into the sea.[62]

· · · · · · · · ·

Summer passed and Labor Day came to signal the beginning of school; trees in Washington Park turned gold and red before their leaves fluttered down and were swept into deep crisp piles that kids weren't supposed to jump into and scatter, so of course they did, then ran like hell from the rickety-legged old man brandishing his rake; and pretty soon it was late autumn and the nights were cold, and brittle stars were close overhead when Mother, Anne-Marie and I walked home through dark streets after Dish Night at the Paramount Theater, where Humphrey Bogart had appeared in a special clip asking us—yes I'm talking to *you*, pal, sitting in that theater seat right now—to dig deep and subscribe to the Third War Bond Drive and help buy the guns and planes our boys need to beat the Japs and Nazis and come back home to the families they love. The lights were turned up, and ushers came down the aisles passing out pledge forms in which you wrote how much you would give. I was always embarrassed that we didn't have enough money to buy war stamps, much less the $18.75 needed to buy the cheapest war bond. But Mother took her pledge form with a friendly smile and put it into her handbag to be used later for keeping pinochle scores.

Through that long, war-weary winter of 1944–45, I taped up the newspaper maps that recorded our army's progress in Europe as I learned of it from nightly news broadcasts and the weekly movie news-reels. I drew and re-drew lines and blocks and curving arrows that de-scribed enemy emplacements and our troop movements as we liberated France. Meanwhile, we fought the Japanese in the Pacific where our young men died in amphibian island-hopping advances against an en-trenched and stubborn enemy; but for my family the essential war was in Europe, where Ben was, and all our hopes for the future.

I finished *Poil de Carotte* and began *Le Comte de Monte Cristo*. Maybe I'd become a rich and famous translator, if only I could work out what this conditional tense was all about.

VICTORY IN EUROPE

MARCH WINDS moaned around street corners, making sooty dust swirls that stung the eyes and were gritty between the teeth. The unseasonably cold wind pushed me down the steep Livingston Avenue hill when I returned from school, my arms spread wide to create more sail surface to let the wind hustle me along rubber-knee'd and pleasantly helpless. The next morning before dawn, that same searching wind made climbing the hill doubly hard because I had to bend low to offer less surface to its force. Radio news commentators informed us in triumphant tones that American and British troops, having survived the harrowing Battle of the Bulge, were driving the Germans eastwards over the Rhine as the Russians pressed them westwards to Berlin. Could victory be far away?[63]

My personal contribution to the war effort was a complex combat game I constructed from shards of those war movies in which actors like Errol Flynn and John Wayne single-handedly mowed down thousands of arrogant Nazis or sneaky Nips. This most athletic, most realistic, most demanding and most satisfying of all my story games was also to be the last one I would ever play.

On the first three Saturdays of that last March of the war I set my clattering alarm clock for four in the morning, dressed quietly, then slipped out of the house to walk through pre-dawn streets all the way up to Washington Park and the flat-topped artificial hill that looked down on its miniature lake and boathouse. As sunrise began to gild the topmost leaves of the park's trees, I would work my way up this steep-sided hill, slipping back on the dewy grass at every second step. When I reached the top the game began with orders coming in over my crackling walkie-talkie stick. (After you spoke, you had to say 'over' and rub the side of the stick with your thumb so the other guy could speak, and you had to make his voice sound metallic and put in some static, not an easy stick to run.) I was informed that my loyal followers and I must hold this hill long enough for a reinforcement column to come up and thwart the Germans' (or Japs') final offensive. I accepted the assignment gravely, knowing full well the terrible sacrifices it would entail. Then I gathered together my old band of followers and told them what was expected of us, my voice tight and bitter because we had been chosen *yet again* for the most dangerous mission of all. Why did we always get the dirty jobs? Why *us?* The likelihood of our coming through this one was slim, but my band was willing to follow me; yes, even to the deepest pits of hell!

I was examining the lay of the land through my telescope stick when I suddenly realized that we were completely surrounded by machine-gun emplacements whose fire was sweeping our flat hilltop from all directions at once. Through this withering fire, I dashed from one side of the hill to the other, shooting clip after blazing clip down on the enemy with my rapid-fire stick while shouting orders and en-couragements to my band. One by one, my followers got hit. Gail died with her head on my knee, looking up at me with a faint smile of admi-ration. I kept up a continual report of our plight to headquarters over my walkie-talkie stick, a task requiring considerable vocal acrobatics be-cause I was also doing all the dialogue for half a dozen heroes and mak-ing the sound effects of the incoming fire that ricocheted just inches from my head. Running crouched down so that my knees almost hit my chin (and once they did, making me bite my tongue...damn it!) I got to the other side of the hill just as Reggie got it. He died with a typically British stiff-upper-lip joke, the punch line of which he was unable to say before he passed away, so I said it for him. The last of my devoted followers to die was always Tonto. There were no theatrical last words between us two Indian blood brothers. No tears. No outward demonstrations of emotion. He just nodded a last farewell, and I nodded back, and he died. Snatching up my machine-gun stick, I rushed from one side of the hill to the other, mowing down columns of ascending Germans (or Japs) until I could see the allied reinforcements slipping into place around the boathouse. The day was saved! Democracy had vanquished Totalitarianism, showing that free men fighting for what they believe in were invincible, because they—

But just then a bullet got me in the stomach, and another in the shoulder, and one in the back, and a fourth in the hip. I spun, pitched, staggered, limped, crawled to the edge of the steep hill and fell, tumbling and bouncing all the way down, collecting painful knocks, twists, bruises and scuffs along the way.

I lay unmoving at the bottom of the hill, my legs and arms splayed at unlikely angles indicating broken bones and torn ligaments. After a long time, I stirred and opened my eyes, then I slowly rose, first to my knees, then, with desperate effort and after collapsing a couple of times, to my feet. Then I staggered and slogged my way back up the steep hillside several times each morning so that this spectacular fall could be repeated, like an action re-play, and only when I was satisfied that I had drained the last drop of heroic bathos out of it did I limp out of Washington Park, past the first early-morning pedestrians, and take the long walk home to clean up my scuffed knees, change my torn clothing, and set off on my Saturday collection round, which I accomplished with the fatalistic gravity of a boy who has been prematurely aged by seeing his closest friends die beside him.

Three Saturdays in a row, I saved Democracy at the top of the Washington Park hill. After the third heroic battle my hips were stiff with accumulated bruises, I had scrapes on my knees and cheek, and I had wrenched an ankle in the final great rolling, bouncing plunge of my bullet-riddled body down the almost vertical flank of that hill and lay at the bottom, the twisted remnants of an unknown hero. Only a handful of early walkers were in the park that last Saturday when I stopped beside the four-man gondola swing and looked back at the hill and the boathouse below it. As I stood there, I felt a tug of bittersweet sadness and my eyes misted as I realized that I would never, never play a story game again. Those inventive, precious, nonsensical moments of escape and adventure were behind me.[64]

As a symbol of my passage from fun-seeking boyhood to responsible manhood, I left the stick that had served as a telescope/machine gun/walkie-talkie/plasma holder against one stanchion of the big wooden swing, and I walked quickly away, down the path, through the gate, to a side street leading to home and responsibilities.

About three blocks from Clinton Avenue, I stopped, turned and ran back up the street, through the gates, across the grass to the swing where, thank God, I found that my all-purpose stick had not been nicked by some kid to play his dumb games with. I carried it back home with me...just in case.[65]

· · · · · · · · · ·

I do not claim that my epic defense of the flat-topped hill in Washington Park was a determining factor in the fall of the Third Reich, but could it really be mere coincidence that on May 7, only a couple of months after I limped away from the last of my early-morning battles, Germany surrendered and the war in Europe was over?

I hawked EXTRA-A-A's, from one corner of Pearl and State streets while other newsies worked the other three corners.

GERMANY SURRENDERS!
VICTORY IN EUROPE
Now let's get those Nips!

We hadn't heard from Ben for a couple of weeks, and Mother had a niggling premonition that something had happened to him. Maybe he had been sent to Germany just before the surrender, and maybe he had been wounded again...or worse. She remembered her father telling her about a young man from Plattsburg who was the last American to die in the Great War, killed by a stray bullet only ten minutes before the armistice came into effect. I assured her that the army wasn't likely to send a twice-wounded man into combat again, but she responded: "Maybe so, but don't forget what they say: Lightning always strikes three times."

"Well, yes...there's that."

On our block, anyone needing to make a telephone call had to use the pay phone on the back wall of Kane's cornerstore. If you wanted long distance (which no one ever did until the war scattered our boys across the nation) you got a fistful of change from Mr Kane, placed your call with the operator, then hung up and sat out on the Kanes' back steps for twenty minutes or half an hour until the operator rang back with your party on the line. Before you could speak, you had to feed coins into the box until the operator said that was enough for three minutes, then you would rush to get your business done as quickly as possible. To prevent kids from fiddling with the telephone (there was a persistent, if never realized, belief that by tapping it in just the right place you could cause a flow of coins to gush out from the coin return slot) it was placed fairly high up on the wall, with the effect that little old women had to stand on tiptoe to get their lips close to the stationary mouthpiece that protruded from the middle of the instrument. It was amusing to see them trying to speak loudly enough for their voices to carry up to the mouthpiece, yet quietly enough to keep what they said from being overheard by Mrs Kane, who always found urgent tasks to perform in the shop when there was a long-distance call, such tasks as counting the cans of tomatoes that were stocked not far from the phone. Occasionally, Mr Kane would receive incoming calls from sons or husbands who had departure leaves before going overseas but who didn't dare send the news by telegram because on Pearl Street telegrams almost always meant that someone had died. When such a call came in Mr Kane would leave the store in his wife's care and rush down the street to tell whoever it was that they'd better hurry up because they had a long-distance call that was costing their son an arm and a leg—perhaps not the best metaphor to use when speaking of a man who was about to go into combat.

We were sitting around our radio, listening to the evening news about the continuing war in the Pacific, when there was a knock on our door. It was Mr Kane. We had a long-distance call. Mother looked at me, her eyes afflicted with fear. "Ohmygod! I told you! I knew something was wrong! Ohmygod!"

Anne-Marie and I ran with her across to the cornerstore. She reached reluctantly for the dangling earphone as though it were a viper and put her lips as close to the mouthpiece as she dared. "Hello?" she said in a frangible voice. Anne-Marie turned away, not wanting to see Mother's expression when she heard what Anne-Marie felt sure would be something terrible, and she stood staring out through the front door of the shop, chewing on a strand of hair. "Yes?" Mother said. Then, after listening for a time she asked, "When?" Anne-Marie looked at me, her eyes brimming. The person on the other end of the line did most of the talking, with Mother saying only 'I understand' and 'Yes, I see'. So frustrated was Mrs Kane in her effort to construct the details of our tragedy from these scanty fragments that she gave up can-counting and leaned on the counter, frankly examining Mother's face for clues. Finally Mother said, 'When will that be?......No idea at all?......I see...... Yes, I see......All right......" There was sufficient ambiguity in this for Anne-Marie to lift her eyebrows at me with a tentative maybe-everything's-all-right-after-all expression. I pushed out my lower lip and shrugged. Then Mother said into the phone, "All right, well, you take care of yourself. Yes, I will. Good-bye. What's that?" She lowered her voice. "Yes...me too," and she hung up. When she turned to us she was smiling. "That was—" But she saw Mrs Kane's gossip-hungry face and she said, "I'll tell you when we get home."

She and Anne-Marie left the shop while I thanked Mr Kane for coming to fetch us.

"No bad news, I hope?" Mrs Kane asked, desperate to know.

I looked into her eyes and frowned, as though trying to find the words to explain everything...but then, too full of emotion to speak, I shook my head, turned and left.

When we got home Mother told us the news. Ben hadn't been the last man shot in Europe, after all. My eyes suddenly pricked with tears, and I realized that I'd been more worried than I had let myself admit. Ben had been shipped back to Fort Dix, New Jersey, and he had called to say that as soon as his records caught up with him, he would wangle some of his accumulated leave and come up to Albany so he and Mother could get married.

So things were working out after all. But I didn't dare count on it. And I found it disquieting to see my feisty, tough-minded mother acting like some bubbly bobby-soxer on her first date. I kept well out of the way the next few evenings while she and Anne-Marie sat together at the kitchen table, babbling about the wedding (...a simple ceremony...no church, of course, because she was a divorced woman...) and about what Mother should wear (...nothing too wedding-ish, just a nice spring suit she could get some use out of afterwards...matching hat and shoes and gloves...not a big hat, just a pillbox with a half veil...). Anne-Marie's experience as Dressmaker to the Stars was invaluable. And no honeymoon, Mother declared. Period, end of sentence! She didn't want to leave us children alone, not even for one night. And anyway, she felt that a honeymoon for a second marriage would be sort of...well, funny. After all, second weddings aren't like first ones. They're more...well, you know...arrangements, sort of. No, she wouldn't have a honeymoon. Just a little reception after the wedding—

"But not here!" Mother said abruptly. "I'm damned if I'm going to return from my wedding to North Pearl Street, Albany, New York. I am not going to be married in a slum and that's final! Period! End of story!"

"But...where?" I asked.

Mother thought for about three seconds, then she pronounced, "I'll be married from my cousin Lorna's house."

"In Granville?" I asked incredulously. "At Tonio's?"

"Lorna can be my matron of honor."

"And Tonio? You think Ben wants him as best man?"

"Tonio doesn't have to be best man. He can be...a witness. It's the least they can do, considering that they haven't lifted a hand to help us all these years."

"Yes, but..."

"I'll write to Lorna tonight."

"But, Mom..."

"I've made up my mind! A woman should be married in the bosom of her family. Maybe that's what went wrong with my first marriage.

Papa didn't like Ray, so we snuck off and got married in Connecticut where we didn't have to wait for blood tests. The whole ceremony took about ten minutes. No family, no friends to wish us well. And look how *that* turned out. No, I want to be married from my cousin's house, and that's that!"

"...period, end of sentence," I added under my breath. "End of paragraph, end of chapter, end of story, end of..."

The week sped by in breathless planning and anticipation. Gab sessions between Mother and Anne-Marie continued late into the night in their shared bedroom, where they talked from one bed to the other, making and refining plans for the wedding, and for what we would do after the war: the tourist cabins and the cafe with its red-checkered tablecloths, Anne-Marie's dance career, my becoming one of Wyoming's leading doctors. Lying on my bed out in the living room, I read to the background murmur of their voices rising and falling, muttering and fluttering, as they lay in Mother's bed side by side, sketching our golden future on the common darkness above them.

Mother wrote to her cousin Lorna and received a return letter full of underlinings and exclamation points. Lorna would *love* to have her and Ben married from their home! Ever since their visit to Albany Lorna had been *hoping* and *praying* that something might come up that would give them a chance to make up and become close again, like they used to be back when they were young girls sweeping all the dancing cups. Remember? We were a *great team*! Knocked their socks off!

Mother didn't seem to notice that her cousin made no mention of Uncle Tonio, so I didn't bring him up.

One manifestation of the hopeful climate of those weeks was the especially long song sessions that began when Anne-Marie and I were doing the supper dishes and sometimes extended for hours, the three of us sitting around the kitchen table, playing 'Name That Tune' and challenging one another on the hits of the last year of the war.[66]

Late one night in mid-July, a sleep-rumpled Mr Kane came knocking at our door. We had a telephone call. Mother rushed across the street wearing pajamas under her old terry-cloth robe. It was Ben calling from New Jersey. He had received two months' back pay and two weeks of leave before he had to report to San Francisco for new duties.

He wanted them to get married as soon as they had their obligatory blood tests. Not only that, but shortly later we would all be going across the United States to California! Two days after the Germans surrendered, Ben received orders transferring him to a communications training center in California. He had worked out all the details of our trip, which, as his legal family, the army would pay for. He would go first to find a place for us to live, then we would follow with such possessions as we were allowed to bring—not much, he was afraid, considering the spatial limitations on wartime trains. As Mother was sharing this news with Anne-Marie and me, I wondered how Ben had reacted to hearing that the marriage would take place at Lorna and Tonio's house in Granville, but I didn't ask because I had a feeling she hadn't told him yet.

Anne-Marie and I had trouble getting to sleep that night, she because of the excitement of California, *Movieland,* and I because despite my natural tendency to gloom-seek, it was beginning to look as though our ship had come in after all. Still, I didn't let myself believe this completely, lest spiteful Fate catch me hoping and decide at the last minute to scuttle it at the dockside.

Ben arrived the next morning, having hitchhiked to Albany through the night. After the first crush of hugs and kisses with everyone talking at the same time, he settled into his place at the table, and the kitchen seemed full of him because he had been gone so long that we had become used to just ourselves around the little table. While Mother and Anne-Marie were plying him with eager questions, I noticed that his hands trembled slightly and that he was thinner and... I guess 'friable' is the closest word. He had seen action in Africa and on the beach in Sicily; he had been wounded twice; he had known the fear of death. These things had aged him, robbed him of his sense of immortality.

Later that night, after Anne-Marie and I were in our beds, I overheard a taut exchange out in the kitchen when Mother revealed that they were going to be married in her cousin Lorna's house. Ben called it Tonio's house, and asked why he hadn't been consulted. I couldn't catch the words of Mother's response, but her voice was captious and exasperated, and shortly after, without a pause at the door for a kiss,

Ben left the apartment and went up to sleep in the top-floor room that used to be his, and that Mother had rented again for the time he would be with us. (She'd be damned if she'd give the block's busybodies something to gossip about!) The feeling at the breakfast table the next morning was that spiky politeness that makes children tighten their neck muscles and try to become smaller, but the tension slowly dissolved during the week-long flurry of planning and list-making during which Ben and Mother went downtown to get their blood tests, and to buy a new suit for him, because he was sick of the army and didn't want to be married in uniform. But when they came back, they brought their bristly tension with them. After a brief but sharp contest of wills Ben had chosen a blue double-breasted suit, an apple-green shirt, a striped tie and two-toned black and white shoes with perforated toe caps. On their way back from shopping, they had stopped off at a restaurant where my mother had done occasional stand-in work, perhaps because Mother wanted to show off her returning hero. While there, Ben did something that embarrassed her, dunked a doughnut or something like that, and Mother said something about people who were born in a barn. Their recent scrape over his taste in clothes still raw, he slapped some money down on the table and walked out of the restaurant, leaving her to explain his behavior to her former co-workers. Walking out on my mother was the very worst thing for him to have done. It was a gesture laden with ominous symbolism.

There were other hints that Mother's habit of controlling everything (for Ben's own good, of course) was meeting resistance. He was no longer the easy-riding, half-joshing cowboy who didn't mind being trained and shaped. And there was something else, something that came to the surface only rarely and briefly. We would be sitting around the kitchen table, all jabbering, and I would glance up to find that he had slipped into what I can best describe as a sudden silence of the soul. An instant later, he would be back, joking and planning and telling yarns. It was as though something had gone slack inside him, before tightening up again. These were passing moments, and I assumed that time would heal him. A more permanent change was that he had lost his taste for the absurd. Something brought us around to talking about the Olympic games, which had been discontinued for the duration of the war, and Mother had said that if long-distance canal skating were an Olympic sport, she would enter and win all the medals. My sense of the absurd prompted me to suggest that she and I enter as a team in the sheet-wringing-out competition, and that induced the image of domestic activities as Olympic sports. I suggested high-speed knitting with its concomitant danger of what champion knitters called skein-burn from the wool rushing so fast between the fingers that it smoked, and there would be a special category for the truly adept, one-handed knitting...with style points. Then I described the super-heavy-weight division of Free Style Knitting in which vaulting poles were used as knitting needles and docking hawser for wool. I glanced over at Ben, expecting him to step in and carry us yet further into the absurd, but there was annoyed confusion in his eyes, as though he were trying to figure out what the hell I was talking about, and that disturbed me even more than his sudden silences of the soul had. The war had changed Ben in subtle but profound ways that Mother didn't seem to notice.

I went to Anne-Marie's last dancing class. When it was over, Mother told Miss LaMonte about our plans to move to California, and asked if she knew any good dance teachers out there so Anne-Marie could continue to prepare for discovery. Pushing a handkerchief down between her breasts to soak up perspiration, the glistening Miss LaMonte said that she didn't know any personally, but she assumed that we might find one or two adequate teachers, although we couldn't expect them to have the professional New York legitimate stage training that had made her studio what it was today. As Anne-Marie was putting her leotards into her carrying bag for the last time, Miss LaMonte's mother turned in her bentwood chair before the old upright piano, peeled the ubiquitous cigarette off her lower lip and, after a short but impressive bout of moist coughing, told Mother between reedy gasps that Anne-Marie would do just fine in California because she had plenty of moxie, and if there was one thing you needed to be a success out in California it was moxie.

One evening while Mother and Anne-Marie were planning the last details of the wedding, Ben and I took a walk around our neighborhood. As we threaded through the narrower back streets, he told me about some of the funny and frustrating things that had happened to him in the army, but nothing about combat or his wounds. When I asked about these, he either changed the subject or slipped into silence, but when I asked what war was like, he described it as months of discomfort and boredom broken by a few minutes of panic and rage, and if your panic and rage made you do certain things, you were called a hero, but if it made you do other things you were called a coward, and that's how it was. He said that from what he had seen, war was just one massive screw-up. The victors didn't really win, they just lost more slowly than their enemy, or had enough stockpiled materiel to go on losing longer. We were comfortable enough with each other to be able to walk in silence for longish periods, each browsing on his own thoughts. I wanted to tell him that I could see how much the war had changed him, and that he should do what he really wanted to do, and not feel obliged to marry my mother because of us kids. I selfishly yearned to hear him say that taking care of my mother was what he wanted more than anything in this world. I wanted to escape both responsibility for my mother's future happiness, and any guilt about Ben's future unhappiness. While I was trying to find the words to express this, he broke the silence to ask how I was getting along with my slide rule, and I confessed that I'd been slack about keeping in practice, like he told me I had to, but I had taught myself to read French...pretty much. The next thing I knew we were approaching our stoop, and I hadn't offered Ben an easy way out of any guilt he might harbor about wanting to leave Mother and us kids. I didn't then admit, even to myself, that I was glad I hadn't given him a chance to liberate himself, for fear he might take it.

The next day Ben withdrew his savings from the bank, and the four of us went down to the echoing, brake-squealing, gas-smelling Central Terminal and boarded a bus for Granville. Mother had strongly advised him to leave most of the money in the bank, but he said that he had never had that much folding money in his pocket before, and what's the point of having money if you can't get a kick out of it? But that explanation wasn't sufficient to keep Mother from returning to the matter and gnawing on it, as was her habit. She always believed that her advice was ignored only by those who hadn't quite understood it.[67] During the long trip up to Granville we kids sat in the front seats just behind the driver because Mother thought that might assuage Anne-Marie's tendency to motion sickness.

It didn't, and this was before buses had on-board toilets, so the driver had to pull over three times to let her vomit by the side of the road while, to Anne-Marie's humiliation, the passengers looked on, their eyes flinching away then back again with that blend of revulsion and fascination people feel towards freshly squashed roadkill. Mother and Ben sat just behind us, and I heard her mention the excess cash Ben was carrying at least half a dozen times. His responses progressed from passing it off with lighthearted joshing, to a flat statement that he didn't want to talk about this any more, to prickly silence that I could feel through the dust-smelling velveteen seat after she said that flashing a big wad of money was nothing but acting like your typical hick.

I scrunched down in my seat and wished I had the power to render my mother mute for just a little while. I tried closing my eyes and focusing all my concentration on the task. It didn't work.

When the bus stopped on Granville's main street, we were met by a nervous, apologetic Aunt Lorna, who had come alone because she wanted a chance to tell Mother that Tonio had made some changes in the arrangements...just a few. Speaking quickly to explain everything before Mother could interrupt, Lorna began by saying she hoped Mother wouldn't get mad and blame *her*, because it wasn't her fault; she had so much wanted things to go just right, especially when her favorite cousin and best friend in this whole wide world would soon go away to California and God only knew when—or if—they'd ever meet again, and it would be a crying shame to let little things ruin what might be the last time they ever spent together, especially considering the bad blood there had been between them, not that she was blaming Mother for that, but...

"What *is* it, Lorna, for the love of Christ?"

Ben returned from getting our luggage from under the bus in time to hear Aunt Lorna explain in a whining, don't-blame-*me* tone that at the last minute Tonio had decided to invite his two brothers and their families for the weekend—to make a real family affair out of it, you see?—and he'd also invited a couple of business acquaintances who happened to be in town—but don't worry, Tonio didn't invite them to the wedding, just to the supper afterwards. Tonio hadn't seen his brothers in a coon's age, although they only lived down in Hudson Falls, and Lorna could hardly tell him he couldn't have any of his family visit when she was having her cousin and her children and—oh, and Ben of course. Hi, Ben, nice to see you! Remember me? I'm Lorna. So! Well, the sleeping arrangements might be a little crowded. Both of Tonio's brothers have kids.

"And the kids were invited to my wedding too?"

Lorna put a temper-soothing arm around Mother. "Oh, *please,* hon. Let's not have any trouble. Things will work out fine and dandy, if you'll just take it easy and not worry. I'll take care of everything. Anne-Marie, you're pale as a ghost. What's wrong, honey? Had a bad trip up? Puke in the bus, did you?"

Mother looked inquiringly at Ben, who puffed out a long sigh, then put his arm around her and pressed her to his side. "Don't worry, hon. I'm sure everything will be fine."

With huge relief, Lorna kissed her cousin's cheek noisily and thanked her for understanding how things were, then she herded us all towards their car—no longer new, so she was allowed to drive it. When Ben said something about the car's 'X' sticker which allowed them almost unlimited gasoline, Lorna shrugged and said that Tonio's friends could arrange things like that. Ben's jaw tightened, but he refrained from comment.

At Lorna's house we were greeted by a screaming herd of children ranging from two years old to ten. Tonio was sitting on the porch with his brothers, two younger, fatter duplicates of himself, even down to the dark Calabrian stains beneath the eyes from generations of vitamin-B deficiency. He waved a curt greeting but didn't get up. We went into the house, wading through a tide of noisy, clutching kids, and met Lorna's sisters-in-law: over-worked, distracted women whose youth and spirit had not survived the third child, but they'd gone on to have five each. We were escorted upstairs to drop off our suitcases, and I discovered that although the house had six bedrooms the only way they could put us all up was to give a bedroom to each of the couples with the biggest for the newlyweds (wink, blush), which left one bedroom for all the boys and another for all the girls. Including Anne-Marie and me, there were seven girls and five boys, and when I asked how five of us could sleep in one double bed, Lorna said we would sleep crosswise. It'll be fun!

Anne-Marie and I exchanged glances. We doubted that.

The wedding was to be that evening, a simple ceremony before a Justice of the Peace with only Lorna there as matron of honor and Tonio as witness. There would be a wedding supper for all the family and the two guys from Troy that Tonio had invited. Aunt Lorna beckoned Mother into her bedroom to have a 'nice juicy gossip', and Anne-Marie and I drifted back downstairs where we found Ben, doing his best to play the social game. He declined a glass of wine and accepted lemonade instead, smiling half-heartedly at the single-entendre suggestion from one of Tonio's brothers that Ben was trying to keep his head clear so he didn't miss anything tonight. Right? Right? Am I right or not? Eh? Somebody tell me if I'm right or wrong here! Tonio's nieces and nephews ran shrieking through the house, crashing into me, trampling my toes and clutching me with sticky fingers, using me as a pivot point and a shield. Like most children brought up to show a well-behaved front to outsiders, Anne-Marie and I had nothing but contempt for kids who were rambunctious in public, and for their feckless parents.

I managed to hide from the mob up in the attic with a book until evening came and we all had to gather on the porch to wish the wedding party well as they drove off to the Justice of the Peace, but not before one of Tonio's brothers complimented Ben on his new blue suit, his blue and pink striped tie and his two-toned shoes, then he turned away and lightly tapped the side of his nose. I cannot recall how Mother looked, but I am sure that even after all these years Anne-Marie would be able to describe to the last detail her wedding suit, gloves and hat with a veil.

When the wedding party returned, dinner was served to the ravenous pack of kids in the steamy kitchen full of wonderfully complex smells. The women put up great writhing plates of spaghetti and meatballs with generous dollops of thick red sauce dusted with feathery ground cheese. The meatballs were made from a family recipe: beef and sausage ground together with bread crumbs that had been toasted with herbs, and each meatball had a bit of olive and a sliver of garlic buried in its center and was seared in smoking hot olive oil to seal it, then cooked in the sauce long enough for the bread crumbs to absorb its moisture and flavor. Ben was sitting with the men around the dining room table, six of them because Tonio's two 'business acquaintances' from Troy had arrived for the wedding feast. Following the traditions of Tonio's family, the men ate alone and were served first. Mother, as the bride and therefore, by rights, the star of the evening, resented having to eat out in the kitchen with the kids and women, and she was annoyed by the way Lorna kept jumping up to put her head into the dining room and ask the men if they wanted anything, then running to their service with bottles of wine, platters of sauce-drenched meatballs, and steaming bowls of spaghetti which she had fished from the cauldron that filled the kitchen with steam because it was kept on a rolling boil so that second and third helpings of pasta could be freshly cooked al dente. "Let them serve themselves, for Christ's sake," my mother said. "Their legs aren't broken."

Anne-Marie and I sat side by side so at least one ear wouldn't be permanently damaged by the kids, whose voices soared to a volume calculated to crack toilet bowls. Much of this cacophony was cheerful animal high spirits, but the joyful noise was punctuated by yelps from kids who had been pinched or kicked under the table; and by that nerve-flaying whine 'Ma-ma-a-a!' 'Ma-ma-a-a!' of spoiled kids who repeat their complaining mewls until the mother finally breaks off her gossiping, wheels on the offender and screams, 'What do you want! What? What? *What?*', which rebuff makes the brat yowl even harder. Beneath the manic din were undertones of soft whimpering from little kids who had spilled their milk or wet their pants, and those taunting sing-song chants of teasing that make the victim finally roar in venomous rage, all this mixed with the voices of the women at their table in the corner, talking louder and louder to be heard over the kids, and over one another, and every once in a while one of the women, driven to exasperation by a child tugging on her skirt and whining for attention while the mother tried to talk through and over the interruption, would suddenly snatch the offending kid by the collar or the hair and thrust her face into his and scream, 'Are you going to give me a minute's peace? Or do you want me to slap that face right off you?!' As the whimpering child pondered these options, guffaws and snorts came from the dining room where the men were exchanging blue stories. A kid experimented to see how far forward he could tip his baby sister's chair. The girl fell out, split her lip and set up a bellow out of all proportion to her pain, but sufficient to get her brother cuffed around the ears by his mother. "That's it! I've had it up to *here!* You want me to smash your head between two bricks?!" As she jumped up from the table to show her sisters-in-law that she was a firm disciplinarian and in no way responsible for the way her kids were behaving, this rattled mother upset a bowl of spaghetti sauce into Aunt Lorna's lap, so the boy got slapped for that, too.

In short, an extended family having fun.

Anne-Marie and I finished eating and tried to excuse ourselves so we could slip away, but Mother whispered harshly that it would be impolite to leave, and it wouldn't hurt us one little bit to stay and make friends with our cousins...cousins that we might never see again, as we would soon be out west. I guess it was this promise that gave us the strength to sit at the table for what seemed like a geological age, our faces frozen in sickly grins that were as close as we could come to smiles.

But even the most enriching experiences must come to an end, so finally, butt-sore, cramped, stuffed and deafened, my sister and I were allowed to go up to bed with the rest of the kids, while the women collected the dishes and began to clean up the devastated kitchen.

"—but not *you,* Cuz!" Aunt Lorna said. "You're the bride! You just sit there and talk to us! You and me, we haven't had a good gab session in *years!*"

As I passed the dining room door I saw that the tablecloth had been removed and cards were being dealt out. There were glasses and wine bottles on the table, but no lemonade pitcher. I glanced at Ben anxiously. His new blue double-breasted suit jacket was hanging open, the top button of his apple-green shirt was undone, and he had tugged down his pink-and-blue tie. His face glistened with sweat, but he was smiling and seemed to be having fun, so everything would be all right. Maybe.

Some time in the middle of that night, I gave up trying to sleep and slowly picked my way out of the sweaty tangle of cousin-limbs. Sleeping crosswise hadn't worked. The bed's slack springs had made us all slide towards the middle, so it had been impossible to keep space between me and the next boy. For the first hour, there had been giggling and punching and pinching and threats to tell mothers and counter-threats about what would happen to you if you did. The oldest of my cousins demonstrated both his primitive idea of humor and his profound stupidity when he clutched the cousin next to him, farted, then pulled the blanket over their heads, sharing with his victim the effects of his droll prank. I took comfort in the knowledge that 'Aunt' Lorna and 'Uncle' Tonio had not been able to have children of their own, so these kids and I shared no common genes. They were 'cousins' by courtesy only.

I found Anne-Marie out in the dark hallway. She had disentangled herself from a crush of squirming girls, one of whom had wet the common bed. We sat together on the top step of the staircase and looked glumly down towards the light and noise of the wedding party, with its snorts and hoots, its harsh laughter and detached drunken words, until she fell asleep on my shoulder and I had to put my arms around her because she was shivering in her thin nightgown. I dozed off in that awkward position, my cheek against the wall.

In the small hours of the morning, my mother found us at the top of the stairs, shivering and clammy. My arm had fallen asleep under the weight of Anne-Marie, and it tingled painfully as circulation returned to it. Mother took us into her bedroom, into her wedding bed, where we all snuggled together to get warm. She and Ben had had a shouting row, and her eyes were red with crying. Characteristically, Anne-Marie reacted to the tension and anger radiating from Mother by withdrawing into a deep sleep, but Mother remained rigid with rage. Whispering into the darkness, I asked what had happened, and she told me that after drinking wine—"and he *knows* he can't hold his drink"—Ben had played poker with the other men. The game had broken up with a fight. Ben had hit one of Tonio's 'business acquaintances' from Troy, and when Mother and Lorna rushed in to break things up, the other friend had his back to the wall, a flick blade in his hand, while Ben faced him, his belt wrapped around his fist and about a foot of belt and buckle dangling like a flail. If Mother and Lorna hadn't been there, things would have gotten nasty, because Tonio and his brothers seemed content with the role of interested bystanders. Uncle Tonio helped the fallen Trojan to his feet and persuaded both of his pals to go to a downtown bar with him and his brothers. Just to let things cool down a little, whaddyasay? Who needs trouble? They left grumbling about 'bad losers' and making threats against 'four-flushing hicks'.

When they were alone, Ben confessed to Mother that he had lost more than half the money they had saved up for their cabins in Wyoming.

"Did you say those guys were from Troy?" I asked Mother.

"That's what Ben said."

"Jesus!" I whispered

"What is it?"

I remembered Uncle Tonio telling me about his 'friends' from Troy. He had bragged that he knew a couple of card sharks who could clean suckers out 'slicker 'n shit'. They let the sucker win for a while, then: "...whadda you know?...his luck turns sour and he ends up stripped to the bone. And if the sucker complains...? Well, you don't complain about *these* guys. They got friends, and their friends got ways. Know what I mean?" He had winked.

I told Mother about this, hoping she would see that it wasn't all Ben's fault. These men from Troy were professionals cheats. But although she had lived with my father for a total of only a few months, he had managed to infect her with the con man's scorn for the mark: the stupid pigeon that deserves to be plucked. Losing money to a couple of card sharks made Ben contemptible in her eyes, and it's hard to imagine a worse basis for a lasting union than contempt. Resentment is less destructive; even hatred. Realizing that nothing I could say would change her view of Ben as a sucker who deserves whatever he gets, I limited myself to asking where he was now.

"Who cares? Wandering around out there in the dark, probably. Feeling sorry for himself. I told him off good and proper for getting drunk and losing all that money! It was mine as much as his! Those cabins were my last chance to make something of myself...to *be* somebody!"

"And what did Ben say?"

"What *could* he say? He gave me some crap about marrying into a family of cheats and thieves, and he stormed out. Just like that! Left me cold!" She began to cry again. No sobbing, just tears flowing down her cheeks into the corners of her mouth. "When I think of the things we went without to save up that money! The gallons of potato soup you kids had to..." Her words squeaked and stuck in the back of her throat, and it was a while before she could add, "...and on my wedding night, too!"

When we went down to the kitchen the next morning the house was empty except for Aunt Lorna, who was busily...too busily...making our breakfast. The atmosphere was taut. She told us that Tonio's brothers and their families had gone back to Hudson Falls first thing that morning.

"And those card sharks Tonio brought in to clean Ben out?" Mother asked.

"Well...I think they took the morning train back to Troy. But, hon, please don't—"

Ben came to the back porch to speak to Mother, but he wouldn't come in because, he said, if he did he might lose control and start busting up things...and maybe some people too. He must have had a bad night, because his new suit was muddy in patches and his trousers had a triangular rip at the knee, where his skin showed through, oddly pale and baby smooth. He told Mother through the screen door that he had spent the night wandering around, and he would be waiting for us at the bus station when she was ready to leave.

I wandered into the dining room, which still smelled of wine and stale cigarette smoke. When I came back into the kitchen, Aunt Lorna was bustling around, serving pancakes to Anne-Marie and babbling away nervously about how there was nothing in the world like a good breakfast to drive the blues away and make the world seem brighter. But Mother would accept only a cup of coffee.

"Well, sit down to drink it at least," Aunt Lorna said. "Your bus doesn't leave for ages."

Mother didn't sit. She stood at the back door, sipping her coffee and staring out across the muddy creek that ate a little further into their backyard every year. "So where's that son of a bitch you married?" she asked.

"Oh, hon!" Lorna said plaintively. "Calling people names won't help anything."

"Don't 'oh, hon' me! Where is he? Off getting his cut of blood money from his card-shark friends?"

Lorna explained that Tonio had been out all night long with them, making sure they didn't come back looking for revenge. He'd done this to protect Ben because he had hit one of them, and that made men like that want to hurt people...bad.

"Oh, so Tonio's a big hero, is that it?" Mother asked. "Trying to help us out, is he?"

"Hon...please! Don't blame *me*. I never thought anything like this would happen."

"What are you going to do about it?"

"What do you mean?"

"You know perfectly well those men cheated Ben!"

Aunt Lorna winced and turned away. I was embarrassed by the way Mother kept bullying Lorna, who was only guilty of marrying Tonio and accepting his domination.

"That was money I'd shrimped and saved for, Lorna! My children went without to build that money up! It was our future...our hopes and dreams! So what are you going to do about it?"

"Good God, hon, what *can* I do?"

"You want to know what you can do? You can make your slimy thief of a husband pay us our money back, that's what you can do!"

"I can't do that. Ben *lost* that money! He gambled and he lost. You can't blame *me*. I didn't know those men were planning anything like...Oh, hon, please!" Aunt Lorna buried her face in her palms and sobbed.

"Come on, kids," Mother said. "We're getting out of here!"

Anne-Marie and I swallowed last forkfuls of pancake and picked up our suitcases.

Mother turned at the door. "And you listen to me, Lorna. I don't ever want to see you again unless you can tell me you've left that son of a bitch for good and all. You've buttered your bread, now you can lie on it! And don't bother to write, because I won't answer. From now on, I have no cousin, no friend, no nothing! I'm alone in the world!" She snatched up her suitcase.

"Oh...*hon!*"

And we left. I was the last one out. The screen door slipped from my grasp and slammed shut. I rushed to catch up with Mother and Anne-Marie, hoping Aunt Lorna didn't think I'd slammed the door on purpose. Though they both lived to be old women, my mother never saw or heard from her cousin again.

There wasn't a word spoken during our long, three-stage bus ride back to Albany. Ben's new suit was ruined. Humiliated and hung over, he avoided looking at us. He stared out his window, his eyes raw and whipped. Mother sat beside him, seething in silence; Anne-Marie and I sat in the seat across the aisle, neither of us daring to talk.

Twice Anne-Marie got sick and the bus had to stop along the road; finally she fell asleep against my shoulder.

Night fell, and I carefully eased out of my seat, lowered Anne-Marie's head so she could sleep across both seats, and went to the front of the bus, where I occupied a recently vacated seat directly behind the driver. I stared out the front window as our headlights cleaved an eternal archway of overhanging branches that vanished into the darkness at the edges of the cone of light we chased down the road. In time, the hypnotic drone of the engine and the rigidity of my stare made it feel as though *we* were standing still and the trees were rushing at *us*, then parting and pouring past us right and left. It was all my fault. I had sensed from the beginning that things wouldn't work out between Ben and Mother. They were both good people, but Mother wasn't the easygoing, forgiving, optimistic woman Ben needed; and Ben wasn't what she wanted him to be: a responsible, reliable version of my slick-talking, sharp-dressing father, to whom she still had an aggrieved but undying attachment. I had sensed all this, but nevertheless I had done nothing to save them from each other. I could have, easily. All I would have had to do was tell my mother that I didn't want Ben for a step-father, and that would have been the end of it. Her loyalty to her children sprang from a deeper place than her feelings for Ben, or for any man. But in the end, I had saved myself instead. I wasn't exactly responsible for Mother and Ben's marriage, but I could have stopped it.

I was responsible, however, for Ben's losing money to those card-shark friends of Tonio. Tonio had told me how these vermin worked, and I'd had a premonition of calamity when I walked past the dining room door and saw the cards and the wine on the table, but I hadn't warned him. So whatever happened now would be my fault. I knew that the guilt would be with me forever. At the moment of accepting that guilt I experienced one of those metaphor-moments that emerge again and again in my nightmares: it is night, and I am being chased through a tunnel of harshly lit tree limbs that rush towards my face, then split and rush right and left, into oblivion at the edge of the head-lights, and this chase, this flight, goes on forever, forever.

It was after midnight when we arrived at our stoop on Pearl Street, Anne-Marie sleep-walking between me and Ben. Without a word, Ben and Mother took bedding from Anne-Marie's bed and put it on the floor beside my daybed. Anne-Marie wriggled in, having emerged only minimally from unconsciousness and eager to escape back into sleep. In no time her breathing was shallow and regular. I could hear the rustling sounds of Mother and Ben undressing in the back bed-room, then the creak of the springs as they got into bed. Ben's voice muttered good-night and something else I couldn't catch. Mother was silent. I sat on the edge of my bed, looking out on the street and feeling miserable. When I closed my eyes I could see those pallid branches rush past me as I hurtled into the darkness. I opened my eyes to dispel the vertigo.

After a long silence, I heard Mother's voice. Ben replied. Then Mother said something curt and sharp. I couldn't make out their words, but there was anger and pain in the sound. It wasn't long before they raised their voices and I overheard swatches of their hurtful quarrel.

"...All right!" Ben said. "I got drunk! I'm sorry. I keep saying I'm sorry! What more can I do?"

"You got stinking drunk on your wedding night and left your wife to sleep with her kids!"

A silence, and I hoped they would stop fighting and let sleep and time start to heal things.

But Mother couldn't let it go. "I can't believe it," she persisted. "How could you throw away the money we worked so hard to save?"

"I think they put something in the drinks."

"Oh, my eye! You just can't hold your liquor. And I told you not to bring all that money with you. But no! You had to show off. The big spender from the sticks in his two-tone shoes! You should've known better than to gamble with strangers."

"But it was your family!"

"Oh, so now it's all *my* fault!"

"I didn't say that; I just— Look, I don't want to talk about it."

"Well, I *do* want to talk about it!"

"Not tonight."

"Yes, tonight!"

"I'm trying to forget that it was your cousin and her husband that stole my money."

"A sucker is a sucker. If Tonio hadn't cleaned you out, the next sharper down the pike would have!"

"Honey, listen to me. I don't want to talk about this any more. You hear what I'm saying to you?"

"Is that a threat? Because if you think you can threaten me, you can think again."

Ben didn't answer. The silence that followed was so long that I had almost fallen asleep when I heard my mother mutter something about Ben being a rube and an easy mark who lacked the street savvy and the polish of her first husband.

"Savvy? Polish? You're talking about a guy who dumped you and the kids into this stink hole and ran off. That's savvy and polish?"

"Well, at least he wasn't dumb enough to let himself be taken by a couple of small-time card sharks!" Ben said nothing, and I tried by force of concentration to will my mother to let it drop and not make things worse. But after a short simmering silence she continued, like a kid who can't stop picking at a scab, "...and he knew how to talk to people...how to wear clothes...how to impress—"

"Honey...we'd better not talk about this any more."

"I'll talk about what I damn well like!"

"You may end up talking to yourself."

"You're saying you're going to walk out on me? Is that it?"

Silence from Ben.

"I haven't forgotten how you walked out on me in that restaurant, and don't you think I have. You're no better than the last one!"

I silently begged Mother to stop talking. Just stop talking! And for God's sake, don't say 'the last one'!

"Well," she continued, "nobody's keeping you here against your will. You can pack your bag and take off any time you want to, and good luck to you."

"I don't intend to...Listen, honey. We're just too het up to talk about this tonight. Maybe tomorrow—"

"If there *is* a tomorrow!"

A long silence, then Ben said, "Good-night, honey."

"Don't 'honey' me!"

Shut up, Mom. Shut up!

I couldn't believe that my mother could possibly prefer Ray to Ben. Ben was an honest, hardworking, compassionate man. How could my mother prefer the irresponsible hustler who had dumped us onto Pearl Street? I couldn't believe it. I fell asleep that night with the conviction that love was not only blind but stupid as well. And all night long I hurtled down the tunnel of harshly lit branches.

The next morning Ben had to catch the train for his new posting in California. He and Mother went down to Union Station while Anne-Marie and I stayed home. After sitting at the kitchen table for a long time, picking at the oilcloth with her fingernail, Anne-Marie asked me what I thought about Mother and Ben's fight last night. While I thought she was sleeping, she had been listening from her bed on the floor beside my daybed, breathing deeply and evenly in an effort to calm her fears. Did I still think things would work out? Were we going to be happy in California? Or would Mother and Ben get a divorce, and we'd end up staying on North Pearl Street for the rest of our lives? I admitted that I didn't know, but if anything bad happened, it wouldn't be Ben's fault. And not our mother's either, really. It was Ray's fault. He had hurt Mother...embittered her.

"Yes, but you think things will work out all right, don't you?" Anne-Marie asked again, unwilling to accept a disappointing answer.

I took a long breath and said, "Sure. They just need to get used to each other. Things will work out. You'll see." In my heart I was sure they were doomed.

But when Mother returned from seeing Ben off, she was her old self, smiling and cheerful. Miraculously, they had kissed and made up. Everything was fine! They had spent the last half hour before his train pulled out sitting in the railroad cafeteria, making plans for the tourist cabins in Wyoming. They had decided that if they started off with just three cabins, they could still manage on what was left of the money.

My knees almost buckled with relief. Adults!

I was less relieved, however, when I asked Mother if she had apologized to Ben for being so hard on him, and she told me, "No, he did the apologizing."

"All of it?"

"Sure. After all, it wasn't me that lost the money."

I wondered how long that could last: two people doing the misbehaving, but only one doing the apologizing.

Mother reached into her handbag and produced the tickets she had picked up at the train station for our trip to California in just two weeks. There were three booklets of them, one for each of us. I asked if I could keep mine, and she let me. But now there were a thousand things to do: deciding what to bring and what to leave, gathering cardboard boxes, packing, cleaning the apartment, giving notice to the rent collector. Mother couldn't wait to shake the dust of North Pearl Street off her shoes.

To avoid getting rushed and flustered if we left things too late, we started packing that very day, only to discover by evening that we had packed away some things that we needed for daily life. But we couldn't remember which box they were in and we had to undo half our packing in the search, so Mother said we'd better quit and start again in the morning, after a good night's sleep. And this time we would list the contents of each box on the outside! It rained that night, and I sat looking out at wet cobblestones varnished by light from the streetlamp across the way. I took my booklet of tickets out of their envelope and examined them reverently. Strips of paper that stood for distant places. Albany–Buffalo, Buffalo–Chicago, Chicago–Salt Lake City, Salt Lake City–San Francisco...you could almost hear the sing-song cry of the conductor calling out destinations on the radio drama series *Grand Central Station*.

I let the leaves of my ticket flutter through my fingers like the pages of my riffle books. I could hardly believe it. I was leaving North Pearl Street, at last!

• • • • • • • • •

As dependents of an enlisted man, we were allowed to take only one suitcase each in our passenger car and three medium-sized cardboard boxes in the baggage car, a fraction of the space that officers' dependents were given. This meant that we had to discard or give away almost all of our possessions. We packed and repacked, trying to fit as much in as possible. Birth and marriage certificates had first priority, followed by Mother's three photograph albums...her memories, most of them captured by the old accordion-bellows Kodak that had passed from her father to her, recording both her childhood and ours. There wasn't even space for our precious 'five-tail' Hudson Bay blankets. Using a big chunk of the travel money Ben sent us, we packed the Hudson Bays in mothballs and shipped them separately by Railroad Express, but either they got nicked along the line or they simply fell victim to the chaotic state of the railroads at the end of the war, because we never saw them again.

Mother let Anne-Marie and me each pick one unnecessary thing to bring to California. We made our choices, changed our minds, then changed them back again, suffering not only the torment of leaving desirable things behind but, in Anne-Marie's case, the shame of abandoning dolls and stuffed animals that she had loved and to which she ascribed reciprocal feelings. And yet, at the last minute, she snatched her 'magic skin' doll out of her suitcase and replaced it with the collection of the paper-doll fashions that she had made from brown paper bags: her life's work in the service of fashion...her portfolio, you might say. And in the end I forsook my copy of *High School Subjects Self-Taught* and brought instead my slowly amassed collection of riffle books.

Mother tried to find a safe way to pack Ben's most treasured possession, his fragile melon mandolin. She looked into having it specially boxed and shipped by Railroad Express, but the cost was prohibitive. Her dilemma was solved one evening when we were trying to organize our choices by dragging the 'bring' boxes to one end of the room and the 'leave' boxes to the other, with an 'I'm not sure' box in the middle. She stepped back to consider which box something should go into, and she tripped over the mandolin, crushing it beyond repair. I refuse to ponder the symbolism of that Freudian trip over Ben's mandolin.

When it became clear that we would have to leave our Emerson behind, I felt particularly traitorous. Not only had that radio brought us much of our laughter and most of our entertainment, music, information and news, but it had exercised my imagination, broadened my experience, populated my fantasies. The entire Second World War had been fought inside that radio, among those glowing tubes. Mother decided to give the radio and everything else we couldn't bring with us to Mrs Meehan, who had lost so much in her life that she could no longer let go of things. I was consoled to think that our Emerson would continue bringing its laughter and magic to North Pearl, even if only to the half-wit Meehans.

I kept both paper routes right up to the end because we needed the money, so each morning at four-thirty I was dragged out of those precious last moments of deep, viscous sleep by the slack clatter of our alarm clock. I dressed numbly and staggered into the kitchen to eat oatmeal before stomping up the Lexington Avenue hill to pick up my papers. Upon returning to Pearl Street I helped with the packing and cleaning. There seemed to be an endless list of last-minute errands to do, each of which had to be accomplished before anything else could be decided on, and we were harried by anxiety because the number of days left before departure was dwindling relentlessly. To make things worse, the city was sweltering beneath a terrible heat wave that sapped our strength, shortened our tempers and made working inside our apartment a torment. My skin crawled with prickly heat despite the cold soaks we took in our cast-iron bathtub.

The night after my last collection, I sat at my bedside table, staring into space, too keyed up to sleep, too worn out to work. I was trying to draw up a list of things that remained to be done, when I became aware of an agreeable humming in my ears, and everything felt soft and strange. I was no longer tired; on the contrary, I felt buoyant. But I knew that I had to get some sleep, so I stood up to go to bed...and I slumped to my knees, overwhelmed by an amusing vertigo that made me laugh a weak whimpering laugh. Although the night was hot and airless after a scorcher of a day, I was shivering. But my face was slippery with sweat. What's going on here? The walls of the room bulged and wobbled. I tried to understand why my teeth were chattering although sweat ran down my cheeks into the corners of my mouth. Salty.

I knelt on the floor beside my daybed, shivering, but the iron leg felt deliciously cool against my cheek, and all I wanted to do was to sleep, so I decided that I would just kneel there for a moment and...just rest for a moment...then I'd get back to that list and...

The following morning my mother found me coiled up on the floor beside my bed, asleep, my pajamas damp with sweat. I was very ill.

For the next three days and nights I alternately froze and simmered, clutching my hastily unpacked Hudson Bay to my chin, or feebly trying to kick the stifling thing away. In a reversal of our traditional roles, I was the one who wheezed and coughed until I thought my ribs would crack with the effort of trying to raise thick, stringy phlegm, while my mother made mustard plasters for my chest and rubbed my back with Balm Bengué. A harassed intern came in response to my mother's telephone call from Kane's cornerstore. He said I had something called 'a tropical ague' that, according to him, I had caught because I was run down. He warned Mother to keep me warm and give me plenty of liquids to fight the fever, lest the pleurisy that made breathing painful develop into full-blown pneumonia. One day blurred into the next as I lay there, slipping in and out of fever. My mother kept the radio on at low volume so I wouldn't feel abandoned while she and Anne-Marie worked in the next room, packing and re-packing as quietly as they could. Fragments of comedy shows, news broadcasts, dramas, popular music and soap operas slithered in and out of my consciousness, sometimes in bewildering tangles, but sometimes fitting together suddenly in a way that let me glimpse a great truth. *The* great truth. And it was so obvious! Why hadn't I always known it? But this great and lucid truth was so fragile that when I tried to recall what it was, it disintegrated and fled my mind. Again and again, or maybe only once with a long echo, I reminded myself that our train would be pulling out in just a few days, by which time I had to be well and strong, because our tickets couldn't be postponed or exchanged for a later date. If we were ever going to get out of Pearl Street, it had to be now. Now or never...or never...never...

In the early hours of the fourth night, I opened my eyes and saw streetlight patterns on the ceiling. They were amazingly sharp and meaningful. I drew a long tentative breath, ready to stop with the first pain. But my lungs didn't hurt, and they were dry. I squeezed my hands into fists, and for the first time in days they didn't feel weak. My hair still hurt at the roots and my eyes were stiff and made squeaking sounds when I looked to the sides, but the fever had broken and, although everything seemed overly intense and strangely 'elsewhere', I knew I had passed through the crisis. I smiled into the darkness and felt both happy and lucky. I considered going into the back bedroom to tell my mother that I was well, but she and Anne-Marie had worked through that day's sapping heat and were deep in the greedy sleep of the truly weary, so I smiled again, closed my eyes and let myself slip into a safe, cozy slumber.

OUR SHIP COMES IN

I WATCHED Albany slip backwards out of our lives as our train pulled away from Union Station on August 3, 1945. We were the only civilians in a car so overcrowded that some of the passengers, mostly soldiers reporting back to duty after leaves, had to squat in the aisles. Two young soldiers got up to give Mother and Anne-Marie their seats. Another offered his place to me, but although I was still wobbly from my illness, I was as tall as he, so I felt obliged to say no, thanks, and I perched on Mother's armrest all the way to Buffalo where, during the bustle of passengers getting off and on, I slipped into the vacated window seat facing my sister.

Earlier that morning Mother and Anne-Marie had stood out on the curb among our boxes and suitcases, awaiting a taxi to take us to the station, while I went back into our apartment for a last look around to make sure we had left nothing behind that we didn't mean to leave behind. In the deep silence of the no-longer-alive apartment I was aware of a soft drip, drip, drip from the cold-water tap. I went into the kitchen and tried to turn it off, but I couldn't, and I wondered if it had been dripping, unremarked, ever since we arrived that March afternoon eight and a half years earlier. While I had remained in bed until the last minute to conserve my energy for the trip, Mother and Anne-Marie had worked since dawn, determined to leave the apartment spotless...another proof that we weren't of the Pearl Street culture. They had left the door of the icebox open so that loathsome icebox smell wouldn't accumulate. Upon leaving, my mother had passed a wax mop over the linoleum floors. The wax hadn't dried completely in the front room, so my rubber soles made slight ripping sounds as I stepped over to my daybed and looked out the window for the last time. The two over-sized wicker chairs stood where they had always stood, in the way and all but useless. A new family would be moving in within the week, and the broken canes would snatch at their clothing as they had snatched at ours for eight years. How many families would sit in those slumping, squeaking chairs before they finally found their way to a dump somewhere? I was touching one of them in farewell when the taxi drew up outside. Snatching my hand away in my haste to start on our adventure, I got a sliver of rattan under my fingernail. Those god-damned chairs got a final shot at me.

As the cab pulled away, I saw Mr Kane standing in the doorway of his cornerstore. He lifted a palm to me in farewell and blessing. I lifted my hand to him.

I owed him more than that. I promised myself I would stay in contact with him. We would exchange letters, so he'd have someone to share his quirky brand of 'enterprise socialism' with, and I'd have the advice of a wise old man.

I never wrote to him.

Because Ben wasn't an officer we had to travel in enlisted men's transportation, which meant that we crossed the United States in worn-out chair cars with no berths to stretch out in at night. What had been a three-day trip in peacetime took us six and a half days because of wartime congestion and because over the preceding twenty years the rolling stock and track had been allowed to run down by the asset-stripping descendants of nineteenth-century robber barons. Our train included four sleeping cars and a dining car, but these were reserved for officers and their dependents who were protected from degrading contact with the lower orders by MPs stationed at the door of the first sleeping car. From the conductor, we learned that these modern, comfortable cars were less than half full, while our car and all those behind us were so crowded that men slept in the vestibules, where they sat on the floor beside rattling toilet doors, bracing themselves against their duffel bags to catch a little sleep as the car jolted and swayed through the night: a further example of unjust privilege to kindle a budding young socialist.[68]

The crowded conditions produced that wartime atmosphere of make-do cheerfulness. As the train followed the tow path of the Barge Canal towards Buffalo, soldiers sang and laughed and exchanged jokes and swigs from pocket flasks, while those lucky enough to have seats played cards on blankets stretched over their knees, or caught snatches of sweaty, uneasy sleep. There was always a line of urgent men at the door of the only toilet that was functioning, and it was sometimes necessary to use the vestibule window they had wrenched open for the purpose.

At Chicago we made a chaotic cross-city change from the New York Central to the Union Pacific, an embarrassing business because our luggage was a mix of cheap cardboard suitcases, string-tied boxes, and soft things knotted up in old sheets, real Route 66 stuff. A predatory taxi driver counted each of our boxes and bundles as a piece of luggage, putting an unexpected dent in the fifty dollars in small bills that my mother carried for the trip. But she made the driver stop at a little grocery store where she bought four loaves of bread, a large jar of peanut butter, a couple of pounds of assorted cold cuts, and two bottles of milk. This turned out to be a wise precaution because there was no dining car in our next train; the railroad company didn't make enough profit from soldiers' meal tickets. From Chicago on, a small group of homesick soldiers clustered around us, forming an ad hoc family of which Anne-Marie was the hub and the star. She sang hit songs for the soldiers to the accompaniment of a guitar and a mouth organ. A monkey-faced corporal who used to be a drummer in a swing band provided the beat using two pencils as drumsticks. His drum set consisted of the arm of his seat, the bottom of an empty Whitman's

Sampler box and the train window, and he produced cymbal rubs by miming the action while making a *tchshshsh* sound through his teeth. Anne-Marie even managed a few simple tap routines in the narrow, lurching aisle.

I had always been disinclined to celebrate openly, lest malevolent Fate decide to teach me a lesson, but I let myself savor a thrill of optimism about our future. Maybe I thought we were too hard a target for Fate to draw a bead on, racing as we were across the continent on glistening steel rails. I was wrong.

The soldiers didn't buy the expensive sandwiches that were hawked down the aisles twice each day because most of them had blown their money on leave, and even those who hadn't were reluctant to eat in front of hungry buddies. They would look out the windows with feigned interest in the passing scene while we ate our sandwiches, but the smell of peanut butter and cold cuts made them swallow their saliva. When I noticed this, I could no longer eat; so after carefully counting up what remained of our fifty dollars and deciding that we could make it to California (just), Mother insisted that each of the soldiers of our little 'family' accept a sandwich every time we ate. They demurred, saying they weren't hungry, but Mother said 'don't try to give that crap to a Mother!' and they capitulated. Our little larder soon ran out, so each time we stopped long enough, I would rush out and buy sandwiches for everyone at the station lunch counter, where they cost half as much as the skimpy, dried-out sandwiches the railroad company hawkers sold. The danger of missing the train added zest to the game. One sullen young man who hovered on the edge of our nonce family refused to 'take food out of the mouths of kids'. When Mother pressed him too much, he slapped the sandwich out of her hand and the soldier sitting next to him drew back to smack him, but Mother shook her head, and he let it go. The sulky young man was the only sailor in our car, but the soldiers didn't taunt him on this account because he had received a nasty face wound, and they had found out during the first night's drinking in the vestibule that his girlfriend had ended their engagement with a Dear John letter, not because she wanted to, she had explained, but for his own good...in the long run. This brooding young sailor managed to sustain himself across the country on a box of Horlick's Malted Milk Tablets. Sometimes late at night when he thought everyone was asleep, he wept silently, save for a slight squeaking sound as he swallowed back his tears.

I jumped off at a two-hour layover to get some bread and peanut butter at a little store near the station. On the way back I bought a newspaper from the counter of the railroad canteen. The soldiers crowded around to read the headlines over my shoulder. One of our B-29s had dropped an 'atomic bomb' on Japan, demolishing a city called Hiroshima. There were whistles of wonder and triumphant yelps as the paper was passed down the car. We didn't learn until after the war that the number of civilians killed immediately was something like 70,000, more than the total death toll of all the air raids on England. Within the next six months, fifteen thousand of those suffering from unspeakable burns would also die, and the toll would continue to mount for many decades, as radiation worked its cancerous way through those damaged in the blast and through the bodies of children still unborn.

Our soldiers talked late into the night about the important things, or the wacky ones, they intended to do as soon as they got home, now that the war must be almost over. The sailor with the slippery-looking scars on his forehead and one cheek just looked out the window at the darkness.

Boredom alternated with helpless rage during the delays we spent in dusty sidings under the stifling sun. We were sitting on a shunt line, waiting for the overdue eastbound to pass us, when there was a buzz of excitement at the far end of our car, and a tipsy conductor came wading through the tangle of men sprawled in the vestibule, announcing that we had dropped a second atomic bomb, this one on Nagasaki. Americans would eventually learn that this bomb was more powerful than Hiroshima's, but Nagasaki's terrain and its smaller population lessened the extent of destruction and slaughter. Only 40,000 people were killed outright and a further 25,000 injured, many of whom would later die of radiation poisoning, and only about forty percent of the buildings were destroyed or damaged so badly they had to be pulled down. A relatively merciful bomb, really.

I had never heard of Hiroshima before the news of its bombing, but I had read about Nagasaki in the "Music Appreciation" part of *High School Subjects Self-Taught*. Puccini's Madame Butterfly had lived in beautiful Nagasaki.

It was after midnight. In the dim glow of the blue nightlights, everyone slept, uncomfortable and unattractive, mouths open, heads and feet counter-lurching with each lurch of the car. From within the narcotic clickety-click of the wheels and the groans of an old train on badly maintained track, a phantom orchestration of 'In the Mood' emerged, only to recede each time my ear sought it out. My long illness was still recent enough that I felt as though my skin didn't quite fit...as though I were slightly elsewhere and otherwise. Slipping in and out of shallow sleep, I half-awoke each time we passed through a town. Perhaps it was the reduction to yard speed that woke me. One time I opened my eyes and was sleepily confused to find the car quiet and still. We were standing in a siding, and out in the oceanic darkness of the plains there was a lone house with a single lit window. I focused back from the house to the blue ghostly image of my face on the train window, and I wondered about this house standing alone in an empty vastness....One lit window. A lonely birth? A last illness? Love-making? Someone too excited to sleep as they plan a new life? Someone too worried to sleep because a son overseas has not written for weeks? A kid tearfully packing up a few treasured things before running away from home?

With a bump and a metallic groan, we moved out of the sidetrack and I dozed again, slipping down through the sound of the wheels clicking over track, down through the distinct yet fugitive threads of 'In the Mood', down to an underlying rhythm of peh-ta-kleet...peh-ta-kleet...peh-ta-kleet that coiled back on itself and became Pearl-a-Street...Pearl-a-Street...Pearl-a-Street, and I knew I would never again walk in the back alley where I had fought rustlers, sneering Nazis, perfidious Arabs and Cardinal Richelieu's swaggering henchmen, never again know an anguish of choice before Mr Kane's penny candies in glass jars, or walk past the storefront churches of Blacktown and hear preachers suffused with the Holy Ghost rasping and gasping out salvation, or look up at the flag in the corner of the classroom at P.S. 5 and drone andtotherepublicforwhichitstands; never again pull my sister's wagon back from the surplus food warehouse, bringing home the ingredients for our safety-net potato soup; never again kneel beside the altar at early mass, or hold the paten beneath the wafer, worrying lest the body of Christ fail to make its precarious passage from Father Looney's trembling hands into the demurely opened mouths of the sisters with Parkinson's disease...mouths open like the sleepers around me in the dim blue light of the train, with its peh-ta-kleet...peh-ta-kleet...peh-ta-kleet, and I was rushing westward, away from Mrs McGivney's sugar cookies and her husband's fine white hair suffused with sunlight as his pale eyes stared into nothingness; leaving behind the bragging hotshots who loitered in the mouth of the alley, waiting for compliant Brigid Meehan...she of the dangerous brother with a milky eye, and the mother who could not let go of things...she of the long, silky left breast; I was leaving the abandoned brickyard with its dune of builders' sand where, although weakened by thirst and multiple wounds, I had performed such feats of courage, feats rivaled only by those I accomplished on the flat-topped hill of Washington Park; leaving the iron daybed where, in my aroused dreams, my face had come closer and closer to Sister Mary-Theresa's until our cheeks touched beneath her winged wimple and, suffused in the fresh-bread-and-yellow-bar-soap smell of nun, I received delicious relief in my sleep; leaving behind the smell of fever and Balm Bengué as my mother hung over the edge of her bed to drain her lungs; and the long walks back from Dish Night at the Paramount Theater, and stories about my grandfather told as late-night trolley cars clanged and squealed through the paperweight snowfall on their way down Clinton Avenue to the turn at Pearl-a-Street-Pearl-a-Street-Pearl-a-Street. Trolley wheels and train wheels repeat the street's name until its essence mixes with 'In the Mood' and both dry up, leaving only a husk of peh-ta-kleet...peh-ta-kleet...peh-ta-kleet.

. . . .

We arrived at the Oakland station stiff, rumpled, bone-bruised and disoriented. After a week of living on sandwiches and developing sea legs to cope with the constant motion of the train, we were weak-kneed, and the polished marble floor of the waiting room felt unreliably solid beneath our feet. Less than two dollars remained in our travel kitty, but we had made it to California. We were finally Out West. Our ship was about to come in.

We waited for three and a half hours in the station, sitting among our cardboard boxes and knotted sheets stuffed with clothes and soft belongings, before we learned from a message left with Travelers' Aid that Ben wasn't going to meet us. He was in Point Barrow, Alaska, where the Army had sent him without warning to help install communication equipment at a weather station. He had been unable to contact us because we were on the train crossing the continent, but he had sent a buddy, who looked as though he had stopped off at every bar between the base and the train station.

The buddy spanked all his jacket pockets twice before he found an envelope from Ben containing a letter and three hundred dollars, all he had managed 'to beg, borrow or steal' in the short time before his departure. Mother read Ben's letter quickly, her eyes stabbing angrily at the lines. He said how sorry he was that he had been snatched away, but the good news was that before shoving off he had managed to buy us a house in a town called Mission San José. Nothing fancy, but a really great investment.

··········

It was after midnight when the rented pick-up turned off the paved road that wound through the hill country south of Haywood, and bounced up a dirt track. Ben's buddy helped us unload our boxes and packages onto the ground, then he drove back down the track, raising dust into the moonlit night, his retreating taillights hopping as he jolted onto the paved road.

Mother, Anne-Marie and I stood looking at our new home. Ben's letter had said how lucky we were that he had found us a place to live, because the housing shortage in California was something fierce, what with all the war industry. The man he bought the house from, sight unseen, had assured him that it was sure to soar in value...they had even had a couple of drinks on it.

The hinges groaned as I tugged open the sagging door of the two-room shack. The interior smelled of straw and what I would learn to recognize as chicken shit. I felt along the wall for a light switch, snorting and flailing my arms each time a cobweb brushed my face.

Back out in the moonlight, I walked around the outside of the shack, then I returned to my mother and sister.

"Well?" Mother asked, her voice infinitely weary.

"There's no electricity."

There was no running water either. Or toilet. Just a slumping wooden outhouse around back.

We bedded down on the floor as best we could, putting coats and sweaters over us for warmth. Anne-Marie snuggled up next to Mother and soon fell into a deep defensive sleep. From across the room, I could feel that Mother was rigid with anger as she stared into the darkness overhead. I fell asleep before she did.

Over the next few days, Mother displayed the resilient energy with which she always responded to emergencies. Crises brought out the best in her, and I admired the brave, can-do way she took charge. A lot of our three hundred dollars went into buying second-hand furniture and replacing the household goods we'd had to leave behind. We spent a full day in the blistering heat, scraping and scrubbing every surface because the shack had done service as a chicken coop.

The dusty town of Mission San José was a mile from our shack, up a road patched with tar that the sun melted to slick and gooey beneath a layer of dust. I went through the town from door to door asking for work, but all I could find was pumping gas at the general store, where I had to snatch a clacking handle back and forth to draw gas up into a calibrated glass cylinder before letting it run down a hose into the car's tank. The old man who ran the place didn't pay wages as a matter of principle, but he gave us a discount on the kerosene for our stove and lamps, and I got the occasional tip for scraping splatted bugs off windshields. When cars pulled up to the pump they had to avoid an old dog that dozed in the middle of the road, spittle dribbling from its tongue into the dust. That dog darkening the dusty road with its drool will forever epitomize Mission San José for me...indeed, all rural life.

I was standing at the pump when an old-fashioned touring car came weaving down the road, its horn blaring. It narrowly missed the old dog, jumped the curb, skidded to a stop, and out piled two reeling sailors and a heavily made-up woman who couldn't stop giggling because she had lost one of her shoes somewhere. They were celebrating the unconditional surrender of Japan. It was V-J Day! The war was over!

The next morning Mother appeared in her bright blue Bette Davis suit with the flopping bell-bottom slacks and set off down the dirt road in search of work. The only job she could find was in a cannery, cutting apricots for twelve cents a lug. At first, she could do only two lugs an hour, but by the time the apricots ran out, she had worked her way up to four, so a twelve-hour day of cutting apricots at full speed brought in five dollars and seventy-five cents. Experienced Mexican women could make twice that. In her effort to rush Mother repeatedly nicked her thumbs with the hooked, razor-sharp 'cot knife until they stung with the acid juice and throbbed so much she had to hold them up above her head to get some relief, so it was hard for her to sleep.

We ate lots of apricots during those first days, with effects on our bowels that one might imagine.

Two weeks later, the apricot harvest was over and Mother lost her job at the cannery. She hitchhiked to towns as distant as Haywood, but there was no work to be had anywhere and, because we had not lived long enough in California to merit public assistance, there was nothing anyone could do for us. What was left of our three hundred dollars would last only a few weeks. We tried to borrow money on the shack and discovered that it was worthless now that the war industry had collapsed and with it the demand for local housing.

I remembered Ben once saying, "Sometimes you almost feel thankful for a little bad luck, because if it wasn't for bad luck, you wouldn't have any luck at all."

One hot, airless evening I was sitting on the front step of the shack. Out over the hills a condor soared, its bald head low between narrow shoulder blades, the tips of its wings fingering the air for up-drafts, its eyes relentlessly scanning for the crippled and the dead. And I suddenly came to the chilling realization that we were poor people. Through all the hard years on Pearl Street I had never thought of us as poor people. We had little money, sure, and we were temporarily down on our luck, but we weren't *poor people*, like destitute characters in

Dickens, or the wretched of *Les Misérables*. But now we were poor, re-ally poor, because this rural poverty was heavier and more hopeless than poverty in a city with museums and libraries and streets that might lead to a bit of good luck. I now felt sure that we would always be poor, and there was no way out.

In response to Mother's crisp, angry letters, Ben had written to say that he had applied for a hardship discharge from the army. As soon as it came through, he would come to Mission San José. But when would that be? How could we survive until he got there, and what could I do to help? Far from contributing to Mother and Anne-Marie's mainte-nance, I was just another mouth to feed, so I decided to follow the Mexican crop-pickers north and send every cent I could spare back to Mother. I promised her I would write often and come home as soon as the apple harvest was over, but down deep I knew that my decision to hit the road had as much to do with escape as with filial self-sacrifice.

Mother must have known it too because, when my last morning in Mission San José came, she didn't say good-bye. She just sat at the kitchen table staring into her coffee cup. I took the packet of sand-wiches she had made for me and bent over to kiss her hair. She didn't look up. I patted her shoulder and left.

After tying off my bindle I stood on the front step of the shack and looked out at the sunburnt hills. I had told myself that I would follow the crops only until Ben came back from Alaska and we could pick up our lives again. But in fact something subtle but irremediable was already happening: the bonds were falling away; the epiphany I had experienced in the golden lamplight beneath the pewter clouds of Snyders Corners was nearing fulfillment. I knew with a sur-logical cer-titude that I soon would be adrift, a drifter and free. I closed my eyes and a wave of bone-deep relief flowed over me.

Anne-Marie came with me down the dirt track to the main road. We walked side by side, our heads down, our shoes kicking up little dust puffs.

"I told you," she said without looking at me.

"Told me what?"

"I said you'd go away one of these days, and I'd be left behind."

"I'm not leaving you behind. I'll be back in no time."

She stopped and turned to me. She searched my eyes gravely. Then she smiled and shook her head.

I squeezed her hand and walked on. As I crested the hill I looked back, but Anne-Marie was no longer there.

And there's the story's natural closing image...the boy going down a patched tar road, walking out of childhood, into the rest of his life. But our lives are continuous and interwoven, and narrative fabric doesn't tear neatly; there are threads to tie off, curiosities to satisfy.

After Ben got mustered out, he and Mother tried to make a go of things in Mission San José, but in the end they had to let the land go for taxes. The 'ruptured duck' lapel pin that showed he was an ex-serviceman was of no use in getting work. For about two years, while defense factories re-tooled, the job market was flooded by people thrown out of work at the end of the war. In addition, there were hundreds of thousands of returning veterans chasing the handful of jobs. The luckiest of these used their GI Bill loans for university or for technical training, and they emerged with qualifications for good jobs in the great consumer boom soon to begin. But Ben couldn't take off two or three years to go to college. He had Mother and Anne-Marie to care for, and it wasn't long before they had two sons of their own as well.

Mother never forgave Ben for squandering their money on that useless shack and scuttling her dream of success in Wyoming, any more than she forgave him for not being my smooth-talking, slick-dressing father. Despite his quick intelligence, his jack-of-all-trades skills and his willingness to work long and hard, Ben never managed to get ahead in life; in fact, he never quite managed to catch up. He chased scheme after scheme but he failed each time for lack of planning and capital, so they had to begin again at the bottom of the labor ladder until they managed to claw their way back out of debt and save up enough to launch themselves into another venture. By the time they ended up with a little subsistence farm on Puget Sound, their dreams had soured into bitterness, and communication had been replaced by the relentless guerrilla sniping of mutual recrimination.

One night, after years of adhering to his self-imposed rule of absti-
nence, Ben brought Mother to a New Year's Eve party with neighbors
where, to be sociable, he drank two hot toddies. Just before dawn, he
committed suicide. He was not yet fifty.[69]

My mother always viewed Ben's death as a desertion. She felt
that he had run out on her, just as her first husband had...and her
eldest son.

I met my father only once, twenty-four years after that day the
three of us sat on the stoop and waited for him to come home bearing
a green cake. We spent about three hours together in a grim tenement
in South Philadelphia. He sat at a kitchen table breathing through a
mask attached to an oxygen cylinder. He told me about his time with
the carnivals, trying to impress me with the colorful and audacious
scams he had run over the years. I'll never know how he got my address, but I had received a letter from him saying that he'd been released from prison early on compassionate grounds (he was dying of
emphysema) and he wanted to see me before he went 'to work the great
tip up yonder'. Curiosity had brought me across the United States on
an Indian motorcycle manufactured in the year of my birth to meet this
man whose absence had shaped my childhood. That, and the promise
that if I came he would tell me tales the likes of which I'd never heard.
As it turned out, I had heard most of his stories of scam and hustle because by then I had done a couple of seasons with the carnivals myself,
and I knew the ways of a con with his mark. But some of his yarns had
bitter, ironic twists, and there were details of scams and stings I wasn't
familiar with, even a few old-fashioned carnie terms I didn't know. He
hadn't anticipated that I might have been 'with it' myself, and he both
resented this and was put off pace by it, as though I were trumping his
ace by not being totally unacquainted with the world of con. It immediately became important to him to show me that he was the real
carnie in this family and that, while I may have drifted with the shows
for a couple of seasons, I was a mere 'forty-miler'...a mark at heart.
After all, if this dying old wreck wasn't a better con man than the son
he had abandoned, then what was he, for Christ's sake?

With considerable relish, he described a scam he had run during

the war when, impersonating a federal officer, he had confiscated illegal slot machines in peaville towns in Colorado and New Mexico, then
he would con the owner of the bar into loading the slot machine into
his rented car as 'confiscated evidence'. (For the true con, inflicting a
last humiliation on the mark, like making him grunt his slot machine
into your car, is the cherry on the top of a genuinely satisfying scam...
the last proof that the mark and the con don't descend from a common
primates ancestor. In carnie parlance, this final humiliation is termed
'making the mark take his shoe off'.) Ray then drove out into the
desert and broke the slot machine open with a sledge hammer...ideally
one borrowed from the mark. The upshot of this scam was that Ray
ended up with both the Feds and the Mob looking for him. And for
what? For a little loose change and the thrill of the sting.

"In the end, I turned myself in to the Feds to avoid the Mob!" He
laughed so hard that he coughed pink phlegm into a wad of toilet
paper and had to spend a couple of minutes sucking at his oxygen.
When he could speak again, he looked across the table at me, his eyes
bloodshot and his lips blue. "You know something, kid? I've spent more
than half of my adult life inside. All in short two- or three-year shots."

"If you were such a scam maven, how come you did so much time?"

"The way I see it is this. The day I was born Malicious Fate condemned me to a life sentence. But my guardian angel had connections
downtown, and she arranged that I do my time on the installment
plan...five years down and a couple of years each decade." He grinned.
When I didn't respond to this rehearsed bit of bitter wit, he became
suddenly serious.

"Look here, kid. I asked you to come because I thought maybe
you'd want to hear my side of things."

"In fact, Ray, I don't."

"You don't want to hear what I've got to say?"

I opened my hands in a gesture of 'whatever'.

"I'm going to be up front with you, kid. I'm a drinker. That's always
been my problem. Unfortunately booze and stings don't mix. I'd have
some mark all sewn up, and I'd take a drink or two to celebrate, and
then I'd get the urge to make the mark look foolish. Tease and bait
him. Make him do what they call in the business..."

"...take his shoe off," I said.

"Oh...you know about that, eh? Well, I'd play the mark, just to see how far I could rub it in without tipping him off. And inevitably the booze would make me push it just a little bit too close to the edge, and the next thing you know, I'm eating rice and grease in some Dixie can. Some people never learn. They say that life is the great teacher, but that's crap. No really good teacher would give you the test before she'd taught the lesson." Even while he was chuckling at this, he was examining me, hefting the moment, ready to make his sting. The tail end of his laugh blended into "...so, tell me, kid. Do you ever think about that Saint Patrick's Day party I threw for you and your sister in Albany?"

"Is that what you remember? Throwing a party for us?"

"I spent hours stringing up green paper through those goddamned water pipes. And there were green plates and napkins and green pop and a green cake."

"There was no green cake."

"Sure there was! I went out to buy one. I remember like it was yesterday."

"You went out to buy a cake, but you never came back. The party never happened."

"What are you saying? I remember it! I can see you kids eating the cake and drinking the pop."

"Some people get very good at conning themselves."

"Tell me about it. A con's got to be able to con himself, or he'll never amount to anything. The only way to build up the confidence and sincerity you need to sell some mark the Brooklyn Bridge is to believe deep in your heart that you own it. Really own it. Know what I mean, kid?"

"I really hate this 'kid' business."

"Do you?"

"H'm."

"Sorry. You're absolutely sure there was no party?"

I told him I was absolutely sure.

He digested this, then shrugged and said, "I'll be damned. Ah, well, you survived it. You didn't turn out so bad. Big motorcycle. Been to university. When I think of what I could have done with a university degree."

"Why didn't you award yourself one?"

"Matter of fact, I did. A couple of times I was professor this or doctor that." He looked at me sidewards, then his voice shifted to a huskier, more sincere timbre. "Jesus, kid, you're right. There was no Saint Patrick's Day party. No green cake. Funny how you can wish something had happened so much that you actually stash it into your memory. I went out that morning meaning to get a green cake, but the first thing you know, there I was, walking along...marks on the street corner...action in the bars...and I was free, white and stepping out. I wanted to go back to that cheap apartment, but I couldn't. I just *couldn't* do it, kid. I loved your mother. I really did. I love her to this day. She was a great gal. Full of life, and a heart as big as all outdoors. Did you ever see her dance? She was what you call life-embracing. That was what she was, life-embracing. And I loved you kids, too. I mean, I didn't really know you kids, but I loved the *idea* of you. My own kids. But...some men have just got to be free, kid. Know what I mean?"

I didn't answer. He was still looking for the right moment to run whatever graft he had in mind.

He gave me a couple more stories of his experiences on the hustle, one of which I had heard half a dozen times while I was with the shows, each story-teller claiming to have been there when it happened. (For the old carnies among my readers, it was the tale of Jimmy Straights, the bucket-game, and the Ferris wheel.)

Then, with just a hint of quiver beneath a brave, stiff-upper-lip tone, he said, "I guess you're surprised to see how low I've fallen. Living in a rat hole like this. Tied to this goddamned air bottle."

I didn't answer. Here it came.

"Well, this is not the lowest a man can fall. There's lower. A lot lower."

"Is that right, Ray?"

"Oh, yeah. Yeah, a man can fall so low that he tries to hit up his kid...his own kid that he hasn't seen since he was a baby...for a couple of bucks to buy a bottle of cheap hooch. Now *that's* low."

"It's pretty low all right."

"But that's how low I've fallen, because I'm sitting here and I'm looking you in the eyes and I'm asking you to leave a little something on the table so your old man can get drunk tonight and forget that he's dying, forget that his lungs aren't worth a damn and that one of these days soon, he'll just stop breathing and never wake up."

I nodded. It was a potent shot, aimed as far below the belt as he could reach. How could anyone turn down a dying drunk's last request? Turn down the man who gave you the gift of life? And this really didn't have anything to do with the money. It was all about proving to himself, and to me, that he was the real carnie, and I was just another mark.

"Well," I said, getting up with a grunt. "I guess I'd better be going. I don't want to be in this neighborhood after dark."

He looked at me out of the corners of his eyes. Then he chuckled. "You're tough, kid. I got to hand it to you, you are really tough. All bone and gristle where other people got heart."

I almost said something corny, like: I learned from a master.

"Yeah," he went on. "Look at you! Young, smart, tough and on your way to the big party I just got home from. Have fun, kid. Life's a gas."

I nodded and left.

I was down on the street, checking my mill over to make sure the kids I'd found standing around it hadn't screwed anything up, when my father appeared at the front door of his tenement, gasping and wheezing from being disconnected from his oxygen. He tried to call out to me, but the effort made him gag and cough, so I walked over to him.

"What?"

"I...ah...just..." Clutching the door frame, he swallowed and blinked. "I just wanted to say that..." His voice clogged up. He raised some phlegm and spat. "I just realized that I never took you to a ball game, kid. Can you believe it? I never took my own son to a ball game!"

I looked at him levelly for a long moment, then I said, "You're really good. You play cards that most people don't even have in their deck."

He grinned. "So who's the real con here, kid? Tell me."

"You, Ray. You're the real con."

He nodded. "I'll see you in hell, kid." He winked and turned back into the building.

I rode out of Philadelphia. Early the next morning, I rolled in for coffee at What Cheer, Iowa, a one-dog town whose name had snagged my eye each time I passed it as I drifted back and forth across America. Sitting over a mug of thin hot coffee in an archetypal mid-American diner with its obligatory sprinkling of retired farmers wearing caps that advertised farm machinery, I jotted down a few swatches of dialogue for a tale about a man meeting his carnie father after many years, and the old man trying to touch him for a few bucks, just to prove that he was the better con.

Back in my attic room above a bar on Seattle's old Skid Road, half the wall above my work table was papered with rejection slips. I didn't find a publisher for *I Never Took You to a Ball Game, Kid*. Until now, that is.

A creaking old grain tramp brought me from Newport News to Europe, where I banged around on a pre-war Matchless until it broke down, marooning me in Sicily for lack of spare parts. I worked my way back to Paris. In the 1950s Paris was still the city of Baron Haussmann, Zola, Proust, and the Lost Generation, having not yet fallen victim to the cultural vandalism of inner-city gentrification or the aesthetic vandalism of egomaniacal politicians desperate to leave their mark on Paris. I wrote in 'brown' cafes without distracting music or clanging games, or I exchanged ideas and prejudices with other unknown but confident writers and painters, each of us making one small coffee last through the morning. I slept in tawdry hotels and sometimes in doorways or beneath bridges where I earned acceptance among the *clochards* by bringing vegetable crates from les Halles to burn in the communal oil drum. We would sit with our backs against the escarpment, swapping late-night lies as flames flickered beneath sooty arches. Winter came and we sometimes slept on the metal grills, where up-drafts of warm air from the Métro kept us from freezing. We lay on flattened-out cardboard boxes so the grills wouldn't bruise our hipbones.[70]

Spring arrived and I met a young woman who wore long dramatic capes, and whose eyes were flecked with the colors of autumn. We walked across Paris one blustery night as the shifting wind alternately billowed her cape out behind her or enfolded her within it, as I wanted to do. Dawn came while we were talking sleepily in a bar used by bakers on the Ile Saint Louis.

Beautiful and cheerful, she was also a talented painter whose attributes and qualities were totally antithetical to mine. Where I was cynical, she was accepting. Where I was judgmental, she was understanding. I drew my energy from anger and frustration; hers came from health and inner calm. I was a congenital pessimist; she was hopeful... no Pollyanna optimist, but a life-embracing woman making a healthy Pascal's Bet. I was tough; she was strong; I had impact, she endurance; I was a man of words, she a woman of images. The only thing we shared, other than physical desire for each other, was a sense of the absurd, the utter nonsense that delights the whimsical mind as much as it annoys the earthbound one. It was my inexplicable good fortune that she was willing to marry me, but everyone warned her that our profound differences could not support a long-lasting union.

For many restless years I dragged her and our children from place to place, forever running from my disappointments and self-inflicted injuries, and sapping her creative energy with the task of continual nest-building as I pursued the career best suited to my nomadic life, story-telling.

Things turned out well enough for the woman and two children you met sitting on the stoop outside their new home on North Pearl Street, their shoddy possessions piled around them.

As the film buffs among you will have guessed, Anne-Marie never did replace Shirley Temple. While still a teenager, she escaped the tensions and recriminations of Mother and Ben's home and fled into an early marriage with a winsome, breezy young man who turned out to have a serious problem with alcohol. Despite the emotional and financial difficulties his drinking caused, they produced half a dozen children, many grandchildren, and a host of great-grandchildren on whom Anne-Marie lavished love and care, and in whom she took, and still takes, great pride. She was widowed relatively young and her life has not been easy, but through all her trials she has developed her ability to find calm within herself. This enviable spiritual resource has helped her to accept life's injustices without bitterness, and she now lives a rich contemplative life.

Her ship has come in, and it is laden with the peace she always sought.

Mother's final decline into the kaleidoscopic ooze of Alzheimer's disease was mercifully rapid. The onset of her dementia had been slow and, in its way, merciful. As sometimes happens, the first things to disappear from her memory were the injustices and resentments she had nurtured and brooded over all her life. Ben vanished from her memory; my father followed soon after; and for the last two years she had no memory of ever having been abandoned or disappointed by any man. She sometimes recalled that she had once been married, but she remained sweetly vague about who he had been, and why he was no longer with her on their little farm on Puget Sound. Sometimes she believed that her husband was the man who was now her doctor, and sometimes her lawyer held this honor, and even, for a short period, the governor of her state. He was always a well-educated man who was also, she would confide with a wink, a great dancer and a real snappy dresser. In fact, she and her husband had won cups for dancing the Charleston. In her later years, she assumed that the big bouquet of Talisman roses and the peck of Northern Spy apples she received on each birthday came from her mythical husband...whichever one it was at the time.

The last year of her life she began to be visited by an Indian princess who came through the dazzling mist of the early mornings to tell her that she was vastly admired by all Indian women, who were grateful to her for getting them the vote. She once showed me a special blade of grass this Indian princess had given her as a token of how proud everyone was of her great success as a tap dancer, a fashion designer and a writer of novels. The fog that thickened around her remained pink almost to the end.

Her ship had come in, and it was laden with the success she had been denied.

After my health declined to the point of being able to work only two or three hours a day, and only with the support of oxygen, I found it difficult to live up to my image as a scrappy outsider going to Fist-city with publisher after publisher over literary, social or political matters. How tough and independent can you be when your wife has to bathe you and help you dress? But I still have good moments. Sometimes, when I have been bundled up and installed on the terrace of my cafe to read or to write letters, I look up and see my wife striding across the *alée* of our Basque village towards me, her cape flapping behind her. As she approaches she smiles at me, there is a rush of warmth around my heart, and my spirits lift.

My ship came in, too, and it was laden with love.

Mendiburua, Pays Basque, 2004

OUT NOW IN PAPERBACK

"A quite superb psychological thriller" *The Independent*

"A tour de force... A story that explores meticulously some of the darker corners of the human soul" *Washington Post*

"Spectacularly entertaining" *Newsweek*